Social Security in Ireland

Social Security in Ireland

Anthony McCashin

Gill & Macmillan

Gill & Macmillan
Hume Avenue
Park West
Dublin 12
with associated companies throughout the world

www.gillmacmillan.ie

© Anthony McCashin 2004

0 7171 3425 3

Print origination in Ireland by Red Barn Publishing

The paper used in this book is made from the wood pulp of managed forests. For every tree felled, at least one is planted, thereby renewing natural resources.

A catalogue record is available for this book from the British Library.

Contents

For Mary with love and thanks; for the next generation, Darragh and Róisín, and the previous generation, Bobby and Carmel McCashin, Daniel and Kathleen O'Shea, and Tommy Kelly.

Preface

I have accumulated many debts in the course of writing this book. To begin with, I took leave of absence from the Department of Social Studies, Trinity College. Dr Shane Butler as acting head of the department agreed to my request for this. I am grateful to him for his cooperation. My debt to the department, however, is not without limit, as my period of leave from 2000 to 2002 was unpaid! As the project neared completion my departmental head, Professor Robbie Gilligan, and other colleagues, graciously endured my preoccupation with it and my distraction from administrative and academic duties.

Many chapters benefited from the advice of individual colleagues. Dr Eoin O'Sullivan commented on chapters one, two and nine. He was also a rich source of data and academic material, and a continual source of encouragement. Dr Sophia Carey read chapters one and two: her input lead to some necessary re-drafting. I also benefited from the assistance of Judy O'Shea. She gave very definite, and very necessary editorial advice on all of the chapters. Anonymous referees responded to a sample chapter, and at a later stage commented on seven chapters. I learned what little knowledge I have of pensions policy from Dr Jim Stewart of the School of Business, Trinity College. Ann Doyle, Executive Officer of the Social Studies Department came to the rescue on word processing matters on a number of occasions.

Throughout the book I have drawn on the work of researchers at the Economic and Social Research Institute, Dublin. They include Professors Brian Nolan, Chris Whelan, Tim Callan, Brendan Whelan, Gerard Hughes, Dr Philip O'Connell, Dr Dorothy Watson, Dr Richard Layte, and others too numerous to mention. I frequently cite, and occasionally reproduce in detail, results from many of their studies on poverty and related issues. Over the years I have learned a great deal, not only from their written work, but also from informal conversations with some of them about their research. Professor Tim Callan also cast an experienced eye over chapter twelve on Basic Income. Dr Geoffrey Cook of UCD, a long-standing friend and academic sparring partner, made his doctoral thesis on the history of social security in Ireland available to me. I acknowledge his generosity and his permission to quote from his work. Mel Cousins allowed me to read draft chapters of his book, *The Birth of Social Welfare in Ireland, 1922–1952*, and discussed his research with me. This helped in the writing of chapters two, five, and eight. None of the above is responsible for the content or opinions in the text, and I alone am responsible for any errors or omissions.

I owe more than the usual author's debt to Gill & Macmillan. The commercial, editorial and production staff, including Hubert Mahony, Marion O'Brien, and Deirdre Nolan, were all very tolerant as I stretched deadlines to near breaking point. I hope that my lapses as an author have not diminished their faith in the final product.

As the first attempt at a general text in this area drawing largely on Irish material, this book will attract criticism. For general readers interested in practical policy improvements the discussion of policy principles may seem too academic in parts; others will be puzzled by the absence of material on some undoubtedly important topics; for the well informed reader the historical material may rely excessively on secondary sources, and throughout I have drawn in an eclectic way on a number of disciplines — sociology, history, social policy, and economics. If these are faults, they can act as starting points for future work. Hopefully, other authors will be impelled to take up where I have left off, and to add to the growing body of indigenous writing on Irish social policy.

The book could not have been written without the patience and support of my wife, Mary O'Shea, and my children, Darragh and Róisín. They excused me from normal family life for much of the past year while gently encouraging me to the very end. I promise them all an immediate down payment on the debt I owe them.

Anthony McCashin
Trinity College Dublin
December 2003

Introduction

This book is about income maintenance in the Republic of Ireland. It is written for students of social policy, practitioners and researchers in the fields of poverty and social policy, and non-specialist readers attempting to understand the history and structure of income maintenance policy in Ireland, and the main policy issues in this field.

Somewhat confusingly, income maintenance in Ireland is administered by the Department of Social and Family Affairs, formerly named the Department of Social, Community and Family Affairs (1997–2002) and the Department of Social Welfare (1947–1996). The latter term, 'Social Welfare', is generally used in Ireland to describe the topic of the book. In fact, in spite of the two recent name changes, 'social welfare' continues to be used in Ireland by students, researchers, politicians, and journalists when referring to this branch of government policy. However, it is not a term that is familiar outside of Ireland. 'Income Maintenance' is a more familiar term to academic readers, but is somewhat unwieldy and conveys too narrow an impression of the functions of policy and the debates about policy in this area. The more general term 'Social Security' seems the most neutral and internationally acceptable term to signify the core topics covered in the book.

Social security refers to *public measures that provide cash benefits to deal with specific contingencies arising from the loss of earnings or inadequate earnings, and to deal with the cost of supporting dependants.* It therefore embraces situations where an individual's earning power or main income source:

- Is lost permanently (retirement, serious injury, widowhood), or
- Is temporarily interrupted (unemployment or illness), or
- Never develops (because of physical or mental handicap), or
- Is inadequate to prevent poverty because of low income or a large number of dependants.[1]

The text is therefore structured around these principle contingencies that give rise to income loss or poverty. However, not *all* cash benefits are dealt with — Maternity Benefit, payments for carers, and allowances in respect of orphans, for example. There are two other points to note. First, although cash benefits are the focus of the book, the government department responsible for these (Department of Social and Family Affairs) also administers some non-cash benefits. The most important of these are Treatment Benefit (for Dental, Aural and Optical services) and the various benefits-in-kind such as allowances for telephone rental and free TV licences for some benefit recipients. To keep the book within manageable limits these non-cash benefits are not discussed. Second, in some countries 'social security' is taken to include a range of functions other than cash benefits, such as health care, rehabilitation, and training, but in Ireland the system of cash benefits is distinct and separate. This book deals only with the cash benefit system.

Part 1 gives a brief historical survey and sets the scene with a summary description of current provisions (Chapter Three) and a review of key concepts and policy objectives (Chapter Four). Ireland's cash benefits system is remarkably complicated. This book does *not* attempt to comprehensively describe the legislative and administrative detail.[2] However, Chapter Three gives a brief overview of the current system. Elsewhere throughout the text discussions of policy are informed by limited descriptions of current benefits and policies. The core of the material, Chapters Five to Eleven, is in Part 2. These chapters adhere, to varying degrees, to a broad framework: historical development, an analysis of policy objectives and controversies, recent trends in relation to benefits and poverty, and future policy. None of these chapters contains a full comparison of Irish policy and provisions with those of other countries. Where relevant, however, international trends are given as a backdrop to evolving policies and debates in Ireland. Part 3, comprising Chapter Twelve, deals with the social security system as a whole, focusing on a very specific question: should Ireland abandon its current system in favour of a Basic Income system, the radical alternative advocated by some?

The minutiae of a social security system can change rapidly. In Ireland the annual budget and other legislation lead to a revision of nominal benefit levels and other changes — usually of an incremental nature. The details given in the text of benefits and entitlements reflect those that apply in 2003 or 2002. Time will render some of these details obsolete, but the historical evolution of social security, and the context and strategic choices it will confront in the immediate years ahead, will not be superseded by routine budgetary and other adjustments. In a fundamental sense, the controversies that have shaped policy in the last decade are likely to persist for some time.

Notes

1.   This formulation is based on Dixon's definition (Dixon, 1999: 3).
2.   General readers who wish to study an overall guide to the Irish cash benefits system should consult the 2003 version of the Department of Social and Family Affairs' booklet: Booklet SW4, *Summary of Social Insurance and Assistance Services*.

Part One

1
Historical Development of the Irish System of Social Security

INTRODUCTION

This chapter offers an overview of the development of Irish social security from the first quarter of the nineteenth century until political independence in 1921. The chapter begins with an account of the nineteenth century Poor Law in the UK and its establishment in Ireland and then shows how the Poor Law became the *motif* for later developments in Ireland and the United Kingdom. Then a summary account of the emergence of old age pensions is given, followed by a brief account of the introduction of national insurance for unemployment and sickness. In Ireland social security was the political responsibility of the government in London until political independence, and of necessity, therefore, the chapter records the development of social security in Ireland largely, although not wholly, as a by-product of political influences and choices in Great Britain.

THE POOR LAW

The first national, statutory system of welfare in Ireland was the 1838 Poor Relief (Ireland) Act that emerged from the establishment of the 'new' Poor Law in Great Britain in 1834. The latter was embodied in the 1834 Poor Law Amendment Act. Some background is necessary here. In 1601 the 'old' Elizabethan Poor Law was introduced in the wake of a series of bad harvests that created widespread deprivation and unrest (Fraser, 1973). Under the Elizabethan Poor Law the local parish gave relief to the poor from local funding. Three important principles underpinned the operation of local poor relief: to receive aid the poor had to prove 'settlement' (permanent residence) in the parish; the principle of the liability of dependants meant that family members were mutually responsible for their well-being and maintenance, and poor relief was utterly minimal. An important addition to the Poor Law was the 1662 Act of Settlement. As a result of geographical mobility in the seventeenth century, many poor people were perceived as moving from one parish to another — specifically, from poorer to richer parishes — to avail of the more generous relief that was available in better-off parishes. The Act allowed the parish to return individuals to their original parish if it was judged that they might become a burden on the local parish.

The old Poor Law gave way to the 'new' Poor Law embodied in the 1834 Poor Law Amendment Act for a number of reasons. (Powell, 1992; McKay and Rowlingson, 1999; Cook, 1990) First, the settlement requirements of the old law became increasingly incongruous in the context of the free mobility of labour that became an inherent feature of the newly urbanised, industrialised economy. Second, the old Poor Law became transformed in many areas in to a 'Speenhamland' system (after the name of the parish in which the arrangement first appeared). In the 1790s, bad harvests and the resulting shortages and inflation led to fears that the new revolutionary spirit emanating from the French revolution of 1789 would engender political unrest. In 1795, in Berkshire, the justices began to allow relief on a much wider scale and also permitted relief to poor, employed labourers to ensure they could afford food. Third, the Speenhamland system was increasingly criticised for its effects on the rural economy, subsidising 'bad' employers for paying below subsistence wages, on the one hand, while artificially driving up the price of bread by subsidising demand, on the other.

The Speenhamland system merely illustrated — for some of its distinguished critics — the fundamental difficulty with the old Poor Law. It was perceived, in today's terms, as too generous, as evidenced by a significant increase in the amount of rates levied to fund Poor Law expenditure. The views of such critics are vividly illustrated in the contemporary writings of a Poor Law overseer, Sir G. Nicholls. In a pamphlet in 1821 Nicholls gave an account of the problems of the old Poor Law and in particular made a detailed critique of its impact in the parish of Southwell.[1] He commences his critique by suggesting that the provision of a workhouse 'at considerable expense' had become 'the resort of the idle and profligate of both sexes' and had generated a 'circle of pauperism'. Pauperism eventually embraced 'nearly the whole population. Self-reliance and provident habits were destroyed, the call for these qualities being superseded by a ready access to the public purse'. Nicholls conveyed a picture of wilful and widespread reliance on the local parish in his portrait of poor families in Southwell (Nicholls, 1898: 228–9):

> A stripling married a girl as ignorant and youthful as himself. They immediately apply to the overseers to provide them a house, and for something also towards getting them a bed and a little furniture. The birth of a child approaches and the overseer is again applied to for a midwife, and for money to help them in the wife's 'down-lying'. Perhaps the child dies, and the parish has to bury it; and if it lives, the parish must surely help to maintain it. And so it was

throughout the whole range of their existence — in youth and in age, in sickness and in health, in seasons favourable and unfavourable, with low prices or with high prices — the parish was still looked to and relied upon as an unfailing resource, to which everyone clung, and from which every man considered he had a right to obtain the supply of every want, even although (*sic*) it were caused by his own indolence, vice or improvidence.

This critique of the 'generosity' of the old Poor Law led Nicholls and his fellow reformers, in their role as overseers in Southwell, to instigate changes in the administration of relief. These reforms included the abolition of the Speenhamland system of supplementing the wages of labourers and the payment of rents for labourers' cottages. However, the core of the changes was the new and harsh regime imposed in the parish workhouse: the division of families within the workhouse, the separation of sexes, the imposition of a rigorous work regime for inmates, and so on. Nicholls summarised the approach to the reform of the old Poor Law in Southwell as follows (Nicholls, 1898: 236):

A well-regulated workhouse answers these two conditions. No person in actual want will reject the relief proffered therein, and a person not in actual want will not submit to the restraints by which the relief is accompanied. Workhouse relief will be more repugnant than labour to persons able to work, whilst to those who are disabled as well as indigent the workhouse will be a welcome refuge.

Prior to the establishment of Royal Commission on the Poor Law in 1832 this critique — and its practical implications in local parishes — became increasingly widespread and greatly influenced the new Poor Law of 1834. Nicholls' critique was legitimised by the influence of the *laissez-faire* school of political economy with its emphasis on the 'invisible hand of the market' and the need for a free, mobile market in labour in the context of Britain's industrial economy. The great exponents of liberal, *laissez-faire* economics opposed the Poor Law and in particular opposed the gradual evolution of the old Poor Law into the generic, Speenhamland system of relief. Thomas Malthus in his classic and influential work published in 1826, *Essays on the Principle of Population* had argued that there was a natural tendency for population growth to exceed the growth of food supplies. The Poor Law, he argued, was a destructive mechanism that was reinforcing the increase in the population of the poor, bringing with it a population burden that could not be sustained. The other great classical economists, David Ricardo and Nassau Senior, were equally vehement in their opposition to poor relief and argued for the abolition of the Poor Law in Britain. Senior, for example, in his famous letter to Lord Howick about poor relief in Ireland set out the three possible grounds that might give rise to poor relief: infirmity and illness; crop failure, and want of employment. He accepted that illness could be relieved, but that old age was foreseeable and hence did not justify public provision (except in the case of provision in infirmaries for illness). In relation to crop failure, he opposed public relief of any kind and in the case of lack of employment, or employment at insufficient wages, among the able-bodied he suggested that public provision would 'destroy . . . industry, providence and mutual benevolence' (Cook, 1990: 5). In the terms of twentieth and twenty-first century debates, this perspective feared the emergence of an 'underclass' and a 'culture of dependence'.

By the early 1830s the old Poor Law was widely unpopular. The cost was rising rapidly and the growing number of the poor seeking relief was giving rise to concern among its intellectual critics about the impact of the Poor Law on the economy and society. However, the Poor Law was still inadequate to meet the needs of the poor in many areas and gave rise to protest and unrest: the local nature of the old Poor Law meant that the poorest parishes had the least finance available to fund poor relief. A Royal Commission on the Poor Laws was established in 1832 and reported in 1834. Its recommendations were implemented in the 1834 Poor Law Amendment Act. The new Poor Law reflected the philosophical influence of classical economics, as the central principle on which the new law was founded was that of 'less eligibility' (Nicholls, 1898: 242). According to this principle, the circumstances of any person receiving relief must be worse than those of the poorest labourer: the circumstances of the recipient of relief 'shall not be made really or apparently so eligible as the situation of the independent labourer of the lowest class'. The Royal Commission outlined what it considered would be the effect of offering relief that gave the poor the same standard of living as that of the lowest paid labourer (cited in Nicholls, 1898: 242):

> In proportion as the condition of any pauper class is elevated above the condition of independent labourers, the condition of the independent class is depressed, their industry is impaired, their employment becomes unsteady and its remuneration in wages is depressed.

Any expenditure on poor relief that breached this principle of 'less eligibility' was, the Commission suggested 'a bounty on indolence and vice'. Accordingly, relief outside the workhouse (outdoor relief) was abolished for the non-disabled (Cook, 1990; Nicholls, 1898).

The principle of 'less eligibility' retained a continuity with the old Elizabethan Poor Law in its harshness, but it offered a new rationale for this harshness in terms which economists would later call labour market incentives: welfare (for those able to work) should be less than the net earnings of low-paid employees. 'Less eligibility', taken together with two other key elements of the 1834 reform, gave the new Poor Law its defining characteristics. Firstly, the workhouse regime was designed to be harsh so that it would act as a deterrent to the able-bodied claiming relief, and, secondly, it was more centralised. The Act provided for the appointment of three Poor Law commissioners and inspectors, and conferred considerable powers on the commissioners in relation to the detailed administration and implementation of the Act. At local level the new Poor Law was administered in Poor Law Unions under the direction of Boards of Guardians.

This new framework was the UK's first national statutory system of welfare and was to remain broadly in place until the beginning of the twentieth century. In Ireland, meanwhile, the general population suffered the most appalling social conditions (Cook, 1990; Burke, 1987). The economy was predominantly agricultural and at the base of this economy was a vast underclass of poverty. About 10,000 landlords who let significant parts of their land to 'middlemen' owned the land. In turn, they sub-let to cottiers who rented cabins and small plots and paid for these partly with their labour. Even the large landless labourer class rented very small patches of land for growing potato and other subsistence crops. This complex agricultural structure had, on the one hand, sustained a rapidly growing population: the population of (the island of) Ireland grew from about 2.5 million in the middle of the eighteenth century to over 8 million in 1841. On the other hand, the existence of the peasant and cottier classes was precarious. There was intermittent famine and continual emigration: from 1815 to 1847, 1.5 million emigrated.

In Dublin, the economy offered a stark contrast to the thriving industrial cities of Great Britain. The Act of Union of 1801 had put paid to any prospect of industrial growth in Ireland's cities and the small wealthy and middle-class segment of the population had begun to desert the city, weakening its economic fabric further. The large period townhouses of these classes began to be inhabited by the poor, some of these fleeing the destitution of the rural economy. By the 1830s, the social and economic problems of Ireland, compounded by religious discrimination and political repression, were well documented. A Select Committee of the House of Commons in 1804 had argued against the introduction of statutory poor relief in Ireland. A later report, in 1819, by a select committee on the State of Disease and Conditions of the Labouring Poor in Ireland, suggested that the best way of dealing with the poor in Ireland was to develop Ireland's indigenous resources in agriculture and fishing. This conclusion was essentially repeated in the 1823 report on the Employment of the Poor in Ireland. A further report was published in 1830: this report, *Report of the Select Committee on the State of the Poor in Ireland*, did not directly address the issue of legal provision for the Irish poor. In turn, this drew a public rebuke of the committee's chairman, Thomas Rice, M.P., from a member of the Catholic Hierarchy, who argued that the committee's own evidence strongly supported the case for statutory provision for the poor (Burke, 1987: 15).

The controversy about the need for a Poor Law in Ireland intensified in the 1830s as social conditions in Dublin deteriorated drastically during the cholera epidemic. These conditions were dramatically highlighted in 1833 when the Mansion House Committee (then the largest and most active philanthropic body in Dublin) published, in graphic and detailed terms, the results of its enquiry into social conditions in the city. With the completion of the 1832 Poor Law inquiry in England and the implementation of its report in 1834, the government dealt with the continuing controversy about poverty in Ireland by instituting a further inquiry, the *Royal Commission of Inquiry into the Conditions of the Poorer Classes in Ireland*, chaired by the Anglican archbishop of Dublin, Dr Whately.

The context in which this inquiry undertook its work was marked by intense controversy about the appropriateness or otherwise of introducing a Poor Law. Irish landlords were implacably opposed, fearing that escalating costs on local rates would ensue, as had happened in the Speenhamland variant of the old Poor Law in England. However, the sheer scale of destitution had led to growing demands for some form of statutory relief. In the event, the Whately committee repudiated both the old and the new variants of the Poor Law, and in the course of three detailed reports offered extensive statistical evidence and vivid illustrations and case material about the extent and nature of poverty in Ireland.

Whately started from the premise that there was no point in imposing a workhouse test on the able-bodied poor as the problem was 'not to make the able-bodied look for employment, but to find it profitably for the many who seek it' (Burke: 29). Furthermore, Whately estimated that the sheer scale of destitution in Ireland was such that a Poor Law system of workhouses would require accommodation for almost 2.4 million people. Whately was also acutely aware of the dilemma of attempting a Poor Law solution in Irish circumstances. This had been highlighted by the classical economist Nassau Senior who had served on the Royal Commission on the Poor Laws in England: the depth of destitution in Ireland was so profound that not even the most rigorous workhouse test would deter the poor from resorting to the workhouse.

Nowadays, Whately's report would be described as recommending 'prevention rather than cure'. Whately recommended, first, a radical series of measures aimed at developing the economy principally through the establishment of a Board of Improvement with wide powers in the area of land improvement and redevelopment, agricultural training, education and rural housing. Secondly, they argued for a comprehensive program of assisted emigration as a means of relieving overpopulation and, thirdly, they proposed a series of largely institutional services for categories such as the aged and the disabled, partly funded through national taxation. In the event, the government rejected the Whately Commission's report. Philosophically, it ran completely counter to the prevailing *laissez-faire* policy, and the minority Whig government then in office would not have risked political defeat in the House of Commons by attempting to implement the Irish Commission's report. Furthermore, the report had provided the government with a tactical reason for rejecting it: the report had evaded the important and contentious question of whether the Poor Law in Ireland should be funded locally from rates collected by Boards of Guardians (Cook, 1990: Burke, 1987).

In response, the government despatched George Nicholls to Ireland — the Poor Law overseer who had been so influential in criticising the Speenhamland system and in introducing the rigours of the new Poor Law in Southwell. Nicholls imposed his new Poor Law analysis on Ireland, and in a series of three reports developed a plan for Poor Relief in Ireland that was modelled on the 1834 Act. This Act, opposed by the Irish landlords, came into effect in 1838. It gave the English Poor Law Commissioners power to appoint officers in Ireland and provide and oversee a national network of workhouses within a framework of Poor Law Unions and elected Boards of Guardians. In each Union the cost of the workhouse was to be met by a Poor Law rate administered by the Boards of Guardians and levied on the Unions' property owners. Under Nicholls' supervision the network of workhouses began to emerge — 92 were provided between 1839 and 1843 — and the process of establishing and collecting rates began.

The 1838 Act — the first national, statutory system of welfare in Ireland — failed. The English model of poor relief was essentially inappropriate in Irish conditions. The sheer scale of destitution was such — even before the calamitous effects of the Great Famine of 1847 — that the workhouse could not operate as a deterrent in the way that it might in England's industrialised, wage-labour economy. Furthermore, the poor rate (the source of funding for the Poor Law) was to be collected from all property owners so that the population at large would have an interest in preventing pauperism. This principle meant, in Irish circumstances, that very small rates liabilities were being extracted, with considerable effort, from vast numbers of small property-owners, as well as established landlords. As Cook has pointed out, 'the distinction between ratepayers and the destitute was barely perceptible' (Cook, 1990: 14). In turn, this considerably widened the resistance to the poor rate and contributed to violence and disorder in the collection of the poor rate in many unions.

To compound the difficulties, the Great Famine created the most intense destitution on a scale that was unforeseen. The workhouses in Ireland came to be occupied by the starving and diseased, giving the workhouses a role and a stigma that had not been anticipated. Finally, whatever scope an English Poor Law might have had to relieve distress in Ireland was reduced by some specific aspects of the 1838 Act that differentiated the Irish from the English Poor Law (Cook, 1990: 26–8). For example, unlike the English Act, the Irish Act did not confer a *right* to relief. In Ireland, a widow was required to have two legitimate children to receive outdoor relief, whereas in England the requirement was one child. Guardians in England were permitted to grant outdoor relief in urgent circumstances, but no such discretion was allowed the Irish Guardians. In England, the families of prisoners and the children of families deserted by their natural heads were allowed outdoor relief, but in Ireland they were not. The net effect of these differences was that the incidence of relief in Ireland (standardised for population size) was considerably *lower* in Ireland than in England, Scotland, or Wales, notwithstanding Ireland's vastly greater level of need.

What is the significance of the Poor Law for the history of social security in Ireland? The chronological significance is that the 1838 Act and the developments in the Poor Law thereafter provided the framework in which income maintenance was first paid in Ireland. Although the first social security legislation proper might be deemed to be the Workmen's Compensation Act (1897) or the introduction of Old Age Pensions (1908), it is more likely that under the rubric of outdoor relief cash payments first began to be made in some areas in the last quarter of the nineteenth century. The emergence of cash relief under the evolving Poor Law had a wider significance, however. Payments from the state first took the form of locally dispensed, discretionary payments, in a legal context that gave no rights to recipients, and in an institutional context that was inextricably associated with the Famine and the harsh Poor Law of the 1838 Act. This imparted to the next generation a deep-seated revulsion of the Poor Law: the indignities and stigma of the Poor Law would in future be invoked as a rationale for improvements in social security and social policy generally.

During the second half of the nineteenth century the Poor Law evolved and spawned a wide variety of initiatives in health and welfare. From the point of view of the development of income maintenance the critical changes were the gradual widening of the grounds for receipt of outdoor relief, commencing in 1847, and the transfer of overall responsibility for the Poor Law to the Local Government Board that was established in 1872. In the 1880s, when the agricultural economy was depressed, outdoor relief was granted to able-bodied landowners, and henceforth able-bodied persons would not be refused outdoor relief at times of agricultural depression. By the late 1880s, expenditure on indoor and outdoor relief were about equal, but this change took place in a framework that was essentially unchanged in ethos and structure since 1838. The number of workhouses had reached 163 in 1850 and from then until 1914 only four workhouses were closed (O'Connor, 1995). The significance of the Poor Law would begin to decline dramatically early in the twentieth century as national legislation incorporated a new method of responding to poverty — national insurance.

THE EMERGENCE OF NATIONAL INSURANCE

In the period 1900–11 the pace of change in social policy in Great Britain and Ireland accelerated and legislation for old age pensions, sickness benefits and unemployment insurance was introduced. This reflects the outcome of the battle of political ideas in Great Britain in the last quarter of the nineteenth and the early years of the twentieth century. This battle centred on the relative roles of the state and the individual. Marshall's (1975) classification of these ideas offers a way of summarising the controversies. At one end of the political spectrum were the Victorian individualists, broadly supportive of the Poor Law. In the debates over social legislation this stance was most clearly represented by the Charity Organisation Society (founded in 1869). This was the largest and most active philanthropic organisation in Great Britain and it looked to individual rehabilitation and self-improvement as the way to ameliorate poverty. The COS regarded the Poor Law as a necessary deterrent against the poor claiming relief, resting this belief on the assumption that in a prosperous country poverty must be unnecessary. Helen Bosanquet, the leading exponent of this view, argued that all those who were not genuinely incapable of work should be held responsible for their own maintenance and that of their dependent relatives. In 1903, in her book, *The Strength of the People*, she rhetorically posed the question as to whether the social and economic system would allow everybody to meet their responsibilities. Her answer was that 'It is a vain and idle hypothesis. The social conditions *will* permit them.' (Marshall, 1975: 39) In the debates about pensions, unemployment and health care the COS and their followers opposed state welfare, or campaigned to have new provisions tied to the Poor Law and to voluntary effort.

In contrast to the COS, the newly emerging working class politicians and socialist intellectuals under the rubric of the Fabian Society campaigned for collectivist solutions. Sidney and Beatrice Webb were the most famous exponents of such views.[2] Their analysis of social problems was socialist: the causes of poverty lay in the capitalist economic system, which needed to be reformed. This analysis led them to offer state, collectivist solutions. The Webbs argued that to deal with unemployment, for instance, state-provided labour exchanges should operate as a direct system of allocating labour. Likewise, in their book about health, *The State and the Doctor*, the Webbs argued for a significant, direct role for the state in the provision of medical care.

The 'new liberalism' of Lloyd George and Winston Churchill and other political leaders of the Liberal Party represented a third political stance. This was essentially classical liberalism with its emphasis on the rights of the individual, free trade and a limited role for the state, qualified by an acceptance that a completely unregulated free market economy was simply not practical. A modern capitalist economy, in this perspective, could not function effectively without a modicum of state intervention such as the provision of infrastructure, housing, basic public sanitation, and so on. As the nineteenth century entered its last quarter, the theoretical ideal of a pure market economy co-existed with growing intervention in the economy and society in the form of such legislation as the Factories Acts and the 1870 Education Act. This increasing recognition of the practical necessity for state intervention extended at the end of the nineteenth century to include social problems. For efficiency as well as for social reasons, the state might need health provisions to cure sick workers and get them back to work, or pension provisions to allow old, unproductive workers to retire, or a system of labour exchanges to get the unemployed back to work more quickly. In policy terms this perspective allowed a limited degree of state intervention as much for practical as for social reasons: many years later a standard analysis of the relationship between ideology and politics would label this perspective 'reluctant collectivism' (George and Wilding, 1976). An example of this analysis was William Beveridge's (1909) analysis of unemployment in *Unemployment; A Problem of Industry*. Here Beveridge argued not about the injustices of unemployment or the exploitative nature of the capitalist labour market, but about the needless waste and inefficiency it entailed. His strategy was to devise an element of organisation in the labour market to help it to operate more efficiently; this perspective would greatly influence policy in relation to unemployment.[3]

New liberalism was as much a political and electoral strategy as a body of coherent thought. The programme of social reform it would implement was strategically constructed to support the working class electoral base of the Liberal Party. This was under increasing threat from the mid-1880s when the electoral franchise was greatly extended and the number of working class MPs began to increase. More fundamentally, however, the political elite in Great Britain began to see that practical social legislation could be an effective political bulwark against socialism. British policy makers (Lloyd George and Winston Churchill notably) learned from Germany at this time about how to organise social insurance, but also learned of Chancellor Bismarck's tactical use of initiatives in this area as a political weapon in the battle for workers' loyalties. As Arthur Balfour, a Conservative politician, observed, 'Social legislation, as I conceive it, is not merely to be distinguished from socialist legislation, but it is its most direct opposite and its most effective antidote.' (cited in Marshall, 1975: 40) Of the three sets of ideas — Victorian individualism, Socialism and New Liberalism — it was the latter which dominated the first two decades of the twentieth century and directly affected the shape of the emerging system of social security.

The debate about political ideas and their implications for public policy was intensified by the revelations of social deprivation in Great Britain. These revelations were at first literary in nature, in the popular novels of Charles Dickens. But from the late 1880s in particular, a new tradition of systematic social inquiry directly influenced political debate. In 1890, General William Booth of the philanthropic body, the Salvation Army, published a popular work on poverty in England, *In Darkest England, or the Way Out* in which he drew parallels between the poor in England and African tribes. Commencing in 1889 and finishing in 1903, Charles Booth, who would later contribute to the controversy about pensions, published a seventeen-volume study, *The Life and Labour of the People of London* (1889). Booth used a quantitative approach and offered a direct answer to the question 'how many are poor?' The figure that struck the public imagination was Booth's estimate that 30% of the people of London were poor. But the impact of Booth's work was superseded by the enormous impact — public and political — of Seebohm Rowntree's landmark study *Poverty: A Study of Town Life*, published in 1901.[4]

Rowntree's work is the precursor to modern studies of poverty and income distribution that attempt to identify 'poverty lines' and the numbers below them. He undertook a census of all working-class households in the city of York and collected detailed information about all of the households and supplemented this with information from employers about wage rates. He applied very rigorous dietary benchmarks to determine the minimum amount of food required and costed these: these costs were supplemented with other necessary costs such as rent. These calculations yielded a figure for the absolute minimum amount of income households of different sizes needed. He then estimated the numbers of families below this minimum. Sensationally, Rowntree estimated that 9.9% of the population of York were below the stringent poverty line ('primary poverty') and a further 17.93% were in 'secondary poverty'.

The impact of *Poverty: A Study of Town Life* can be attributed not only to the estimates of poverty it reported and its innovative use of social scientific methodology, but also to the way in which Rowntree put poverty in context. In his discussion of 'the immediate causes of poverty' he showed that poverty was endemic — it was a general problem affecting the working class because of underemployment, low pay, and the absence of wage earners (Rowntree, 1901: 119). Most famously, he outlined the existence of a typical life-cycle which generated greater needs at particular times — when wage earners have young children, for example. He pointed out that '*the wages paid for unskilled labour in York are insufficient to provide food, shelter, and clothing adequate to maintain a family of moderate size in a state of bare physical efficiency*' (Rowntree, 1901: 133, emphasis in original) He was careful to record that the 'poverty line' he identified was strict:

> It will be remembered that the above estimates of necessary minimum expenditure are based upon the assumption that the diet is even less generous than that allowed to able-bodied paupers in the York Workhouse, *and that no allowance is made for any expenditure other than that required for the maintenance of merely physical efficiency*. (Rowntree, 1901: 133; emphasis in original)

Rowntree also reported case studies of individual families and gave an in-depth analysis of health and housing conditions in communities in York, showing the intimate connection between poverty and ill-health and mortality, contrasting the mortality rates in the poorest and richest areas. In reporting his findings, Rowntree correctly anticipated that the COS and it supporters would repudiate his research. He therefore presented his work with a view to countering the individualist philosophy of the COS and in one extended passage he carefully stressed again how menial his poverty line was by dramatically listing all of the social needs which his calculated minimum would not allow (Rowntree, 1901: 134):

> A family living upon the scale allowed for . . . must never spend a penny on railway fare or omnibus. They must write no letters to absent children because they cannot afford to pay the postage. . . . They cannot contribute anything to church or chapel or give any help to a neighbour. They cannot save. . . . The father must smoke no tobacco. . . . The mother must never buy any pretty clothes for herself or her children.

He also emphasised the impact the life cycle has on poverty and he showed that it was not possible for many workers with families to stay above the primary poverty line at prevailing wages: 'But the fact remains that every labourer must pass through a time, probably lasting for about ten years, when he will be in a state of 'primary poverty'; in other words, when he and his family will be *underfed*.' (Rowntree, 1901: 135; emphasis in original)

Rowntree's book had a profound impact politically, generating a widespread controversy. Lloyd George was a personal friend and very aware of the contents of *Poverty: A Study of Town Life*. He referred to the book in some of his speeches and he was particularly struck by the fact that Rowntree, an industrialist who was concerned with the health and productivity of workers, stressed that workers were actually undernourished. His association with Sidney and Beatrice Webb further amplified the impact of Rowntree's work. The latter had worked with Charles Booth on his study of the poor in London and was an active adherent of the emerging discipline of quantitative social science, emphasising the collection and reporting of large-scale survey information as the basis for social inquiry and policy debate. As members of the Royal Commission on the Poor Laws, the Webbs carried the policy debate about Rowntree's findings into the centre of official debate about poverty. The COS was also represented on the Royal Commission, however. The Commission's deliberations therefore became a battleground on which the Webbs and the COS rehearsed their respective arguments about the causes of poverty, invoking Rowntree's research as evidence for their views.

Rowntree emphasised the efficiency implications of the widespread poverty he described. Poor health, slum housing, and low levels of nutrition posed a threat to the efficiency of industry and the economy. This theme was dramatically reinforced in 1904 when the Report of the Interdepartmental Committee on Physical Deterioration was published (Marshall, 1975: 33–4). The Annual Reports of the Inspector General of Recruiting in the period leading up to the Boer War (South Africa) had revealed that a high proportion (42% in 1896) of prospective recruits to the army fell considerably short of minimum physical and health requirements, and the military authorities suggested that physical standards in the population generally were in a state of deterioration. While the official report of 1904 expressed disagreement with the specific estimates made by the recruiting authorities, it nevertheless confirmed the shocking truth of widespread poor health among people of working age. Rowntree in a chapter entitled 'The Relation of Poverty to the Standard of Health' (Rowntree, 1901: 182–221) had made this very point. He illustrated the link between the social and health conditions of workers and national economic efficiency, by pointing out that America was then emerging as one of Great Britain's competitors and that this was partly because 'her workers are better nourished and possess a relatively higher efficiency' (Rowntree, 1901: 221). The cumulative effect of these findings was to forge a link in the public mind and in reformers' agendas between social needs, on the one hand, and economic efficiency and national self-interest, on the other.

The mix of ideological debate, popular controversy and new knowledge of social conditions provided the impetus for the reform of the Poor Law in Great Britain and Ireland. A Vice-Regal Commission on Poor Law Reform in Ireland was established in 1903. It reported in 1906 and effectively recommended the abandonment of the Poor Law. The report proposed the abolition of the workhouse system, the establishment of separate institutions for the different categories of inmate, the removal of the aged and infirm from the workhouses and the establishment of separate county institutions, and a considerably greater emphasis on the use of outdoor relief. The Royal Commission on the Poor Laws and Relief of Distress was instituted separately in 1906 and reported in 1909. In a minority report to the Royal Commission, the Webbs, informed by their collectivist ideology and armed with the evidence of Rowntree, Booth and others, offered an analysis that essentially supported the 1906 report on Ireland's Poor Law and recommended the abandonment of the Poor Law. The contrasting arguments of the Vice-Regal Commission and the Minority and Majority reports of the Royal Commission helped to keep Poor Law reform on the parliamentary agenda and there were abortive attempts to have an Irish Poor Law bill passed in the House of Commons between 1908 and 1912.

The gradual erosion in the effective role of the Poor Law began with the introduction of national social security legislation. This removed increasing segments of the population from the remit of the Poor Law. A modest beginning in this direction was the Workmens' Compensation Act of 1897, but the key developments were the introduction of Old Age Pensions in 1908 and Unemployment and Sickness Benefit in 1911. Ireland was to benefit significantly from these reforms introduced by the Liberal government of 1906–1911 (Gilbert, 1966: 159–231).

OLD AGE PENSIONS

The background to the introduction of pensions in Ireland is that in England from the late 1870s a campaign for the introduction of pensions began. Canon Blackley, an Irish-born cleric who was involved in work with the poor in East London, published a pamphlet advocating pensions in 1878. This pamphlet had little impact because of the conservative influence of the Friendly Societies, reinforced by the opposition of the Charity Organisation Society. The Friendly Societies were an integral element in the culture of the prosperous Victorian working class and offered their members sickness insurance. The societies were socially conservative and intensely concerned to distinguish their respectable membership from the pauper class that would depend on the Poor Law. Any proposal for an old age pension scheme that was contributory in nature was opposed by the Friendly Societies, as this would be competing with them for the savings of the working class. In effect, the societies had a veto on the emergence of old age pensions.

The idea of a tax financed, non-contributory pension did not appear until the end of the century and any proposals for pensions were contributory in nature and thus invoked the resistance of the societies. For example, Joseph Chamberlain leader of the Unionist Party published a pamphlet in 1891 proposing a system of voluntary pensions with subsidies added by central government. This was rejected by the societies. In the same year Charles Booth, the renowned social investigator and reformer, in a paper to the Royal Statistical Society in London proposed a non-contributory pension scheme for the elderly, financed from national taxation. In the 1890s, the resistance of the Friendly Societies continued to thwart the emerging efforts to introduce some form of State pensions. The Aberdare Commission (the Royal Commission on the Aged Poor) was set up in 1892 and reported in 1894, but it did not reach agreement, as Booth and Chamberlain — authors of fundamentally different proposals — were both members of the Commission. Moreover, in 1894 before the Commission reported, the Friendly Societies reiterated their opposition to state pension provisions. Aberdare concurred with the Friendly Societies that pensions should be their responsibility.

In office again in the mid-1890s, Chamberlain established a Treasury Committee under Rotschild to examine the issue of pensions, but limited the terms of reference to contributory plans. *De facto* only four out of 100 submissions (those dealing only with contributory schemes) could be considered and the Committee could not agree about these. By 1896 the prospect of pension reform seemed remote, but in 1908 a national, non-contributory pension was legislated for, and in 1909 it was implemented. A variety of circumstances led to this. First, the practicality of a pension paid for by the state became clear in 1898. The Governor General of New Zealand, William Pember-Reeves, was visiting London and gave a public talk about the pension system that had been introduced in New Zealand: this was a tax-financed, non-contributory scheme. The organisers of this event arranged a further meeting in 1898 at which Charles Booth spoke, and out of this a national campaign emerged. A practical example was now available of a pension scheme that offered an alternative to the Poor Law for old people and that did not directly compete with the Friendly Societies for contributions.

Second, a nationally organised campaign developed with the full support of the Trade Unions and the Cooperative movement. This campaign was all the more effective because of Charles Booth's ability at defining and then popularising the policy reform being demanded. In 1899 he published a pamphlet titled *Old Age Pensions and the Aged Poor* in which he set out the case, and gave costings for a pension for all old people over 70. Furthermore, Booth's work gave reinforcement to the popular arguments being advanced in favour of state pensions: state pensions would considerably reduce the costs of indoor and outdoor relief under the Poor Law, would greatly enhance the health of the elderly, and would preserve the Friendly Societies. In 1899 the TUC demanded a pension as of right for all people over 60 and in 1901 the Cooperative movement did likewise.

Third, by the end of the nineteenth century the Friendly Societies were in a more difficult situation financially. Life expectancy had risen significantly in the latter half of the century and the Societies were now incurring greater numbers of claims from members experiencing greater longevity. Nor could the Societies deal with this problem by increasing contributions from members, as individual societies would not increase these for fear of losing members to competitor societies. The underlying insolvency of the societies was hidden for much of the 1890s as they profited from high interest rates on their reserves. But by 1900 there was a realisation that they were, in effect, paying pensions in the form of sickness payments (for which they had not made actuarial provision). The societies now accepted that a non-contributory pension would not displace the savings of their contributors, and in 1902 they offered public support for pensions for the first time.

Fourth, the electoral and political dynamic of social policy changed markedly very early in the twentieth century as the Liberal party's grip on the working class vote began to slip. In 1903, Will Crooks, a member of the National Committee campaigning for pensions, was elected to the House of Commons in what had previously been a staunchly Unionist constituency. In the same year, a working-class representative was elected in Durham to a seat normally held by a member of the local Liberal oligarchy. The general election in 1906 resulted in the return of an unprecedented number of working-class MPs. Keir Hardie had founded the Labour Representation Committee in 1898 as a forum for the newly emerging category of working class elected representatives. After the 1906 election there were 29 such MPs formally affiliated to the LRC and a further 24 sitting officially with the Liberal Party. The Liberal Party had not come to office as a party united on a platform of social reform. On the contrary, in the election the Liberals had studiously avoided an overall commitment to social reform. The eventual emergence of pensions legislation was, Gilbert's detailed account suggests, 'principally the story of forcing upon the traditional Liberals in the cabinet the conviction that pensions were not only theoretically desirable, but politically essential, if the reputation of the liberals as a party of social reform were to be improved' (Gilbert, 1966: 204). The new working-class MPs were not in a position to impose their will, but the more reform-minded members of the Liberal cabinet were aware that the working-class votes that had supported the LRC 'had to be bought back, and quickly. Part of the price was old age pensions.' (Gilbert, 1966: 202) This political pressure intensified in 1907 when the Liberals lost further by-elections, Booth published a further pamphlet proposing a tax-based pension, and the TUC again publicly demanded a national pension scheme.

The development of actual pensions legislation began in 1906 when the Prime Minister met two of the leaders of the campaign and gave an assurance that a scheme would be introduced. The Treasury was put to work on the costs and related issues and at this point the only unresolved issue was what *type* of pension scheme would be legislated for. In 1907, the TUC publicly warned the Prime Minister not to take seriously the proposal being advocated by a banker, Lord Avebury, for a voluntary scheme administered by the Friendly Societies. In 1908, the King's Speech to Parliament made a commitment to legislation and in April that year the Chancellor set out proposals for the Cabinet. These proposals were close to the substance of the eventual legislation and reveal the influences shaping the Government's thinking. The cabinet note pointed to the savings in Poor Relief and the wholesale unpopularity of the Poor Law. It noted the success of the New Zealand scheme and argued against a contributory scheme, reflecting Treasury advice, on the grounds that there was no administrative infrastructure for the administration of a system of contributions. Significantly, it followed the opinion of the Webbs who were then members of the Royal Commission on the Poor Law and argued against local Poor Law type financing, but equally it opposed a completely universal pension and opted for a means-tested pension, tax-financed and subject to a test of character. This strategy drove a mid-way course between the radicals such as Booth, the Webbs and the progressive wing of the Liberal Party, and the conservatives such as the Friendly Societies, the Charity Organisation Society and the traditional wing of the liberal party and the Tories — the latter wanting a closer link between pensions and the Poor Law.

The legislation received its first reading in May 1908 and its second reading in June 1908. It provided for pensions for all persons of 70 years and over with an income below a stipulated annual figure, subject to proof of non-imprisonment and non receipt of poor relief in a specified period.[5] The key changes made to the legislation before it was passed were: first, married couples were granted a full pension each rather than the 'one for one person/one-and-a-half for a couple' formula in the original bill and, second, a sliding scale of pensions according to means was substituted for a simple cut-off point of means. The pensions were to be administered by Local Pension Committees representing the elected members of local authorities.

The pensions came into effect in 1909 in Ireland and the UK and represented the first significant departure from the Poor Law to national, statutory income maintenance provisions. In fiscal terms the pension provisions were very significant for Ireland, as Guinnane (1993) has shown. The Irish population was older and poorer than the British and therefore Ireland had more pensioners per capita than Britain. Also, the amount of the pension was set with the incomes and living costs of British urban workers in mind, and it comprised a higher proportion of the earnings of Irish labourers and agricultural workers.

NATIONAL INSURANCE FOR UNEMPLOYMENT AND SICKNESS

Two other important elements in the unfolding system of social security in Great Britain and Ireland were put in place by the Liberal Government: unemployment insurance and health insurance. The unemployment legislation was remarkably uncontroversial given its significance (Gilbert, 1966: 233–88). Here too the Poor Law was a starting point for reform. Although the percentage of paupers in the population began to decline at the turn of the twentieth century, the number of able-bodied workers in the workhouses in the larger cities, London especially, remained high and continued to rise. This was criticised on the grounds of its cost and because workhouse conditions were manifestly not acting as a sufficient deterrent. During the 1880s and 1890s the increasingly common response to the cyclical patterns of unemployment to which the British economy was now prone was the use of relief works, most commonly under charitable auspices. It became obvious that such schemes could not be offered on a sufficient scale. In 1904 the Local Government Board organised local committees in the metropolitan boroughs and in London representing the Poor Law authorities and local government. These took on the task of organising poor relief for the unemployed, creating local work schemes, assisting with emigration and establishing new farming and agricultural colonies to train and 'rehabilitate' the unemployed.

This system received no central government funding, but its essential principles were embodied in the Unemployed Workmen Act of 1905. This Act required every borough to establish Distress Committees and permitted the local authorities to fund the Committees' activities partly through funds from rateable income. These new committees had a similar range of discretionary powers, as well as new powers to establish labour exchanges and employment registers to bring employers and workers together. Circumstances combined to ensure that this labour exchange system evolved into the national system established in legislation in 1909. The level of unemployment rose significantly in 1907 and this showed the limitations of small-scale, locally organised and funded responses to unemployment. William Beveridge, later to be the architect of the British system of social security after the second World War, was involved in the central committee overseeing the 1905 Act and his observation of the operations of the schemes informed his ongoing research on the nature of the unemployment problem. In his book on unemployment Beveridge (1909) had identified what would now be labelled 'underemployment': the existence of very large numbers of workers in chronically vulnerable employment circumstances — unskilled, and reliant on work in casual, seasonal and very disorganised trades. He argued that the state should have a continuing role in organising the labour market to counteract underemployment.

In 1908 Winston Churchill took the post of President of the Board of Trade with responsibility for employment matters. At this point Churchill was a zealous reformer, and both publicly and privately argued for a programme of social reform that would include health insurance, unemployment insurance and labour exchanges. He appointed Beveridge to the Board of Trade, and a bill legislating for the establishment of labour exchanges was drafted in 1908 and enacted in 1909. Beveridge was made director of the new labour exchanges service in the Board of Trade and oversaw the expansion in the number of exchanges and in their role. In 1910 there were 61 exchanges and this grew to 430 by the end of 1913 (in addition to the much larger number of small rural branch agencies.) The 1909 Act empowered the authorities to establish exchanges and to offer a range of services. Workers could be given financial assistance to travel to seek work; the act permitted workers the freedom to refuse any job that might be offered at less than the trade union rate of pay and the exchanges maintained strict neutrality between worker and employer by refusing services to employers seeking 'scab' labour in a strike.

A number of points should be noted about the early history of labour exchanges. Firstly, Beverage clearly envisaged labour exchanges as a social service to aid the worker in the labour market and to make the labour market more efficient. Historically, and to this day, the exchanges have become associated specifically with unemployment payments — the 'dole'. While it is true that a system of unemployment payments was devised for Ireland and Great Britain in 1911 and administered through the exchanges, it is clear that Beveridge and his political masters accepted the need for some form of labour market organisation quite independently of any consideration of payments for the unemployed. Secondly, in this initiative the Liberal reformers again steered a middle course between the same political ideologies that competed to influence the pensions legislation. On the one side were the Webbs who wanted a fully comprehensive system that made it compulsory for employers to use the exchanges and who advocated much more direct systems of labour allocation. On the other, the anti-reformers in the Cabinet and the Liberal Party were generally disposed not to support the overall programme of reform to which Churchill and Lloyd George were now committed. Thirdly, the development of the labour exchanges revealed clearly for the first time the influence of German experiments on British policy. Churchill publicly adverted to the successful experiences of Germany in 'Social Organisation' and in his and Beveridge's preparation of the labour exchanges system they looked to Germany. The legislators also consulted the TUC, which sent a delegation to Germany in 1908 to look at their arrangements in relation to health, and social insurance for sickness and old age. The German 'solution' of social insurance had been ignored in the case of the initial pension reform, but by 1911 insurance was adopted as the mechanism for dealing with social security for health and unemployment (Gilbert, 1966).

Social security payments for unemployment were introduced in the form of unemployment insurance in 1911, as part two of the National Insurance Bill. The proximate source of the initiative was the enthusiasm of Churchill, Lloyd George and the trade unions for the German experiment with social insurance. After the passage of the pensions legislation in 1908 Lloyd George had personally visited Germany and this visit reinforced his growing interest in social insurance. However, the introduction of social insurance for unemployment was by no means inevitable. Although Germany had unemployment insurance, it was not a national, statutory system, and the existing local and embryonic schemes in Great Britain and Europe were either trade union based or organised at town or municipal level. The central features of the 1911 Act were as follows:

- Employers and employees would pay matching contributions to a national unemployment fund.
- The state would add a third contribution.
- The contributions paid and benefits received would be flat rate.
- The coverage of the Act would be limited to specific trades.
- The state would subsidise private (typically trade union) schemes to encourage the unions to offer higher benefits than those available under the state scheme.
- Employees were entitled to one week's benefit for every five contributions paid subject to a maximum of 15 weeks benefit in any twelve-month period, after a waiting period of one week.
- Employees on strike were not entitled to benefit, but equally the act allowed a worker to refuse to take up employment in a firm engaged in a trade dispute.
- A worker unemployed through his own 'misconduct' or who left employment 'without just cause' could be disqualified from benefit, although the act provided for an appeals system (Gilbert, 1966: 265–89).

The administration of contributions commenced in July 1912 and the first benefits became due in January 1913. This scheme remained largely unchanged until 1920 when the 1911 Act was repealed and the Unemployment Insurance Act was introduced (Farley, 1964: 44–8). The coverage of the scheme was widened to include all employees aged 16 or over in a contract of employment, although the key exclusions from the scheme (agricultural employees, domestic servants, public employees) meant that the effective coverage for unemployment insurance in Ireland remained limited in contrast to Great Britain. Under the 1920 Act the numbers insured in Great Britain and Ireland rose to over 12 million compared to just over two million under the 1911 legislation. It is difficult to estimate what proportion of the Irish workforce was insured for unemployment, but Farley (1964: 47) suggests that by 1926 only 37% of the Irish workforce was covered by the legislation. The 1920 legislation also altered the levels of benefit and changed the details, but not the substance, of the earlier legislation. In 1921 there were amendments to the 1920 Act: the levels of benefit were substantially increased; as expenditure rose rapidly during 1921 the benefit levels were revised down to their 1920 levels again, the waiting period for payment was increased to six days and contribution rates were increased; additional allowances were introduced in respect of dependant spouses and children of the unemployed. The broad architecture of unemployment insurance introduced at this time has remained substantially unchanged.

The application of national insurance to health-related costs in Part 1 of Lloyd George's 1911 Act proved to be contentious. This part of the Act set out to offer social insurance to meet the costs of sickness benefit (income for workers when out of work sick) and medical benefit (the costs of doctors and medicines for workers and their families). The Act proposed an insurance framework for sickness analogous to that for unemployment for broadly the same sections of the workforce. At the time the legislation was introduced it was unclear how many in Ireland would be affected by its provisions. In her account of the bill, Barrington (1987: 42) notes that estimates varied from 800,000 to 1.3 million. The 1911 Census would later show that the total number of employees affected was 933,000. Workers, employers and the state would contribute to a fund and become entitled to sickness benefit based on their contributions, with both benefits and contributions set at flat rates. The benefits available were sickness benefit for 26 weeks subject to a specified number of contributions; a long-term payment, disablement benefit, could also be paid where stricter contribution requirements were met. In addition, a lump-sum maternity benefit was payable and a separate sanatorium benefit administered by TB sanatoria was provided for.

For both Great Britain and Ireland the legislation stipulated that the Friendly Societies would act as the agencies for the payment of sickness benefit. The persons required to become contributors could choose which society to apply to, but the societies were free to refuse membership to any individual (but not on grounds of age). A separate system of collecting and recording contributions in Post Offices was necessary for those contributors, 'deposit contributors', who could not obtain membership of a society. Relying on the societies had distinct advantages in Great Britain, but experience was to show that in Ireland this created distinct problems that would require national legislative action. From the time the bill was enacted until political independence the structure of the scheme remained unchanged, with modifications being made in the level of benefits, the contribution amounts and the income ceiling governing membership.

The new sickness benefit scheme brought considerable benefits to workers and their families, but in both Great Britain and Ireland it was the most politically contentious of all the new national insurance provisions. Briefly, in Great Britain the original proposals had included provisions for widows and orphans, but these were abandoned in the face of opposition from the Friendly Societies and private insurance companies (Gilbert, 1966: 289–399). As well as conceding on this major issue, the Government also had to negotiate with the medical profession and the Friendly Societies on the terms of their involvement in the medical benefit aspect of scheme — the part of the scheme governing workers' access to treatment by doctors. The legislation enacted in Great Britain was significantly different to the Government's original plans. The Government had intended to use Local Health Committees (under the local authorities) as the vehicle to administer medical benefit, but opposition to this eventually led the Government to administer it through the Friendly Societies, with the doctors paid on a contract basis by the societies for each sick worker treated.

Irish workers were *not* included in the medical benefits aspect of national health insurance at all. This element of national health insurance was rejected by the medical profession, by the Catholic hierarchy and by the Irish Party in the House of Commons (Barrington, 1987: 39–66). The political dynamics that led to the rejection of medical benefits in Ireland have been fully recorded in Barrington's authoritative study and need not be recorded here. Barrington points out that in Ireland the existing medical services and their organisation differed significantly from those of Great Britain. Specifically, Ireland had a Poor Law based, local dispensary system of medical care for the poor alongside an emerging system of voluntary hospitals and private general practice. Ireland, however, did not have a dense network of Friendly Societies. The Irish Party and the medical profession would not accept the extension of state-funded medical care that medical benefit would have entailed. Barrington's account suggests that in fact many general practitioners in Ireland (the Poor Law dispensary doctors) would have benefited from the proposed shift to insurance-funded capitation payments. However, the campaign against the legislation was ill-informed and overly influenced by the interests of the small group of private-practice consultants who opposed the perceived threat to private care (Barrington, 1987: 39–66).

The rejection of medical benefit had one long-lasting, important effect on the character of Ireland's social security system. It separated the systems of social insurance and health care at an early point in their development. In the future, many countries would build on medical benefit arrangements to develop equal access to health care through social insurance for all of the population. The repudiation of medical benefit in Ireland led not only to the separation of income maintenance system from the health care system, but also to the continuation of separate health care for the poor and the well off. As Barrington (1987: 65) has stated:

> The decision to exclude medical benefit meant that insurance funds would play little part in financing general practice or hospital services in the future and that the remuneration of doctors by capitation fee was never firmly established. No special arrangements were made to meet the medical needs of the working classes and the dispensary system had demonstrated its resilience once again.

The last addition to the emerging social security system prior to political independence was the introduction of separate pensions for the blind. Under the Blind Persons Act in 1920, people aged over 50 unable to work because of their disability became entitled to a pension on the same terms as which people aged over 70 received the old age pension.

CONCLUSION

The emergence of social *insurance* as an instrument of social security was important. Historians of the British welfare state have stressed the fundamental nature of the initiative (Marshall, 1975: 53–4; Fraser, 1973). In the first instance, national insurance required a qualitative change in the labour market: the state was now intervening on a large scale in what had up to that point been a simple capital-wage nexus between the worker and the employer. By levying contributions on employers and extracting contributions from employees the state would henceforth have a direct effect on the cost of labour to employers and the disposable income of employees. More importantly, the use of the notion of insurance was significant. 'It led people', Marshall suggests, 'to exaggerate the distinction between social insurance and social assistance, and helped to maintain the flavour of inferiority that clung to the latter.' (Marshall, 1975: 55) This caused, Marshall also suggests, 'a widespread misunderstanding of the nature of social insurance which bedevilled discussions of social policy for many years' (Marshall, 1975: 55).

One of the attractions of national insurance is that the term 'insurance' had connotations of prudence, thrift and self-help — the virtues emphasised by the Friendly Societies, the private insurance companies and the COS — but this obscured the nature of the 'contract' between the citizen and the state. National insurance required its participants to 'contribute' and allowed them to benefit according to certain rules. This relationship was in practice not a commercial, actuarial one, in which the benefits received by individual recipients were calibrated according to their individual 'insurance premiums'. The contributions were, in reality, rules of entitlement, but the fact that workers paid contributions in a quantifiable way reinforced the insurance character of the new rights. The insurance 'rights' workers began to accrue were subject as much to political as actuarial considerations.

By developing social insurance as they did, the policy makers simultaneously addressed a number of conflicts of policy logic and practical politics. Social insurance could be presented as the opposite of the dreaded Poor Law. It was not discretionary welfare at the behest of the local Poor Law guardians, but a set of entitlements that recipients could claim to have 'earned'. The new insurance benefits, while clearly superior to the Poor Law, were not radically redistributive either: in fact the contribution system of flat rate contributions at all wage levels required disproportionate contributions form the lower-paid and was therefore regressive. An element of redistribution arose indirectly as a result of the sharing of the costs of unemployment, sickness and so on, and social insurance could therefore be characterised as a form of collective provision. However, the provisions were constructed to complement rather than displace private provision and hence they could also be presented as inherently compatible with an individualist philosophy and a free market economy. Furthermore, while the legislators presented the new measures as the undoubted reforms and improvements they were, they could also point to the contributory — and therefore 'prudent' and 'responsible' — nature of the reforms. These made the initiatives partly self-funding: compulsory national insurance generated a continuous flow of revenue out of which the payment of current benefits could be made.

Before moving on to examine the period after political independence, it is useful to make some general observations about developments up to that point. Clearly, the emerging social security system in Ireland was British, but it is important to distinguish the dimensions of similarity or 'parallelism' in the early development of the two countries' systems, following Cook's analysis (Cook, 1986: 67). Parallel *introduction* refers to legislative initiatives that are introduced at the same time; parallel *provision* refers to identical legislative content, and parallel *enactment* to legislation being enacted and enforced in the two systems simultaneously. Parallel *outcomes*, however, refer to the actual effects of the legislation in the separate contexts of Ireland and Great Britain. Significantly, the period till 1921 shows instances where outcomes in the two countries differed, despite strongly parallel introduction and provision. Notably, the considerably lower proportion of the workforce in waged work in Ireland greatly reduced the effectiveness of the national insurance legislation in meeting the needs of the poor population in Ireland. Where the degree of parallel provision in the specific content of legislation was low, with strongly differentiated legislation, this seemed to be to Ireland's disadvantage. The Irish Poor Law was notably more restrictive than its British counterpart, for example; the medical benefits of national health insurance were not extended to workers in Ireland and the impact of the formal legislation was therefore much less in Ireland than in Great Britain.

By 1920 the emerging social security systems in Ireland and Great Britain contained the seeds of different types of social security systems. The Poor Law remained in place for the large numbers of people for whom the embryonic social security system had not yet made specific provision. Alongside this ran the new old age pension arrangements, financed out of general taxation and based on a means test. Then social insurance for two contingencies, sickness and unemployment, were added. Given the co-existence of tax funded pensions, national insurance benefits and the Poor Law, it was by no means pre-determined what system Ireland would develop in the future — leaving aside the fact that political independence would transfer political responsibility for social security to the new Irish government.

A final reflection concerns the British origins of Ireland's system of social security. Ireland's long-standing colonial link with Great Britain did not make it inevitable that its social security system would be as British as it was at political independence, because the events that shaped the emergence of social security were highly contingent. If, as seemed possible at the turn of the twentieth century, Ireland had achieved Home Rule before the Liberals' social reform programme got underway, then a native government would not have inherited the British reforms — and might not have imitated them — and the subsequent path of social security development might have been different. Alternatively, it is possible that the Liberal Party might not have won the political argument about legislation for national insurance, or might not have won it until the years after the Great War of 1914–18. These alternative scenarios provide an appropriate point at which to turn to events after political independence.

Notes

1. Sir R. G. Nicholls, a Poor Law overseer, was influential in shaping the Poor Law in Great Britain and Ireland. He wrote a two-volume history of the Poor Law, later supplemented by a third volume by T. Mackay. This account of the 1821 pamphlet is taken from the third volume (Nicholls, 1898).
2. The Fabian Society was founded in London in the early 1880s by Thomas Davidson. It offered a forum for left-wing and socialist writers and activists to debate political issues and to publish pamphlets; its first pamphlet was *Why are the Many Poor?* The Society would later develop strong links with the British Labour Party, publishing many authoritative social policy documents in the twentieth century.
3. William Beveridge was author of the most widely cited social policy report during the twentieth century in these islands, the 'Beveridge Report', published in 1942. He was a most influential figure in the development of

social policy in Great Britain. Like many of the new liberal reformers he became involved in these issues through his personal involvement with the poor in London's East End. He played many roles in British social policy in the twentieth century, starting with his work as leader writer in the *Morning Post* newspaper from 1906 to 1908. He was a civil servant in the Board of Trade from 1908 to 1909, during which time he researched the unemployment problem and advised the Government on the development of labour exchanges and wrote *Unemployment; A Problem of Industry*. Later he was a civil servant in the Ministry of Food, a director of the London School of Economics, and during the Second World War was an advisor to the Government on post-war reconstruction and social planning. It was during this era that he wrote the famous 'Beveridge Report', *Social Insurance and Allied Services* (1942). The biography of Beveridge is *William Beveridge: A Biography* (Harris, 1977).

4. Benjamin Seebohm Rowntree was an industrial chemist employed in the cocoa works in York at the turn of the twentieth century. During his life he combined a deep philanthropical commitment to the poor with a political commitment to practical 'new liberal' reforms. His industrial experience gave him great cause for concern about the efficiency of labour in British industry and his primary aim in researching *Poverty* was to examine the diets and social conditions of British workers — hence the emphasis in the book on defining exactly the basic needs of workers. Rowntree was an active supporter of the Liberal party and advisor to the party in government and opposition. His research on poverty had a direct impact on the British social security system: his 'poverty lines' were updated in later versions of his study and influenced the levels of benefit incorporated into the Beveridge-led reforms of social security after the second World War. *Poverty* spawned a whole series of local studies in Great Britain and the general approach to the analysis of poverty that he pioneered — now called 'budget standards' — has remained influential. Rowntree's biography is *Social Thought and Social Action: A Study of the Work of Seebohm Rowntree, 1871–1954* (Briggs, 1961).

5. In the terms of the currency then in place, the amount of the pension was 5 shillings, or one quarter of £1 sterling. The annual income limit was £26 sterling.

2

Social Security in the Twentieth and Twenty-First Centuries

INTRODUCTION

This chapter deals briefly with the development of social security from the foundation of the Free State until the present day. A number of works already contain chronologies of this period or historical accounts of the development of social security (Cook, 1992; Cousins, 1995; Cousins, 2003; Powell, 1992; Commission on Social Welfare, 1986). Therefore, this chapter focuses on broad sub-periods and major influences, rather than on historical detail. Much of the timing and detail of policy developments is contained in the policy-specific chapters in Part Two. Each of the four sections below deals with a historical period, and the last section offers some reflections on the social and political influences that have shaped social security in contemporary Ireland.

FROM LAISSEZ-FAIRE TO STATE INTERVENTION: THE FIRST 25 YEARS

The first two decades offered contrasting experiences. The incoming Free State government inherited Sinn Féin's preoccupation with the Poor Law. Sinn Féin added the adjective 'foreign' to the list of pejoratives that the Poor Law had acquired. In 1919, the first policy pronouncement of the emerging state was the *Democratic Programme of the First Dail*, promulgated at the embryonic meeting of the incipient parliament, following Sinn Féin's comprehensive success in the 1918 general election. This programme was initially drafted by Thomas Johnson, leader of the Labour Party and redrafted along less labourite and Marxist lines by Sean T.O'Kelly, later to become President. It noted the right of every citizen to an 'adequate share of the produce of the nation's labour'. It promised too to abolish the 'odious, degrading and foreign Poor Law system', and identified as the 'first duty' of the new state its obligation 'to make provision for the physical, mental and spiritual well-being of the children, to secure that no child shall suffer hunger or cold from lack of food or clothing or shelter' (Lee, 1989; Powell, 1992; Cook, 1992).

The somewhat social-democratic tone of the Democratic Programme did not find its way into the 1922 Constitution, which was largely liberal-democratic in ethos. Prior to independence key nationalist figures ascribed less political significance to the social content of the programme than the Labour Party and trade unionists. The Free State government, therefore, did not have an indigenous programme for social policy. On the contrary, the new regime was to reveal a distinct antipathy to the development of social security. This was not due to a low level of economic and social development. In fact, the new state had a higher income per capita than small, comparable European countries (although its per capita income was about two-thirds that of Great Britain's), modern banking, transport and administrative infrastructures, a high level of savings and high standards of literacy and education (Lee, 1989). The conservative nature of the Free State's social policy was underpinned by three key influences.

First, if the Free State government did not aspire to a social revolution this was because a social revolution had already occurred prior to political independence — the transformation of the Irish peasantry into landowners in the succession of Land Acts that commenced in the 1880s. The attachment to property that this sustained was strengthened by the sharp increase in agricultural incomes in the decade prior to independence. Second, the political elite of the Free State was conservative. On the one hand, its economic policies gave pre-eminence to the interests of the large farmer class and the urban, professional middle classes. On the other, the administrative elite in the inherited government departments held orthodox views on matters of fiscal and financial management. In this orthodoxy, free trade driven by agricultural exports was at the core of economic policy. It was not the role of the state to intervene to develop the economy or to impose costs on the trading sector of the economy through taxes or social security contributions.

Third, the Labour party and the trades unions were weak and divided. The 1922 election left the Labour Party with 17 of the Dail's 122 seats, reflecting a 21% share of the popular vote. In the snap election of 1923, to an expanded Dail from an enlarged electorate[1], Labour's share of the vote and of Dail seats declined: it had fourteen of the Dail's one hundred and fifty-three seats. The trade union movement was weakened by industrial unrest in 1923, and the return of James Larkin, leader of the Transport Union in the general strike of 1913, precipitated a formal secession from the union of Larkin's supporters and the founding of the Workers Union of Ireland.

Cumann na nGaedheal (later Fine Gael) led the governments of the first decade of independence. In social policy terms this was a harsh regime. Lee (1989: 124) summarises his detailed account of the first decade of Free State social policy:

The Cabinet pursued a clear social as well as economic policy. It took the view that the poor were responsible for their poverty. They should pay for their lack of moral fibre. The existing distribution of income, and of opportunities, largely satisfied the demands of social justice . . . The Cabinet waged a coherent campaign against the weaker elements in the community. The poor, the aged, the unemployed, must all feel the lash of the liberators.

The government implemented a conservative financial policy aimed at a balanced budget at the lowest level of public expenditure. For example, Government expenditure was reduced in 1923 and 1924 and this facilitated a substantial reduction in income tax in 1926. This then required a greater role for indirect taxes — and these bore more heavily on the lower income groups. Agricultural land was de-rated in 1926 and 1931. These tax policies were to the distinct benefit of the larger farmers and the more secure, higher income employees — Fine Gael's electoral support base. More generally in economic policy, the government persisted with a development policy based wholly on agricultural exports; the case for intervention to develop industry and create employment was not seriously examined, and the urban working classes in particular suffered from the rise in unemployment during the 1920s (Lee, 1989; Powell, 1992; Kennedy, Giblin and McHugh, 1988).

In social policy, the opportunities that offered themselves to the new administration to improve policies and services were not taken up. The old age and blind pension was actually reduced in 1924, resulting in savings, although the reductions were partly rescinded in 1928.[2] The government also lowered its subsidy to the National Health Insurance scheme in 1924, and in 1929 it responded selectively to the report of the Committee on Health Insurance and Medical Benefits by implementing only the recommended changes that could deliver economies. In the 1929 National Insurance Act, Sanatorium benefit was abolished — notwithstanding Ireland's high rate of TB — and married women's entitlements were also curtailed. Maternity benefit was abolished and women's membership of an Approved (Health Insurance) Society was ended on marriage, in return for a one-off marriage benefit, requiring employed married women to commence a new insurance contribution record (Powell, 1992; Lee, 1989).

The commitment to the abolition of the Poor Law took a particular turn in the hands of the government, whose emphasis on economy and retrenchment effectively vetoed any serious attempt that might have been made at reform. In 1923, the voting disqualification for poor relief recipients was abolished and the discredited title 'workhouse' was replaced with 'county home'. These changes were merely symbolic and they took place in a wider context of rationalisation and retrenchment in Poor Law provisions, with Poor Law institutions being closed or amalgamated. The Poor Law was reorganised around county units, and local government became responsible for poor relief and health services. However, local government expenditure was reduced in 1923 and 1924 and this resulted in an effective reduction in some local services. In response to criticisms about the 'reformed' Poor Law, the government established the *Commission on the Relief of the Sick and Destitute Poor* (also known as the 'O'Connor Commission') in 1925. The Commission reported in 1928 and made a wide range of recommendations about the standards and organisation of health and social services. It noted the effect of the retrenchment policies in terms of a very uneven service in different parts of the country. Critically, the Commission documented the transformation in the Poor Law, with the majority of cases now dealt with as outdoor relief and a continual growth in the level of outdoor relief.

The growth in outdoor relief and the expenditure implications of this had led the Commission to consider the basis on which outdoor relief should be dispensed. On this critical issue of the right to relief of the able-bodied poor the Commission adopted a strictly conventional stance. It argued that relief should only be afforded as a matter of urgency after most careful investigation 'of all the circumstances of the applicant' and that it should be possible for the authorities 'in the case of the able-bodied to devise a scheme of work for such which might be as effective a test as the workhouse was intended to be' (O'Connor, 1925: 54). This recommendation about work tests raised two difficulties. First, it meant that the able-bodied poor would receive relief on the condition of 'less eligibility' — their circumstances could not be improved relative to that of the lowest class of labourer. Second, a 'work test' implied that work would be available, and to implement this condition would have required mass provision of work schemes for the growing body of the unemployed. This ran counter to the non-interventionist ethos of the government; while the government dabbled in the limited provision of work schemes linked to outdoor relief, it could not countenance very large-scale employment schemes (Cousins, 2003).

The O'Connor Commission was the first government inquiry after political independence to touch on issues relevant to social security. It has been presented as punitive and puritanical in some commentaries because it recommended the institutionalisation of unmarried mothers (Powell, 1992). In fact, the view it adopted of social security issues was a balanced one. In relation to outdoor relief, it advocated rigour in the administration of claims and suggested that some of the increase in outdoor relief expenditure might have been due to administrative disruption when the Poor Law was transferred to the local authorities. However, it did not accept the complaints submitted to it that the removal of the old workhouse test 'had led to great extravagance and that the cost of Home Assistance was now altogether excessive' (O'Connor, 1925: 53). On a wider front, it firmly recommended the removal of poor widows with children from the Poor Law system and the establishment of Mothers' Pensions payable by the state. This recommendation was not implemented.

The first decade of social policy was consistently harsh, as the government adopted a low tax, non-interventionist policy. It adhered to this approach in spite of the unpopularity of some of its policies and in the face of some unrest as dependence on the Poor Law escalated during the decade. The pace of social policy development quickened noticeably in the 1930s; Fianna Fáil had abandoned its abstentionist policy in 1927 and entered the Dail. In the 1932 election it campaigned on a programme that promised employment and improved social services, and entered government, at first governing with the support of the Labour Party and then as a majority party.[3] The Fianna Fáil regime proved to be more pragmatic and responsive to popular demand for improved social rights. On the general economic front it embarked on what has been described as a 'drastic experiment in economic nationalism' (Kennedy, Giblin and McHugh, 1988: 41). This comprised a protectionist policy in industry, a legal prohibition on foreign ownership of Irish industry, and the establishment of state-owned industrial enterprises in transport, energy, and food processing.

This stance was practical, rather than ideological. State owned industries were viewed as filling the gap left by private enterprise[4]. Protection of Irish industry by tariffs and quotas was not a strategic approach to implementing the 'infant industry' argument whereby small, indigenous industry is allowed to grow, protected in the domestic market, until it reaches an international exporting scale. The objective was more practical — to allow industry preferential access to the home market and to sustain employment in such manufacturing industry as did exist. The expansion in the building and construction sector was a practical measure to both increase employment and to address one of the social issues that had featured in the 1932 election — slum clearance and the need for housing. In the event, the economy grew modestly in the period from 1932 to the beginning of the Second World War and total industrial employment rose.[5] However, unemployment remained high (at its peak the unemployment register recorded an unemployment total of 146,000), because of the fall-off in emigration triggered by the Great Depression.

The Fianna Fáil government attempted to respond to popular demands. As a result, a number of critical elements in the emerging system of social security were added in the period 1932 to 1944. First, persistently high unemployment and the harshness of the Poor Law led to widespread protests. The practical limits to work schemes and the limited coverage of unemployment benefit left the government searching for other policy initiatives that would ameliorate the situation. In 1933 unemployment assistance was introduced, Sean Lemass being the main instigator. Cousins' detailed account of the emergence of Unemployment Assistance shows the pragmatism of the Fianna Fáil approach (Cousins, 2003). It was conscious of its electoral mandate and of the hostility directed at the previous government because of the lack of provision for the unemployed. Lemass argued that Poor Relief (now renamed Home Assistance) was simply degrading and therefore unpopular, that direct employment schemes were impossible given the scale of unemployment, and that unemployment benefit was limited in coverage. A scheme of unemployment assistance could overcome these problems and could be targeted at the unemployed without any means. Means-tested Unemployment Assistance provided a solution that was pragmatic without being generous or comprehensive. In fact, within a year of its introduction the government introduced restrictive measures in response to concern about the cost of UA and its abuse by claimants.

The recommendation by the O'Connor Commission in the 1920s to introduce Mother's pensions was not adopted at the time. In 1932, the government established the *Committee of Inquiry into Widows' and Orphans' Pensions* (chaired by Joseph Glynn, a member of the O'Connor Commission). It reported in 1933, and legislation introducing pensions for widows was enacted in 1935. The logic of introducing widows' pensions ran in parallel to that of Unemployment Assistance: it removed widows and their children from the Poor Law. Glynn's 1933 report had a majority and two minority reports. The majority proposed a non-contributory scheme funded from central taxation, one minority report suggested a contributory pension for wage earners only, and the other argued against a separate widow's scheme and in favour of an augmented Home Assistance service. In 1935 the government legislated for *both* a non-contributory and a contributory scheme; the pension was payable to widows aged 60 or over and to younger widows with dependent children (Cook, 1990; Farley, 1964).

The 1930s also saw the re-structuring of National Health Insurance (Cook, 1990; Farley, 1964). Despite a flurry of legislation in the 1920s dealing with the detail of national health insurance, the most significant change up to 1932 was the 1929 legislation that curtailed women's benefits and abolished Sanatorium benefit. A *Select Committee on the National Health Insurance Bill 1933* documented again many of the problems that had plagued health insurance since its introduction in 1911: the high cost of administration because of the large number of Approved Societies with a small membership; the practice in some societies of accepting only good risks; the variation in benefits paid due to the diversity in the financial circumstances of the societies.[6] The government moved quickly to address these problems. In 1933, it established one overall National Health Insurance Society under a representative board, and this took control of the assets of the pre-existing societies and commenced the administration of a uniform system of benefits.

In 1944 Children's Allowances (later re-named Child Benefit) were introduced and their emergence reveals much of the underlying dynamic of social policy development at this time. The Fine Gael T.D., James Dillon, raised the issue in the Dail in 1939, referring to the financial problems of large families and proposing that allowances be introduced for families with four or more children with an income below a certain threshold. In the same year De Valera also discussed the idea of a family allowance (Cousins, 1999), and the Department of Local Government and Public Health reported to the government on the subject. This led in turn to the establishment of a Cabinet sub-committee comprised of members broadly in favour of the idea. This committee made little progress and prompted Sean Lemass to draft his own proposals, suggesting a contributory scheme for wage earners and the self-employed. However, these proposals were not well received — at the level of principle or detail. A further committee was established in 1940 and it produced a comprehensive and analytical report in 1942, the *Report of the Inter-Departmental Committee on Family Allowances*.

The 1942 report and the response to it gave rise to a discussion at government level about the options for a possible scheme. In the event, while the Committee recommended a means-tested allowance for large families with low incomes to alleviate poverty, the government chose a universal scheme, and introduced it in 1944, a choice in which De Valera had an active part (Cousins, 1999). The political background to the initiative was Fianna Fáil's loss of seats and votes in the 1943 election, in which the government self-consciously chose to avoid promises in the social services area. In this election social issues featured very strongly and Fianna Fáil lost some of its natural electoral support (Lee, 1989; Cousins, 1999). Fianna Fáil learned an electoral lesson about the political salience of social policy issues. In 1944, it legislated for children's allowances in the form of a monthly allowance for each child for third and subsequent children in all families. The allowance was accompanied by a 'claw back' on the income tax relief for children — this reduced the net benefit of the initiative to higher income families.

The design of the scheme was strategic. A contributory scheme would only have benefited those paying social insurance, and would have excluded farmers and the self-employed, and a scheme for only the poorest families would have entailed a means-test of many families' income to give a benefit to only a few. Children's Allowances were diffused throughout the population and benefited the social groups with larger family sizes (farmers, farm labourers and the working class) — Fianna Fáil's core support base — and the claw back of tax relief made the scheme more targeted and affordable. The higher earners affected by the reduction in tax relief were not Fianna Fáil supporters in any case[7]. The legislation for the allowance was passed in 1944 before the surprise election in the summer of that year.[8] In the election campaign, Fianna Fáil reversed its 1943 strategy, emphasising its commitment to social reform and invoking the new allowance for families as an example of the government's commitment to the development of social policy. Fianna Fáil returned to power again in 1944, recouping much of the electoral ground it had lost.[9]

TOWARDS A NATIONAL SYSTEM

In the period from the early 1940s to the early 1950s the possibility of an overall national system of social security gained political currency in Ireland, culminating in the 1952 *Social Welfare Act* that provided a unitary national framework for social security. Internationally, the 'Beveridge Report' published in the UK in 1942 dominated the debate about social security at this time. This report was the most widely sold official government publication of the twentieth century. In conjunction with its associated reports the Beveridge plan offered a framework for the UK, not only for social security, but also for social and economic reconstruction generally. Beveridge summarised his plan as follows (Beveridge, 1942: 9):

> The main feature of the plan for social security is a scheme of social insurance against interruption and destruction of earning power and for special expenditure arising at birth, marriage or death. The scheme embodies six fundamental principles: flat rate of subsistence benefit; flat rate of contribution; unification of administration responsibility; adequacy of benefit; comprehensiveness and classification . . . Based on them and in combination with national assistance and voluntary insurance as subsidiary methods, the aim of the Plan for Social Security is to make want under any circumstances unnecessary.

Beveridge's plan for social security entailed a comprehensive, national system of social insurance, offering flat-rate social insurance benefits for flat-rate contributions in respect of illness, widowhood, retirement, unemployment and industrial accidents. In this scheme all of the workforce would contribute to national insurance and become entitled to the suite of insurance benefits. These benefits would be based on subsistence costs. Beveridge's plan also envisaged a universal system of children's allowances paid for out of general taxation, a national system of health care and the maintenance of full employment.

In Britain, in 1944, a White Paper reflecting the Beveridge programme was published, and legislation giving effect to the Beveridge social security plan was implemented in 1946. In Ireland too a debate took place about the future of social security, influenced by the Beveridge report. Beveridge's plan was widely cited in the media in Ireland, and it was studied by officials and politicians (Lee, 1989; Cousins, 2003, Bew and Patterson, 1982). Copies of the Beveridge report were circulated to the Cabinet in December 1942, and in 1943 Sean Lemass publicly accepted that the Beveridge report had portrayed Irish social security provisions in a poor light. Politically, the government was conscious of the demands of the Labour Party in the 1940s for improved pensions and a comprehensive social security system. The close labour market ties between Ireland and Britain and the implementation of Beveridge's recommendations in Northern Ireland heightened its influence in the Republic.

The government refrained from endorsing Beveridge, and McEntee and other government representatives made three key criticisms (O'Cinneide, 1999). Firstly, the proposal would have entailed a threefold increase in expenditure. Secondly, it was unsuitable for Ireland, which had a large self-employed and farming population, and thirdly, it entailed excessive state intervention.

Beveridge's plan was not the only one to emerge, however. Dr John Dignan, Bishop of Clonfert, and Chairman of the National Health Insurance Society published a pamphlet *Outlines of a Scheme of National Health Insurance* (Dignan, 1945). This offered a radically different scheme to Beveridge and to the limited provisions then in place. Dignan's plan was, in essence, European rather than British. It envisaged an *earnings-related* system of benefits and contributions, universal social insurance cover and the independent management of the system by an autonomous, representative, 'vocational' organisation. The intellectual origins of the Dignan plan lay partly in the *Report of the Commission on Vocational Organisation*, which had strongly reflected Catholic social teaching in its advocacy of subsidiarity (Commission on Vocational Organisation, 1943). The Commission had reported in 1943 and outlined a detailed structure for the incorporation of vocational organisations into wide areas of public administration.[10] Underpinning the Commission's elaborate framework for the involvement of vocational organisations was a theological rejection of unnecessary state power (whether Fascist or Communist) on the one hand, and of unrestrained markets on the other. The Papal Encyclicals *Rerum Novarum* (1891) and *Quadragessimo Anno* (1931) identified centralised state power and uncontrolled markets as 'extremes', and advocated subsidiarity — the establishment of vocational organisations — as a balance against market power and excessive state power. Dignan's scheme mirrored this emphasis on subsidiarity in proposing that the social security structure would be devolved to an autonomous, non-governmental body. The Commission's proposals were not well received by the Fianna Fáil administration and they cast a long shadow on the political reception of Dignan's social security proposals (Whyte, 1972; Riordan, 2000; Cook, 1990; Lee, 1989).

A violent public controversy took place between Bishop Dignan and Sean McEntee, Minister for Local Government and Public Health, about the content of Dignan's plan and the Minister's view that Dignan had exceeded his remit in publishing his plan on his own initiative. The origins of, and culpability for this controversy is the subject of detailed historical argument (Riordan, 2000; McKee, 1989). As regards the substance of the Dignan plan, it did not survive the detailed scrutiny of the Minister and his department. In reality, it was a vision rather than a plan. It set out a model of a fully comprehensive social insurance system, administratively decentralised, and managed by a board of vocational representatives. However, the Dignan document did not address the issue of costs at all and the government was then able to dismiss it as not being a meaningful plan. Furthermore, Dignan had naively applied the subsidiarity principles of the Commission on Vocational Organisation and proposed a wholly subsidiarist structure for social security. This would have removed social security from the direct control of the government and the Dail: Minister McEntee was on firm ground in arguing that this central aspect of the government's services should be directly accountable to the Dail and under the direct control of a Minister. Dignan was not re-appointed as Chairman of the National Health Insurance Society.

The net effect of the public controversy over Dignan was to extend and enliven the debate about the future of social security in Ireland that Beveridge's report had instigated. As the substantive debates about the need for a social security plan continued during the 1940s, political developments led to the establishment of the Department of Social Welfare. In the early 1940s, the government had concluded that one new, overarching social services department would be of little benefit in terms of cost or efficiency. However, a momentum built up, with the growth of substantial new statutory schemes from the mid-1930s onwards — Unemployment Assistance, Widows' Pensions, Children's Allowances — and the establishment of the National Health Insurance Society. This momentum quickened after Beveridge, as his plan was predicated on the establishment of a separate ministry for social security. This aspect of Beveridge was also fed into the Irish debate, and, in 1944, the Labour Party leader, William Norton, requested the government to consider the need for a separate department for all social services. The government at that point refused, although the political pressure continued. In 1945 the Dignan plan was published and controversy ensued, a critical element of which was the government's rejection of Dignan's organisational proposals. This meant, however, that the government required a political response, not only to the general clamour for improved social security, but also to the specific question of departmental responsibility for the future development of social security.

In 1945 the government established an Inter-Departmental Committee to consider the advisability of allocating responsibility for social services to a single ministry. A majority of this committee recommended a unitary department for all of the income maintenance services such as unemployment payments and widows' pensions. Cousins' account of the Committee's work shows that the Committee (or at least its chairman) anticipated future significant developments, the planning of which would require centralisation and direction. The government endorsed the majority view and in 1946 passed the necessary legislation to establish the Department of Social Welfare (Cousins, 2003). The department was formally established in January 1947 and took over all of the functions in relation to existing income maintenance schemes.[11]

Within a year of the establishment of the department Fianna Fáil was defeated in the election of 1948 and an inter-party government with 'a makeshift majority' — to use Lemass's terminology — was formed, under the leadership of John A. Costello of Fine Gael (McCullagh, 1998). The government was headed by Fine Gael and had Ministers from Fine Gael, Labour, National Labour, Clann na Poblachta, Clann na Talamhn and Independents.[12] This government agreed a ten point programme that included the following: 'Introduction of a comprehensive social security plan to provide insurance against old age, illness, blindness, widowhood, unemployment etc'. It also promised a modification of the means tests for blind persons' pensions, old age pensions, and widows and orphans pensions (McCullagh, 1998: 37). In the first budget the government increased pensions. It incorporated sickness benefit into the new department and abolished the National Health Insurance Society in the process. One year later the proposed plan for the future of social security in Ireland was published in the White Paper, *Social Security* (Department of Social Welfare, 1949).

The White Paper was Beveridgean. It proposed a national insurance system, entailing a unitary system of insurance contributions and flat-rate benefits for unemployment, sickness, and widowhood, as well as a maternity benefit. The most significant proposed innovation related to pensions. Here the White Paper proposed a retirement pension based on social insurance contributions, suggesting eligibility at age 60 for women and 65 for men. The paper gave details of the proposed rates of benefit and insurance contributions. In one critical respect, the White Paper departed from Beveridge: it confined its proposed social insurance system to employees, facing squarely the difficulty of attempting to include the large agricultural and self-employed sectors in the scheme. The authors of the White Paper, while clearly influenced by Beveridge, had looked further afield and learned of the experience of other countries in this respect. It noted that social insurance 'may have only a limited application, in as much as certain classes of the population may have no cash income at all, or have insufficient cash income to allow them to participate in a scheme for which a regular and perhaps substantial contribution is necessary' (Department of Social Welfare, 1949: 11). The White Paper noted that in Ireland this matter was of 'considerable importance' because a 'large proportion of the population — notably those on small agricultural holdings — live in circumstances which do not provide a regular cash income' (Department of Social Welfare, 1949: 11). Farmers and the self-employed were therefore excluded, ostensibly on practical grounds, but in drafting the White Paper the Minister may also have wished to avoid a political clash with farmers and Fianna Fáil. Prior to the White Paper, Lemass and McEntee and others had argued against Beveridge on the grounds of its unsuitability in an economy with a large farming and self-employed sector. (The White Paper also left open the possibility that certain civil servants and other public sector workers might not be included in the scheme.)

There was some opposition to the White Paper. Prior to its publication, the Department of Finance had made its opposition on economic grounds clear, and the other two key economic ministries, (Industry and Commerce and Agriculture) also expressed opposition. Likewise Fine Gael — one of whose senior members, Patrick McGilligan, was Minister for Finance — was opposed. After its publication, it was criticised on a number of grounds. Some individual Catholic clerics criticised it as statist and therefore *contra* the principle of subsidiarity. However, there is no historical evidence that the Church or the Catholic hierarchy intervened in the way that it did in the infamous controversy about the Mother and Child Scheme (O'Cinneide, 1999). The exclusion of farmers from social insurance became a subject of some debate. On the one hand, the White Paper was criticised by some trade unionists for excluding this group; low-income farmers and the self-employed would, it was pointed out, be eligible in the usual way for means-tested payments paid for out of general taxation. Those who were being excluded were thus accused of *benefiting* from non-inclusion. On the other hand, some of the farmer TDs in the Dail wanted farmers *included*, on the grounds that the scheme would be partly funded by general taxation and it would be unfair to exclude any sector of the workforce.

In the event, the Bill that finally reached the Dail in 1950 excluded a large segment of the workforce (civil servants and other public sector workers) and the self-employed. Some of the independent farmer TDs threatened to vote against the Bill on its second reading. However, the Minister induced these opponents to support the legislation by amending the Bill at this stage with other improvements that were in demand — improvements in the level of old age and blind pensions and a relaxation in the pensions means test (McCullagh, 1998: 194–5). Fianna Fáil's position was to support the principle of the scheme, but Dr James Ryan, the Fianna Fáil spokesman argued the merits of improving the existing benefits and assistance payments through general taxation. The Bill never became law, as the government fell in 1951 in the wake of the controversy over the Mother and Child Scheme, and Fianna Fáil returned to office with Dr James Ryan as Minister for Social Welfare.

Fianna Fáil flirted with a complete departure from a social insurance plan in favour of a greater reliance on tax-financed social assistance (Cousins, 2003). However, the momentum in favour of extending social insurance prevailed, and in 1952 the Fianna Fáil government passed the 1952 *Social Welfare Act*. This reflected the social insurance strategy that Norton and the new department had pursued. Norton had moved some way from a Beveridge system in the 1951 legislation by excluding farmers, other self-employed workers and public sector workers. The 1952 legislation moved even further in two critical respects. First, the retirement pension proposals were dropped entirely and, second, an income limit for non-manual employees was imposed with those above the limit being excluded from contributing. These changes meant that the 1952 legislation was considerably less comprehensive and redistributive than the grand plans that had stimulated debate in the 1940s. The importance of the 1952 Act was that it provided a 'structural framework on which Irish social security was to be based for two subsequent decades' (Cook, 1990: 102). In summary, the developments that culminated in the 1952 legislation left Ireland with a social insurance system offering coverage for some employees from unemployment, sickness and widowhood in the context of a unified and centralised system of insurance contributions. This truncated version of social insurance meant, accordingly, that social assistance and Home Assistance would continue to have a very significant role in social security.

CONSOLIDATION 1960 TO 1982

Ireland's social security system languished during the economically depressed 1950s and the momentum did not resume until 1961. The period from the early 1960s to the early 1980s was a process of continual extension of the limited social security system established in 1952. The chart below summarises some of the key developments — these are outlined in more detail elsewhere (Cook, 1990; Cousins, 1995; Commission on Social Welfare, 1986). In the late 1950s the entire underpinning of economic and social policy changed with the publication of *Economic Development* in 1958 and then the *First Programme for Economic Development* in 1959. These ushered in significant changes in economic policy — notably the adoption of strategies to integrate the Irish economy into the world economy. These policy changes — combined with the generally benign world economic situation — resulted in a rapid transformation in the economy. Ireland entered a period of sustained economic growth, rising incomes and rising levels of employment. From 1960 to 1973, GNP grew at an annual average rate of 4.3%, and industrial and services sector employment grew rapidly as employment in agriculture declined (Kennedy, Giblin, and McHugh, 1988).

This change in economic fortunes dramatically altered the context in which social security evolved, conferring considerably greater freedom on government to develop the system. In the event, the years 1957 to 1982 were almost wholly years of Fianna Fáil government.[13] The Fianna Fáil leadership passed to Sean Lemass in 1959 and his government (and successive governments) enthusiastically adopted the economic modernisation programme inaugurated in 1959, and systematically extended the social security system. By the early 1980s the social security system had been considerably extended. For example, social insurance pensions were introduced and the income ceiling on membership of the social insurance system removed, widening access to the social insurance system; a range of schemes was introduced to cater for a number of categories of women, and the residual Poor Law (then named Home Assistance) was abolished in 1975, replacing it with the Supplementary Welfare Allowance and conferring a legal right to a minimum payment; the unemployment payments system was enhanced with the establishment of Redundancy Payments system, and a social insurance payment for long-term sickness was introduced.

A number of threads shaped policy developments during this period. In the 1960s in particular, developments in social security were seen as an integral part of the general programme of national development. The *First Programme for Economic Development* had stressed the need to constrain public expenditure and to focus on economic development, but the later programmes explicitly addressed

Chart 2.1: Selected Changes in Social Security Provision in Ireland 1960–1980		
Year	Change	Key Points
1961	Contributory Pension	Pension at age 70; pension age lowered to 66 from 1973 to 1977 and Separate retirement pension at age 65 introduced in 1970
1967	Occupational Injuries Scheme based on Minority report of the Commission on Workmen's Compensation, 1962	Social insurance provision for all employees for work-related injuries and illnesses
1970–3	Schemes for Lone Mothers	Insurance-based payment for 'deserted wives', assistance schemes for unmarried mothers and deserted wives
1970	Pension for Long-term sickness	Invalidity pension for long-term sickness to supplement Disability benefit
1974	Pay –related benefit for Unemployment and Disability	PRB added to flat-rate benefit as a per cent of previous earnings (between 'floor' and 'ceiling')
1974	Extension of Social Insurance	Income limit on non-manual workers abolished
1975	Supplementary Welfare Allowances introduced	Legal right to a minimum payment; right to an appeal: more standardised, centralised system in place for SWA.
1979	Pay-related social Insurance	Flat–rate contributions replaced by contributions calculated as a per cent of earnings

social policy, including social security. In fact, there was an acceptance that an improved level of social services generally was a central policy objective, economic growth being the key to its achievement, and there was a clear recognition that the introduction of certain social security reforms (redundancy payments, pensions for older workers) would actively *facilitate* improved productivity and economic restructuring. It is clear also that there was no desire to return to the debates of the 1940s and early 1950s about what type of social security system Ireland should have. On the contrary, the framework of policy development remained firmly and unquestioningly within social insurance. As the *Third Programme for Economic and Social Development* stated, 'As far as possible, services will be financed by methods of insurance so that benefits may be granted without test of needs or means' (Government of Ireland, 1969: 207–8).

The question of what *type of social insurance* — flat-rate versus income-related benefits — did arise, however, although governments during this period articulated no consistent policy argument. In the area of unemployment and disability, income-related benefits were added to the system of flat-rate benefits in 1974. These remained in place until their final abolition in 1994. Pay-related benefits required more substantial insurance contributions than flat-rate benefits. When first introduced in 1974, PRB was calculated at a rate of 40% of an employee's previous earnings (the 40% rate was applied to 'reckonable weekly earnings', i.e. not all earnings but earnings between a 'floor' and a 'ceiling') and was payable for 24½ weeks as long as flat-rate benefit was still in payment. PRB was also payable with Maternity Allowance. However, these changes did not herald a general conversion to income-replacement or a general public demand for an income-replacement system. In the area of pensions, a Green Paper, *A National Income Related Pension Scheme*, discussed the future of social insurance pensions and explicitly set out the arguments for, and the possible organisation of a comprehensive income-related pension system (Department of Social Welfare, 1976). The Green Paper was intended to lead to a White Paper, but a White Paper was never published and, as Chapter Ten shows, pensions provision moved in an altogether different direction in the subsequent two decades.

Gender loomed large in the developments in this period. As Chapter Seven shows, many of the individual schemes introduced at this time were directed at categories of women not previously dealt with in the social security system. The *Commission on the Status of Women* identified many of these needs and also documented areas in which the existing social security provisions discriminated against women. The Commission's report added considerable momentum to developments in social security, and this momentum was strengthened by the impact of the EC's Directive on Equal Treatment in Social Security, signed by Ireland in 1978. This Directive was to have considerable impact on the structure of social security, although the practical steps required in Ireland to implement the Directive did not commence until the mid-1980s.

Finally, although there was no long-term policy enunciated about the rate of increase in social security payments the cumulative picture conveyed in a number of studies is that they increased more than proportionately with national income. Annual budgetary increases in payments tended to exceed the rate of inflation. In his analysis of income maintenance payments, Walsh (1974: 221) calculated that for the period 1953–71, they rose significantly more rapidly than national income per capita, concluding, 'as the nation has become more prosperous the lot of those supported by transfer payments has improved at a faster rate than the overall growth rate of income'. For later years the NESC reports, *Towards a Social Report* (1977) and *Income Distribution: A Pilot Study* (1975), gave detailed case studies of the relative levels of social security payments and other incomes. The consistent picture is that from 1966 to 1976 the real value of social security payment rose cumulatively. These increases took effect in a context where average and marginal tax rates on employee incomes rose and the consequence was that social security payments tended to raise as a proportion of the disposable income of employees. In his analysis of trends in pensions, unemployment benefit, and disability benefit from 1951 to 1981, Hughes (1985: 84–93) showed that there was a high statistical correlation between the growth in benefit levels and increases in gross earnings. The increases in taxation on earnings over the period then meant that benefits rose significantly more rapidly than *net* earnings. For example, the ratio of Unemployment Benefit and Disability Benefit to net earnings for a married couple with two children rose from 35% in 1961 to 52% in 1981. In relation to pensions, the contributory old age pension for a couple was 33% of net earnings in 1961 and 51% in 1981.[14] In summary, in this period of consolidation, not only did the scope of the system widen considerably, but also the living standard afforded by social security recipients converged towards that of the average employee.

THE COMMISSION ON SOCIAL WELFARE AND BEYOND

In the late 1970s and early 1980s systems of social security were coming under increasing scrutiny in many countries as governments coped with the implications of slower economic growth; moreover, the budgetary costs and potential inefficiencies of social security had come on to the agenda of governments in some countries. A Conservative government came to power in the UK in 1979 (lead by Margaret Thatcher), intent on 'rolling back the welfare state'. Amongst its initiatives was the establishment in 1984 of a review of social security with a strong emphasis on costs and efficiency. Against this background, the coalition government of Fine Gael and Labour that had come to office in 1982 and lasted until 1987 established a commission to review the social security system.[15] A number of factors contributed to the establishment of the Commission. The Commission offered a compromise course on which the parties in government could agree. Fine Gael was intent on resolving the crisis in the public finances that the coalition had inherited from the Fianna Fáil government of 1977–81. The Labour Party, however, wanted to continue to improve social security and had ministerial responsibility for this area (as it had in the 1973–77 coalition).

More immediately, the very rapid rate of development of the Irish system had made it very complex, and by the early 1980s it was by no means clear how further *ad hoc* development could cope with the structural challenges the system would have to face in the future. For example, the implementation of the EU's Directive on Equal Treatment challenged the historic gender divisions on which the Irish system had grown up. In 1978, the Green Paper on income-related pensions had been published, and in the absence of a subsequent White Paper a policy vacuum existed both in relation to pensions and to the more general question of flat rate *versus* income-related benefits. The benefits system had become so complex that in a number of areas there were serious anomalies and inequities that required resolution: for example, a proliferation of rates of payment for child dependant additions; two separate rent allowances for tenants in private rented accommodation alongside a subsidised rents regime for local authority tenants; three different lone parent payments for categories of women, but no provision for lone fathers; exclusion of many contributors from long-term social insurance payments because of the historic exclusion of large segments of the labour force from the social insurance system.[16]

The Commission had wide terms of reference (and a relatively short time period in which to complete its work) and started its work against the background of the rapid and *ad hoc* developments of the previous two decades: 'the social welfare system has been allowed to develop without the benefit of a comprehensive review' (Commission on Social Welfare, 1986: xiii). The Commission described its approach as 'evolutionary' and opted to recommend development of the evolving social insurance system. Like its companion body established in 1979 to analyse the system of taxation (the Commission on Taxation), the Commission on Social Welfare considered alternative systems such as Negative Income Tax, or Social Dividend schemes (these are discussed more fully in Chapter Twelve), but concluded that 'the development of social welfare in Ireland is best pursued by expanding and significantly improving the present system' (Commission on Social Welfare, 1986: 184). The Commission's analysis (in the terminology then current in international debate about social security reform) could be described as advocating a 'Back-to-Beveridge' strategy (Atkinson, 1969; Judge, 1980). In the Irish case this strategy entailed a reform of the system centred on a fully comprehensive social insurance regime, adequate benefits, and an improved system of child income support.

There were a number of key elements in the changes the Commission proposed. First, it offered a specific calculation about what the minimum level of social welfare payment ought to be, drawing on a range of illustrative calculations and, in 1985, recommending a range within which, ideally, all payments should fall. The benefit system should also be flat rate, rather than income-related. Second, it proposed that the fragmented system of social insurance should be extended so that the self-employed, public servants, part-time employees, and so on, should be included and it argued that the tri-partite funding system (employers, employees, and the state) should continue. Third, it proposed that the adequate system of payments it recommended should be supplemented in a number of key respects; the introduction of a national system of housing benefit (means-tested) in place of the discretionary rent allowance being administered by the regional health boards; the payment of lump-sum payments to meet the 'capital' needs of very long-term recipients with dependants; an improved system of child income support that would incorporate age-related child benefit payments and the eventual rationalisation of Family Income Supplement and Child Dependant Additions.

The Commission's report was published in 1986 at the height of the fiscal and unemployment crises: in 1985 the national debt/GNP ratio was 134% of GNP, unemployment was approaching 18% and emigration had resumed on a significant scale. In this context the Commission's analysis was bound to have an impact. On one side, the sheer scale of dependence on social security payments in society created a constituency for many of the changes recommended by the Commission — not least its recommended minimum payment level. On the other, the state of the public finances constrained government from implementing the Commission's report outright. Furthermore, the political debate about fiscal policy was enlivened by the presence of the newly formed Progressive Democrats party — defined by its neo-liberal emphasis on reducing taxes and public expenditure. Tensions between the Labour and Fine Gael parties in government on the issue were heightened by the mishandling of the publication of the Commission's report by the Fine Gael minister responsible for social welfare (the minister had been appointed in a Cabinet reshuffle in place of a Labour minister). In the policy community the report received a mixed reaction. At a special policy symposium of the Social and Statistical Inquiry the report was castigated by one economist — apparently advocating a means-tested system — who argued that it was 'not the result of deep study or an honest analysis of the design and implementation of the social welfare system' (Dowling, 1986). Another economist, at the same event, pointed critically to the commission's 'reluctance to abandon the social insurance concept' (Honohan, 1986).

A further spate of analytical commentary was published in the journal *Administration*. Here the Commission's report was dismissed by one commentator as mere 'administrative housekeeping', reflecting an uncritical adherence to a social insurance/social assistance system (Cook, 1986). A very authoritative commentator in the same symposium compared it with the corresponding Fowler review of social security in the UK and described the commission's analysis as a 'more intellectually coherent report' and 'a more rounded piece of policy analysis'

(Bradshaw, 1986). Likewise, a Northern Ireland academic expert on social security broadly concurred with the Commission's analysis (Ditch, 1986).

The Commission's analysis was widely reported in the popular media and its analysis and recommendations received sympathetic coverage.[17] In 1987 the Fine Gael-Labour Coalition lost office and Fianna Fáil returned to power, forming a minority government with Charles Haughey as Taoiseach.[18] The commission's report significantly influenced government policy in the following decade, for a number of reasons. First, the Fianna Fáil government embarked in 1987 on the first of a series of national social partnership arrangements that offered an agreed framework for the evolution of pay, taxation, social security and related matters. The first agreement, *Programme for National Recovery*, was devised as a response to the economic crisis. It legitimised the government's retrenchment policies in the eyes of trade unions and the public by trading off income tax reductions for low nominal pay increases and expressing commitment to 'greater social equity' (Government of Ireland, 1987: 13). This Programme committed the government to 'maintain the overall value of social welfare benefits' and stated that the government would 'consider special provision for greater increases for those receiving the lowest payments'. The Government and the social partners negotiated further national agreements and the Commission's recommendations in relation to the adequacy of the payments (and some other recommendations) featured in these agreements. *The Programme for Economic and Social Progress* (Government of Ireland, 1991: 22) explicitly referred to some of the Commission's recommendations and committed the government to adopt the priority recommendations in relation to payment levels in the short-term and thereafter to 'increase social welfare rates further and progressively in accordance with the recommendations of the Commission on Social Welfare'. The later partnerships institutionalised the Commission's report as a frame of reference for developments in relation to payment levels and to wider aspects of social security policy.[19]

Second, Fianna Fáil had returned to government in a context in which social expenditure and redistribution were politically contentious — the proximate reason for the fall of the Labour/Fine Gael government was a lack of agreement on how fiscal retrenchment should be effected. Fianna Fáil was sensitive to the political and electoral consequences of its stance on social welfare and was also intent on facilitating and renewing the social partnership agreements. The sensitivity of the government was heightened by the sheer size of the welfare constituency. In the late 1980s, 880,000 adults (recipients and their adult dependants) were in receipt of payments. Therefore, at an early juncture in the 1987–1989 government, the Minister endorsed the Commission's general analysis and key recommendations. In the Dail in 1987 the Minister for Social Welfare stated: 'I will be taking the Report of the Commission on Social Welfare and all the views I have received on it fully into account in planning the reform and development of the social welfare system' (cited in McCashin, 1992: 12). Policy changes in subsequent years were announced with reference to the Commission's report. For example, one year later in the 1988 Social Welfare Bill the government implemented a key element in the broadening of the social insurance system, as envisaged by the Commission, and the Minister stated: 'The introduction of social insurance for self-employed persons represents precisely the sort of broadening of the social insurance base which was recommended by the Commission' (cited in McCashin, 1992: 13).

A third set of circumstances conspired to reinforce the policy impact of the Commission. From the late 1980s onwards a programme of academic research on poverty in Ireland commenced. The first major publication arising from this work appeared in 1989 (Callan, Nolan, Whelan, *et al* 1989). Further, updated work appeared in 1996 (Callan, Nolan, Whelan *et al*, 1996) and again in the late nineties and beyond. The impact of this research was to generate public awareness of the extent of poverty and to ensure that the issue of social welfare payments and reform of social security stayed on governments' policy agendas. The emerging evidence about poverty did not in itself support the detail of the Commission's report. However, the appearance and re-appearance of 'headline results' about income poverty provided a focus for bodies such as the Combat Poverty Agency and a wide range of voluntary organisations in their advocacy and lobbying for an improved social security system.

By the end of the 1990s the agenda set out by the Commission had been implemented to a considerable extent. In the first half of the 1990s public servants and part-time employees were incorporated in the social insurance system. Simultaneously, the remaining elements of pay-related benefit for unemployment and disability were phased-out. At this juncture the Irish social security system had become almost wholly a Beveridge-type system, entailing a comprehensive range of social insurance flat-rate benefits, complemented by a system of social assistance allowances and a programme of child income support. A number of issues shaped the agenda of social security debate from the mid-1990s onwards, issues that remain contentious and unresolved. The first of these is related to housing costs and the role of rent allowances in particular. This specific topic has been the subject of no less three official reports (and some independent research) since the mid-1990s. Chapter Nine discusses this issue in some detail.

A further series of contentious questions concerns the nature of dependency in the social security system and the mix of individual and family-based rights. Formally, dependency is now defined in financial terms — spouses can be claimed as 'dependants' if they are not the main earner in a family. However, this approach to dependency is combined with a payments structure built around an adult-plus-dependant scenario, with the amount accruing for the dependant being less than a full personal rate of payment. In turn, this means that conventional couple-type beneficiaries may be treated less favourably than comparable households where there are (for example) two unrelated individuals receiving two full personal payments. This kind of comparison has been invoked to argue that the adult-plus-dependant benefit system favours lone parents relative to couples. This question touches on the subject of 'individualisation' — whether and how the social security system should be more fully built around individuals rather than families.

Finally, during the last decade of rising prosperity, social security payments rose more rapidly than inflation and thus the real value of benefits increased significantly. However, the combination of rising real incomes and a declining burden of taxation meant that *disposable incomes* grew more rapidly than gross incomes. Therefore, as Chapter Three reports in some detail, the poverty line measured in terms of a proportion of disposable income also rose. The growth in social security payments was not sufficient to keep pace with this rising poverty line and poverty grew. This situation has raised the issue of indexation — the formula by which social security payments should be adjusted. The Commission on Social Welfare did not agree on this question, but the recent period of prosperity and the medium-term prospect of a continued growth in incomes have brought this issue on to the policy agenda again.

INFLUENCES ON THE DEVELOPMENT OF SOCIAL SECURITY

This chapter and Chapter One outlined the development of social security in Ireland, but did not explain *why* it developed at the rate it did and in the way it did. Explaining Ireland's experience would require an application of the theoretical research on welfare state development that has emerged in the social sciences. This research is both complex and controversial. A number of themes recur in it that are relevant to the Irish case. First, in understanding the *emergence* of social security and the welfare state more generally, research from a variety of theoretical stances has tended to focus on the inter-play of industrialisation, urbanisation, and political responses to the new needs and demands that these forces create (Flora and Heidenheimer, 1981). A common frame of reference is to view the emergence of social security in European countries as the outcome of a political dynamic, in which the urbanised, industrialised working class succeed in their struggle for expanded social and economic rights. Some interpretations of the European experience offer a particular variant on this perspective. Rimlinger (1971) in his classic study points out that it is the political elites rather than the working class whose influence is decisive. For example, Bismarck, the German Chancellor, introduced social insurance as a political palliative, attempting to dampen demands for enlarged political rights.

In relation to the later expansion of social security, the theoretical debate has focused on the relative roles of political factors (broadly defined) as opposed to economic and demographic factors. On the one hand, Wilensky (1975) in a comprehensive study stressed the 'automatic' influence of ageing populations and increased economic growth: these create the needs and the resources that lead to social security development. On the other, some scholars (Esping-Andersen, 1975; Esping-Andersen, 1990) have stressed the importance of political choices, arguing, for instance, that countries with stronger left-wing political parties and higher levels of trade unionism developed their welfare states (including their social security systems) earlier and to a more comprehensive degree. The former perspective emphasises the way in which economic growth and demographic change creates *convergence and modernisation* across states with very dissimilar histories and politics, while the latter stresses the *divergence* between developed nation states in their rates of social security development and in the type of social security systems they devise. Marxist scholars form a sub-set of the political school, acknowledging that the working class can obtain social rights, while emphasising that there are inherent *limits* to the extent of social security development in capitalist economies (Gough, 1979).

The research on social security development has become increasingly comparative. This has been driven in part by the influence of the so-called institutionalist school of welfare state politics. Research in this vein points to the different institutional arrangements that nations states have and argue that institutional arrangements (in the widest sense) exert an independent influence on welfare state development. For example, the political system may be federal or unitary in structure, it may have weak or strong bureaucracies, and it may or may not have a written constitution. These institutional factors may not determine policy outcomes in isolation from broader economic and political factors, but they shape the context in which policy choices are made and constrain governments' administrative, legal and bureaucratic capacities (Skocpol, 1995; Heclo, 1974).

It is by no means clear how the Irish case should be theorised. There is a serious dearth of fundamental historical research and little in the way of comparative analysis, but a number of points can be made about how the 'facts' of the Irish case might be interpreted. It is clear in the first instance that the origins of social insurance in Ireland (the 1911 legislation) lay in the general British developments of the time. There were no indigenous forces — such as industrialisation or class-based politics. Irish social insurance was, at first, simply transplanted from Great Britain, reflecting the strategic political response of the Liberal Party to the growing politicisation of the working class and the popular clamour for an alternative to the Poor Law.

But what were the key forces at work *after* political independence? Recalling that during the period from 1922 to 1948 some significant developments in social security took place, these can hardly be ascribed to the effects of large-scale industrialisation and the class-based politics to which it has given rise in many European welfare states. On the contrary, a broadly based, nationalist party, Fianna Fáil, implemented these developments. This is not to suggest that welfare politics in Ireland are non-political, and therefore exceptional, but to question *how* welfare politics are viewed in much of the research literature. The Irish experience surely testifies to the fact that class interests can be mobilised and expressed through *non-class* parties such as populist parties (as Skocpol points out in relation to the US) or cross-class parties such as Fianna Fáil. A consistent thread in the development of social security in Ireland has been the capacity and willingness of Fianna Fáil, in contexts of electoral competition and constrained resources, to attempt to respond to popular demands for reform and improvement. A telling historical comparison is that when Fianna Fáil was in power, Ireland implemented children's' allowances *before* its richer, industrialised neighbour; likewise, national legislation for unemployment assistance.

Popular demands in the Irish case, of course, refer not only to urban workers' demands but also to the interests of farmers and rural workers. Any attempt to understand the pattern of social security development in Ireland must also incorporate an analysis of *agrarian* politics and interests. Furthermore, agrarian politics should not be thought of *a priori* as antagonistic to the development of social security. On the contrary, the Irish agrarian polity was historically very receptive to large-scale state intervention — in the redistribution of land, as Fahey has pointed out (Fahey, 1998). Furthermore, the needs of the *rural* population loomed large in the design of unemployment assistance and children's allowances — the two key initiatives in the period before a national system was introduced. More recent research on the politics of social security, notably Baldwin's (1990) authoritative study of social insurance in European welfare states, has begun to question the emphasis on the politics of the working class, and to put the organisation and political mobilisation of farmers and agricultural workers centre-stage in accounting for social security development.

Turning to the events of 1948–52, a very limited Beveridge system was introduced in contrast to the comprehensive plan enacted in the UK. In the light of the theoretical issues raised above it is tempting to retrospectively describe the policy outcome in 1952 as a 'failure' to establish a full national social security system. However, viewed from any theoretical stance there are no grounds for supposing that Ireland should have had a fully established system at that point. In fact, given its level of economic development, and the weak, divided nature of its left-wing parties (and the low level of trade unionisation in the workforce as a whole) it would run against the grain of theoretical expectations if Norton had implemented the plan in the White Paper.

The difference between the White Paper proposals and the 1952 provisions can also be examined in the light of the theoretical debate between institutionalists and Marxists. Famously, one interpretation of the 1935 New Deal social security legislation in the USA argues that the economic interests of 'monopoly capitalists' were decisive in shaping the legislation to their own interests (Quadagno, 1984). However, writers of an institutionalist persuasion have questioned this interpretation (Scokpol and Amenta, 1985). The latter argue that while economic interests and class relations cannot be ignored, they must be analysed in relation to the federal structure of the US state, the role of Congress in the national state system and the influence of individual states' previously developed policies and policy-making systems.

This theoretical controversy about the relative influence of the state and organised economic interests is relevant to Ireland. One line of inquiry about the 1952 Act is that the private insurance industry may have effectively vetoed the more comprehensive proposals in the 1949 White Paper. In fact, Cook records that when the Fianna Fáil minister was advancing the 1952 legislation after the fall of the Inter-Party government and the demise of the Norton Bill, Norton referred to the influence of the insurance companies. According to Cook, 'Norton saw the exclusion of retirement pensions and death benefits as revealing the countervailing power of insurance companies. In fact, he saw the situation as one in which the insurance companies had won and the workers of the country had lost.' (Cook, 1990: 100–1) There is no theoretical analysis of the 1952 legislation that examines it in the light of the political power of business, but clearly further research on this topic would benefit from applying more explicitly the theoretical stances that have enriched research on social security internationally.

The period of rapid social security development in Ireland after 1960 also invites theoretical consideration. It appears to offer support for a straightforward modernisation account of social security development, with the system expanding rapidly at a time of significant industrialisation, economic growth and accompanying urbanisation. However, this perspective would fail to show how, and to what extent, political and electoral factors might have had an influence on social security development. For example, an institutional perspective would focus on the apparent autonomy of the state in broad economic development policy, suggesting that the program of social security development was part of this general state-led initiative. Equally, an argument for political influences could be made. The 1960s was a decade of marked electoral competition. Fianna Fáil was in a small minority relative to all other parties combined and this may have accelerated the responsiveness of the governments of the time to demands for improved social security. On a wider front, the Fianna Fáil party was attempting to secure its electoral support in the context of a changing social structure: the urban, industrial workforce was growing rapidly and trade union membership (and industrial militancy) also grew (Bew and Patterson, 1982). The rapid growth of social security in this period might be seen, not merely as an accumulation of *ad hoc* improvements, but as a central element in a national political and economic strategy.

Finally, what role did Catholicism and Catholic social teaching have? The difficulty here is that the Church-State controversy over health care and the Mother-and-Child scheme in the 1940s and 1950s has cast a long shadow on the way social policy development in Ireland has been generally considered. For example, a well-known textbook description of the Irish welfare state portrays the Church as a defining influence in social policy development in Ireland

(McLaughlin, 2001). Recent work on the development of the 1952 Social Welfare Act shows, however, that in this formative period the Church did *not* attempt to exert influence in this key area of policy (Cousins, 2003; Ó Cinneide, 1999). In fact, the government decisively rejected the proposals that emanated from Church sources — the Dignan Plan. Later, in the 1960s, the Church actively advocated expanded social security provisions (Whyte, 1972; McCashin, 1982).

But does this mean that Catholicism and the Catholic Church are irrelevant to an understanding of the development of social security? International comparative studies point to the positive influence of Catholicism on welfare state development. Castles' comparative statistical analysis of OECD countries for the post-war years shows a positive correlation between Catholicism and social security development (Castles, 1998). Likewise, Van Kersbergen's study of Christian Democracy shows that Catholic parties and Catholic workers' movements were central to the emergence and development of social security and social policy generally in some European countries (Van Kersbergen, 1995). Clearly, these issues require further research.

CONCLUSION

By the end of the twentieth century Ireland had developed a comprehensive social insurance and assistance system. However, the political, social and economic factors that have shaped this system are very under-researched and in particular the Irish experience would be better understood if it were analysed in a comparative context. Chapter Three offers a description of the current system, and Chapter Four outlines some analytical principles. Chapters Five to Eleven in Part Two focus in more detail on the development of specific areas of social security and on policy problems, while the final chapter in Part Three reviews the debate about alternatives to the present system.

Notes

1.   The 1922 constitution extended the vote to all women over the age of 21. The 1918 electorate was 1.37 million and the 1923 electorate 1.72 million. The Dail also increased the number of seats to 153, although the 44 elected Sinn Féin deputies exercised an abstentionist policy.

2.   The background to this now infamous welfare 'cut' should be noted. It was well known in official circles that after the introduction of the pension in 1908 there was considerable over claiming of pensions in Ireland due to fraudulent behaviour on the part of claimants, the difficulty of establishing applicants' ages because of the absence of civil registration, and the lax use of discretion by the local pension committees that decided on claims. In addition, pensions expenditure was the largest single fiscal burden

transferred to Ireland at independence and before independence some nationalists had raised the issue of the affordability of the pensions under the Free State's narrower fiscal base (Ó Gráda, 2002).

3.   The 1932 election resulted in the following disposition of the Dail's 153 seats: Fianna Fáil, 72; Fine Gael, 57; Labour Party, 7; Farmers' Parties, 4; Others, 13. In 1933 De Valera called another election and increased Fianna Fáil's seats to 77. Fine Gael had 48, Labour, 8 and Farmers' Parties and Others 11 and 9 respectively.

4.   In the 1930s the following state companies were established: Aer Lingus, Bord na Móna, Sugar Company, Ceimici Teoranta, Irish Life Assurance Company, Industrial Credit Company, Irish Tourist Board.

5.   There is some dispute about the exact extent of the employment growth. Kennedy, Giblin and McHugh (1988: 47) point out that the Census of Industrial Production records an increase in industrial employment from 110, 600 in 1931 to 166, 100 in 1938.

6.   See Farley (1964: 36–8) for a summary of the problems with national health insurance and a brief account of the 1933 National Health Insurance Act.

7.   As Cousins (1999: 51) in his detailed account suggests 'As we have seen, Fianna Fáil had lost much of its radical lustre by the early 1940s. A system of children's allowances payable universally to all larger families would be of benefit to those voters specifically targeted by Fianna Fáil, i.e. farmers and the working class. The 1946 census indicates that farmers were the most fertile category of family followed by general labourers and semi-skilled workers. Thus a universal payment of children's allowances funded in part by specific (albeit limited) withdrawals of income tax relief from higher earners would be likely to provide benefits to those voters targeted by Fianna Fáil while at the same time directing some of the cost of the allowances towards better-off Fine Gael voters who were not going to vote for Fianna Fáil in any case.'

8.   The legislation was enacted in February 1944, the election of that year was held in the summer and the first payment of Children's Allowances was made in August 1944.

9.   In the 1943 election Fianna Fáil's share of the first preference vote fell from its 1938 figure of 51.9% to 41.9% and the number of seats it had fell by 10 from 77 to 67. Fine Gael also lost 10 seats and its share of the vote fell from 33 % to 23%. The Labour Party, Farmers' Parties and Independents gained votes and seats. In 1944, Fianna Fáil's share of the vote increased back up to 49% and the number of seats to 76, one short of the 77 it had in 1938.

10.   The Commission (7–8) defined vocational organisation as a 'form of organisation of human beings based on their occupation or vocation and designed to enable them to fulfil some activity concerned with the occupation. . . . Now when members of a vocation associate for some

purpose concerned with their vocation and form an organic body with power to speak and act for the vocation we have a vocational organisation.'

11. The first draft of the bill used the term Department of Social Services.

12. The 1948 election led to the following distribution of seats across the parties: Fianna Fáil, 68; Fine Gael, 31; Labour, 14; National Labour, 5; Clann na Talmhan, 7; Clann na Poblachta, 10; Others, 12.

13. In 1957 Fianna Fáil were returned to power with almost 50% of the first preference vote and over 50% of the Dail's seats, but from 1961 to 1965 they governed as a minority government having lost seats in the 1961 election. In the 1965 election Fianna Fáil gained seats and increased its share of the vote, allowing it to govern with a majority of one. Fianna Fáil gained further seats in the 1969 general election (although its share of the vote declined slightly) and it a majority of six in the 1969–73 Dail.

14. These figures are calculated from Tables A2, A4 and A6 in Hughes's study (Hughes, 1985).

15. In 1981 and 1982 there were three general elections with Fianna Fáil and Fine Gael led by Charles Haughey and Garret Fitzgerald respectively, and the Labour Party led by Frank Cluskey, Minister for Social Welfare in the 1973–77 coalition. The political instability came to an end with the formation of the 1982–87 coalition between Fine Gael and Labour, with Garret Fitzgerald as Taoiseach. In the 1982–7 Dail the distribution of seats was as follows: Fianna Fáil, 75; Fine Gael, 70; Labour, 16; Others, 5.

16. The influential social services organisation The National Social Services Board in its magazine *Relate* had been highlighting the many anomalies in the social security system and calling for a fundamental review of social security. In the event the Director of the NSSB, John Curry, became the chairman of the Commission.

17. For a detailed account of the media and political response to the Commission see McCashin (1992).

18. The disposition of seats after the 1987 election was as follows: Fianna Fáil, 81; Fine Gael, 51; Labour, 12, Progressive Democrats, 14; Others, 8.

19. The impact of the partnership agreements on social security policy was to last beyond the government of 1987–9. There were changes of government in 1989, 1992, 1994, and 1997. Fianna Fáil was in government (under various arrangements) during these years of partnership agreements with the exception of 1994–97 when the 'Rainbow Coalition' of Fine Gael, Labour and Democratic Left was in office.

3
The Irish Social Security System in Context

INTRODUCTION

This chapter describes the Irish system today and places it in context. The first section locates Ireland in a European context and describes its social security system. This forms the backdrop to the overview of the Irish system that follows: the description here gives aggregate data on expenditure and a brief account of the structure of the system. The next section focuses on the key issue of the level of benefits. The last section reviews some of the contexts in which social security now operates — social, economic, and political. An important preliminary point concerns the predominance of social insurance. Dixon's detailed description of social security systems across the entire globe shows that there are very few countries that do not have some social insurance provision (Dixon, 1999: 81–91). As a form of income maintenance, it is predominant in Europe (East and West), North America, Latin America and the Middle East; it is also predominant in Africa and Asia. South East Asia and Australasia are the exceptions. Of the 165 nation states he includes in his survey, 86% have at least one social insurance provision in place

THE IRISH SYSTEM IN EUROPEAN CONTEXT

Is the Irish system of social security different? How does it compare with those of other countries? To place Ireland in context it is useful to outline different types of social security regimes across a range of countries and offer some detailed examples of how Ireland compares — for convenience the European Union's membership at 2001 is taken as the frame of reference. In a report on social protection the European Commission (1995) identified four clusters of countries with identifiable types of social security systems as follows:

- *Scandinavia*: These countries have very comprehensive systems (sometimes described as 'universal'), a strong focus on work participation and generous, income-related benefits.

- *Continental Europe*: This group, sometimes described as 'Bismarckian' after the historical instigator of social insurance, includes France, Germany, Austria, Belgium, Holland and Luxembourg — these countries' systems are very largely based on social insurance, the benefits are income-related and their social insurance structures are categorised by occupation or sector.
- *The UK and Ireland*: For obvious reasons, Ireland is paired with the United Kingdom — both owe their policy designs to William Beveridge and have historically built their systems around insurance (alternatively described as 'national' or 'social' insurance), both have flat-rate benefits and an important role for social assistance.
- *Southern European Countries*: These countries' systems also have an element of social insurance, but their provisions are far from comprehensive and the systems lack basic minimum income arrangements.

At the risk of some over-simplification, detailed comparisons of benefit levels, duration of entitlements and some other factors would suggest that the overall quality of systems follows the descending order in the presentation above, with the Scandinavian countries having the more developed provisions and the Southern European countries the least. One other point of contrast that distinguishes Ireland and the UK is the separation of income maintenance from health care.[1] In contrast, in many European countries, the social insurance system is a mechanism for funding health services as well as income maintenance, and insurance contributions in these regimes are related to health service entitlements. These institutional differences clearly have implications for the organisation and management of social security and for the nature and content of policy debates.

To allow a fuller comparison, the paragraphs below, with the aid of Charts 3.1 and 3.2, give an outline of how Ireland and three other countries provide for old age pensions and unemployment. These two areas are chosen for closer comparison because, taken together, they offer a picture of the core of the countries' systems. The details in the charts give broad support to the classification given above.

There are a number of key comparisons to note about the Irish provisions for old age. In the first place, Irish social security pensions are built largely around *private sector employees and the self-employed* — public sector employees' pensions are financed and structured differently. The latter will by-and-large have income-related pensions while social security recipients' pensions will be flat rate. Many other countries, such as Finland, have more unified arrangements across the sectors of the labour force. Second, all three comparison countries have income-related pensions. This does not mean, however, that Ireland's pensions are in general lower relative to income, as the Irish system has additional flat-rate payments in respect of spouses and children. Third, Ireland has no provisions for deferred or earlier pensions (either full or partial). The only age differentiation is between the Retirement Pension payable at age 65 for a greater contribution record and the Contributory Pension payable at age 66; Ireland is the only country in the selection with a central element in its pensions entitlements payable at an age greater than 65.[2]

The chart also reflects one other important feature of pension arrangements: the more mature systems incorporate the self-employed as well as employees. This does not apply to Greece: therefore, while the Greek system is income-related rather than flat rate, the large share of both agricultural and non-agricultural self-employment in the Greek economy means a low coverage for the pensions system. The chart also highlights a structural feature of Scandinavian social security — the provision of a general guarantee supplemented by income-related provisions.

Chart 3.1: Social Security Provisions for Old Age, Selected Countries, 2001

Country	Key Provisions
Finland	Dual system with (a) insurance pension for all employees and self-employed, and (b) national, guaranteed pension; pensions are integrated so that universal pension is withdrawn when insurance pension exceeds a limit; no exemptions from scheme for employees, self-employed may be exempted only for first four months of self-employment, depending on income.
	Minimum national pension requires three years residence after age 16; full national pension 40 years; full employment pension requires 40 years employment/self-employment; very limited scope for credited contributions.
	Standard pension age is 65; early pension at 60, actuarially reduced; deferred pension allowed, actuarially increased; earnings do not affect amount of pension.
	Amount of national pension based on length of residence, municipality, amount of other pensions; insurance pensions related to past earnings, with target of 60% of earnings for 40 years contributions; pensionable salary based on last ten years (from 2005).
	No adult or child supplements; care allowances for home care needs and housing allowances based on income and housing costs.

Finland *(cont.)*	Pension income assessed for tax, with special deductions for those with national pension; care allowance and housing allowance not taxed; sickness insurance premium levied at 1.5% of taxable income and 1.2% of pension income.
Germany	Compulsory social insurance for all employees and some self-employed (limited part-time employment excluded); minimum membership of 60 months. Standard retirement age of 65; provision for early pensions (full and partial) according to gender, age, health, employment status. Pension is earnings-related and calculated on a statutory formula based on past earnings and the pension paid to an average earner; credited contributions allowed for sickness, higher education, unemployment. No statutory maximum or minimum pension and no supplements for adult or child dependants; earnings up to a limit may be combined with pensions. Pensions are taxable, with tax calculated on the basis of interest credited on the accumulated contributions; sickness insurance and long-term care insurance (0.85%) deducted from pensions.
Ireland	Social insurance coverage for all private sector employees; small number of very low-income self-employed and part-time employees excluded. Contribution rules specify a maximum age of 55 for commencing contributions, a minimum number of contributions and an average annual number of contributions; credited contributions allowed for periods of sickness, unemployment, care work. Pension age is 66 for insurance pension; more contributions required for retirement pension at 65; pension benefit is flat rate; additional payments for those aged 80+ and those living alone; pensions funded from general social insurance fund; means-tested pension available at 66 for those not qualified for insurance pension; pensions have additional payments for adult and child dependants and extra, non-cash benefits; except for Retirement Pension, no restrictions on employment. Pensions included in taxable income, no social insurance contributions on pensions.

Greece	Pensions based on compulsory social insurance for all employees; different contribution rules for those insured before/after 1992; minimum period of membership is 4,500 working days; full pension of 80% of pensionable income for pre-1992 insured, and 60% for post-1992 insured, requires 35 years membership.
	Retirement age is 65 for post-1992 members; for pre-1992 members, age is 65 for men and 60 for women; early pensions, full and partial, available for men and women under certain conditions; credited contributions for periods of unemployment, sickness, military service.
	Amount of pension related to earnings and contributions, subject to minimum and maximum; rules for minimum pensions vary between pre- and post-1992 members; additional amounts for adult and child dependants.
	Pension may be reduced according to amount of employment, depending on year of retirement, age, and age at which work resumed; pensions included in taxable income, social insurance contributions payable.

Source: European Commission, (2001A).

Turning to unemployment payments, some of the same features are repeated. Here too the Finnish system is more comprehensive. It incorporates employees and the self-employed, and has a basic allowance, an income-related payment, and special provision for the young unemployed. None of the other three countries have provision for the self-employed. Of the four countries, Ireland, again, is the only one with flat-rate payments. Germany, for example, has a simple formula that equates the benefit with a percentage of net earnings. Also, Ireland's duration of entitlement to benefit is comparatively limited; it is set at 390 days in comparison with Finland's 500 days, and Germany's sliding scale with a maximum of 64 months. One point to note is that Finland has a general provision that excludes young people even from the residual Labour Market Assistance if they have not completed training or refused labour market support. Therefore, although Finland and its Scandinavian neighbours have more comprehensive schemes, they also actively enforce their strong cultural mores about work: generosity and comprehensiveness are combined with the obligation to work. This serves as a reminder that no one element of a country's provisions should be taken as its defining characteristic.

Both sets of comparisons also show that the countries have much in common. Social insurance plays a role in all four countries, notwithstanding their historical,

Chart 3.2: Social Security Provisions for the Unemployed, Selected Countries, 2001

Country	Key Provisions
Finland	Three elements of provision: Earnings-related Allowance, Basic Unemployment Allowance and Labour Market Assistance; earnings-related payments for employed and self-employed members of unemployment insurance funds aged 17–64, basic allowance for employees and self-employed aged 17–64; labour market assistance for those not fulfilling the conditions for earnings-related payments or who have exceeded the period of entitlement to basic allowance; labour market assistance not available to 17–24 year olds who have not completed training or refused to accept labour market measures.
	Minimum period of work — 43 weeks in last two years and minimum of 18 hours weekly; for self-employed minimum of two years in last four; seven-day waiting period during eight consecutive weeks for Basic Allowance, five days for Labour Market Assistance; five-month wait for first entrants to labour market, unless vocational training completed.
	Earnings–related payment based on previous 43 weeks earnings, previous 24 weeks income for self-employed; Earnings-related payment is Basic Allowance + earnings related supplement of 42% of earnings between certain limits; Basic Allowance set at a daily rate; Labour market assistance set at daily rate with different rates for single persons and families; additional payments for children under Basic Allowance and Labour Market Assistance. Limit of 500 days for Basic Allowance — paid to 60 years of age if recipient reaches 57; no time limit on Assistance; provision for partial Allowance for part-time work; separate unemployment pension for long-term unemployed 60 and over.
	Payments may be combined with some other allowances; payments included in taxable income.
Germany	Unemployment Insurance and Assistance for employees; for insurance minimum of 12 months insurance in last three years, for assistance receipt of insurance in last year; no waiting period for insurance or assistance; duration of insurance benefit related

Germany *(cont.)*	to age and contribution record to a maximum of 64 months; duration of assistance entitlement one year, with right to re-apply. Insurance benefit is 67% of net earnings for those with children and 60% for those without; earnings decided on average weekly wage for last 52 weeks, income from part-time work reduces insurance benefit; Assistance is 57% of net earnings (with children) or 53% (no children); no additional payments for dependants; benefits not liable to taxation, recipients' contributions for sickness and care provisions paid by Federal government. Partial unemployment provisions for seasonal unemployment and part-time work. Special employment scheme for unemployed 55 and over and retirement at 60 for the unemployed.
Ireland	Unemployment Benefit payable to insured persons except self-employed and public servants; eligibility based on social insurance; minimum age of eligibility 16, maximum 66; minimum contribution of 39 paid and 39 paid in previous year; limited to 390 days; waiting period of three days. Flat-rate benefit plus adult and child dependant payments depending on spouse's income; benefit included in annual taxable income; benefit, at half rate, may by combined with some other benefits. Rent allowance may be payable — also Fuel Allowance. Partial Benefit payable for short-time working and part-time working; unemployed aged 55–66 entitled to Pre-Retirement Allowance after 15 months unemployment. Unemployment Assistance payable for those with insufficient contributions or after Unemployment Benefit period is ended, age limit of 18-66, subject to means-test; waiting period of three days (except where period of Unemployment Benefit has ended). Flat-rate assistance plus adult and child additions subject to spouse's income; two rates of Unemployment Assistance, long-term and short-term.

Greece	Payment available for insured employees and first-time claimants aged 20–29; minimum requirement of 125 days work in last 14 months or 200 days in last two years, or 80 days work in last two years for first-time claimants.
	Earnings-related system based on monthly pay for salaried workers and daily pay for manual workers; salaried workers receive 50% of monthly wage, manual workers 40% of daily pay, subject to minimum of two-thirds of minimum wage and maximum of 70% of reference wage; maximum includes supplements of 10% for each dependant.
	Duration of entitlement based on length of previous work, maximum duration of 12 months, extra duration with lower benefits based on employment history; benefit for five months for new first-time claimants aged 20–29; part-time work for three days weekly allowed with benefit receipt.
	Benefit may be combined with other payments; benefit included in taxable income; social insurance contributions not deducted.

Source: European Commission, (2001A).

political and economic differences. In the case of unemployment provisions, the countries share a number of quite specific arrangements: they have all adapted their provisions to incorporate part-time employment; they also have differentiated treatment for the older long-term unemployed, and minimum entry criteria based on past employment or insurance contributions.

One other important aspect of social security should be noted — whether or not a country provides a 'last-resort' minimum payment for those without specific coverage under insurance or assistance categories. Although this part of social security is not the most significant in terms of expenditure or number of recipients, it deals with the most severe level of need and perhaps the most vulnerable claimants. The arrangements here are not easy to summarise and vary significantly. However, one fault-line that divides more developed from less developed systems is the presence or otherwise of a national legislative framework for such 'safety net' provisions. Ireland has such a framework in the *Supplementary Welfare Allowances* legislation. This gives a legal right, subject to a means test, to a statutorily-determined payment, and permits additional payments for exceptional needs and emergencies. Germany has the *Federal Social Assistance Act* and Finland the *Social Assistance Act* for broadly similar functions. In contrast, Greece has no statutory scheme, and Spain and Italy have arrangements at regional level, with considerable discretion and inter-regional variation.

A very unusual aspect of the Irish system, not found in other countries is the use of *non-cash benefits* (the 'free schemes' in popular parlance) as supplements to the cash payments. They comprise a range of provisions such as a universal free (public transport) travel scheme for pensioners, seasonal fuel allowances for welfare-dependent households and for pensioners living alone or with adult or child dependants or a carer, a free television licence, telephone rental and an allowance for electricity or gas. In 2002 total expenditure on these benefits-in-kind amounted to €296 million.

THE IRISH SOCIAL SECURITY SYSTEM TODAY

This section briefly reviews the main features of social security in Ireland today, beginning with a brief profile of the organisational structure. The relevant details about individual benefits are dealt with in the context of the policy discussions in specific chapters in Part Two.

In Ireland social security is the responsibility of the Minister for Social, Community and Family Affairs. The department of that name (see Chart 3.3) has a central policy section and a separate Social Welfare Services office headed by a Director-General: this office is responsible for the operational activities of the department. Benefits and allowances are administered in some cases centrally and in others through local offices and employment exchanges: decisions about applications for benefits and allowances are made by Deciding Officers, who have a legal identity separate from that of the department. The SWA service, although legislated for centrally, is delivered locally on an agency basis by staff of the Regional Health Boards. There is also a legally independent Appeals Office. Increasingly, the payments system is automated, with 25% of all recipients receiving their payment via electronic fund transfer.

Social Insurance is the core of the system and is based on funding from the contributors, employers, employees and the self-employed, and the state. Table 3.1 records the key aggregates for social insurance for 2002. There are over 2.4 million contributing to social insurance: a very large majority (75%) are 'Class A' contributors, creating entitlement to the full range of social insurance benefits. The employees' contribution rate in 2002 was 4% of their gross pay (subject to a ceiling) with their employers making a matching contribution of 10.75% to the fund.[3] In 2002, the total income was €4.79 billion and expenditure on (contributory) social insurance benefits was €4.38 billion, leaving a surplus of €420 million. The surplus reflects the exceptional buoyancy of the economy in recent years. It is not a legal requirement that the fund is balanced in accounting terms and, in practice, until 1995 the fund was typically in deficit and subsidised from the central exchequer.

Chart 3.3: Organisation of the Irish System of Social Security

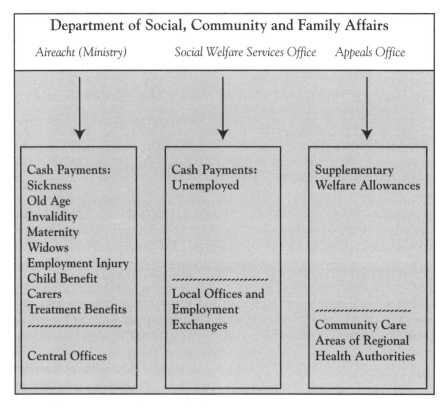

Department of Social, Community and Family Affairs
Aireacht (Ministry)   *Social Welfare Services Office*   *Appeals Office*

Cash Payments:
Sickness
Old Age
Invalidity
Maternity
Widows
Employment Injury
Child Benefit
Carers
Treatment Benefits

Central Offices

Cash Payments:
Unemployed

Local Offices and Employment Exchanges

Supplementary Welfare Allowances

Community Care Areas of Regional Health Authorities

Social Assistance is the second dimension of the system. This is comprised largely of means-tested allowances, funded from general taxation, that are counterparts to the insurance benefits. However, social assistance also includes means-tested payments for low-income employees, a range of employment supports, and the Supplementary Welfare Allowances scheme. SWA operates as a payment of last resort and a mechanism for meeting exceptional and emergency needs, and also contains the increasingly important Rent Allowance paid to social welfare recipients in the private rented sector.

Child Benefit is in a separate category. Funded from general taxation, it is payable monthly to all families, untaxed and without a means test. In 2002 over one million families received it and at €1.46 billion it is the largest single item in the social security budget.

Table 3.2 summarises the data on expenditure by broad category. The two largest programmes of expenditure are for Old Age and Families, each of these accounting for over one quarter of the total. Retirement and Contributory Old Age pensions amount to almost €1.7 billion. An important feature of the table is

Table 3.1: Key Data on Social Insurance in Ireland, 2002

Social Insurance	
Contributors (000s)	
Class A	1,809
Other	621
Total	2,430
Social Insurance Fund €m	
Employers	3,521
Employees	974
Self-employed	253
Other	51
Total	4,798
Expenditure on Benefits	4,379
Balance	(+)420

Source: Department of Social, Community and Family Affairs, 2003.
Notes: The data on contributors refer to 2001; €635 million of the 2002 revenue was transferred to the Exchequer.

the size of the insurance benefits spending compared with the figure for assistance: the figure for insurance benefits now considerably exceeds that for assistance. Chart 3.4 summarises the expenditure data.

Total spending on social security in 2002 (administration included) was 29% of gross current government expenditure and 9.1% of GNP. The latter figure represents a one-percentage point rise on the figure for 2001. However, from the early 1990s until 2001, the trend had been a continual fall in the figure: a decade ago, in 1992, it was 13.9%. The fall was due to a number of factors. By the early 1990s the system was comprehensive and no substantial new schemes were added. Economic growth and the dramatic fall in unemployment then reduced expenditure pressures significantly. With GNP increasing at a historically exceptional rate and unemployment falling sharply, the arithmetic effect was a cumulative decline in expenditure relative to GNP. This trend was then reinforced by the pattern of increases in benefits; while benefits rose, they did not rise as sharply as national income.

The description of social security here needs to be set in the context of what has been described as the 'social division of welfare'. In a celebrated paper Richard Titmuss pointed out that *direct expenditure* by the state on benefits (what he termed 'social welfare') is paralleled by *fiscal* welfare and *occupational* welfare (Titmuss, 1954). Fiscal welfare in this context refers to the indirect expenditure by the state through the tax system to meet needs or costs similar to those being addressed by social security. For example, the tax system contains allowances, credits and

Table 3.2: Expenditure (€m) on Social Security by Category, Ireland 2002

Category	Insurance	Assistance	Other	Total	Total %
Old Age	1,689	624	161	2,474	28
Widows	761	117		878	10
Sickness/Disability	866	582		1,448	16
Unemployment	485	680		1,165	13
Families	200	670	1,463	2,333	26
SWA and Other	61	544		605	7
Total	4,062	3,217	1,624	8,903	100

Source: Department of Social, Community and Family Affairs.
Notes: Administration expenditure is excluded; Pre-retirement allowance included in Old Age (Assistance); Unemployment includes employment supports and redundancy payments; The Non-cash 'Free Schemes' are in Old Age (Other); Farm Assist is in the SWA and Other row (Assistance) and Treatment Benefits are in the SWA and Other (Insurance) row.

Chart 3.4: Social Security Expenditure

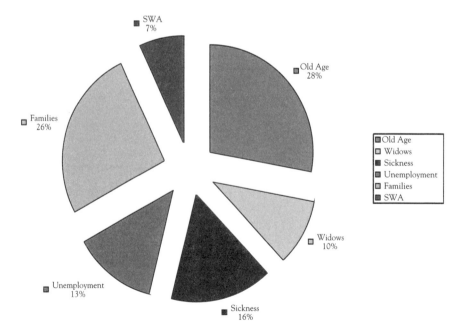

exemptions for pensions, sickness insurance, housing costs, caring responsibilities, and so on. However, these allowances are more likely to benefit higher income households, and in conventional budgetary accounts they are not costed, or represented as expenditures. The critical point is that references to expenditure on social security payments ignore these indirect expenditures, and this in turn gives an incomplete picture of the distribution of total government spending.

This has important implications. For example, discussion of the cost of pensions that focuses exclusively on the state's contributory and non-contributory pensions ignores the cost of a variety of tax supports for private pension provision. Therefore, the description of social security and the analysis of policy options and reforms must consider the parallel system of fiscal welfare. Some relevant examples of fiscal welfare include: the tax allowance for employees' contributions to occupational pensions; the tax credit in relation to the rent costs of tenants in private rented accommodation; the tax credit for relatives undertaking care work in the home. The role of such allowances will arise in the policy discussions in Part Two, but at this point it is important to note that the costs of fiscal welfare (in terms of revenue foregone by the exchequer) can be significant. For example, the NESC records a cost of €456 million for the tax allowance on employees' contributions to approved superannuation schemes: this compares with €490 million for the old age non-contributory pension in 2001 (NESC, 2003: 342).

As regards occupational welfare, many employees also benefit from employer-provided welfare in the area of pensions, maternity benefits, sick pay, and so on. With the exception of pensions there has been no analysis in Ireland of the extent of this form of welfare, but, as in the case of fiscal welfare, it is likely that higher income employees benefit from such provisions, and that occupational welfare may also impose costs on the state because they are facilitated by tax measures. In practice, in many employments these occupationally provided benefits (pensions, for example) are integrated with direct state welfare, but the net outcome of the co-existence of occupational welfare and social welfare is that those on higher incomes receive enhanced benefits.

BENEFIT LEVELS, INCOMES AND POVERTY

Benefit levels form a hierarchy in Ireland, as Table 3.3 illustrates. At the top of this hierarchy are the long-term insurance benefits for pensioners and at the bottom the benefit and assistance payments for the unemployed. Table 3.3 shows the amounts of benefit for individual recipients, and to give these a context, the table also shows the ratio of the payments to average net earnings. These ratios are all in the range under 40%. While this suggests that benefits are low relative to incomes in general, it is important to note that the comparison between the benefits and net earnings is given merely to put current benefit levels in context. These illustrations do not take account of the additional payments for adult and

Table 3.3: Benefits in 2003: Amounts for Individual Recipients, % of Net Average Earnings, and Change in Real Value 1993–2003

Benefits	Amount € Weekly	% of Net Earnings	Real Change %
Old Age Pension (age 80+)	163.70	34.7	29.9
Old Age Pension (age 66–80)	157.30	36.1	33.0
Widow's Pension (age 66–80)	155.80	34.3	21.4
Non Contributory Pension (aged 66–80)	144.00	31.7	41.9
Carer's Allowance	129.60	28.6	27.6
UB/DB/UA	124.80	27.5	30.9
Child Benefit (one child, weekly equivalent)	31.40	7.0	266.3

Source: Central Statistics Office; Department of Social, Community and Family Affairs.

Notes: The Child Benefit/net earnings figure is based on a married, one earner couple; all other examples are single people. Net earnings = gross earnings minus tax and PRSI.

child dependants, nor do they incorporate the monetary value of non-cash benefits. Also, the benefit levels cannot be taken as representative of the incomes or recipients and their families, as individual recipients may be part of wider families or households and may have other sources of income.

A further point about Table 3.3 is the rate of increase in the real value of the payments over the decade to 2002 — i.e. the increase after taking price inflation into account. The real increase is significant in some cases. What is the link between the benefits, poverty, and changing real value of the payment over time? Figure 3.1 shows the link between two benefits and the trend in prices, average net earnings and average gross earnings. The chart tells a simple story. Benefits increased more rapidly over this decade than prices, as Table 3.3 illustrated. They also outstripped gross earnings — earnings, that is, before tax and social insurance are deducted. However, *net* earnings rose most rapidly of all of the series given in the chart. This was the decade of substantial tax reductions and changes to PRSI, and the combination of rising earnings and reduced tax liabilities led to a very marked increase in net earnings.[4] Benefit levels, although rising more rapidly than prices, diverged from net earnings.

The implications of these trends are summarised in Table 3.4, which combines information on benefits and relative income poverty. In the top three rows of this table, figures are given for the proportion of persons in the population falling below these relative income poverty lines. These require some explanation. The

Figure 3.1: Benefits, Earnings, Prices, 1990–2002

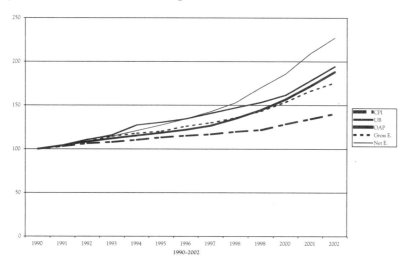

methodology here is informed by the relative income approach to poverty developed by Peter Townsend and elaborated in his famous book *Poverty in the United Kingdom* (Townsend, 1979). In this approach, poverty is due to a *lack of resources* leading in turn to *social exclusion*, i.e. an inability to buy the goods and services and participate in the habits, activities and life-style that are customary or approved. According to this definition, poverty, according must be judged in

Table 3.4: Percentages of Persons below Relative Income Poverty Lines and below Constant Real Poverty Line, and Benefits as % of Relative Poverty Line, 1994–2001

Poverty Percentage of Persons below:	1994 %	1997 %	1998 %	2000 %	2001 %
40% Poverty line	5.2	6.3	8.2	8.5	8.1
50% Poverty line	17.4	18.1	19.3	18.0	18.4
60% Poverty line	30.4	30.1	27.8	27.1	27.5
Constant Real 50% Poverty line (1994)	17.4	7.8	5.6	3.1	2.4
UB/DB as % of 50% Poverty Line	94.3	81.9	77.1	71.3	69.4
Pension as % of 50% Poverty Line	110	94.7	90.7	88.3	86.0

Source: Whelan, Layte, Maitre *et al*, 2003; Department of Social Community and Family Affairs.
Notes: The UB/DB and Pension data are based on the personal rates for recipients only: Poverty lines based on mean income.

terms of prevailing living standards.[5] The first element in this approach is lack of resources; most importantly lack of income, and the use of relative income poverty lines is the central aspect of this approach to poverty.

Briefly, this type of analysis entails the collection of large-scale, representative social survey data on the incomes and other circumstances of the population, and then the following procedures are applied:

- Average income, then *average disposable income* (i.e. income net of taxes etc), is calculated from the survey.
- To take account of the fact that individuals live in households of varying size and composition, per capita equivalent scales are used to adjust incomes and this procedure *yields average disposable income per capita equivalent.*[6]
- Using average disposable income per capita equivalent income as a benchmark, alternative *poverty lines* are specified and the proportions of the population below these lines are estimated.

There is no objective basis for the choice of one poverty line over another: the common practice in this kind of research is to present estimates of poverty based on a number of lines to show how the results vary according to the poverty line chosen. The income data derived in this form of survey are representative of incomes generally — unlike, for example, the illustrative data in Table 3.3 that refer only to earnings.[7]

The first three rows of Table 3.4 show the rate of poverty for three lines, 40%, 50% and 60% of the average adjusted income figure. At all three lines the rate of poverty rose in the period up to 1998. In other words, in a context in which the real (inflation-adjusted) value of benefits rose, relative income poverty also rose. The final two rows of the table show how this came about: the level of benefits fell as a proportion of the poverty line (the 50% line is chosen for illustration). Since 1998 the poverty rate has stabilised. Significantly, the pattern of poverty conveyed here is based on a *relative* income concept. A very different link between benefits and poverty emerges if a different concept of poverty is adopted, one in which the poverty line is *fixed* in real terms. In the case of Table 3.4, this means defining the poverty line in 1994 terms and then adjusting it in later years only for price increases. As the fourth row in the table shows, if a fixed poverty line is applied the rate of poverty fell markedly over the 1990s.

In summary, the level of benefits in Ireland is low relative to incomes in general. Their real value has increased cumulatively over the last decade, so that recipients relying over this time on a benefit payment as the sole source of income experienced an increased standard of living. However, in relation to incomes in general, benefits declined and this contributed to rising poverty, when poverty is viewed in relative terms.

THE WIDER CONTEXT

The sections above gave a descriptive overview of the current social security system in Ireland. At this point it is useful to outline the wider context in which the system functions and in particular to record the key trends of the last decade that have shaped, and may continue to shape the system. Table 3.5 contains some stylised facts to guide the discussion.

The economic base of social security has dramatically altered in the last decade or so, with GNP per capita rising significantly and unemployment falling to historically very low levels. This has directly affected social security. The growth in employment led to a surge in revenue into the social insurance fund and by 1997 a surplus had emerged in the fund — a surplus that grew in the subsequent years. This surplus reduced the need for an Exchequer subsidy. The high level of employment led to an expansion in the contributing membership of social insurance and in turn this has shifted the system further in the direction of social insurance and away form social assistance. The majority of the expenditure is now insurance-based.

The *pattern* as well as the level of employment has also changed as the indicators suggest. Notably, the rate of female participation in the workforce has grown markedly — this applies in particular to married women, including those with children. Associated with the growth in female labour force participation, there has been a rise in the extent of part-time employment.

The economic developments of the last decade have consolidated the *resource* base for the social security system. But, if the resource situation has evolved, so too has the level and pattern of *needs*. As Table 3.5 indicates, the level of aged dependency (the proportion of the population aged under 65) declined, reflecting the growth in the prime working-age groups. This demographic scenario is already changing, and in the years immediately ahead Ireland will experience a gradual ageing of its the population. The social security system is beginning to adapt to this change.

However, the aggregate dependency rates are at best an indicator of overall potential need. An equally important dimension of the demographic situation is the changing family structure. An increasing share of families in Ireland is comprised of one-parent families, and women head the vast majority of these. Structurally, these families are less well placed to avail of employment opportunities and their reliance on social security is likely to be higher. If Ireland follows the international pattern of a continuing increase in the number of lone parent families, then they may form an increasing share of the social security population. This more recent change is challenging the social security arrangements built around the conventional two-parent family. Also, the rise of cohabitation and the increasing acceptance of single-sex relationships means that the social context in which social security must function is becoming more varied and complex. The notion of financial 'dependence' has been integral to the social

Table 3.5: Summary Indicators of Social and Economic Context

Indicator	Circa 1990	Circa 2000
Economy		
GNP per Capita as % of EU average	73.5	99.8
Unemployment Rate %	12.9	5.7
Demography/Labour Market		
% Married Women with young children in Work	42.2	55.2
Number of One Parent Families (000s)	41.4	90.0
Age Dependency ratio	18.5	17.6
(number 65+ as % of number 15–64)		
Inequality Trends		
% Share of Wages and Salaries in National Income	66.8	60.1
Earnings dispersion; ratio of high wage to low wage	3.68	3.93
Gini coefficient of inequality	0.377	0.373

Source: National Income and Expenditure, CSO, various issues; *Labour Force Survey and Quarterly National Household Survey*, CSO, various issues; Nolan, 2000B; Barrett, Fitzgerald and Nolan, 2000; NESC (1991); Fahey and Fitzgerald (1997). *Note:* All the data are within three years of the 1990 or 2000 dates, except for the work participation data for married women where the earlier date is 1995.

security and tax systems in Ireland and these changes in family formation patterns have posed policy choices and problems that are still being resolved.

A potentially significant change in context is the emergence of strong pressures towards income inequality. On a broader international front, there is a wide range of commentary arguing that modern welfare states in the increasingly competitive, globalised economy are prone to forces that increase economic inequality (Yeates, 2001; Mishra, 1998; Pierson, 1994).[8] There is considerable debate about this internationally, and in Ireland claim and counter-claim have been made about whether and to what extent the recent experience of economic growth and integration into the global economy has created greater income inequality and social inequality (O'Hearn, 1998; Kirby, 2002; Allen, 2000; Nolan, O'Connell and Whelan, 2000).

The discussion here does not attempt to review this controversy, but assesses to what extent social security in Ireland may now be operating in a context of widening income inequalities. Some indicators in the table reflect different aspects of inequality. First, the share of national income accruing to wages rather than profits or self-employment income fell during the period of the Celtic Tiger. However, these figures measure the functional rather than the personal distribution of income. Turning to the distribution of pay among employees, the extent of wage inequality has risen, as indexed by the ratio of low pay to high pay. Table 3.5 also shows the values for the Gini coefficient of inequality. This coefficient varies from 0 to 1, with higher values indicating greater inequality, and conversely. It takes into account income from all sources, and in Table 3.5 it reflects the impact of the tax and social security system, summarising the degree of income inequality in disposable income. The values for the coefficient have remained remarkably stable over time, despite the rise in earnings inequality, and the shift to profits from wages. Research on income distribution (Nolan, 2000) suggests that in Ireland employment is critical here. During the 1990s employment rose markedly in the lower reaches of the income distribution: for example, some households that had no employees in the early 1990s might have two or more in the late 1990s. Employment growth ameliorated the effect of pressures towards inequality.

Could budgetary policy in tax and social security have also contributed to the stability in disposable income inequality? In the period since 1994, while increasing the real value of benefits, governments have implemented a range of tax cuts and adjustments to tax rates and tax bands: notably, marginal rates of income tax have fallen from 27% and 48% in 1994 to 20% and 42% in 2002. The evidence of the many income distribution studies undertaken in recent years is that in the distribution of resources as between benefit increases and tax reductions, budgetary priority has tended to favour tax reductions to the detriment of lower income and welfare-dependent households (Callan, Keeney, Nolan *et al*, 2001; Callan, Keeney, Walsh, 2003; Callan, Nolan, Walsh *et al*: 1999). In one study, ESRI researchers assessed the distributive impact of tax and social welfare policies, by posing the question: over and above the resources required to index the tax/benefit system to wages, how have budget 'packages' been distributed as between tax cuts and welfare increases? They found that over period from 1994 to 2001 the tax system (and Child Benefit) received substantially *more* than was necessary (for indexation) and the welfare system *less*.

Table 3.6 reports some detail from an analysis by the ESRI of the budget packages of successive governments. The figures record the average percentage gain or loss in net income by households at different levels in the income distribution, ranked by quintile (i.e. according to the lowest fifth, second lowest fifth, and so on) against a benchmark of indexation of benefits and taxes to wages. In 1993 and 1994 lower income households benefited slightly while higher income households lost. The more recent budgets, however, show a much clearer pattern. The cumulative effect of the 1995, 1996 and 1997 budgets was a *loss* for the two lowest quintile households in contrast to gains for the remainder. In the 1998–2002 series of budgets the lowest quintile gained slightly on average, but the higher quintiles gained very substantially: 2.3% for the lowest and 10.6% for the highest. Social security is one instrument of income redistribution and can counteract underlying income inequalities, but the emphasis in recent budgetary

Table 3.6: Average percentage Gains/Losses for Households in Different Income Quintiles from Budgetary Tax and Benefit Changes

Quintile	Budgets 1993–94	Budgets 1995–97	Budgets 1998–2002
Lowest	1.3	–1.9	2.3
Second	1.1	–1.0	6.4
Third	0.4	2.0	11.5
Fourth	–0.4	3.0	10.9
Fifth	–0.7	1.9	10.6
All	–0.1	1.6	9.7

Source: Callan, Keeney and Walsh, 2003, Table 3.6.

policy of prioritising tax reductions over benefit improvements weakened its redistributive impact.

CONCLUSION

The social security system is based on social insurance and still strongly reflects its British origins. In the last decade the system reached maturity, with the balance of expenditure now attributable to insurance benefits. Benefit levels have increased significantly in real terms, although the system now operates in a wider context of higher overall levels of prosperity and profound changes in social, employment and family structures. The next chapter considers how social security policy and provision should be analysed.

Notes

1. This is not a strict separation in Ireland's case. Social insurance contributions cover entitlement to Treatment Benefits (Dental, Aural, and Optical Benefits) for some categories of contributors.
2. The Pre-Retirement Allowance is a qualification to this description.
3. In addition a Health levy of 2% is payable by employees below a certain income level.
4. The reductions were delivered through a combination of adjustments to tax bands and tax allowances, and a significant reduction in tax rates: the marginal rates of tax in 1991–2 were 29%, 48% and 52%, and 2002 they were 20% and 42%.
5. Townsend's widely-cited definition of poverty is as follows: 'Individuals, families and groups in the population can be said to be in poverty when they

lack the resources to obtain the types of diet, participate in the activities and have the living conditions and amenities that are customary, or at least widely encouraged or approved, in the societies to which they belong. Their resources are so seriously below those commanded by the average individual or family that they are, in effect, excluded from ordinary living patterns, customs and activities.' (Townsend, 1979: 31)

6.   In Table 3.4 the scale used is: 1.0 (first adult), 0.66 additional adults, and 0.33 for all persons aged 0–14. This is the scale implicit in the structure of social security payments in Ireland. For example, if a household had a disposable income of €500 and comprised a man, wife and one child under 14, the per capita equivalent income is the unadjusted income divided by the scale, giving 500/(1+0.66+0.33), or €251.25.

7.   Callan and Nolan (1994: 9–42) contains an overview of the conceptual and methodological issues in defining and measuring poverty.

8.   For example, competitiveness requirements are constraining welfare states from imposing costs such as taxes and social insurance contributions on business; the freedom of multi-national corporations to change location leads states to compete for investment by controlling wage and other costs; the emphasis on competitiveness has led to a less significant role for the state in the economy, leading to a decline in the role of stable life-long employment; the search labour market flexibility has led to greater employment insecurity and a stronger link between employees' wages and performance, contributing to greater wage dispersion between employees.

4
Analysing Social Security

INTRODUCTION

This chapter deals with the aims and objectives of social security. A recent textbook on social security in the UK suggests 'It is misleading to talk about the "aims of social security" as if they are something that exist on their own, providing a set of universal criteria against which we can evaluate the social security system now or at any given time in the past' (Sainsbury, 1999: 34). A chapter on income maintenance in a recently published textbook on Irish social policy makes no reference at all to the aims or objectives of the income maintenance system (Mills, 1999: 27–48). The reasons for this difficulty about listing policy objectives are not too hard to find. There is dispute about the aims of social security, and controversy about the relative importance of various objectives. To complicate matters, the objectives that might be identified may change over time in response to changing circumstances. Furthermore, official policy documents or political pronouncements may not be specific or clear about the aims of policy.

Despite these complexities it remains the case that in much of the analysis and political and public commentary about policy focuses on issues of poverty and low-income. An analysis of social security solely in terms of poverty, however, would not reflect the diversity of the system or the range of policy debates and controversies it engenders: nor would it be a particularly simple task. This chapter does not set out a list of objectives, inferred from how the social security system operates, or imputed to policymakers and government on the basis of their actions and statements. It sets out a general framework for the analysis in later chapters. This framework outlines different levels of policy analysis and allows a discussion of controversies and debates about the objectives of policy. However, it does not contain formal criteria that are applied uniformly across the social security system, recognising that there may be controversy about objectives and aims, that objectives may be implicit or explicit, and that they may be expressed with varying levels of precision across different areas of policy. Each area of policy is different and has its unique problems and controversies and the framework set out here (summarised in Chart 4.1) will therefore be applied differently in each chapter.

GENERAL SOCIAL OBJECTIVES

A preliminary point to note is that social security may be an instrument of broad political strategies. As the history of social security in the first two chapters shows, ideology and politics play a part in defining the role of the social security system in society and the economy as a whole. Beveridge, for example, explicitly argued for a system that should complement private effort and be an instrument of labour market and economic policy. Ultimately, Beveridge envisaged that one of the objectives of the social security system was to facilitate the reform and maintenance of the capitalist economy. Other viewpoints in political economy would articulate a different link between social security and society. Thus, countries with strong traditions of social democracy give the social security system the role, broadly, of helping to transform rather than reinforce the workings of the capitalist economy. These 'higher level' objectives influence quite specific aspects of social security policy.

Turning to the framework in Chart 4.1, social security can be identified as one instrument of quite specific policy goals at national and international levels. In Ireland in the 1960s, national economic development became the overriding goal of public policy and during this period social security policy in general, and quite specific aspects of it, were viewed officially as tools of the general programme of development. The Third Programme for Economic and Social Development (Government of Ireland, 1969: 17–18) pointed out that the distinction between 'economic and social objectives' can be 'exaggerated' and that many social developments contain elements, which are 'essential to economic progress'. The programme argued that social development acts as a motor of economic development by 'helping to convince people that growth is a worthwhile objective'. A very direct instance of the pursuit of national economic policy by social means was the series of improvements in unemployment payments, notably the introduction of a Redundancy Payments scheme for some workers made redundant as a result of the planned restructuring of the industrial sector. The programme linked the welfare and economic aspects of this initiative in social security, referring to its main objectives as 'alleviating hardship for workers who become redundant and of helping to reduce the resistance of workers to changes which are necessary for increased efficiency' (Government of Ireland, 1969: 132).

A more recent example of this link between broader policy goals and the role of social security is the European Union's emphasis in its policy statements on the link between employment and social policy and social protection. In 2001, the European Union referred to the 'dynamic interaction between these three policy areas — economic, employment, and social' (European Commission, 2001B: 13) and stated, 'A high level of social protection and well targeted social policy is essential for adapting the economy and providing an efficient and well trained labour force.' Of course, statements such as these are not uncontroversial and

Chart 4.1: Framework for the Analysis of Social Security

Analysis	Examples in Irish Social Security Policy
General Societal Objectives	1960s Programmes for Economic Expansion see social security system as an instrument of national development.
Broad Social Policy Aims	Social Security policy identified as central to the pursuit of Ireland's National Anti-Poverty Strategy.
Financial Functions:	
Poverty Relief;	Official Government document states that people 'should have sufficient income to enable them to live in a manner compatible with human dignity.' (DSCFA, 1998:24)
Redistribution;	Commission on Social Welfare (1986:123) argues that 'the attainment of significant redistribution of resources is a widely accepted aim of social policy in Ireland. Social welfare payments are an important part of the redistributive process.'
Income Replacement;	Replacement of lost income, as distinct from provision of a sufficient income, is not listed in government documents as an aim of policy.
Life Cycle Redistribution;	Official review of Child Benefit (DSW, 1995:) gives 'assistance towards the costs of children' and 'sharing the financial burdens of parenthood' as criteria for assessing Child Benefit.
Equity/Efficiency Evaluations	Expert Working Group on Integration of Tax and Social Welfare (Expert Working Group, 1996:4–6) offers equity and efficiency as criteria for evaluating systems of social security; efficiency analysis focuses on impact of social security on employment.
Secondary Objectives	Administrative and quality-of-service issues listed in the aims of policy in reviews of social welfare: Commission on Social Welfare stressed need for a 'simple' system: NESF argued for improved delivery of services as a key aim of income maintenance policy.

represent a political vision of the role that social security might play in the modern economy. The same official documents that advance this vision may also refer to the costs of social security and to the need to subordinate social security to economic goals such as competitiveness.

SOCIAL SECURITY AND SOCIAL POLICY

The second row in the chart refers to the more common and more topical issue of the link between social security and broader social policy goals. In 1995, the Irish Government committed itself to the development of a National Anti-Poverty Strategy (NAPS) following its participation in the United Nations World Summit in Copenhagen. At the summit, Governments agreed to the goal of 'eradicating poverty in the world, through decisive national action and international co-operation as an ethical, social, political and economic imperative of humankind'. An Interdepartmental Committee subsequently formulated the Irish government's national anti-poverty strategy, *Sharing in Progress* (Government of Ireland, 1997). This document starts by adopting a relative concept of poverty as formulated by Townsend (see Chapter Three) and then outlines a policy programme in which social security has a role.[1]

The NAPS set out a number of developments that were envisaged as central to the pursuit of the overall programme. First, in relation to the critical issue of the adequacy of social security payments, the NAPS incorporated a poverty target based on the research on relative income and relative deprivation in Ireland. This research generated the concept of 'consistent poverty'. The 'consistently poor' are those whose incomes are below a specified (relative) income poverty line and who also suffer a certain degree of basic deprivation. Basic deprivation means an inability to afford certain things (such as heat for the home or hot meals) that are widely endorsed as necessary. NAPS specified that one of its targets was the reduction in consistent poverty in the population from a figure in the range 9% to 15% (as reported by the ESRI for 1994) to a figure in the range 5 to 10%, over the period 1997 to 2007.[2] This target has both an income dimension and a consumption or deprivation dimension. NAPS does not explicitly relate the consistent poverty target to a specific target about the adequacy of social security payments: it reiterates the agreement of the government and the social partners to adopt the (inflation-adjusted) rates of social security recommended by the Commission on Social Welfare.[3]

Sharing in Progress also refers to other social security issues that it deems to be central to the overall anti-poverty strategy. These include, for example, a stronger focus on transitions to work, reforms of the tax and benefits system to avoid disincentives and poverty traps, and individualisation — the right of individual adult dependants to receive payments in their own right. However, these issues are referred to, as problems to address and no particular policies in these areas are set out as important to the overall anti-poverty programme.

THE FINANCIAL FUNCTIONS OF SOCIAL SECURITY

The data on poverty levels in Chapter Three gave evidence about the extent of relative income poverty in Ireland This section focuses on the type of poverty-related objectives that policy makers and policy advocates might have. At the outset, it is clear that official policy in Ireland is framed in Beveridgean terms — the objective of policy is not to redistribute incomes from rich and poor or to replace all of the income lost through unemployment (for example), but to offer financial relief and prevent outright destitution. The evidence for this is the adherence to a system of modest flat-rate payments over a long period of time. But, are there more precise financial targets that can be discerned for the level and structure of social security payments. Is it clear, in other words, what exact costs and needs the payments are supposed to cover?

The first issue here is the link between poverty-related objectives and benefit levels. In this context the central point to note is that there are no official statements about what specific standard of living the social security payments system is intended to sustain. This reflects the fact that no Irish government has ever undertaken any formal calculations about payments levels and how they relate to living costs and living standards for payment recipients. It is striking that at critical junctures in the development of the system this analysis was not undertaken. For example, the level of payments established in the 1952 Act were not presented in any context, for example, in relation to calculations of living costs, or prevailing living standards, or income levels. Unlike the UK system established by Beveridge the Irish payment levels do not appear to have had any clear rationale.[4]

Later, in the 1970s, when the residue of the Poor Law, Home Assistance, was being abolished and replaced with Supplementary Welfare Allowances, a further opportunity arose to undertake research on living costs and living standards and to relate this to payment levels. The purpose of the legislation was to confer on all citizens for the first time a legal right to a payment for basic needs. In his introductory speech on this legislation the Minister stipulated that the new SWA scheme should guarantee 'to all persons who have to depend on the service, a standard basic minimum income as of right' (McCashin and O'Donoghue, 1979). The legislation (SWA Act, 1975: S.5) stated that 'every person in the State whose means are insufficient to meet his needs and the needs of any adult or child dependant of his shall be entitled to supplementary welfare allowances'. However, the Act simply incorporated a pre-existing payment, the rural rate of unemployment assistance — the lowest payment level, and no analytical exercise was undertaken on what 'needs', or 'minimum income' might mean in terms of social security payment levels.

In the 1980s, the Commission on Social Welfare pointed out the historic neglect of payment levels and undertook a range of calculations to estimate a range within which a minimally adequate payment level might fall (Commission on Social Welfare, 1986: 189–194): the Commission attempted to 'establish a level of income which would be sufficient to maintain a single adult in independent circumstances at a standard of living which is linked to living standards . . . in society generally' (Commission on Social Welfare, 1986: 191). The calculations yielded an estimate of a minimally adequate income and this estimate received quasi-official recognition when the (inflation-adjusted) rates were incorporated into the nationally agreed programmes in the 1990s. However, the Commission pointed out that its calculations were not based on any 'agreed statistical procedure or theoretical foundation as, ultimately, in our view, any calculated minimum will be somewhat arbitrary' (Commission on Social Welfare, 1986: 193). For example, the Commission took some implicit official standards of minimal adequacy — the threshold for medical card eligibility and the minimum wage rates in certain sectors — and with certain adjustments adopted these as indicators of a minimum. It also calculated a minimum based on a variant of the official US budget standards procedure: a necessary amount for food is first calculated and then the total minimum budget required is estimated.

The Commission's report was widely cited and had some influence on policy in relation to payment increases, but two key points should be noted. First, while the Commission's analysis of a minimum was used as a benchmark by poverty advocates for payment increases, the calculations also showed that some welfare payments were already in the range of adequacy as estimated by the Commission, and that the addition of the benefit-in-kind schemes (free fuel, free electricity etc) enhanced the living standards of those categories of welfare recipient whose payment levels were already at or close to the adequacy target. Second, although poverty and the specific issue of policy targets have both received considerable attention in recent years, the position in relation to the specific financial objectives of social security payments remains as it was at the time of the Commission's report. There is no official benchmark on which the social security payments are based and no official set of calculations about the needs the payments are estimated to meet.

Turning from the rationale for the level of payments to policies about increases in the payments, the evidence in Chapter Three shows that they have increased substantially in real terms. However, there is no statutory obligation on the Government to index the payments to any external yardstick such as consumer prices or earnings. The Commission on Social Welfare did not come to an agreed conclusion on this point: some members suggested that social security legislation should specify that payment levels be indexed to inflation. More recently, an official working group on indexation considered this issue again (Government of Ireland, 2001). The group did not reach agreement, and recorded two broad approaches. One point of view was that it is inappropriate to establish a formal benchmark, and a contrary view was that an explicit link should be established between benefit levels and average earnings as a fundamental right, so that the incomes of welfare recipients keep pace with those of the wider community. The majority of this working group argued that it would be reasonable to have a target of 27% of gross average earnings for the lowest social security payment, and proposed that this target be reached in full by 2007.

A further aspect of the link between social security payments and poverty concerns the structure of the payments. The Irish system is not unusual in having a tiered system of payments with local social assistance, general non-contributory, assistance payments and contributory benefits in ascending order. Within these different tiers, however, there are arbitrary variations in the standard of living afforded by the payments. For example, to anticipate an issue that arises in Chapter Nine, it is unclear what the relationship is intended to be between the level of payments, the treatment of housing costs and the living standards of recipients before and after they have met their housing costs. Recipients might have very different incomes after payment of rent or mortgages; some will have zero housing costs, young owner occupiers would typically be facing mortgage payments that are high relative to income, and local authority tenants will have very modest rents because of the impact of the local authority differential rents scheme. One group of recipients will have a living alone allowance payable in addition to their 'main' payment: if the logic of this is to recognise the higher unit costs of one-person households, then recipients in one-person households not in receipt of this allowance may have a lower standard of living. A similar anomaly exists in relation to the benefit-in-kind schemes (free travel, fuel vouchers, free electricity and telephone rental).

It can be argued that in Ireland the absence of an official, arithmetical benchmark for social security payments is not a significant obstacle to the assessment of the social security system or its impact on poverty because of the availability of representative data on the incomes and financial and social circumstances of the population. These data have facilitated a wide range of studies of poverty and inequality and, as was noted above, allowed the formulation in the NAPS of a very specific poverty-reduction target. Admittedly, the stream of research material on poverty since the 1980s has informed public debate and policy formulation, but there is no statutory obligation on the government to undertake or fund such research. Furthermore, these data, although providing important contextual and evaluative information, are still at one remove from official expectations of what living standard is supposedly affordable for recipients of social security. In short, Irish governments have had representative data available on the incomes of the population since the program of poverty studies first commenced in the late 1980s. Governments could have used the data from these studies to specify a target for benefit levels based on these independently derived poverty lines. However, the target it chose, as noted earlier, does not have a direct implication for benefits.

In principle, a government could adopt a poverty line derived from social research as its criterion of adequacy. In practice this is unlikely, and it is important to note the distinction between research-based standards such as relative income poverty lines and legal or administrative standards, as Veit-Wilson points out (Veit-Wilson, 1998). Relative income poverty lines and similar analytical measures represent the findings of social science research about 'the minimum income levels at which the whole population show or state they can live adequately, whatever the political implications of the findings'. Official standards, however, are often 'political criteria of adequacy, whatever the political implications of the findings' (Veit-Wilson, 1998: vii). An important implication of this distinction is that if a government has a legal minimum payment, such as the SWA system in Ireland, this minimum is not a poverty line in the analytical sense. A legal or administrative minimum is one useful criterion for evaluating social security, but this type of minimum should not be mistaken for a measure of poverty. For instance, to show that a given per cent of the population in Ireland is above or below the SWA payment rate is not the same as offering an estimate of poverty.

To place Irish official practice in context, the way in which governments in other countries specify the link between poverty and social security payments can be considered. Chart 4.2 summarises some key points from Veit-Wilson's ten-country study of how selected governments fix minimum income standards. (Veit-Wilson (1998:1) defines a Minimum Income Standard as: 'a political criterion of the adequacy of income levels for some given minimum real level of living, for a given period of time, of some section or all of the population, embodied in or symbolised by a formal administrative instrument or other construct'. His study shows that there are potentially three levels at which governments might specify standards of adequacy — in descending order these relate to: pay/minimum wages; pensions/social insurance benefits; social assistance allowances. Governments could have standards at none, some, or all of these tiers. The rationale invoked for a standard will depend on the tier at which it is set. Standards set in relation to pay will derive from principles of minimum reward for work and will also reflect the 'less eligibility' principle that income from work should be greater than income from welfare. The influence of social insurance on adequacy standards has meant that some countries have a middle tier distinguishing minimum pensions (and other insurance entitlements) from social assistance. Insurance benefits are contribution-based and are set at a higher level than standards based only on need. In very many countries there is a third, lower tier (sometimes local rather than national or federal, and discretionary rather than statutory) in the form of social assistance and usually rationalised as meeting the most basic needs.

Chart 4.2: Income Maintenance Provisions and Minimum Income Standards in Ten Countries

Upper Tier Minima

Belgium	Academic Study of Public Attitudes to Minimum
France	Minimum Wage
The Netherlands	Minimum Wage
Sweden	Official budget for 'reasonable' level of living

Middle Tier Minima

Australia	Henderson Poverty Line/Male earnings index
Finland	Minimum Pension
New Zealand	Basic benefit level (pre-1990 Universal benefit)

Lower Tier Minima

Germany	Federal recommendations for social assistance
New Zealand	Brashares/Aynsley/ food budget method
USA	Poverty Guidelines/Lower Living Standard/Thrifty Food Plan/Median family income percentages

Source: Veit-Wilson (1998: 83).

The chart shows the tiers at which the ten countries studied set minimum standards and summarises the detail of the link between these standards and levels of social security payments. Examples[5] of how some of these countries operate these minima give an indication of the specific ways in which the financial functions of social security can be set out. Holland, for example, has had a minimum wage over a very long period with an automatic indexation system. Under certain conditions the indexation system would be set aside and negotiation between trade unions, employers and government (twice yearly) would determine the increase in the minimum: after 1980 these negotiations explicitly used the trend in real average earnings as a benchmark for negotiation.

Every four years the government was obliged to review the development of the minimum wage. The minimum was framed in terms of a stereotypical 'family wage' for a man with a spouse and two children and was supposed to allow a socially acceptable standard of living. Since 1971 many social security payments were directly linked to the wage-based minimum. A series of formulae were used to convert the gross wage to a net benefit and standard equivalence scales were applied to arrive at benefit levels for households of different sizes. From the mid-1970s to the early 1990s local social assistance levels were also linked to the minimum.

Turning to a middle tier minimum, the minimum standard in New Zealand from 1972 was the Basic Benefit Level (BBL) for social security benefits. In New Zealand the approach of governments has been to outline a principle of adequacy expressed in terms of Townsend's concept of poverty: benefits should provide adequate resources to participate in society. The government has not always implemented this when it has been politically difficult. A Royal Commission in 1972 argued that the focus of policy should be to identify a measure of average living standards (rather than to define a minimum) and that the measure of average standards should be the benchmark for social security benefits. The Commission chose a specific earnings yardstick and set the BBL for a couple at 80% of the net wage figure, and for a single person at 60%. This set the minimum standard for most social security benefits from 1972 to 1991, with the initial BBL being related to prices rather than earnings over time. In the early 1990s, a new and separate minimum was created for unemployment benefit — a lower tier minimum based on a subsistence approach to estimating and costing 'basic' needs.

The USA provides the most widely cited example of a minimum standard set at the lower tier, the Orshanky Poverty Line (after its author, Molly Orshanky). In 1965, Orshansky took a 1950s recommended diet for a family of four, costed this diet and multiplied it by three (one-third being the 1950s share of food in household expenditure). This figure, indexed, was adopted as the official US statistical definition of poverty, and in the USA's War on Poverty in the 1960s it was used for planning and statistical purposes. Notwithstanding the considerable changes in incomes and living standards since then, the OPL has only been indexed to prices and has not been rebased — the basic composition of the 'shopping basket' has not been changed to reflect current lifestyles. The OPL is subject to considerable criticism among policy critics and poverty researchers. There are two other subsistence-type standards in the USA. One of these is the Agriculture Department's Food Plans, based on surveys of actual food consumption patterns and adjusted to reflect cost and nutritional considerations: this was last rebased in 1983. A further standard is the Bureau of Labour's family budget figures published since 1911, last rebased in 1967. Here a moderate family budget is identified and higher and lower cost budgets are derived as percentages of the moderate figure. These standards have been used in a number of ways to determine eligibility for services and benefits. For example, the OPL figures are used to determine eligibility for the Federal Food Stamps program and the amount of stamps awarded is based on a family's net income and the Food Plan income threshold.

In summary, the international experience is that some governments use highly formalised Minimum Income Standards for a variety of purposes, including setting levels of benefits and establishing criteria for assessing the adequacy of social security payments. Ireland, in contrast, has no such official minimum standard, explicitly derived. Consequently, it is unclear what the specific financial target of Ireland's payments system is. However, Ireland does have the multi-tiered system of 'minima' found in other countries, although these minima are informally calculated. First, there is a national minimum wage of €6.35 per hour — or €254 for a forty-hour week. Then the rate for the social insurance old age pension is €157.30 for one person (more for a person aged over 80), and a variety of insurance based payments are in the range €125–€157. At the lowest end of this hierarchy is the legal minimum to which a person is entitled subject to a means test: currently, this minimum is €124.80.

REDISTRIBUTION

Clearly, one of the effects of social security is to bring about a degree of redistribution: the distribution of income is different to what it would be if there was no social security system. To put the redistributive role of social security in context it is necessary to describe the redistributive process more fully.

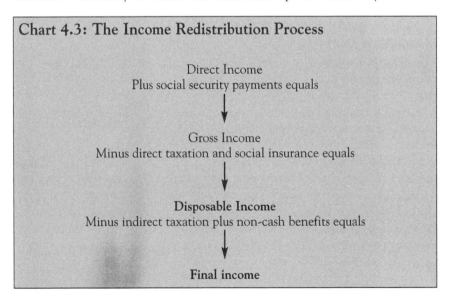

Chart 4.3: The Income Redistribution Process

Direct Income
Plus social security payments equals

↓

Gross Income
Minus direct taxation and social insurance equals

↓

Disposable Income
Minus indirect taxation plus non-cash benefits equals

↓

Final income

Chart 4.3 outlines the role of social security in the wider process of income distribution. This process is one in which households and families have an initial, direct income: this is the income (such as pay or self-employment income) that they receive from direct economic activity. For some households this figure might be zero — the unemployed and social security pensioners, for example. Households may also receive benefits, of course, and when these are added to Direct Income they yield Gross Income. However, tax and social insurance is deducted from income and this leaves households with their Disposable Income. (A final stage noted in the chart is included for the sake of accuracy, but is of less relevance in this context. Out of their disposable income people also pay indirect taxes on their expenditure: they may also receive income-in-kind such as medical services and free schooling for children, giving a Final Income.)

The central point to note about this framework is that social security is only one in a series of interventions. Therefore, if the distribution of disposable income changes over time or varies from one country to another this could be due to a number of factors. For instance, if unemployment rose, inequality in gross incomes would tend to rise. The social security system offsets the initial distribution of income, but the extent to which this happens is an empirical matter. Critically, the greater the level of benefit relative to average income and the greater the number of recipients in the population the more impact the social security system will have.

Income distribution studies measure the extent of income inequality at each stage and summarise the inequality in the form of an index. The most common of these is the Gini-coefficient. This coefficient varies from 0 to 1: the higher the coefficient, the greater the inequality. Nolan's study of income distribution shows that the distribution of disposable income (indexed by the Gini Coefficient) in Ireland is more unequal than in most EC countries (Nolan, 2000B). The coefficient will be lower for gross than direct income, and lower again for disposable income. However, the critical issue is how much lower the coefficient is at gross income stage. In Ireland, in 1997, the coefficient was 0.536 for direct income, 0.417 for gross income and 0.373 for disposable income. The biggest decline in the co-efficient happens at the direct-gross stage. Therefore, the social security benefits system, rather than the income tax system, is the more powerful mechanism of redistribution.

In terms of current policy in Ireland, there is little agreement as to the extent of redistribution of incomes that should be sought and of the role of social security in this process. The Commission on Social Welfare, for example, argued that social security should explicitly adopt redistribution as one of its policy aims: but later official documents do not endorse that view. For example, *Social Inclusion*, the DSCFA's strategic document for the National Anti Poverty (DSCFA, 1998: 14–21) identifies 'key issues' and 'key action points' but redistribution is not one of these. Clearly, the extent of income redistribution to be attained is a matter of policy choice and one of the critical choices a country makes with regard to redistribution is the type of social security system it develops. The Irish system was influenced by the progressive liberalism of British social security reformers (rather than the egalitarian radicalism of European socialism) and Irish policy-makers adopted a Beveridgean approach to social security. This focuses on poverty alleviation based on a system of modest, flat-rate benefits, leaving wide scope for private provision and private effort. There is no evidence of any concerted demand for a more strongly redistributive approach to social security. A greater emphasis on redistribution would imply a social security policy aimed at reducing the gap between social security recipients' incomes and average incomes, a more progressive system of financing the social security system, and a benefit structure incorporating an earnings-related element.

INCOME REPLACEMENT

Income replacement is not articulated as a policy objective *per se*, although like income distribution one of the financial effects of the Irish social security system is to achieve an element of income replacement. The benefit structure is largely predicated on recipients' loss of income, and the effect of the benefit system is to ameliorate the impact of this income loss. An income-replacement element exists in practice in the current Maternity Benefit scheme, in which the amount of benefit is 70% of reckonable earnings, but there are no indications that income replacement will be adopted more generally as a financial function of the system.

It is important to note that parts of the benefit system were temporarily structured in an income-replacement fashion and then re-structured as flat-rate, poverty-alleviation benefits. In the early 1970s both unemployment and disability benefit were supplemented with a Pay-Related Benefit, creating a substantial income-replacement effect for some beneficiaries. But these PRB payments were finally abolished in 1994, having been curtailed from the early 1980s onwards, and there has been no demand since then for their reinstatement. At one juncture in the late 1970s, policy makers explicitly considered the arguments for a significant addition to the income-replacement role of the Irish social security system in the form of an Income-Related Pension scheme for the elderly (Department of Social Welfare, 1976). But this consideration never proceeded beyond the official Green Paper and it is only in recent years (as the chapter on pensions shows) that the possibility of a state income-replacement pension of some kind has returned to the policy agenda.

LIFE-CYCLE REDISTRIBUTION

This financial function of social security benefits is the most universally accepted function of the social security system. The concept — and the policy implications to which it gives rise — originated with Rowntree's *Poverty: A Study of Town Life*. In his analysis of the incomes of the poor, he drew attention to what he termed the 'alternating periods of want and comparative plenty' (Rowntree, 1901: 136–7). This referred to the broad phases in the life cycle associated with changing levels of needs and resources — as summarised in Figure 4.1.

Figure 4.1: Incomes over the Family Life Cycle

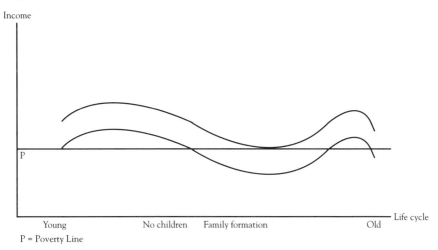

P = Poverty Line

Rowntree describes the typical family life cycle as follows: A young adult person without children will have limited needs and no dependants, and may be sharing living costs by residing in the parental home. When this person marries and establishes a separate home, living costs will rise because of the expense of a separate home and the cost of household formation. With the birth of children, a household enters a long period of greater need that may not be met by a rise in household income: during this period workers and their families face a serious risk of poverty. This phase ends when older children enter the workforce and begin contributing to the family income, bringing a period of relative prosperity to the household. As these young adults leave to form new households the now elderly household faces old age, retirement and, again, a decline in income. Rowntree pointed out that this cycle was universal, applying not only to the very poor, but also to the ordinary worker. In Figure 4.1, therefore, there are two stylised cycles, one for a 'low' income household which is portrayed as falling below the poverty line during the high needs phases, and one for a 'high' income household which experiences the same cycle but remains above the poverty line.

Rowntree's description of the life cycle preceded the introduction of benefits for children and the retired. In other respects too his depiction of the phases of the life-cycle is outdated: family sizes are smaller, although the period of child dependence on parents is longer now; the wage that Rowntree analysed was a man's 'family wage' in contrast to the extensive number of two-earner households today; the natural family cycle that he described (single–married–married with children) may now be complicated by lone parenthood; the period of old age and retirement is now more extended. However, the underlying imperative that Rowntree outlined remains. Since then governments have responded by introducing life-cycle related benefits and the focus of policy debate is on how and to what extent these needs should be addressed. In Chart 4.1, the illustration given of a policy focus on life-cycle redistribution is the explicit acknowledgement in the Child Benefit Review Committee's report of the life cycle function of Child Benefit. This function is also referred to in the context of both child-related payments and pensions in a wide range of official reports (Commission on Social Welfare, 1986; Expert Working Group, 1996; Department of Social Welfare, 1995). There are two critical aspects of life-cycle redistribution that now command attention. There is considerable debate, first, about the relative importance of targeting social security benefits on the poor, as opposed to targeting based on general life-cycle redistribution to the elderly or families with children. Second, and related to the targeting debate, the *instruments* of life-cycle redistribution have been debated, with debate focused on the most appropriate mix of social security benefits and taxation.

EFFICIENCY

A highly analytical style of policy analysis, underpinned by micro-economic principles, is frequently applied in contemporary analysis of social security. These principles lead to quite clear definitions of equity and efficiency. Therefore, it has become increasingly common to use formal equity/efficiency criteria, and it has become possible to adopt this approach because of the growing availability of quantitative data: furthermore, policy-makers are often primarily concerned with the economic impact of social security.

Briefly, efficiency has two important aspects. First, in relation to allocative efficiency, a starting point for formal economic analysis of social security provision is to question whether state provision of social insurance benefits is justified on efficiency grounds.[6] Efficiency will be maximised under market provision if a number of conditions hold. These conditions (referred to in the texts as 'the standard assumptions') are: perfect information, perfect competition and no market failures. Critically, the conditions are very relevant to insurance markets. For a market to be efficient, consumers and producers must have full information about prices, quality and about the future. Perfect competition requires that there is a large number of consumers and firms, that no one producer (or consumer) can determine the price and that there are no barriers to entry to the market against new consumers or producers. Also, the agents in the market must have equal power — i.e. there should be no discrimination in favour or against any consumers or producers because of (say) race, political influence, gender, and so on.

The absence of market failure refers to the character of certain goods and activities that create externalities. They impose costs or confer benefits on other persons. For example, a landlord with derelict and dangerous property that might have a high market value is imposing costs on neighbours and the community. Other goods are pure public goods that exhibit very specific technical attributes (non-rivalry in consumption, non-excludablility and non-rejectability), which means that the goods will not be produced at all or produced inefficiently in the market. For example, the marginal cost of an extra consumer of some goods is zero; it is impossible to exclude consumers from using certain resources. Generally these public goods characteristics apply to services like the army or the police and to goods like fresh air, open spaces, the environment, and so on. Finally, in relation to pure public goods, certain goods are produced under increasing returns to scale, creating a tendency to monopoly and thus a reduction in choice and higher prices. The textbook examples of this process usually refer to public utilities such as energy or transport.

It is easy to see that in certain areas, not least in insurance, these conditions may not be met. For example, in the case of the market for pensions, it is probable that consumers will have very incomplete information about costs, interest rates, and so on, making it difficult for them to behave as 'sovereign consumers' exercising free choice. Although the public goods and externality criteria can be most obviously invoked in areas such as health and housing provision, some interpretations of these principles also identify an externality relevant to social security provision. (Barr, 1987: 86–9) If the welfare (formally, the utility) of a rich person is affected not only by his own income but also by the income of a poor person (in a simplified, two-person world) then redistribution from rich to poor may be efficient.[7] Specifically, where the increase in the rich person's welfare as a result of the rise in the poor person's income exceeds the loss of welfare to the rich person as a result of the decline in the rich person's income, then redistribution to the poor person is efficient. This logic applies in the first instance to the case for voluntary (that is, charitable) redistribution, but the principles have been extended to show that the welfare of the rich may be affected not by the income of an individual poor person but by the character of the income distribution in society overall (Thurow, 1971; Barr, 1987).[8] This gives rise to an efficiency argument for state redistribution to the poor.

It is important to note that if one or more of the three conditions for efficient markets fails, then a theoretical case for intervention in the market arises. Equally important, a theoretical case for intervention on efficiency grounds does *not* automatically imply direct state provision. For example, if the market for sickness insurance or pensions is inefficient because of imperfect information or lack of proper competition due to discrimination against some consumers, this might be redressed through regulation or other means. Also, efficiency grounds for intervention are quite separate from equity grounds. State intervention (including provision) on efficiency grounds might result, for example, in a more equal distribution of income among the elderly, but even if equity is not the aim of policy-makers the efficiency rationale for intervention still holds.

The second aspect of efficiency concerns the incentive effects of social security. As Barr and Whynes (1993: 4) state, 'where institutions are publicly funded, their finance and the construction of benefits should minimise adverse effects on (i) labour supply and employment, and (ii) on saving'. There is a wide and controversial literature on these issues. The most widely cited — and most controversial — aspect is the incentive effect of unemployment benefits on labour supply. These benefits may affect the willingness of the unemployed to accept jobs at prevailing wage rates, as the level of benefits sets the 'reservation wage' — the wage at which the unemployed person is indifferent between accepting a job or remaining unemployed. The link between benefits and unemployment has generated a wide variety of research, and the issue has received considerable attention in Ireland also, in both official reviews of the social security system and in independent research. Chapter Eight addresses this issue in detail.

Two other equally contentious issues concern the impact on national savings of state pension contributions and the impact on employment of employers' social insurance contributions. In the case of pensions, a research and policy debate commenced in the mid-1970s about the effect of state social insurance pensions on aggregate savings in the economy (Feldstein, 1974). The first research in this area argued that state pensions (which typically have pay-as-you-go financing with pensions paid for out of current revenue rather than being pre-funded) diminish the incentive for workers to save and thus lower national savings and investment (and hence economic growth) in the long run. A body of research has since grown up attempting to tease out the mechanisms through which these effects could happen and to examine the evidence in a variety of countries and pension systems (Barr, 1993). The empirical and theoretical issues in this area remain unresolved. The immediate policy question arising from the research is whether pensions should be fully funded, and the importance of this policy question has grown as governments' pensions costs have grown. Chapter Ten deals with pensions policy.

As regards employment and social insurance, the efficiency concern arises from the fact that social insurance systems are typically financed on a tri-partite basis, with employers and employees making contributions to a social insurance fund and the state also contributing from general taxation. The employer's contribution is — in effect — a payroll tax: it adds to the cost an employer must pay for labour and therefore diminishes the demand for labour. This reasoning critically depends on the assumptions made about the real incidence of the employers' social insurance costs, i.e. whether the employer can pass on the social insurance costs to consumers in the form of higher prices or whether the effect of the tax is to result in lower pay or reduced demand for employment. The Commission on Taxation in Ireland broadly argued that the Irish system of social insurance contributions affected the level of employment (Commission on Taxation, 1982). However, the empirical work on this issue suggested that the employment impact of Ireland's payroll taxes was small and that reducing employers' social insurance contributions would not be an effective response to unemployment (Hughes, 1985).

Finally in relation to efficiency, a parallel stream of analysis is concerned with other social and behavioural effects of social security — effects that are not directly economic but which may come to seen as deleterious for other reasons. The existence of separate payments for lone-parent families has been seen as contributing to the rise in the number of lone-parent families, for instance; the availability of rent allowances for poor tenants has been blamed for the departure of young, unemployed people from the family home and thus the 'break-up' of the family. Some of the more general neo-liberal critiques of the welfare state — for instance Charles Murray's *Losing Ground* (1984) — conflate the direct efficiency issues with these wider behavioural issues. These critiques then ascribe a whole range of social and economic problems in modern society to state social security provisions.

In the last two decades in the United States, and in the last decade in the UK, this critique has had some influence. It shaped President Clinton's restrictive welfare reforms and this in turn influenced Prime Minister Blair's 'New Deal' policies in social security. What this has meant in practical terms is a much greater emphasis on 'activation' in social security, i.e. welfare to work. As Prime Minister Blair expressed it, 'work for those who can, welfare for those who cannot'. At a wider level this critique of the welfare state has led to a search for a 'Third Way' between the 'old Right' efficiency critiques and 'old Left' egalitarian defences of state welfare generally. A body of ideas reflecting the Third Way has now emerged and is increasingly influential (Giddens, 1998). The implication for social security is that in the future the emphasis in welfare will be as much on the duties and responsibilities of citizens as on their rights. State social policy will focus on the 'social investment state' (Giddens, 1981: 99–128) by emphasising education, training, and work participation, and focusing on 'positive welfare' — i.e. ways of ensuring that the dependent population are active and contributing to society. The influence of these ideas can be seen in the shift towards 'activation' in some areas of Ireland's social security provisions.

EQUITY

Discussions of equity start with a conventional distinction between vertical and horizontal equity. Vertical equity refers to the important issues of poverty and inequality: the extent to which social security is supposed to achieve vertical equity is a matter of discussion, as suggested above (Barr and Whynes, 1993). A number of aspects of social security arise here — the level of payments relative to incomes at large, the joint, net redistributive effect of the benefits and taxation regimes, and the type of benefit system that might be desirable (for example the balance in the social security system between means-tested payments and insurance benefits).

Horizontal equity refers to how the benefit system differentiates between recipients on the basis of relevant needs and characteristics. The essential point of horizontal equity is to see whether the benefits system treats like situations alike. Does the Carer's Allowance treat carers with similar incomes and similar caring responsibilities in the same way, for example? Do the various mechanisms of giving subsidies for housing costs result in households in similar circumstances having different disposable incomes after they have received benefits and paid for housing?

Also, under the general rubric of equity, social security addresses needs that may not be inherently financial in nature and that are unlikely to be met through private provision. While the core of social security is concerned with protecting against income loss, some aspects deal with social needs. For example, payments for one category of lone-parent (unmarried women with children) were introduced to allow women with children to live independently rather than relinquish their children through adoption. Likewise, benefits for carers facilitate people to provide full-time care for relatives, as this is increasingly seen as a socially desirable way of meeting the caring needs of elderly and dependent persons.

Are equity and efficiency intrinsically at odds with each other? The essential point to note is that equity and efficiency can be used as tools of analysis in social security: they help to clarify the aims and the impact of policy. It would be misleading to suggest that the two principles are merely flags of convenience for different ideologies, the Right emphasising efficiency and the Left equity, although in practice this is often the case in popular debate. In fact, equity and efficiency may converge in the policy conclusions they yield or may reinforce each other: a policy change that increases equity might also advance efficiency and vice versa. The most balanced representation of the equity-efficiency link is Okun's legendary work *Equality and Efficiency: The Big Trade Off* (Okun, 1975). Okun invokes the image of the 'leaky bucket'. If one person with plenty of water attempts to give water to another person without any this can be done up to a point: he simply carries water in a bucket and transfers it. However, the more the water that is redistributed the greater the spillage and leakage. Some water is thus lost to both people. By analogy, the greater the redistribution sought, the greater the likelihood of efficiency problems. Equity–efficiency trade-offs are therefore a matter of empirical detail in specific contexts.

The nature and extent of the equity that should be sought is undoubtedly a political matter. In the international theoretical literature there is a wide continuum of philosophical and political positions. At one end are radical libertarians such as Robert Nozick (1974) who advances a philosophical argument that state provision is coercive and that any redistribution or income provision to the poor should be voluntary. Close to this position are traditional liberal economists such as Milton Friedman (1962, 1980). They argue that only very clear departures from the conditions for markets to work efficiently permit state intervention and, when such intervention is permitted, it would only allow minimal provision to avoid incentive problems. At the other end are socialists and social democrats: these view social security as one instrument in a wide range of equality-driven policies. This perspective advances a relative definition of poverty and seeks to have high levels of income replacement, funded through progressive systems of social security and taxation (Barr, 1987). In Ireland the continuum of political debate is narrow and policy discussions reflect different emphases rather than competing ideologies.

SECONDARY OBJECTIVES

Chart 4.1 also refers to secondary objectives. Most commonly, these objectives refer to the delivery and management of benefits — the need to provide benefits in a way that is simple, dignified and efficient. The important point is that social security is complex and this may give rise to ignorance and confusion on the part of applicants, as well as high administrative costs. Many of the analyses of social security stress the complexity of the system and use simplicity as a criterion for evaluation and reform (Commission on Social Welfare, 1986). However, the importance of this criterion is often weighed in the balance against other more substantive criteria. For example, complexity may be an inherent part of a system that attempts to target a range of needs, and simplicity may be achieved only at the cost of other problems. One of the difficulties of looking in detail at these objectives in Ireland is the absence of detailed studies of the impact and operation of the social security system as recipients themselves experience and perceive it. In Part Two, therefore, there is little attention given to these secondary objectives because of the absence of detailed material.

CONCLUSIONS

This chapter introduced the various ways in which social security is debated and analysed. There is no one set of 'objectives' or problems that are universally acknowledged and applied to all aspects of social security. The chapters that follow in Part Two will broadly reflect the framework introduced here.

Notes

1. *Sharing in Progress* offers this formulation of relative poverty: 'People are living in poverty if their income and resources (material, social and cultural) are so inadequate as to preclude them from having a standard of living which is regarded as acceptable by Irish society generally. As a result of inadequate

income and resources people may be excluded from participating in activities which are considered the norm for other people in society' (Government of Ireland, 1997: 2). This text is very close to the widely cited definition first given by Peter Townsend in *Poverty in the United Kingdom* (see Chapter Three).

2.   The ranges 9 to 15 % and 5 to 10% refer to the proportions consistently poor at lower and higher relative-income figures (40% and 50% of average income respectively).

3.   The CSW's rates were explicitly adopted as part of the national social partnership agreement and published in *Partnership 2000 for Inclusion, Employment and Competitiveness* (Government of Ireland, 1996).

4.   The author has examined the official Department of Social Welfare files for the 1949–1952 period and there is no file that offers any suggestion that a formal exercise was undertaken to underpin the level of social welfare payments in the 1952 Act. However, Hughes has pointed out that the results of a National Nutrition Survey were published in 1950 and they showed that the costs of food for pensioners were less than pension levels and were greater for the unemployed. The Fianna Fáil spokesman on social welfare in the 1950 Dail Debate on the Social Welfare Bill dealing with payment increases, James Ryan, referred to the survey and accepted that the level of benefits proposed would provide enough for a decent standard for the groups concerned (Hughes, 1985: 88). However, no attempt was made to analyse the National Nutrition Survey to calculate a minimum for consumption overall.

5.   The exact year to which the most recent descriptions of the countries provisions refer varies from one country to another, but it can be taken that the accounts hold until the mid-1990s.

6.   There are numerous standard works on the relevant body of theory, but, briefly, efficiency would refer to the maximisation of total welfare and this would occur at a point in the production of welfare where the marginal social cost (the resource cost of an extra unit of welfare) would equal the marginal social benefit. (Le Grand and Robinson, 1984: Ch. 1; Barr and Whynes, 1993; Barr, 1987: Ch.4)

7.   Assuming here for purposes of argument that this is a two-person world.

8.   The argument here is somewhat technical.

Part Two

5
Child Income Support

INTRODUCTION

This chapter deals with payments to families in respect of their dependent children. Currently, there are three such payments: Child Benefit, paid monthly to *all* families, untaxed and without a means test; Family Income Supplement (FIS) paid weekly to *low-paid employees with children*, subject to a means test; and Child Dependant Additions (CDAs) paid as *supplements to weekly benefits and allowances* to benefit recipients with dependent children. The next section considers policy objectives in this area and the link between social security policy and family policy. The third and fourth sections outline the emergence and development of policy and the final two sections briefly review key policy problems and the options for future policy.

One of the roles of social security is to redress imbalances between incomes and needs at critical phases in the life cycle. A critical phase of the cycle is the phase in which adults in the prime age groups are attempting to meet not only their own welfare, but also that of their dependent children. In modern society children are economically dependent on their parents and, in line with international trends, the extent of this dependence has risen in Ireland in recent decades with the significant increase in educational participation.

This phase of the family cycle gives rise to costs in a variety of ways. First, adults with children must meet the additional costs of feeding and clothing their children, and the incomes of most parents — from earnings and self-employment for example — will not be differentiated in accordance with their family circumstances. Furthermore, modern societies impose distinct standards on parents in regard to the maintenance of their children. Children are not permitted to work to contribute to the family income: on the contrary, they are required to attend school, to wear school uniforms, to participate in school-related activities and so on, all of which impose costs on parents that adults without children do not incur. Second, although the labour market participation of married women with children has risen in Ireland, the participation of mothers is lower than that of married women without children and of women in general. This reflects either the desire or necessity of one parent in the family to withdraw from the labour market, in full or in part, permanently or temporarily, to care for children. This gives rise to an 'opportunity cost': parents must either forego the income they would earn in the workforce or directly meet the substantial costs of child care to allow both parents to be in the workforce. Third, in the case of Ireland and the United Kingdom, in both of which private owner-occupied housing is the most common housing tenure, the cycles of housing costs and child-related costs converge. At precisely the time when many parents are attempting to meet the costs of mortgages to purchase homes they are also more likely to be rearing young children.

In the area of child income support, therefore, the objectives of policy relate not only to the general issues of poverty and income adequacy, but also to a range of issues associated with 'horizontal' redistribution — how well families with dependent children relative to households without children.

POLICY RATIONALE AND OBJECTIVES

The first question to arise here is the rationale for a State policy in this area. In the other areas of social security it is relatively easy to discern the policy arguments for state provision and, in particular, for state social insurance payments. Unemployment and sickness and the lack of income on retirement are *risks* faced by the population at large. Private markets may offer some scope for people to buy insurance protection against such risks but, as Chapter Four pointed out, in most modern economies a substantial element of market failure exists and the state provides social insurance and social assistance payments to deal with the financial needs that arise. But the costs of rearing children are clearly not in the category of risks. Is there an analytical case for state intervention in some form, or should the costs of children fall solely on their parents?

The standard policy principles can be brought to bear in considering this question. In particular, the notion of *externalities* is relevant here (Barr, 1987; Le Grand and Robinson, 1984). This refers to situations where there is a divergence between the *private* and *social* costs and benefits of particular activities. While not always stated in those terms, much of the argument about child income support implicitly invokes this principle. In this analysis there are benefits to society as a whole if adults have children, and rear and sustain them. Today's children, according to this logic, are tomorrow's workers, consumers, and producers. This kind of argument can be — and in some historical contexts has been — expressed in social and demographic terms: society needs to reproduce itself, and unless parents are supported with the costs of children the number of children will decline over time, leading to demographic ageing and fewer young people. More generally, it is claimed, societies with declining numbers of young people are likely to be less productive, innovative and dynamic.

The classic statement of this perspective is in Wynn's *Family Policy* (Wynn, 1970), in which she trenchantly argues that the economic support of families with children should be a distinct and central aim of state policy, and that the economic and financial well being of families is a collective responsibility. Wynn and later advocates of family policy suggest that the generous, non-financial instincts that give rise to having children are in opposition to the natural economic forces in modern societies. According to Wynn 'It does not pay to have children in our society in any narrow economic sense whatever. Parents, when rearing their children, behave quite contrary to what might be expected of "economic man". . . . A parent is less able to accumulate property, less able to provide for his old age, less likely to be socially mobile upwards than the non-parent' (Wynn, 1970: 273).

This line of reasoning, at a general level, is now uncontroversial. Most modern governments would support such views and to some degree translate them into specific policies such as free education for younger children, support in varying forms and degrees for child health care, and provision to some extent for the income and housing needs of families.

Countries vary in the extent of their generosity towards families. Ireland has been consistently placed at the lower end of indices of family provision. This raises the second aspect of policy objectives — the link between policy objectives specifically in the area of family *incomes*, on the one hand, and broader social and political objectives in relation to the family on the other. The comparative research on child and family income support stresses that countries' policies in this area are shaped by their policies and objectives about the family more generally: 'family policy' is as important as social security policy in determining countries' approaches to child income support.

The standard international classification of family policies (Kamerman and Kahn, 1979) places countries into one of three categories. One set of countries has *explicit and comprehensive family policies*: these countries include Sweden and France. In contrast, there are countries whose family policies are *implicit and reluctant* — Britain, the USA and Canada typify this group. There is also an intermediate set of cases, including Austria, Finland and Denmark. It is the distinction between the two extremes of explicit/comprehensive and implicit/reluctant, and the implication this has for child income support, that is most relevant here.

France is the most widely cited case of the former category. French public policy has long been characterised by an emphatic national emphasis on the family and on the need to sustain large families and the overall size of the total population. This historic commitment to strongly pro-fatalist policies lies deep in French history. In the French agricultural economy large families have played a very significant role. Also, the military and political elites, with perceptions shaped by war and the military needs of an imperial power, have traditionally adopted aggressively pro-natalist views and portrayed families, especially large families, as in the national interest. These interests have then been articulated in the context of a Catholic culture that has added a powerful moral reinforcement to these influences (Pedersen, 1993). In France, the influence of these forces is reflected in an accumulation of policies towards the family that amount to very strong economic, social and practical support for parents with children (Baker, 1986). The *Quotient Familial* is a formula used to calculate tax liability according to family size. High-income families, if large, avoid income tax. Such a policy, as Baker (1986: 437) has summarised it, 'lowers the barriers to parenthood rather than provides for children in need'.

France and other countries with comprehensive policies offer financial support to families in general through the tax and social security systems and through other means. Housing subsidies are differentiated according to family size; pre-school education is universal; ante-natal and maternity services are universally available; in employment, parenthood may count as experience or seniority for promotion, and parents of three or more children get enhanced pensions; physical planning requirements are also more child-centred and there are concessions and reductions in prices in public and semi-public services.

This policy regime contrasts with that of the United Kingdom, the exemplar of the *implicit and reluctant family policy*. Here the defining aspect of family policy is its association with poverty. The historical forces that led to the introduction of income support for families were by and large concerned with poor children and with the needs of families on low incomes. One of the standard accounts of the introduction of child benefit in the UK describes it as an act of 'historic justice' (Land, 1975) rather than a natural expression of national concern with the number of families and children or the quality of families lives' in general. In the UK, no association is made between supporting parents with children and the size of the national population: on the contrary a growing population would be feared for its potential cost. Nor is the system of child income support related in public policy or popular debate with other family-related issues. Britain lacks a national statutory system of pre-school education, offers limited child income support through Child Benefit and the tax system, and has no national system of public provision of child day care. In Britain, policy debate about income support in respect of children tends to be dominated by one of two issues. One issue is whether or not Child Benefit should be 'targeted' on a limited set of low-income families. The other is about incentives: how to structure income support for families so that welfare recipients have an incentive to take up work or remain in work. In recent years, however, the general problem of low income among families has returned centre-stage and policy initiatives have focused on tax credits for working parents, as a way of simultaneously addressing both incentives and family poverty.

The policy contrasts between 'comprehensive' and 'reluctant' family policies were not reduced by the impact of feminist ideas and politics and the changing role of women in the labour market that affected all advanced economies from the 1970s onwards (Lewis, 1983; Pedersen, 1992). Feminist interpretations and critiques of policy adapted to and reflected these fundamental policy contrasts. In France, active and comprehensive policies to link the family and the labour market were adopted and the broad objective of policy evolved into one of sustaining family life, including high levels of marital fertility, in a context where women were participating to an increasing extent in paid employment outside the home. French feminism, and the specific policy responses it engendered, was less ambiguous about children and the family. Having children was seen as one of the *rights* of women which public policy is obliged to support. Anglo-Saxon feminism, more influenced by a view of the family as oppressive to women, emphasised the formal rights of women in the areas of pay, employment rights, and so on. The lower levels of marriage and declining family size that accompanied women's greater economic freedom in the UK were seen, in part, as a victory and, in part, as an inevitable outcome of women's new choices. The UK, then, is characterised by limited attempts to positively adapt family life to the contemporary labour market.[1]

In this typology Ireland can be characterised as having an implicit and reluctant family policy. As in the UK, family policy in Ireland has been strongly shaped by concerns about poor families. The telling historical illustration here was the manner in which Children's Allowances (now Child Benefit) were introduced in 1944[2]. In 1942, the *Report of the Inter-Departmental Committee on Family Allowances* was published, the committee having been established in 1940 in the wake of emerging political concern about family poverty, falling population and the effects of wartime inflation on living standards. The committee firmly rejected a European, pro-natalist rationale for family allowances, arguing that Ireland's decline in population should be ascribed not to low average family size, but to emigration as a result of general economic factors. It suggested that the rationale for family allowances should be the alleviation of poverty in large families (Inter-Departmental Committee, 1942:28–29).

> We consider, therefore, that for the purpose of mitigating distress in large families with low incomes, some form of assistance to the heads of such families is desirable.

The committee was also very clear that family allowances should have a limited role, arguing as follows:

> We conceive family allowances as a means of reducing the incidence of hardship due to child dependency, not of ensuring that no family will ever feel the pinch of want. Indeed, we consider that any scheme of the kind should be such as would not absolve parents from their duties and rights in the care and upbringing of their children.

In the event, the committee recommended a means-tested scheme. However, in the wake of its report a debate ensued about the most appropriate form of allowance and in 1944 (after a general election in which social policy issues were prominent) the Fianna Fáil government introduced a scheme of Children's Allowances, without a means test, giving the allowances in respect of third and subsequent children. The scheme was accompanied by the *restriction* of tax allowances from which many employees benefited, giving the overall initiative a 'targeted', poverty-related character. Furthermore, the committee explicitly rejected other, wider perspectives on child income support. Notably, it recorded the international influence of the feminist campaigner Eleanor Rathbone, founder of the Family Endowment Society. In her famous pamphlet, *Family Allowances* (1940), Rathbone had argued a feminist case for generous family allowances as an explicit recognition by society of the work of women in the home as wives and mothers. She argued that these services should be recognised independently of the wage-earning system, by means of a generous and universally applied system of allowances to women with children. The Inter-Departmental Committee merely noted that this argument ran 'counter to generally accepted principles concerning the responsibility of parents for the rearing and education of their children and the father's position as head of the family' (Inter-Departmental Committee, 1942: 16).

Since the 1940s, the details of child income support have changed, but policy and debate about policy issues remained, for a long time, firmly in the domain of poverty-related policy rather than family policy *per se*. Additions to the range of child income support measures since then have been largely targeted at particular poverty-relevant categories: Child Dependant Additions for social welfare recipients and Family Income Supplement for low-paid employees with children. It is striking that the most frequent form of policy initiative is the attempt to make the system of child income support *more* targeted and focused on less well-off families. In every decade since the 1940s political leaders and policy commentators have raised the question of the universality of Child Benefit, and of the need to tax it or means test it so that less well-off families might benefit more. These suggestions have never been translated into policy.[3]

The historical pattern reveals an adherence among policy-makers to a quite restrictive view of child income support, leading to a persistent questioning of the justification for payment of Child Benefit to all families. This fundamental orientation to family policy did not significantly alter in later decades when the role of women in society and the economy changed. While an increasing proportion of women began to participate in the paid labour market, they have done so without general state provision or subsidisation of childcare, and in a context where Ireland's provision of maternity leave and maternity pay are modest by European standards. In fact, some of the legislative provisions in taxation, social welfare and employment to facilitate and reflect these changes were *imposed* by the Courts or by EC Directive.

The question arises as to *why* Ireland had this approach to family policy, given the constitutional, cultural and moral significance of the family in Ireland. In Ireland, as the history of church-state relations has shown, there is an underlying tension between state-based improvements to services for families and Catholic social teaching emphasising the need for the State to complement rather then supplant the family. Any direct state interventions in the family need to be framed in this context in Ireland. This is not to suggest that the Catholic church has acted as an outright obstacle to social policy development — such an explanation would then beg the wider question as why *other* countries, the UK included, had similar policies. However, the Church's moral and ideological influence may have reinforced the impact of other influences shaping social policy that were referred to in Chapter Two. These factors would include the level of development of the economy and the weakness of Trade Union and Leftist forces in Irish politics. Also, the historical impact of the land struggle, combined with the identification of Catholicism and nationalism, led to the idealisation of a particular model of family life in Ireland — the large, rural farm family, economically independent and property-owning (Lee, 1989; Fahey, 1998B). This was not conducive to general support for state intervention in families' finances.

Finally, the indirect influence of the Catholic Church through its impact on the constitution and the legal aspects of the family may be relevant. Much of the public and political debate about family policy has concerned the *legal and moral regulation of the family*. In the past twenty years, for example, there have been two referenda about divorce, three referenda about abortion, a High Court challenge to the constitutionality of income support for unmarried mothers, a Supreme court intervention in the tax treatment of married women, a Green Paper on Marital Breakdown, and a High Court intervention in the treatment of married and cohabiting couples in the social security system. This focus on the regulation of the family may have had the effect of distracting public and political attention from the social, economic and practical supports for families. Arguably, it has been very difficult to agree on the broad *objectives* of family policy while political debate has been focused on the treatment of one *type* of family as opposed to another. A justice of the High Court, for example, was impelled to argue in 1988 that:

> The State's constitutional duty to protect the family is not discharged just negatively by avoiding unconstitutional legislation but may involve the positive obligation to protect the family by means of appropriate welfare services and income support.[4]

Turning to the specific financial objectives of child income supports, there was one quite specific financial objective set out in the early development of child income support — the supplementation of the incomes of earners (and the self-employed) with large families. On the introduction of children allowances in

1944, a government minister, Sean Lemmas, clearly spelled out the financial purpose of the scheme, pointing out that since wage levels are related to market forces 'the amount which the wage earner can provide is frequently inadequate for the reasonable requirements of a large family'[5]. The *relief of poverty* in large families is therefore the first financial objective that was identified by policy makers.

A further financial objective later became quite important — ensuring that the system of child income support did not undermine work incentives. This became an important issue as the role of child additions to social welfare payments grew over time. With social welfare recipients receiving weekly child additions to their main payments, the gap between their incomes and the net incomes of low-paid employees with children narrowed over time. From the late 1970s onwards concern was expressed that the system of Child Dependant Additions was creating disincentives and, by extension, compounding the unemployment problem. After Family Income Supplement was introduced in the 1980s the disincentive issue became more complex, the concern being that the means test for FIS would be a disincentive for employees to work longer hours or to seek to increase their gross pay. For example, the official government plan of 1985, *Building on Reality*, explicitly referred to the area of child income support, and in advancing one set of reform proposals argued (Government of Ireland, 1985:105) that it would help to 'improve the incentive to work'. Later reports and commentaries echoed this focus on incentives (Commission on Social Welfare, 1986; Blackwell, 1988; Expert Working Group, 1996).

The range of financial objectives began to widen in the 1980s, reflecting the new feminist critiques of social security (Pascall, 1986). Specifically, Child Benefit came to be seen in the context of concerns about the distribution of income *within* families. Where a husband's earned income or social security payment is a family's main source of income, this income may be allocated and spent according to husbands' preferences, leaving women and children in financial need. As the research evidence accumulated in this area, and public concern about women's right to an individual, personal income grew, Child Benefit began to be seen as the only income to which many mothers in the home have direct, independent access. In 1988, in reviewing the system of child income support, Blackwell (1988: 149) pointed out that Child Benefit 'redistributes income within the family towards mothers'. Some years later a Combat Poverty Agency study examined the distribution of income in Irish families and found that while income sharing is the norm, 'In most households, Child Benefit is in the control of the wife and is also the sole independent source of income available to her. Husband control of that money is virtually unknown.' (Rottman, 1994: 103) The fact that Child Benefit is now regarded as the 'mother's money' is now routinely referred to in contemporary discussions of child income support (Commission on the Family, 1998) and this attribute of Child Benefit has become, for some commentators and advocates, a financial *objective* of the system of child income support.

Finally, as the labour force participation of married women with children grew, child income support was considered increasingly in terms of how childcare for working parents should be provided and funded. Because Child Benefit is paid directly to mothers — those working in the home as well as those in paid employment — its potential role as a neutral *subsidy for childcare* has come on to the policy agenda. An official study of married women's work participation pointed out that if Child Benefit were increased substantially (with the increase financed by abolishing the marriage tax allowances), it could take on this role (NESC, 1991). For mothers working in the home, an enhanced Child Benefit would become their 'pay' for child care, and for mothers working outside the home it would be a subsidy to the cost of child care services. In recent budgetary debates the cost of child care for working parents has been a significant issue, and these costs are now widely invoked as a rationale for improving Child Benefit; *helping with the costs of child care* is therefore the latest financial objective with which Child Benefit is associated. This new link between Child Benefit and child care services is not universally accepted, however, as any conceivable level of Child Benefit would not be sufficient to be seen as a realistic subsidy to the costs of child care or a realistic 'payment' for mothers' work in the home.

One perspective about child income support stresses its role in *horizontal* redistribution: at any given level of gross income the tax and social security systems should differentiate the net incomes of those with children from those without children. For example, the Commission on Taxation, in considering whether Child Benefit should be subject to income tax, stressed this form of redistribution (Commission on Taxation, 1982: 240):

> There is an argument on grounds of horizontal equity for not charging child benefit to tax. This is because it is properly regarded as a means of discriminating at all levels of income between the ability to pay tax of families with children and those without children to support.

It is clear that the range of objectives in this area of has become very wide. Moreover, different interests emphasise different objectives and this takes place against a broad backdrop of political sensitivity about the fundamental objectives of family policy. In practice, public and political debate largely revolves around the balance to be struck between income support for families in general (horizontal redistribution) and income support for poor families (vertical redistribution), while analytical and expert studies have recognised both forms of redistribution and brought the question of incentives into the picture (NESC, 1980; Commission on Social Welfare, 1986; Expert Working Group, 1996).

CHILD INCOME SUPPORTS 1944–1985

Since the foundation of the state both taxation and direct cash benefits have been used as instruments of policy. From the 1940s, when children's allowances (now Child Benefit) were introduced, till the mid-eighties, child tax allowances and children's allowances co-existed alongside child dependant additions. In the mid-eighties the structure was changed: tax allowances were abolished and Family Income Supplement was introduced. A summary of these instruments of income support is given in Chart 5.1.

Chart 5.1: Overview of Child Income Supports				
	Child Tax Allowances	Child Benefit	Family Income Supplement	Child Dependant Additions
Introduced	1923	1944	1985	1952
Target Group	Tax-paying parents	All families	Low-paid Employees	Social Welfare Recipients
Cost €m 2002	(abolished 1985)	1,463	42.4	390
Number of Children		1,019,551	26,531	405,158

When the children's allowances scheme was introduced in 1944, the system of child tax allowances had already been in place since the 1920s. CTAs were built into the system of income taxation alongside the system of personal tax reliefs and offered the taxpayer with children an offset against their tax liability in respect of their dependent children. From the 1920s till their abolition the CTAs were intermittently altered in a number of ways. First, after children's allowances were introduced the amount of the tax allowance was sometimes limited for some taxpayers (a 'clawback', as it became known): this arrangement was in place from 1944 to 1954 and again from 1969 to 1974; it was abolished and temporarily reintroduced in 1979. Second, the allowances were varied according to the age of the child, with a higher allowance given in respect of children aged over 11; this provision was in place from 1966/7 to 1973/4. Third, during most of the period from the 1920s to the 1950s the amount of the allowance was differentiated according to birth order; with a higher allowance for the second and subsequent, or third and subsequent child.

However, the critical observation to make about CTAs is that over time their long-term *real value* (money value deflated by changes in the Consumer Price Index) was eroded, as Table 5.1 and Figure 5.1 show. In fact, the real value peaked in 1935/6, and while it rose again in the 1960s it never again came near to that peak. From the late 1970s onwards, not only did the CTA erode in the face of inflation with the current allowance fixed in money terms from 1975 to 1979, but the current money value was actually *reduced* in a series of budgets commencing in 1979. The child tax allowance was finally abolished in the 1986 budget — the nominal value per child in its last year was £100.[6]

A corollary of the real decline was its declining significance in relation to earnings and in relation to the value of tax allowances for non-family households. At its peak in the 1930s the allowance was over 40% of averæ e earnings and this meant that the income tax system was offering strong horizontal redistribution — clearly giving higher disposable incomes at any given earnings level to families with children. This capacity for redistribution towards families with children weakened, and by the mid-sixties the CTA was a mere 1% of average earnings. The decline in the role of CTA was not due to a more general decline in personal tax allowances. Table 5.2 below shows that the CTA declined also *in relation to tax allowances for single persons and couples*. In the mid-forties, the CTA (first child) was 50% of the personal tax allowance for single persons and 22% of the married couple's allowance. These proportions reached their maximum (67% and 32% respectively) in the late 1950s and then declined, with the rate of decline accelerating in the early 1970s. Tax-paying families with children were therefore losing out compared to taxpayers without children, and losing out in real terms.

Turning to Child Benefit, when it was first introduced (under the title 'Children's Allowances') in 1944 it applied only in respect of the third and subsequent children. In the 1952 Social Welfare Act it was extended to the second child and payment was put on a monthly basis. In 1963 it was extended to the first child. The latter extension was the most significant widening of the scheme in its history: it incorporated an additional 300,000 children. In 1974, when the payment level was being significantly increased, the age limit was extended from 16 to 18. From its introduction, the payment was made to the father and in 1974 payment was vested in the mother. There has been intermittent restructuring of the payment, the most common structure being the current one, of one payment rate for the first and second child and a higher rate for third and subsequent children.

The pattern of adjusting benefit levels has been *ad hoc*, as Table 5.3 and Figure 5.2 below show. The payment levels have tended to remain constant or fall for periods of three or four years and then to display a sharp, temporary increase. Figure 5.2 shows the long-term trend in the real value of Child Benefit. By the mid-nineteen eighties the benefit had not regained the value it had reached in 1973. In that year the payments were substantially increased after a number of years of decline. This pattern applies to figures for the two-child and four-child illustrations. Table 5.4 shows the benefit's link to earnings. Here too the pattern is one of instability. For the two-child family, the ratio of the allowances to earnings reached a peak in 1954 when it was 27% for the two-child family and over 66% for the four-child family. By 1984, these percentages had fallen very significantly. In parallel with the decline in child tax allowances, this cash payment to mothers experienced serious decline.

It is important to note that many families would be affected simultaneously by *both* trends, as the disposable income of families with taxable incomes would be affected by the tax allowances and in addition they would receive Child Benefit. Figure 5.3 shows the trend in Child Benefit and Child Tax Allowance combined for families paying tax at the standard rate. For two child, four child and six child families the period from the mid-seventies to the mid-eighties was one of decline in total child income support.

The system of Child Dependant Additions (CDAs) to the main social welfare payments (such as unemployment benefit and assistance and other schemes) is the other instrument of child-related income support. This system has had a chequered history. Prior to the 1952 legislation that consolidated the emerging social security structure, there was little differentiation among recipients according to the number of children. In 1952, allowances for adult and child dependants were introduced for two children for all schemes except old age pensions. These provisions were later extended: in 1960 the additions were conferred on third and subsequent children and in 1964 pensioners' children were included. The age limit for school-going children eligibility was raised in 1969 from 16 to 21 for widows, and in 1970 the general age limit was raised to 18. As new schemes were added to

Table 5.1: Long-term Trend in the Value of Child Tax Allowances

Year	Current £	Real (constant 1978 prices)
1925	36	386
1935	50	654
1945	60	414
1955	100	497
1965	120	447
1975	230	326
1980	195	144
1985	100	41

Notes: See NESC (1980) and Kennedy (1989) for detailed time series data. The CTA figures are for one child and, where relevant, refer to the first child.

Table 5.2: Child Tax Allowance as a Per Cent of Married Couple's and Single Person's Allowance, Selected Years

Year	Married	Single
1935/6	22.2	40.0
1944/5	21.8	50.0
1954/5	28.3	56.7
1964/5	30.5	50.3
1974/5	25.0	40.0
1984/5	5.5	2.6

Source: Annual Reports of the Revenue Commissioners.

Table 5.3: Children's Allowances as a Per Cent of Earnings, Selected Years

Year	Two children	Four children
1944	0	8.9
1954	27.4	66.4
1964	6.2	19.0
1974	16.6	40.5
1984	14.6	29.3

Source: Annual Reports of the Department of Social Welfare and Irish Statistical Bulletin, Various issues.

the main social security structure in the 1960s and '70s the child additions were incorporated. The system of CDAs grew in its complexity so that by 1986 there were thirty-six different rates of payment, with variation by scheme, number of children, and insurance versus assistance payments. It is therefore difficult to give a fully representative picture of trends in the payments.

Table 5.4 below offers some evidence about the value of the CDAs relative to the personal rates of payment. The contrast with children's allowances and tax allowances is striking, as the CDA system very markedly supplemented the incomes of social welfare recipients with children. For example, the total amount of CDAs paid to a recipient with four children in 1984 was 145% of the personal rate paid to the recipient.[7] Child Benefit would also be paid to this family. This tendency to add to the child-related incomes of social welfare recipients increased sharply over the decades since CDAs were introduced. These figures show very clearly the nature of child income support policy, highlighting the tendency to

Figure 5.1: CTA Real Value

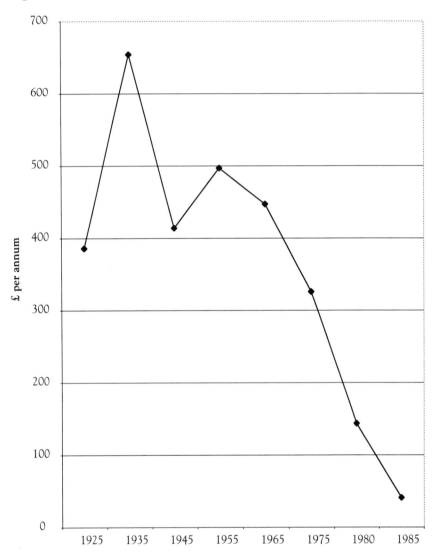

supplement the incomes of lower income families, but not to use the tax and Child Benefit system to do likewise for families in the earning and tax-paying category. As noted earlier, this system of CDAs became subject to criticism, as the CDA payments to welfare recipients with children were not matched by similar levels of child income support for people in work. This contributed to a narrowing of the gap between welfare income and net earnings, this narrowing being more pronounced the larger the number of children.

Figure 5.2: Child Benefit Real Value

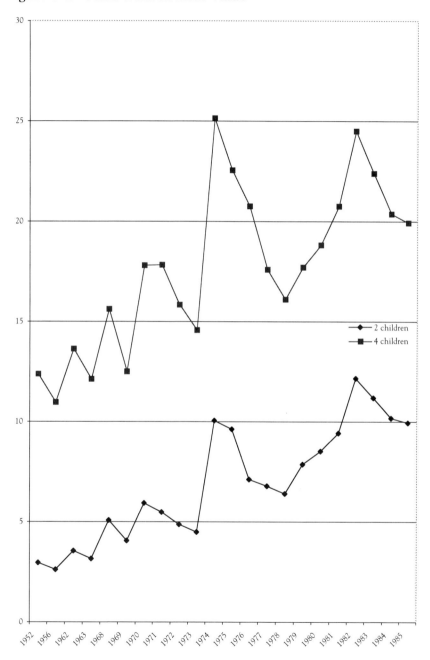

Note: Real value at 1978 prices

Figure 5.3: Tax Allowance plus Child Benefit

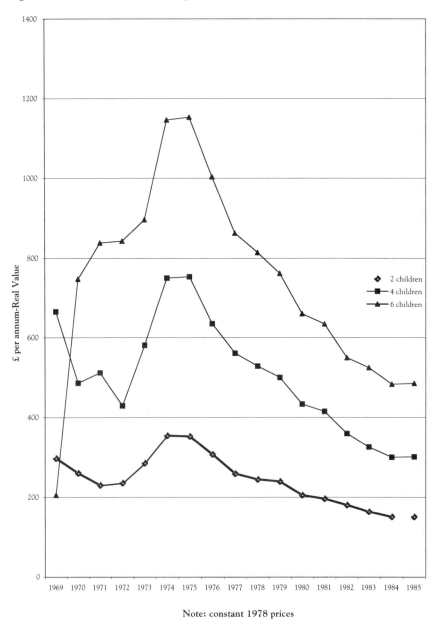

Note: constant 1978 prices

Figure 5.4 shows the trend in relation to the real value of CDAs over the time period. After their introduction in 1952 their nominal value remained unchanged until 1956, when they were increased again. This sequence set the pattern until

Table 5.4: Child Dependant Additions as a Per Cent of the Personal Rate of Social Welfare, Selected Years

Year	Two Children	Four Children
1954	58.3	58.3
1964	61.9	98.8
1974	56.8	103.2
1984	77.6	145.5

Source: Annual Reports of the Department of Social Welfare.
Note: The data refer to recipients of Unemployment and Disability Benefit.

the early 1970s of the nominal value remaining unchanged for two or three years: from 1972 onwards the nominal amounts were increased annually (with one exception). As Figure 5.4 shows, the trend is less dramatic than in the case of Child Benefit or Child Tax Allowance. The long-run trend up to the mid-eighties shows a gradual increase, and while the real value declined from 1980 to 1985 the decline was much less significant than in the case of CTAs or Child Benefit.

CHILD INCOME SUPPORT 1985–2002

There was a transition from 1984 to 1986 in child income support arrangements. In 1984, in the context of the abolition of food subsidies, the Government announced the introduction of Family Income Supplement for low-paid employees. The phasing out of Child Tax Allowances was completed in 1985/6 when the tax allowance was finally abolished. Since 1986, therefore, the current three-cornered system of child income support has been in place: Child Benefit as a universal payment for all families, Child Dependant Additions for social welfare recipients with children, and Family Income Supplement for low-paid workers (with children). Before looking in detail at the evolution of these instruments of policy it is important to note the marked differences in context between this period and the period up to 1985. Incomes have grown very rapidly in the last decade and the labour market reached full employment by the end of the 1990s.

This contrast in context brought with it shifting and conflicting emphases in child income support policy. The unemployment crisis brought with it an awareness of general deprivation and the need for social security to offer adequate incomes — this was a central theme of the Commission on Social Welfare's work (1986). However, the scale of the public finance crisis also focused policy makers in the 1980s on the costs of social security. This reinforced the historical tendency to search for more 'targeting' in child income support measures and to look for improved incentives in the child income support system as a contribution to

Figure 5.4: CDA Real Value

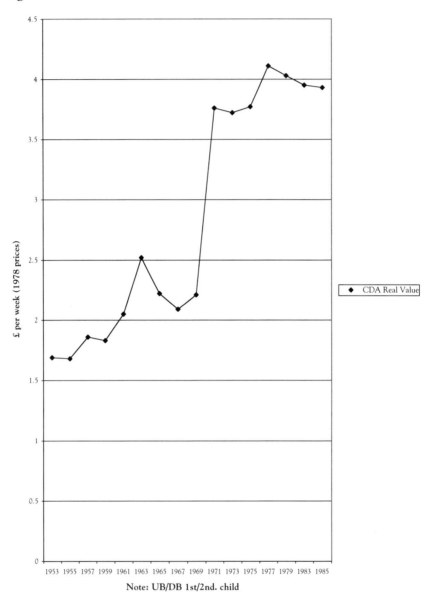

Note: UB/DB 1st/2nd. child

solving the unemployment problem. The government's plan, *Building on Reality*, emphasised these concerns and they remained a concern of policy makers into the mid-nineties. For example, in relation to CDAs, the Minister for State at the Department of Social Welfare explicitly stated in 1994 that, since they are withdrawn when parents return to work, 'this contributes to work disincentives for certain families'.[8] The *complexity* of the system also became an issue; this was raised by the Commission on Social Welfare (1996), the Expert Working Group (1996) ten years later, and by CORI in their advocacy of a complete overhaul of the social security system (Healy and Reynolds, 1994; Healy and Reynolds, 1995).

As the economic boom, and the likelihood of its continuation, took hold, the question of how the benefits of growth should be shared became more topical. Notably, in recent budgets Child Benefit and the need to substantially increase it so that families would share in the increasing prosperity became a central issue. For example, the Rainbow Coalition government of 1994–1997 included a specific commitment to substantially increase Child Benefit, and in 1995 and 1996 payments were cumulatively increased by 45%. In 1999, a policy adviser to the Progressive Democrats called for a substantial increase in child benefit and argued that it should remain 'free of tax, contrary to the suggestions in some quarters that child benefit should be taxable'.[9] In the Budget of 2001, the Minister for Finance referred to the Child Benefit and other provisions as the 'greatest ever package of supports for children' (Budget 2001), and increased the Child Benefit rates by over 50%. These policy initiatives in relation to family incomes, and the views underpinning them, need to be viewed in the light of broader budgetary strategy in recent years. As Chapter Three pointed out, this has emphasised *general* tax reductions and consequently households and tax-payers without children may have benefited more from budgetary policies in the recent boom. In 2002, the total numbers in receipt of the three different forms of payment were: Child Benefit, 522,000 families; FIS, 12,043 families; CDAs, 405,158 individual children.

Turning to Family Income Supplement, this was introduced for three reasons. First, food subsidies were abolished in 1984, and FIS was seen as a form of compensation for the potential loss in living standards for low-income families. Second, the structure of child income support was seen as creating disincentives to work for unemployed workers with families — and at this time unemployment was 12% and rising rapidly. This disincentive was considered to arise partly from the fact that the unemployed with dependent children (and other social welfare recipients) were in receipt of CDAs. On taking up unemployment they would lose these CDAs, and for employees with children this meant a significant narrowing of the gap between net earnings, on the one hand, and social welfare on the other. Third, FIS was envisaged as a temporary measure pending the introduction of an overall reform of child income support. This overall reform was not implemented; FIS remained in place and expenditure and recipients grew over time.[10]

FIS is a means-tested payment, which was originally structured as follows. The gap between an employee's earnings and a 'target' gross wage was identified — this target varied according to the number of children. Then a proportion of the difference between earnings and the target wage was calculated and this amount paid as FIS on a weekly basis. When FIS was first implemented an employee was given 33% of the difference between the target wage and the actual wage. Conversely, an employee then in receipt of FIS would lose 33% of any increase in gross pay, as FIS would decline as gross pay rose. A number of changes were made to FIS. The requirement to work full-time (thirty hours) was relaxed to part-time (nineteen hours), the proportion of the gap between earnings and the target wage (used to calculate the amount of FIS) was incrementally increased to 60%, and the income ceilings were increased more rapidly than increases in earnings. Also, the requirement about the minimum hours of work was changed in 1989 so that it could refer to a couple's total hours rather than one person's. In 2000 the formula for assessing entitlement was switched to a *net* earnings rather gross earnings basis. The cumulative effect of these changes in the scheme was to contribute to an increase in the number of families in receipt of the payment, which grew from just under 5,000 in 1986 to 12,000 in 2002.

For low-paid employees with children FIS could be a more significant part of child-related income than Child Benefit and, as FIS is means-tested, the potential loss of some or all of it as earnings increases creates an incentives problem.

Table 5.5 summarises the key changes in FIS from 1986 to 2002. In the latter year FIS was paid to over 12,000 families in respect of 26,500 children, and expenditure was €42m. In real terms, expenditure has grown very rapidly and this reflects the various changes made to the scheme since its introduction. As the figures show, the growth in FIS has slowed noticeably in recent years. The total number of children is marginally higher in 2002 than in 1996: by contrast the growth in recipients and expenditure was very rapid from 1986 to 1996.

Tables 5.6 and 5.7 summarise the key trends in relation to Child Benefit and Child Dependant Additions respectively. In relation to Child Benefit, total expenditure in 2002 was €1.46 billions. This was a very substantial real increase on the figure for 1996 and was due primarily to the increases in level of benefit. While the number of Child Benefit payments for individual children fell, the real payment per child rose very significantly from 1996 to 2002. As pointed earlier,

Table 5.5: Trends in Family Income Supplement 1986–2002

FIS Trend	1986	1996	2002	% Change 1996–2002
Children (000s)	18.4	29.8	26.5	−11.1
Total Real expenditure (index)	100	558	655	17.4
Real Average Payment per child (Index)	100	233	283	21.4

Source: Statistical Information on Social Welfare Services, Department of Social Welfare.

Table 5.6: Trends in Child Benefit 1986–2002

Child Benefit Trends	1986	1996	2002	% Change 1996–2002
No. Children (000s)	1,177.1	1,065.5	1,019.6	–4.3
Real Expenditure (Index)	100	141	351	149
Real payment per 1st Child (Index)	100	148	373	152
Child Benefit as % of earnings, 2 children	4.1	5.3	11.7	121
Child Benefit as % of earnings, 4 children	8.2	11.4	26.4	132

Source: Statistical Information on Social Welfare Services, Department of Social Welfare.

Table 5.7: Trends in Child Dependant Additions 1986–2002

CDA Trends	1986	1996	2002	% Change 1996–2002
Number of children (000s)	460.2	473.4	405.2	–14.4
Real Expenditure (Index)	100	137	87	–36.5
Real rate p.w.	100	108	88	–18.5
2 child rate as % of Personal Rate	48.4	40.9	28.3	–30.8
4 child rate as % of Personal Rate	90.8	81.9	56.6	–30.9

Source: Statistical Information on Social Welfare Services, Department of Social Welfare.
Notes: CDA expenditure data are estimated.

in one Budget alone the nominal level of Child Benefit doubled. Equally significant, however, is the increase in benefit relative to earnings for two-child and four-child families, shown in the last two rows of the table. For both categories, the benefit rose very significantly in relation to earnings. This recent trend reverses the decline of the period up to the mid-eighties and brings the benefit/earnings ratio considerably above the figure for the mid-eighties. The benefit levels rose sufficiently rapidly to allow the benefit/earnings figure to more than double from 1986 to 2002 even in the context of significant earnings increases.

The real value of Child Dependant Additions had contracted somewhat in the period to 1985. From 1986 to 1996 there was a small real increase in the rate of CDA and this led to a growth in total expenditure. Policy decisions later reversed this pattern. There were reductions in the nominal value of CDAs and by 2002 the real rate was lower than in 1986. Also, the number of children fell, and the combination of falling numbers and lower rates led to the substantial decline (36%) in total expenditure As the final two rows of Table 5.7 indicate, the ratio of the CDAs to the basic personal rate of benefits declined very sharply.

These detailed figures show the change in the *structure* of child income support. The role of Child Benefit has been enhanced and that of CDAs reduced: in the mid-1980s CDA rates were 35% of Child Benefit, and by 2002 this figure had declined to 14%. Policy has therefore changed in two senses. First, the considerable improvements in Child Benefit have reflected a strategic emphasis in recent years on families in general. Second, incentives issues have also shaped policy. Reducing the role of CDAs and increasing that of Child Benefit restructured the income package of the welfare recipients with families and widened the gap between welfare income and income from work. Similarly, in the case of FIS, introducing a payment specifically for employees with families, and then improving it as well as increasing Child Benefit, was directed in part at improving the net income of low-paid workers with families and thereby minimising disincentives.

POLICY PROBLEMS: POVERTY, INCENTIVES AND THE COST OF CHILDREN

A key issue in the discussion of child income support is the extent of poverty among families. Table 5.8 classifies households by type and shows the risk of poverty for persons in each type of household. In the context of child income support, the key feature of the table is the relatively high risk of poverty for persons in larger families and for those in one-adult with children households. There is some evidence that the rate of increase in poverty moderated between 1998 and 2001. These figures refer to persons rather than individual *children* (those aged 0–14): however, the available data on individual children also shows that they experienced a substantial rise in the risk of poverty over time. The proportion of individual children living under the 50% poverty line rose uninterrupted from 8% in the early 1970s to 26% in 1997 and then fell for the first time in 1998 (Nolan, 2000A).

The data in Table 5.8 also show the *incidence* of poverty in 2001 — the distribution of the poor among different types of household. If all of the two-adult and child households are aggregated, then 35.3% of the poor are comprised of

Table 5.8: Percentage of Persons Below 50% of Median Income by Household Composition 1994–2001, and Incidence of Poverty 2001

Type of Household	1994	1997	1998	2000	2001	2001 Incidence
1 adult	1.7	3.6	19.5	24.4	31.0	17.8
2 adults	2.8	3.7	5.3	11.3	13.7	16.5
3 or more adults	1.2	3.3	1.3	3.9	5.2	6.9
2 adults, 1 child	3.5	5.8	13.3	10.5	16.9	9.5
2 adults, 2 children	3.9	6.5	6.6	11.0	8.7	8.6
2 adults, 3 children	6.5	13.9	10.0	13.0	9.4	6.7
2 adults, 4 or more children	18.3	27.5	22.5	22.9	20.0	10.5
1 adult with children	8.4	24.0	42.8	39.5	37.9	12.0
3 or more adults with children	7.6	9.4	7.5	6.7	7.4	11.4
All Households	6.0	8.6	9.9	12.0	12.9	100

Source: Whelan, Layte Maitre *et al* (2003).
Notes: The equivalence scale used here is 1/0.66/0.33 for first adult, additional adults, and children 0–14 respectively.

people living in two parent families with children, and this figure would be higher if the age definition for children of 0–14 were widened to include 14–19 year olds. While people in one-adult and child households have the highest *risk* of poverty, they comprise just 11.1% of the poor, reflecting their relatively smaller numbers in the population at large.

It is important to stress that the patterns of family poverty are due to a wide range of factors of which the system of child income support is only one. For example, high levels of unemployment, growing numbers of lone-mother families, and a historically low level of labour force participation among women with children would all have combined with child income support measures and other factors to generate high levels of child poverty. Likewise, the stabilisation in rates of family poverty would arise from a host of factors, of which the improvement in Child Benefit is one. The fact that child and family poverty remain at significant levels means that the policy trade-off between targeting poor families and redistributing to all families is still very real.

The rate of child poverty in Ireland is high by European standards. In the 1990s, Eurostat (the EC's official statistical agency) produced standardised data on child poverty rates[11], and these reveal that in 1994 Ireland had the highest child poverty rate in the EC. The rate for Ireland, as Figure 5.5 shows, is 30%, compared with an average of 19% across all countries and the lowest rate of 5% for Denmark.

These strikingly high poverty rates confirm a more general finding in the comparative research that Ireland's policies in relation to children are relatively ungenerous. In their study of the EC countries (nine at the time of the study) in the early 1980s, Bradshaw and his colleagues analysed the social security, taxation and child income support arrangements for a wide range of illustrative families and concluded (Bradshaw and Piachaud, 1984:129):

> If countries are compared in their rank order of provision at three different income levels and three family types, Italy and Ireland are consistently the least generous countries, coming eight and ninth respectively in the league table of support, almost whatever the income or family composition. Belgium, France, and Luxembourg are equally consistently the most generous countries.

In relation to how progressive the child support systems were, the study concluded that Ireland's was the 'most regressive' (Bradshaw and Piachaud: 134).

This comparative study is now dated, not least by the fact that Ireland's child support system has considerably changed. However, a later study using data for the early 1990s and taking account not only of the tax and child benefit systems but also of housing costs and subsidies, and health care costs, concluded again that Ireland's provision for children is relatively limited (Bradshaw, Ditch et al, 1993). Ireland's average rank for a range of child support measures, on a scale from 1 to 15, was 11.4, placing it in a group of countries with the 'least generous child benefit package'[12] (Bradshaw, Ditch, et al, 1993: 265).

The comparatively poor outcomes for Ireland in terms of poverty rates and redistribution to families are due, in part, to Ireland's policies. However, other factors also affect differences in poverty rates between Ireland and other countries. Notably, in the 1970s and 1980s most Irish children lived in single-income families, whereas some countries with low child poverty rates (Denmark, for example) had already achieved high rates of work participation among mothers, leaving families in these countries less vulnerable to financial poverty.

A further important difference across countries is the average size of family. Until the mid-eighties Ireland had a high proportion of children in families of three or more, and differences in family size between high and low income families are quite marked in Ireland, with the bigger size of low income families adding to their risk of poverty. These factors were compounded by Ireland's uniquely bad experience of unemployment. The scale of unemployment (ascending to 18% by the late 1980s) and the presence of mass, long-term unemployment into the 1990s

Figure 5.5: Per Cent of Children Below 50% Poverty Line, 1994

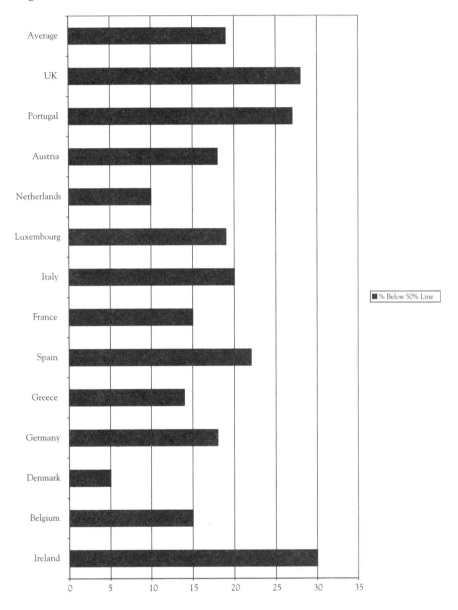

Source: Eurostat (1999).

meant that Ireland had large numbers of children in households that had a high risk of poverty. In 1986 there was close to a quarter of a million children in respect of whom unemployment-related CDAs were being paid, and in 1996 the figure was still in excess of 200,000. On a number of these fronts — family size and structure, employment patterns, income levels — Ireland has converged towards the higher income European countries, but what the impact of these changes and of recent child income support policies has been on child poverty in Ireland is not yet clear.

An alternative perspective on child income supports focuses on the additional costs that families with children incur. There are a number of ways in which these costs can be identified and here it is useful to note the two approaches that have been applied in the Irish context. The first type of research uses large-scale representative data on household income and expenditure patterns and applies econometric techniques to calculate the cost of a child. These estimates can then be used to derive equivalence scales for standardising the incomes of households of different sizes and composition. Conniffe and Keogh (1988) undertook such an exercise for Ireland using the 1980 Household Budget Survey data. Their calculations for 1980 showed, firstly, that the costs of children significantly exceeded the total level of state child support and, secondly, that the costs of older children are considerably greater than those for younger children. For example, the costs of a child over five were approximately 1.5 times the costs of a child under five.

The second type of research on costs attempts to document in great detail the budgetary practices of poor families. In this approach researchers collect very detailed information from a small number of low-income families about their expenditures, and attempt to derive a minimum family budget, identifying necessary expenditure associated with children.[13] The Irish study in this vein (Fitzgerald, Kiely, Quinn, Carney, 1994) documented the spending patterns of some low-income Irish households and compiled a minimum budget for a child. This minimum budget (at 1992 prices and social welfare rates) was significantly greater than the child income support (CDAs and Child Benefit combined) on offer to low-income families. The data confirmed the finding in the econometric study that older children impose greater costs, and also updated the Conniffe and Keogh cost estimates to 1992, showing that these estimates were still significantly in excess of child support levels.

The findings of these studies do not of themselves offer an objective answer to the question about how much child income support should be given, or how. The answer to that question (as the authors of the studies point out) derives from *policy judgements* about what the objectives of policy should be and how they should be balanced against other objectives.

There are two well-documented incentives issues in child income support. One concerns the structure of FIS. Recipients receive FIS on the basis of family size and net pay. Currently, the FIS rate is 60% of the difference between net pay and the target net wage for that family size: a one-child family with a net income less than the weekly target wage of €379 is paid 60% of the difference between its actual net pay and the target. Therefore, if a recipient receives an increase in gross pay, the amount of FIS falls by 60% of the increase. This 60% withdrawal rate then interacts with the tax and social insurance system and with the means-tests for other social services (medical cards and local authority housing, for example). Therefore, a rise in *gross* income for a FIS recipient may result in a reduction in the amount of FIS and other benefits, and higher tax and social insurance deductions. These losses may offset the gain in gross income in whole or in part, leading to what is referred to as a high *marginal tax-benefit withdrawal rate* (MTBWR).

Theoretically, the MTBWR[14] rate could exceed 100 per cent for a recipient. In such a case, the reduction in FIS and the loss of other benefits combined with increased deductions are greater in total than the gain in gross income, and the recipient would have a *lower* net income as a result of the higher gross income. The conversion of the FIS targets to a net income basis ameliorated this problem. However, FIS imposes a minimum MTBWR of 60% on its recipients. A detailed analysis of the FIS population showed that four out of five of those eligible for FIS have a MRTBWR between 60 per cent and 70 percent. The remainder are close to 80 percent because of the combination of the FIS withdrawal rate of 60 percent and the standard tax rate of 20 per cent (Callan, Keeney *et al*, 2001: 39–43). These complications may affect employment incentives and also reduce the take-up of FIS.

The other incentives problem arises from the fact that CDAs are withdrawn from recipients when they take up employment. CDAs affect the Replacement Ratios faced by the unemployed. The ratio is simply the amount of social security income an unemployed person receives as a per cent of the *net* wage they would receive if in work. Where an unemployed person receives benefit they also receive CDAs in respect of their children. Therefore, the net income of an unemployed person with children is significantly higher than the corresponding one without children, and the RR will be higher for the person with children when comparing their welfare income with the net wage from the same job. A larger number of children can push the RR quite high. In 2003, for example, weekly Unemployment Benefit was €274.80 for a man with a non-earning spouse and four children, and €124.80 for one adult. At average earnings, their RRs are approximately 57% in the case of the person with a spouse and four children and 28% in the single person's case, although not all of the difference is due to the CDAs. This problem has been somewhat reduced in the last decade as a result of the reductions in CDAs. However, the structure of CDAs can still lead to high RRs for the unemployed who are offered low wages on returning to work.

The two points about incentives do not imply that the system of child income support creates widespread work disincentives. (Chapter Eight discusses the incentives issue in more detail.) At this point it is important to note that if an incentives problem does exist it may impinge in particular on low-income families. The structure of child income support may be reinforcing their difficulties in taking up work or reducing their net return from paid work, and this is as much a question of poverty and equity as it is of efficiency and incentives.

FUTURE POLICY

This section gives an overview of the critiques and analyses of child income support policy. Past policy developments may give some insight about future change and in this respect it is important to recall that in the social security system as a whole (see Chapter Two) policy development has been *ad hoc*, with policies and schemes usually changing incrementally. There are no examples of overall structural reform in the past. In child income support, furthermore, policies have tended to change in response to other policy imperatives (the introduction of FIS to offset the removal of food subsidies in the 80s; the extension of Child Benefit to compensate for imposition of turnover tax in the 60s, for example).

It was only in the 1940s that a single, specific objective was given in this area — the relief of poverty in large families. Now policy advocates and analysts impute a wide range of objectives to the system. The criticisms of policy, and proposed reforms of policy, depend on the objectives, or mix of objectives, being advanced. A number of key, and inter-related objectives can be identified in the debates.

Horizontal equity: this refers to redistributing 'across' the income distribution from those without children to those with children. A strong emphasis on this objective might be associated with an argument in favour of child tax allowances or tax credits — these differentiate between tax-payers at a given level of gross income on the basis of the number of children.

Poverty, and the need to direct some of the child income support resources to poor families, is a second broadly stated objective. One interpretation of this objective would imply a preventative approach to poverty by means of a generous, universal Child Benefit payment; another interpretation would give a greater role to targeted payments such as FIS or CDAs (since these are directed at low-income families) or to means-testing or taxing Child Benefit. This perspective would argue that all of the 'cost of a child' should be met for poor families only.

Third, a concern with *incentives* is central to some reform strategies. This focus could lead to arguments for either wholesale reform or moderate restructuring. Reform might comprise the complete abolition of FIS and the CDAs — because of their incentive effects — and the consolidation of all income support into one work-neutral payment. Moderate restructuring could entail the reduction of CDAs or the reform of FIS, or the merging of FIS and CDAs into a single means-tested for low-income families.

Fourth, facilitating *women in the home with children to have an independent income* is a newer aspect of policy. This issue emerges from the concern that mothers are more likely to leave the labour force to care for children than fathers and to rely on child benefit as their sole source of independent income. Furthermore, mothers are not adequately 'paid' for the social value of the care they provide.

Chart 5.2 gives an overview of some of the approaches to reform. Each of these reforms is informed either by a very strong emphasis on one objective or an attempt to re-balance the mix of objectives being pursued. A Unified Child Benefit, for example, was outlined in 1985 in the Government's plan, *Building on Reality*. Here Child Benefit would be very substantially increased and then assessed as taxable income. FIS and CDAs would be abolished. The reasoning here is that if Child Benefit is greatly increased it can subsume FIS and CDAs, without recipients of these payment losing in net terms. Redistributing and taxing Child Benefit would be more redistributive and targeted: low-income families would gain more Child Benefit, and higher income families would lose from the impact of the increased Child Benefit being taxed. The abolition of FIS and CDAs would remove the poverty traps and disincentives in the system of income support. In addition, the system would be simple. This overall reform was therefore seen as an

Chart 5.2: Reform Options for Child Income Support

Option	Taxation	FIS	Child Benefit	CDAs
Unified Child Benefit	No change	Abolished	Increased and taxed	Abolished
Integrated Child Benefit	No change	No change	Increased and taxed	No change
New Child Benefit Supplement (Means-tested)	No Change	Replaced by new payment	No change	Replaced by new payment
Cost-based Reform	No change	No change	Related to age of child	Related to age of child
Refundable Tax Credit	Child tax credit for Employees	Abolished	No change	No change
Tax/Child Benefit Realignment	Greater Individual-isation	No Change	Significantly Increased	No change

attempt to meet a range of objectives — redistribution, improved targeting, better incentives and a simpler system. (The feasibility of this type of reform clearly depends on whether Child Benefit can sufficiently increased to compensate for the loss of weekly FIS and CDAs; in turn, this could hinge on whether the reform was attempted on a nil-cost basis or if net expenditure was allowed to increase).

Integrated Child Benefit is a variant on the unified scheme. This term was coined to describe a reform driven largely by targeting and poverty concerns. The reform would leave CDA and FIS unchanged, but would make Child Benefit subject to tax while also increasing it substantially. One study of the issue (Callan, 1991) indicated that Child Benefit could be increased by 40% on a no-cost basis if it were assessed for income tax. Low-income families would gain from this reform and high-income families would lose. A strong argument in favour of this strategy is that with high levels of child poverty it is important to use the tax and benefit system jointly to target poorer families.

The focus of the third possible reform is primarily the question of incentives. Starting from the position that some form of targeting on poor families is desirable, this reform attempts to ameliorate the incentives problems inherent in CDAs and FIS. The studies informing this proposal have confirmed that a significant proportion of low-income and welfare families face potential incentive problems and that this is due not to the overall level of social welfare payments but to the *structure* of child income support. (Callan, O'Neill and O'Donoghue 1995; Callan, 1997). The reform requires the integration of CDAs and FIS into one overall, means-tested supplement to Child Benefit for low-income families, thereby removing the in-work/unemployed distinction and allowing targeted child income support to be targeted on the basis of income rather than employment status. (The details of this reform would be critical to its success — at what income level the new CBS would be payable, with what rate of withdrawal, and so on.) Welfare recipients returning to work would, in this scenario, be eligible for the proposed Child Benefit Supplement (and continue to receive Child Benefit), whereas under the current arrangements because they simply lose CDAs on taking up employment.

The costs-based reform attempts to restructure Child Benefit so that it is related more closely to variations in the costs of children. It builds on the evidence that the needs of children and the extent of poverty are related to the ages of children in families and to family size. The Combat Poverty Agency study and the Child Benefit Review Committee adverted to this issue, and both noted the option of having age-differentiated payments for Child Benefit and CDAs. (Fitzgerald *et al*, 1994; Child Benefit Review Committee, 1995). This reform would leave the other parts of child income provision unchanged.

The Refundable Tax Credit reform would focus on the problems of FIS and replace it with a child tax credit for those in employment. This kind of reform would be similar to the Child Tax Credit system recently introduced in the UK.

It is not a return to the earlier regime of child tax allowances: these were of greater benefit to people paying higher rates of tax, and of no benefit to earners with incomes so low that they were no paying tax at all. The Refundable Credit instrument would confer a fixed cash reduction in tax for employees with children. For low income employees, the credit would become refundable: if their tax credit exceeded their tax liability then the credit would be paid as a benefit added to their pay. This reform strategy and how it might apply in Ireland, was discussed in a recent study (Callan, Keeney *et al*, 2001). The clear advantage is that it abolishes FIS, which has problems of incentives, complexity and low take-up. It also allows the benefit to be targeted at lower incomes, because it is refundable in the case of low-paid workers. Employers would administer the credit through the wage system. This policy reform has some prospect of materialising, because of the recent changes in the tax system that have converted tax allowances to tax credits. Child Tax Credits would be an extension of the emerging structure of the tax system — although its refundable element would be new.

The last reform option envisages a realignment of Child Benefit and the tax treatment of marriage. A key objective of this reform would be to greatly enhance the role of Child Benefit in families' incomes and thereby improve access for women in the home to an independent income. A second objective concerns horizontal equity: to redistribute income away from households *without* children to households *with* children. At present the tax system confers double tax credits on all married couples *whether or not they have children*. Proponents of this reform argue for some reduction in the 'double' treatment of marriage combined with a very substantial increase in Child Benefit. The revenue gained from the tax change would fund the improved Child Benefit. This would give women with children in the home a larger direct income and make the tax and benefit system as a whole more targeted on children. An added advantage is that the enhanced Child Benefit could be, in effect, a voucher for mothers who could choose to use it as a subsidy for childcare costs if they work outside the home.

A pure version of this strategy would be to implement complete individualisation — tax credits and bands of taxable income that would not be related to marital status. The tax revenue generated would then be paid only to families with children, allowing a very significant enhancement of Child Benefit and a fundamental re-direction of the tax-benefit system to families with children. This more radical proposal has not been advocated in Ireland, but critiques of the tax/benefit system have stressed that the arrangement in place in Ireland until 2000 (double tax bands and allowances for all married couples and modest levels of Child Benefit) was badly targeted if the objective of policy was to support families with children (Callan, Keeney, *et al*, 2001; NESC, 1991). In recent years policy has implicitly accepted this critique. In 2000, an element of individualisation was introduced into the tax system and Child Benefit was substantially increased: the rationale for the change was the improved incentives to spouses to work outside the home. Official policy is committed to achieving a greater degree of individualisation by allowing every *individual* a standard rate tax band, but one that is not transferable between spouses. If this policy is implemented, and Child Benefit is further improved, it will result in a significant re-alignment of the tax/benefit treatment of the family.

At the beginning of this chapter it was stressed that policy in this area derives as much from 'family policy' as from social security policy. Is there any evidence that family policy in Ireland is changing? Is it possible that in the future Ireland's family policies will be described on the international continuum as 'explicit and comprehensive'? The fact that employment-family links are now key issues, that an official Commission on the Family was established, that Child Benefit has featured as an issue in recent budget debates, that the Department of Social and Family Affairs now has a role in 'family affairs', all suggest that family policy might become a significant, separate element in public policy. If this were to happen, then a new child income support policy linked to a more explicit set of objectives and priorities might emerge. However, there are still fundamental disagreements in Irish society about the objectives of public policy in this area, as the violent controversy about the introduction of a degree of individualisation in the tax system showed.

Notes

1. See Drew, Mahon and Emerek (1998) for details of some European countries' current policies regarding reconciliation of work and family life.
2. Accounts of this episode in Irish social policy can be found in Cousins (1999) and Lee (1989).
3. The following are some examples. In 1968 the Minister for Finance in his budget speech pointed stated that an examination was underway 'to see whether a more selective scheme would be drawn up' and one year later in the 1969 budget speech stated 'I have decided against the introduction of a means test but I propose to make a start towards selectivity': the Minister then restored the 'clawback' of the children's allowances through the income tax system, reducing the benefit to middle and higher income families. The Labour Party Minister for Social Welfare, Barry Desmond, adverted in the Dail debates on the Social Welfare Bill 1983 to the fact that children's allowances 'was across the board, irrespective of income, and we spend a great deal of money on children's allowances. We must find some rational way of dealing with this question'. In 1987 the social policy spokesperson for the Progressive Democrats, Mary Harney, argued: 'Nobody could justify payment of children's allowances to people earning £40,000 per year, while some families have to live on £40 per week'. The Minister for Finance in the early 1990s also raised the possibility of taxing children's

allowances, but refrained from doing so. (See McCashin, (1988) and Blackwell, (1995) for detailed accounts of the development of policy.)

4. Declan Costelloe, High Court justice, addressing the conference *Progress Through the Family*, Dublin, 1988, quoted in the *Irish Times* 23 May 1988.

5. Quoted in Department of Finance (1976).

6. These figures were the amounts of the allowance in contemporary currency. The *cash equivalent value* of the allowance is the product of the tax rate multiplied by the allowance. Thus, in 1979 a taxpayer paying tax at a rate of 35% would get £70 cash equivalent, i.e. 35% times £200, the value of the tax allowance.

7. In that year the personal rate of Unemployment and Disability benefit (on which the example is based) was £37.25 weekly: a recipient with four children would have received an additional £8.85 per week for the first two children and £8.20 for the next two, giving a total of £35.15 CDAs.

8. Address by Minister for State at the Department of Social Welfare, Joan Burton, T.D. to the conference *Family Income Support — 50 Years On*, Dublin, 1995.

9. Address by Dr. Martin O'Donoghue to conference on 'The Future of the Celtic Tiger and The Family', University College Dublin, 13 November 1999, quoted in the *Irish Times*, 15 November 1999.

10. An outline of the reform that was announced and then abandoned, and the detailed implications of the aborted reform, are discussed in McCashin (1988), and Blackwell (1988).

11. These standardised results are based on annual disposable income for the previous year using 1.0/0.5/0.3 equivalence scales (Eurostat, 1999).

12. The term 'child benefit' in this context refers to the overall support for families not just the regular cash payments that are made to families with children.

13. This form of research is in the tradition of poverty research pioneered by Rowntree (see Ch.2); the definitive study of child related costs in this tradition is *The Cost of a Child* (Piachaud, 1979).

14. A variety of terms are used in the research — Marginal Effective Tax Rate, Poverty Trap, amongst others.

6
Gender and Social Security

INTRODUCTION

This chapter deals with women and social security. In the context of the UK social security system, McLaughlin has pointed out that 'Women are, and always have been, the main users of social security provision, although most social security systems and sub-systems have been created with men in mind as the primary claimants.' (McLaughlin, 1999: 177) The significance of McLaughlin's point is not so much the mix of male and female benefit recipients, as the fact that women are less likely than men to have an independent source of income. For example, in Ireland, in 2002, a majority (over 54%) of the 938,000 direct recipients of social welfare payments were women. This group includes widows, unemployed women, women pensioners, carers, lone mothers, and so on. In addition, there were 126,000 adult 'dependants' of recipients, the vast majority of whom are women; and, finally, there are non-employed married women in the 'working' age groups. This gender pattern in social security is accentuated by women's labour market status — their greater incidence of low pay and part-time employment.

As Yeates (1997) has pointed out, the gendered nature of social security can be traced back to the operation of the nineteenth-century Poor Law. Women's access to poor relief was contingent on their status as dependants of men. They were deemed 'deserving' of indoor relief in the workhouse only by proving that their husbands had either failed to provide for them or had abandoned them for twelve months or longer. When access to outdoor relief was widened during the famine years, widows with two or more children were the first group to become entitled to it. The basis for access to this earliest form of statutory welfare was women's family and marital status: the underlying assumption was that the family was the primary provider and that marriage, in effect, protected women from poverty. The reality was that women far outnumbered men in the workhouse, as Burke's (1987) account shows.

Gender differentiation was also built into the emerging national system of social security that began to replace the Poor Law early in the twentieth century. The National Insurance Act (introduced in 1911 and extended in 1920 and 1921) explicitly provided for different rates of contribution and benefit for men and women. For example, single women contributed the same as single men but had lesser benefits; married women were defined as dependants of their spouses and were entitled to protection only on the basis of their legal relationship to an insured spouse. In the 1920s, changes to the system of social insurance included the introduction of allowances for male recipients in respect of 'dependent' spouses and the 'marriage bar'. The effect of the latter was to require women in public sector employment to resign from employment on marriage. In the case of social insurance, women's insurance records were 'closed' on marriage and women were awarded a marriage grant; women continuing to work after marriage were dealt with as new entrants to the social insurance system. These gender-based rules had the effect of restricting women's access to the developing system of social insurance (Yeates, 1997; Cousins, 1995).

In the 1930s when unemployment assistance was first introduced it was overtly discriminatory against women. A married woman was debarred from entitlement (unless her husband was infirm or disabled) and single women and widows were excluded unless they had at least one dependent child. The immediate impact of these restrictions was to consign large numbers of women to the local, discretionary Home Assistance system (as the Poor Law became known after the Public Assistance Act of 1939).

The assumption of male prerogative and female dependence was also invoked during this period as a rationale for specific welfare reforms for women. Women's inferior access to employment and social insurance meant that widowed women, dependent on spouses' earnings, were left to rely on the Poor Law. In 1927 the Commission on the Relief of the Sick and Destitute Poor had acknowledged the need for a pension scheme for widows and, by the early 1930s, the continuing absence of a pension meant that there were over 10,000 widows in receipt of Poor Law relief (Commission on Social Welfare, 1986: 33–4). A Committee of Inquiry into Widows' and Orphans' Pensions was established in 1932 and reported in 1933. It resulted in the introduction of both a contributory and non-contributory pension for widows and orphans. The underlying logic of the schemes was the need to acknowledge the dependence of women on their husbands and to replace the husband's income lost on his death.

By the 1940s then, the Irish social security system had institutionalised gender discrimination against women. Moreover, this pattern was reinforced by the operation of the income tax system. This was based on the assumption that married women were effectively outside of the workforce. Their incomes were attributed to their spouse and aggregated with that of their spouse for purposes of assessing income tax liability. The overtly discriminatory Conditions of Employment Act of 1935 then compounded the impact of the public sector employment 'marriage bar'. While introducing regulations for hours of work for adults and young workers and for minimum annual holidays rights, the Act also gave the relevant Minister the power to prohibit the employment of women in certain industries and to fix the proportion of women to men in an industry (Powell, 1992: 208–15). The social security system therefore became part of a wider apparatus — constitutional, social, and economic — that prescribed a domestic life for married women in particular.

This pattern of male prerogative was not confined to Ireland and not overwhelmingly due to 'Catholic power', as Powell seems to argue (Powell, 1992). On the contrary, the assumption that men were the 'breadwinners' and women the 'homemakers' acted as a powerful organising principle in other countries' social security systems also. The male breadwinner assumption was also at the core of the post-war Beveridge system that was constructed in the UK. In Ireland, however, the domestication of women received considerable legal, moral and ideological reinforcement from specific clauses in the constitution and from Catholic social teaching, both of which idealised women as mothers and homemakers. The Constitutional framework devised in 1937 at the peak of Roman Catholic dominance, and the general body of Catholic social teaching which prevailed at that time were not, however, the source of the deepening gender discrimination. The effect of this reinforcement of gender division in Ireland was felt later, when the division proved to be deeply institutionalised and the constitutional provisions in relation to marriage and the family complicated the task of making social security more gender neutral.

WOMEN AND THE BEVERIDGE 'MALE BREADWINNER' SYSTEM

As Chapter Two outlined, the system of social security that developed in Ireland in the latter half of the twentieth century was significantly shaped by the British system (as formulated in the Beveridge report). Beveridge made very distinct assumptions about the roles of men and women in the new national insurance system. He constructed a special place for married women in the reformed system as follows (Beveridge, 1942: 48–9):

> Recognition of married women as a distinct class of occupied persons with benefits adjusted to their special needs, including:
> (a) In all cases [marriage grant], maternity grant, widowhood and separation provisions and retirement pensions;
> (b) If not gainfully occupied, benefit during husband's unemployment or disability;
> (c) If gainfully occupied, special maternity benefit in addition to grant, and lower unemployment and disability benefits.

Beveridge was explicit about the logic that differentiated married women from men and single women (Beveridge, 1942: 48–53). The primary role of women after marriage was a domestic one: women, after marriage, perform 'vital unpaid service' in return for which they acquire not only the legal right to maintenance by their husbands but also protection, through their husband's social insurance contributions, from the new risks of widowhood and separation. He reasoned that, 'The attitude of the housewife to gainful employment outside the home is not and should not be the same as that of the single woman. She has other duties' (Beveridge, 1942: 51).

Even where married women are employed their earnings are secondary to those of the husband and are not the family's means of subsistence 'but of a standard of living above subsistence, like the higher earnings of a skilled man as compared with a labourer'. Furthermore, the earnings of married women were liable to interruption by childbirth and, he argued, expectant mothers should be under no financial pressure to remain in work or to return to work after childbirth. Accordingly, maternity grants and benefit were the key social security provisions for married women. Although he assigned married women to a domestic role, Beveridge couched this in a logic of partnership, describing a married man and wife as 'a team', and referring to the 'vital though unpaid' work of women in the home as work 'without which their husbands could not do their paid work and without which the nation could not continue'.

In this perspective marriage for women is the key to protection against poverty. They obtain access to a male wage as the 'first line of defence against poverty', and through their husbands' social insurance contributions they acquire a 'second line of defence' against poverty arising through his death, illness or unemployment. Beveridge therefore constructed women's citizenship around their domestic and mothering roles, in contrast to men's citizenship, which he defined in terms of paid work. He described his plan as supportive of marriage (Beveridge, 1942: 52):

> Taken as a whole, the plan for Social Security puts a premium on marriage, in place of penalising it. The position of housewives is recognised in form and substance. It is recognised by treating them, not as dependants of their husbands, but as partners sharing benefit and pension when there are no earnings.

Beveridge stressed the contrast between married and single women. Married women were 'protected' from poverty by their husband's income and they received specific rights to benefits associated with marriage. However, this spousal protection available to married women meant that if they had employment outside the home they required less benefit than single women. He proposed to pay lower rates of benefit to married women (for unemployment and disability) because the basis of the benefit system was to provide for minimum needs and: 'It is undeniable that the needs of housewives in general are less than those of single women when unemployed or disabled, because their house is provided by their husband's earnings or by his benefit.' (Beveridge, 1942: 51)

This gendered perspective then translated into a set of social security provisions for women in Great Britain and Ireland structured around the following:

- Exclusion of women from unemployment assistance.
- Lower levels of benefit and shorter periods of entitlement.
- Dependant status, sharing husband's benefits.
- Women responsible for unpaid home care.

Chart 6.1: The Male Breadwinner Regime

Type of System	Country Examples	Examples of Policies
Strong male breadwinner	Ireland, Great Britain	No public provision of childcare; marriage bar in public sector jobs; lower benefits for married women; single women barred from Unemployment Assistance.
Modified male breadwinner	France	Generous family policies for one and two-income families; general public provision of childcare.
Weak male breadwinner	Sweden	Active encouragement of all women to work; universal childcare provision; individual rights in taxation and benefits.

Source: Cook and McCashin (1997) based on Lewis (1992).

Although the details of the treatment of women and men in social security varied from country to country, there is an underlying continuum which reflects the extent of countries' adherence to this 'male breadwinner' system (Lewis, 1992; Lewis, 1993; Sainsbury, 1994). Lewis offered a critical, comparative overview of European welfare states' relative treatment of men and women and constructed the typology given in Chart 6.1. In her analysis, modern welfare states historically based their social policies around a 'male breadwinner' system, assuming that men are the prime earners of families' incomes, that women's earnings are lower, and that women withdraw from the labour market on marriage and assume full responsibility for care of children and other dependant relatives. Social security provisions comprise *one* set of policies reflecting this broader regime of male preference; the regime is the combined effect on women's social and employment status of a wide range of policies in childcare, taxation, labour markets, and social insurance.

Some countries, Sweden for example, operated a 'weak' version of the male breadwinner system, characterised by the presence of some policies to facilitate greater equality in the labour market, and, in particular, by public childcare provisions for working mothers. Other countries, Ireland and Britain most notably, are classified in this analysis as 'strong' male breadwinner regimes because of their adherence over a long period of time to a wide range of policies that institutionalised and reinforced women's exclusion from work and social security. Lewis (1993: 17) summarised the Irish regime in these terms:

> Adherence to the male breadwinner model was perhaps strongest and most long-lived in Ireland, where a marriage bar prevented married women from working in the civil service until 1977; where those (relatively few) married women who did succeed in entering the labour market faced exceptionally harsh treatment under the income tax system, with high marginal rates and very low tax-free allowances; and where, until the mid-1980s (under pressure from EC law), married women received lower rates of benefit, shorter lengths of payment of benefit, and were not eligible for Unemployment Assistance. Indeed, Ireland was the only European country to pay dependants' benefits regardless of whether the wife was in paid work. Thus in Ireland, the government assumed active responsibility for enforcing the traditional division of labour between men and women.

POLICY RATIONALE — CHANGING THE MALE BREADWINNER SYSTEM

A gender-based critique of countries' social security systems is essentially an analysis of how different regimes have responded to the challenges posed to the male breadwinner model. Changes in social and economic circumstances posed one set of challenges, gradually eroding the context that was so essential to the operation of a Beveridge-type system. For example, family structures changed. The number of one-parent families began to grow rapidly in many countries from the 1960s onwards, and, by the early 1990s, most developed countries had experienced a significant growth in the incidence of lone parenthood due to the growth of non-marital births and marital breakdown (Bradshaw, Kennedy, et al, 1996). Social security was ill-equipped to cope with this change, as these new forms of family life represented a man/woman/child/ configuration to which Beveridge-type systems gave little attention. In Beveridge's system, marriage offered financial security to women and children, and in Beveridge's time the most prevalent form of lone parenthood was widowhood. Protection against the income lost on the death of the husband was built into social insurance. But the 'new' forms of lone parenthood raised awkward questions. Should unmarried women with children be treated as workers or as mothers? If the former, then it implied that (lone) mothers were required to be in the labour market and, as 'workers', required to be available for work, and so on: if the latter, then it required a method of giving income protection to non-widowed women with children. This in turn raised new issues about the nature of social insurance. For example, could marital separation and pregnancy outside of marriage be classed as 'risks' that should be 'covered' under social insurance?

The growth in the nature and extent of the care work undertaken by women was a further important change. Care of children was the focus of the domestic role Beveridge ascribed to married women, but in recent decades a combination of policy changes and underlying social changes brought *care work in general* onto the social security policy agenda. Long-run demographic changes lead to a significant increase over time in the numbers and proportion of older and dependent people in many countries. Also, the shift of policy away from institutional care towards community-based support for the elderly and dependent population brought a significant increase in the numbers of persons requiring ongoing care and support. The sheer scale on which this care work began to be undertaken, and the emerging knowledge about its demands and costs, generated a host of questions about care work and social security. Should care of older people, for example, be simply assumed to be another part of women's 'other duties'? Could social insurance be reformed so as to 'value' care work and create social rights based around a new valuation of care? Should social security systems offer payment to carers their for care work, and if so, on what basis — as a token of the value of the care, as payment for the earnings lost by carers, as a compensation for the demands and stresses of caring?

Another assumption in the Beveridge model was that women withdraw from employment on marriage. This assumption, and the social security structures it engendered, became increasingly untenable in developed economies from the 1960s onwards as married women's participation in employment rose. Henceforth, married women would be less likely to be wholly financially dependent on their husbands and this became increasingly at odds with the status accorded to them in the system of social security. Governments would have to find ways of adapting to these changed circumstances: on the one hand, married women in the labour force would need to be included in social security as workers and contributors and, on the other, women who remained in the home would still require social protection. These questions challenged the marriage-based unit of entitlement in social security.

Finally, Beveridge's approach was predicated on full employment (by which he meant male employment) at a family wage. Developed economies began to experience high levels of unemployment again in the 1970s — and in Ireland's case mass unemployment and long-term unemployment in the 1980s and 1990s. Countries' labour market experiences varied considerably, of course, but a common experience was the increasing inability of governments to secure permanent full employment using national macro-economic policy. In addition, some economies that had developed comprehensive social security systems also experienced structural changes. These changes resulted in the loss of large-scale, traditional manufacturing employment, a reduction in secure, public sector employment and the emergence of less secure, low-paid service employment. The detail of how these broad patterns affected individual countries need not be outlined here. What was critical for social security was the demise of guaranteed full employment for men, and the emergence of flexible, low-paid sectors in the labour market. Together these undermined the *man's family wage* as the building block for social security. This accentuated the emerging role of women's work, earnings and social security (Blackwell, 1994).

In parallel with these material changes in social and economic conditions feminists challenged the male breadwinner model. At first, this challenge was part of the wider anti-discrimination critique of society that emerged in the civil rights movements in many countries in the 1960s: it led to a focus on removing formal, legal discrimination against women, in the area of employment in particular. However, in the last two decades a formidable body of feminist analysis of social security (and, more generally, social policy) has emerged (Drew, Emerek and Mahon, 1998; Finch and Groves, 1983; Glendinning and Millar, 1992; Lewis, 1993; Millar, 1989: Pahl, 1983; Brannen and Wilson, 1987; Brannen and Moss, 1991; Sainsbury, 1994).[1] This work offered important insights that have shaped the policy and research agenda in social security in Ireland and internationally.

Critically, feminists questioned the potential of social insurance to act as a *gender-neutral system* of social security. Inherently, social insurance was constructed around male, life-long employment at a family wage. It is by no means clear — even with more equal access to work for women — that social insurance can be modified and reformed to adequately encompass the persisting differences in the patterns of men's and women's lives. Women are more likely to have incomplete work histories and social insurance records, because of their greater tendency to withdraw from work, to undertake care work, and to have atypical or part-time work (Blackwell, 1994; Land, 1994). These gender-related limitations on social insurance contributed to the emergence of a policy debate about alternatives to social insurance. In Ireland in the 1990s, for instance, one organisation repeatedly advocated the complete abolition of the social insurance and assistance system and its replacement by a system (variously titled Basic Income, Citizen's Income, Social Dividend) built on a universal, non-means-tested payment to all adults, no matter what their gender, employment status, or marital or 'dependency' status (Healy and Reynolds, 1994; Healy and Reynolds, 1995). While this proposal was not advanced primarily within a gender framework, it nevertheless would address some of the gender-related criticisms of social insurance, and in the work of some advocates of this type of radical reform the benefits to women are stressed (Parker, 1989).

Feminists also criticised the assumption that women could receive their 'protection against poverty' solely through their reliance on the *man's* wage or social security payment. Feminists pointed out that, theoretically, it simply cannot be assumed that men will share the family income with their wives and children. In conventional thinking[2] the 'male-headed' family is assumed to behave as one economic unit. In technical terms the family is assumed to have a single utility function for all family members — a function that is expressed on behalf of the family by its (usually male) head. This assumption of the family as one unit was critiqued and modified. According to the 'new home economics' school (Cantillon, 1997: 198–202), families maximise their welfare in a framework where the spending of the family's income is completely independent of who earns it, and spending reflects collective preferences. In this model, even if the income is not shared, there are no effects on spending as everyone acts altruistically, i.e. according to the family's utility function. The bargaining model is another approach. This suggests that individuals enter into collective units for spending and consumption only when they can do better than remaining on their own. The approach allows for conflict between individuals' inherent preferences. Here the household utility function arrived at depends on the relative bargaining power of the individuals: a stronger bargaining position — from the individual who earns the higher income — confers more influence in decisions about expenditure.

The feminist critique points out that the notion of collective, aggregated, family utility functions relies on the assumption of altruism on the part of the man. However, the broader framework of economic theory assumes that the typical male agent in the workplace will be competitive and income-maximising. Therefore, the observed patterns of household spending may reflect male power or competition within the family for resources. Even where a conflictual bargaining perspective is adopted, it assumes that the bargaining takes place among equals, in a context that has no institutional, social, or legal underpinnings for male prerogative. Moreover, the bargaining analysis leaves the position of children unresolved.

This feminist critique is associated with a body of empirical research that has explicitly abandoned the assumption of the family as an entity with equal 'internal sharing' of resources. There are a number of inter-related themes in this research. First, a somewhat technical body of work focuses on the *unit of analysis* in poverty and income distribution research. As summarised in Chapter Three, conventional poverty estimates start with data at the household level — the numbers and proportions of households/families in the population that are poor on the assumption that all income in the household is available to all household members. For example, Davies and Joshi (1994) analysed the UK Family Expenditure Survey for households comprising couples, and explored the implications of making contrasting assumptions about the extent to which the incomes of men and women are shared. The analysis showed that these assumptions have powerful effects on the measures of poverty among women. To illustrate this approach: when they assume that couples' resources are pooled then married women have a 15% risk of being below the specified line (1986 data), whereas the figure is 52% if they assume that there is minimum sharing (Davies and Joshi, 1994: 327). This kind of study relies on data about households and families where no direct data is included about whether and how incomes are shared. However, this kind of 'what if' analysis is sufficient to reveal that estimates of the extent of poverty among women based on data about households and families, critically depend on the assumptions made about income distribution within the household.

Second, more sophisticated studies combine data about the household with data on *individuals within households* — their income, expenditure, consumption, and access to and use of resources (Cantillon and Nolan, 1998: Cantillon, 1997). These studies suggest that ignoring the issue of sharing (or otherwise) within families does *not* neglect a reservoir of 'hidden poverty' among individual women within families. In other words, if the actual patterns within households are analysed they do not conform to the extreme scenario of higher-measured poverty based on a 'no sharing' scenario. However, they also suggest that there is *unequal* access to income and resources (Rottman, 1994).

Third, a range of studies (both quantitative and qualitative) by sociologists have analysed families' and couples' incomes and attempted to describe and explain *the internal dynamics of family finances* and their impact on the financial well-being of women in particular (Pahl, 1983; Vogler and Pahl, 1994). The important insight from these studies is that families have 'systems' of economic decision-making and these vary by class, income level, stage of the life cycle and the labour force status of men and women in the household. Furthermore, the systems of decision-making have implications for the extent of women's access to and control over the family's income. At one end of a continuum is the traditional scenario where the male (and only) earner in the household retains ownership of the family wage, gives the spouse/housewife an 'allowance' for all household expenses and child-related costs, and retains the balance for personal use. At the other end of the continuum is the dual income couple, pooling their earnings and sharing all expenses.

A related body of work on lone-mother families has highlighted the role of *financial independence* in enhancing the welfare of lone mothers (Marsden, 1973; McCashin, 1996). This research shows that lone mothers value the financial autonomy that comes with being 'alone'. It is striking that lone mothers may actually trade-off the relative poverty and other problems of being on a low income against the freedom and control they experience in managing their own income. One lone mother in McCashin's (1996: 125) study pointed out about her own low income: 'it's not a lot, but at least it's mine'. Poverty, then, in these women's eyes is not only about the *amount* of resources they have, but also about their individual right to direct *access to and control* over their income. Feminists' questioning of the assumption of sharing within families, therefore, goes beyond the issue of the unit of measurement and raises deeper questions about the nature of poverty. As one contributor has suggested, this feminist perspective implies a new emphasis in the definition of poverty — one that concerns each individual's right to 'a minimum degree of potential economic independence' (Jenkins, 1991: 464).

The feminist perspective on this aspect of poverty and social security has raised a variety of policy implications about individual women's access to income. One part of this agenda, clearly, is the general stress on securing women's access to employment and the associated access to social security rights. A further element in the agenda is the individualisation of the general tax and social security systems: this aspect of policy is concerned with the *structure* of these systems. Should the income tax system, for instance, adopt the married couple as the unit of assessment, and if so what effect does this have on the relative income of men and women in one-income and two-income families? In social security, how can the system move away from treating married women as 'dependants' and accord them greater personal rights, while the same time acknowledging that women (especially those with children) may continue to experience prolonged periods of financial 'dependence' on their spouse or partner. Since married people are legally obliged to maintain each other, should policy makers design the tax and social security systems to ensure that each person directly receives a fair share of family income, or should the systems be designed only to intervene when specific cases of neglect arise?

The issue of child income support is also related to these questions, as the previous chapter showed. If the typical 'male head of the family' fails to discharge his responsibility to his children, arguably the system of child income support should be strengthened. In particular, it could be argued that more of the 'family income' should be channelled through the child support system directly to mothers and less through the husband's wage. Child benefit payments — their adequacy, structure and administration are therefore on the policy agenda of feminist analyses of social security.

The core of the feminist critique of social security has been separation of the male and female worlds of work and home respectively, and the social security system's role in the reinforcement of that separation. The focus of policy reform has been the strengthening of women's role in the labour market. But this emphasis on employment is beginning to be questioned by feminists and conservatives alike (Lewis, 2001A and Lewis, 2001B; Fukayama, 1999). One thread in this development is the realisation that the woman-as-worker model can be easily appropriated by a narrow agenda of reducing 'dependence' on welfare, and increasing the supply of workers in the low-skill, low-wage part of the labour market. Even if such an agenda resulted in a significant increase in employment among women it is not the same as reducing poverty. For example, a strategy of reducing poverty among lone mothers by getting them into employment may fail, if they are unskilled and receive low pay, and pay the market cost for childcare.

There is also a realisation that the employment agenda may be at odds with an agenda focused on social care. Quite simply, as Lewis (2001A: 53) has pointed out, 'the demand for care is increasing at a time when its supply, both in the public and private, non-market sectors, is decreasing' in many welfare states. This is because many welfare states have high levels of female work participation *and* a growing demand for care services. Ireland is one such instance, as Fahey has suggested in relation to childcare (Fahey, 1998A). Policy is simultaneously oriented to increasing the participation of women in the labour market *and* attempting to facilitate women providing home-based childcare and those caring for dependent relatives.

'Care' work is also being interrogated. The initial emphasis among feminist commentators was on the under-valuation of care and the need for care work to be recognised and supported. However, the complexity of caring is now recognised. Some feminists now stress the strong sense of duty and the emotional and reciprocal aspects of caring (Lewis, 2001A). For some writers, women's impulse to care reflects a 'gendered moral rationality' different to the individualistic rationality reflected in men's economic behaviour. The danger for these critics is that an emphasis on integrating women into the labour market and 'rewarding' carers may undermine the social basis of care by formalising and commercialising care work. Curiously, this line of reasoning converges with the concerns expressed by conservative commentators bemoaning the loss of a sense of family obligation in the face of growing individualism (Fukayama, 1999). In the conservative perspective, the altruistic nature of care work is being eroded by feminist individualism that is drawing women out of the family and into the competitive world of work. The debate about care is therefore related to wider debates in the social sciences about the supposed decline of the family and community and the rise of materialistic individualism.

POLICY DEVELOPMENT — REMOVING DISCRIMINATION

Starting in the early 1970s, the process of reforming the Irish system of social security began. A simple way of highlighting the nature and pace of the reform is to consider the relevant reports of the Commission on the Status of Women. The Commission was established in 1970 with a brief to make recommendations to 'ensure the participation of women on equal terms and conditions with men in the political, social, cultural and economic life of the country' (Commission on the Status of Women, 1972: 7). Its report recommended a wide range of changes in public policy and devoted a full chapter to social security policy, making 32 recommendations in all. The broad approach the Commission adopted was to recommend the abolition of formal differences in treatment between men and women while avoiding the introduction of new forms of discrimination, and to 'ensure that women, or particular categories of women (such as widows, deserted wives) are provided for in relation to the risks to which their position in society makes them particularly vulnerable' (Commission on the Status of Women, 1972: 136).

To understand the policy implications of the Commission it is useful to look at its recommendations in the light of the challenges to the male breadwinner model. In this context, the key points in the Commission's analysis were as follows:

- It recognised the growing number of lone mother families and argued for the introduction of a social security payment specifically for unmarried mothers.
- It endorsed the introduction in 1970 of a separate means-tested payment in respect of women deserted by their husbands — the Deserted Wife's Allowance — and recommended a reduction in the time period of desertion required to create an entitlement.
- Critically, it recommended a range of changes in social insurance to strengthen the rights of individual women, such as abolition of the historic practice of closing women's social insurance record on marriage, and the elimination of the discretionary lower rate of social insurance payments to married women.
- It also recommended equalisation of men's and women's rights in relation to unemployment benefit and assistance, notably, the removal of the ban on single women receiving unemployment assistance and the abolition of the restrictions on women in agriculture and domestic service receiving unemployment benefit.
- In relation to children's allowances (later re-named Child Benefit), the Commission argued that payment should be made directly to mothers.
- It recommended that 'credited' contributions be added to the social insurance records of women leaving employment to care for (certain categories of) elderly relatives.

The agenda of policy change formulated by the Commission influenced developments for over a decade and almost all of its proposals were implemented, but a more general point should be noted[3]. The commission's analysis of social security was embedded in a wider analysis of women in society and the economy and it offered a wide range of recommendations (most of them implemented) directed at expanding the involvement of women in the labour market and the economy. These recommendations included equal pay for men and women, improved maternity leave, and removal of the marriage bar in public sector employment. In social security, its recommendations reflected this broad concern to enhance women's income and employment.

However, the male breadwinner approach proved more resistant to change and influenced policy makers' response to some of the Commission's recommendations.

Widows' pensions, for instance, were firmly constructed on the assumption that all widows would 'remain out of the labour market, as the pensions were not conditional (then or now) on the age of the women or whether they had children. The Commission said (Commission on the Status of Women, 1972: 151):

> We have been struck by the fact that there is no restriction whatever placed either in relation to age or dependency on the payment of the contributory widow's pension. A young widow without any dependants whatever is eligible to receive the pensions for life or until she remarries to becomes eligible for old-age pension, even though her financial position is no different from that of a single person.

The Commission then argued that some age or dependency restrictions should be applied to the widow's pension, and that widows who would not then be entitled to a pension should be deemed to be 'quite capable of re-entering employment'. In its scenario the Commission envisaged (some) widows as workers — and therefore eligible for unemployment payments if unable to obtain work. But the relatively generous treatment of widowhood, based on the assumption that women should not have the same link to employment as men, remained in place and continued to reinforce gender differentiation in social security. Even the argument that the Commission made about the costs of provision for widows was not sufficient to move policy to a point where some widows might be required to participate in the labour market.

The reluctance of policy makers to think of women with children as workers as well as mothers is further illustrated by the fate of the Commission's recommendations about unmarried mothers. Here the commission recommended that single women with children should be given an allowance to facilitate them to keep custody of their child. It suggested that the allowance should be for one year, after which the women would be available for employment. In fact, the government introduced the Unmarried Mothers' Allowance in 1973 with no time limit on entitlement (other than the normal age of reaching adulthood), no requirement to have any link with employment or training, and a very limited disregard of earnings in the means test. Over twenty years later one commentator pointed out that these provisions strongly reinforced the semi-permanent exclusion of this group of women from the labour market (McCashin, 1993).

By the early 1980s, therefore, changes had been implemented. These changes either removed overt discrimination against women or added on new schemes to respond to the needs of specific categories of women. Gender continued to act as a focus in social security during the 1980s and 1990s and further changes were made: the schemes for lone mothers were rationalised; payments to women carers were extended and reformed, and maternity benefit was introduced. In addition, wider policy changes improved women's social security status: the extension of social insurance to part-time employees and new public sector employees in the early 1990s brought more women into the social insurance system. However, a more complete understanding of how policy changed requires an account of policy development in a number of critical areas. One of the areas — the implementation of the EC's Equal Treatment Directive — is dealt with in the next section. Chapter Seven deals with lone mothers.

IMPLEMENTING EQUAL TREATMENT

The manner in which the EC's Equal Treatment Directive was incorporated into the Irish social security system gives an insight into the gender dynamics of social security policy[4]. Before examining the implementation of the Directive, it is useful to note the data in Table 6.1. It summarises the very rapid rate at which women's role in the labour market changed during the two decades (the 1970s and 1980s) when gender equality measures were central to reform. The participation rate of married women in paid work and their share of the female labour force rose three-fold from the early 1970s to the early 1990s.

Table 6.1: Trends in Female Labour Force Participation, by Marital Status, Ireland 1961–1990

Year	Participation Rates			Share of Female Labour Force		
	Single	Married	Widowed	Single	Married	Widowed
1961	59.3	5.2	26.2	80.0	8.5	11.5
1966	61.0	5.3	22.2	81.4	8.9	9.6
1971	59.8	7.5	19.3	77.7	13.6	8.7
1981	56.4	16.7	11.4	65.3	30.2	4.5
1986	54.1	21.3	8.5	62.0	34.1	3.9
1990	51.0	25.3	6.9	55.3	42.0	2.6

Source: Censuses of Population and Labour Force Surveys.
Note: 'Married' includes separated etc.

In 1979, as Ireland was in the process of reforming its social security system along the general lines of the Commission on the Status of Women's report, the European community adopted EC Directive 79/7 on *The Progressive Implementation of Equal Treatment for Men and Women in Matters of Social Security.*[5] The Directive applied to the working population as well to the retired and the invalided, and encompassed social insurance for sickness and invalidity, unemployment, old age, and occupational injury, as well as social assistance for these contingencies. General family benefits — such as widows' pensions — were not included. Significantly for Ireland, however, family benefits paid as supplements to general payments (adult and child dependants' allowances paid with weekly social security payments) were included. The comprehensive terms of the Directive offered a challenge to the structure of the Irish social security system. It raised a fundamental question as to nature of 'equality' in social security, and the manner in which Ireland gave effect to the directive needs to be set in the context of the widely different interpretations of equality that might be invoked.

Following Abel-Smith's analysis, a number of definitions of sex equality in social security can be distinguished: (Abel-Smith, 1982)

- *Actuarial sex equality* allows the differentiation of the sexes in benefits received because of the differences in the costs of providing such benefits. If women are more likely to be sick, or unemployed, or to live longer, then lower benefits may be paid to women compared to men, or women may, as a group, be actuarially required to pay higher contributions to cover their greater risks of claiming.
- A second type of sex equality is the pooling of risks between men and women, resulting in *insurance status sex equality*. Here, men and women have the same rights to benefits based on their contribution records. However, different life and work patterns may preclude many women from building the same contribution records as men.
- *Citizen sex equality*, allows identical benefits for women and men, although women's contribution records may be distinctly inferior.
- With *positive sex equality*, special social insurance credits are allocated to women in respect of the work they do as carers, while men would also claim social security credits if they discharge these socially vital roles.
- *Sex role equality* aims to make roles more equal between the sexes. In this form of equality the social security system facilitates men and women in sustaining both work and family roles: paternity as well as maternity benefits are paid, and men may be obliged to discharge their childcare roles by partial retirement from the labour market in order to facilitate women's pursuit of a career. Sex role equality in social security is an attempt not merely to reduce the double burden on women of pursuing a career and rearing children, but of ensuring male responsibility for, and share of, the double burden.

The introduction of the old age pension in 1908 in the United Kingdom and Ireland represented a distinct breakthrough for sex equality. As Abel-Smith pointed out, the old age pension was a model of sex equality. The introduction of national insurance in 1911, on the other hand, represented the introduction of actuarial sex equality which intensified as the scope of national insurance broadened after political independence. This actuarial sex equality in social insurance has been modified by various *ad hoc* changes. The 1979 Directive opened up the prospect of insurance status sex equality, and even citizen sex equality, and should have given rise to a debate about the meaning of sex equality in social security.

Social insurance is employment and contribution based, and any inferiority in earnings or employment is directly reflected in access to benefits. There is also the problem of entry or re-entry to the labour market for women with children. Even when a woman obtains employment, there are problems building up an adequate contribution record, if this record is interrupted by childbirth and periods of absence from the workforce. Actuarial sex equality in social insurance schemes would tend to reinforce Irishwomen's second-class status compared with men, when faced with certain contingencies for which the social insurance system gives a benefit. Even insurance status sex equality would still see many women disadvantaged because they might not have the opportunity to build up a significant level of contributions.

One type of social security system, Basic Income, does confer complete citizen sex equality. Basic Income is quite simply a weekly payment to all men and women, of all marital and economic statuses, without means tests or social insurance contributions. The arguments for such an approach to social security are dealt with in chapter twelve. Here it is important to note that, before the Irish government signed the Equality Directive, the NESC had already considered the rationale for such a radical approach and outlined a scheme that might apply in Ireland's circumstances.[6] The government did not accept this approach. Therefore, the option of adopting a social security scheme that would have fully incorporated sex equality was rejected. This was not a rejection of the aspiration to sex equality *per se*, but a refusal to contemplate a proposal with very significant costs that outweighed the advantages of a simple, gender-neutral, comprehensive system.

The usual way of incorporating all women into social security is the award of *credits* for socially useful activity like caring for children or sick relatives. The whole rationale of a credit system is to overcome low market valuation of female labour. Market rates of remuneration do not reflect the social value of women's work. Yet credit systems are obliged to cope with many thorny issues like part-time work and the balance between household work and paid employment. The most difficult issue with credits is the question of financing. In fact, there are strong reasons in any credit system for a subsidy from the taxpayer. The credit system represents the social valuation of the privatisation of child-rearing and the social care of dependant relatives. The social valuation must be high enough to ensure that benefits based mainly on credits are adequate, yet not be so generous that massive disincentive effects in the contributor workforce are created. While such a system would be very expensive to implement, it would overcome, firstly, low levels of benefits to those with patchy earnings and contribution records and, secondly, the dependency of most women on derived rights from their contributor husbands.

The central feature of the Ireland's sex equality policies was the absence of any fundamental debate about the concepts and strategies outlined above. The focus of policy was to delay implementation of the Directive and to conform to its legal requirements, while minimising costs. Central to the interpretation of the directive in Ireland was the comparatively low level of female labour force participation and the importance of dependants' allowances in the social security system. Recipients with children were allowed Child Additional Payments along with their personal payment. Furthermore, married recipients were entitled to Adult Dependant Allowances, and these were paid to married men *whether or not their spouses were in employment*. In the Irish system at the time of the Directive, all married women were dependants, by definition, and men could only be dependants if they were permanently disabled. Table 6.2 below shows the payment structure in 1979 (the year after Ireland signed the Directive) for unemployment benefit and unemployment assistance for married men and their spouses, and married women.

Table 6.2: Unemployment Payments in 1979

Unemployment Assistance (Urban)	£IR Per Week
Person without dependant	14.15
Adult dependant	10.20
Child dependant	4.40
Increase for each child in excess of two	3.40

Unemployment Benefit	£IR Per Week
Basic Rate	17.05
Basic Rate per person under 18 years without dependant, or married woman dependant on her husband	15.00
Adult dependant	11.05
Child dependant	4.95
Increase for each child in excess of two	4.10

Note: The figures given are in the currency of the time, at current prices.

Ireland's implementation of this Directive was prolonged, controversial and litigious. Some of the most straightforward inequalities were rectified first. Thus, under the *Social Welfare Act (No. 2) 1985*, reduced rates of benefit paid to women were equalised to the male rates in the unemployment benefit, disability benefit, invalidity pension and occupational injury schemes. The duration of payment of unemployed benefit to married women was made the same as for other claimants. These provisions became operative in May 1986. Married women were also allowed to claim unemployment assistance but this only became operative in

November 1986, almost eight years after the Directive was issued.[7] Most difficult of all, the Irish Government tried to resolve the complex debate on dependency by specifying that after November 1986, a husband could not claim a social security payment in respect of his wife if she earned more than a specific amount or if she was in receipt of a social security payment (with some exceptions). Also, a claimant's spouse who was not a dependant in the terms of the new legislation could only receive *half* of the child dependant addition which would have been payable if his spouse was an adult dependant. The logic here was that if a recipient with children had a spouse who was not a dependant — in the new meaning of the term — then the children were only half-dependent on the recipient!

These provisions resulted in the reduction of the total net incomes of some of the poorest and most vulnerable families in Ireland. To mitigate the losses, the Government introduced a transitional scheme, whereby a man whose wife earned more than the dependant threshold would have the full child dependency additions restored to him together with an additional payment. An additional IR£20 (€25.40) per week was payable to a husband on social security whose wife claimed social security in her own right, and each parent could claim half the total child dependency additions. Special provisions were also made under the transitional scheme for some men claiming unemployment assistance with a working wife. As Figure 6.1 and Table 6.3 show, the new arrangements locked the recipient couples into a poverty trap. These data show the impact of the

Table 6.3: Married Women with Unemployed Husbands: The Poverty Trap, 1992, (IR£ weekly)

Spouses' Earnings		Assessed Means	Max. U.A. Entitlement	Long-term U.A.	Net Family Income
Gross £	Net £	£	£	£	£
20	20.00	0.00	112	112.00	132.00
40	40.00	0.00	112	112.00	152.00
60	60.00	2.50	67	64.50	124.50
80	73.80	9.40	67	57.10	130.90
100	92.25	18.62	67	48.40	140.65
120	110.70	27.85	67	39.20	149.90
140	129.15	37.07	67	30.00	139.15
160	140.93	42.97	67	24.10	165.05
180	150.34	47.77	67	19.30	169.84
200	163.39	54.29	67	12.80	176.39
220	176.64	60.82	67	6.20	182.84
240	189.69	67.34	67	0.00	189.69

Source: Department of Social Welfare.

Figure 6.1: The Poverty Trap (1992), Unemployed Recipient, Working Spouse, Two Children

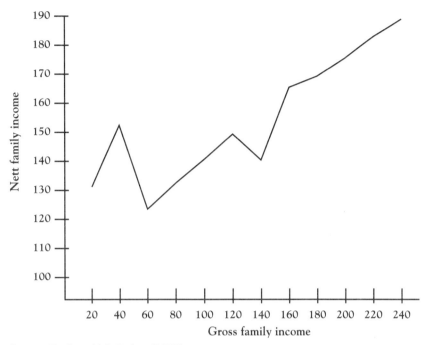

Source: Cook and McCashin (1997)

means test and the loss of the adult and child dependant allowances on the net income of the couple in 1992, after the full implementation of the changes. Where the spouse's earnings are negligible they have the effect of simply adding to the net family income, but as the earnings level rise the impact of the means test and the loss of the dependants' allowances result in a poverty trap — a *fall* in net family income arising from an increase in gross earnings. These data are given for one type of family for one year — but they illustrate a more general pattern implicit in the post-equality treatment of spouses' incomes and the definition of dependency.[8] The effect of this poverty trap would be to *discourage* low-income individuals with unemployed spouses from entering employment or increasing their earnings. An attempt to apply the principle of equality ended up creating a new work disincentive for some low-income women. In fact, the work participation rate for women with unemployed husbands *fell* from 20.1% to 16.7% from 1987–1994 (the period immediately following the introduction of the Directive) while the participation rate for women in all other income categories *rose* — and in some income groups rose very significantly (Nolan and Watson, 1999:84).

The implementation of the Sex Equality Directive also necessitated changes in the procedures for the *assessment of means* and provision was made for the *limitation of the entitlement of married couples* to take into account the sharing of household expenses. The equality legislation stipulated that where both of a married couple living together qualified for unemployment assistance in their own right, the total amount payable to the couple would be limited to what they would receive if only one spouse claimed and received *an allowance for the other as an adult dependant*. In this situation, each person would receive half of the total 'married rate' of payment. A similar limitation was introduced where one of a married couple was a social insurance recipient or was a means-tested old age pensioner and the other was a recipient of unemployment assistance. In this latter case the amount of unemployment assistance was to be reduced to stay within the limitation. This limitation *only* applied where at least one of the couples was an unemployment assistance recipient. In a situation where both partners of a married couple were entitled to a social insurance payment in their own right by virtue of separate contribution records, each partner would receive the full personal level of payment. The limitation only applied in the case of married couples: cohabiting couples and other 'pairs' of recipients in a household were not subject to the limitation.

This situation became subject to legal review in the Hyland case, in which the constitutionality of the arrangements was successfully challenged. The Supreme Court held that these limitation arrangements discriminated against married partners in comparison with partners who were cohabiting and receiving the full personal rates of payment, and that such discrimination against married partners violated the Irish Constitution's commitment to the institution of marriage. (Under Article 41 of the Constitution, the State recognises 'the family as the national, primary and fundamental work of society, and pledges itself to guard with special care the institution of marriage in which the family is founded and to protect it against attack'.) In the Hyland case, *explicit* reference was made to the Supreme Court judgement in the Murphy case in relation to income taxation; the Murphy judgement in 1980 had held that in relation to tax allowances married couples could not be treated less favourably than cohabiting couples.

In the wake of the Supreme Court judgement in the Hyland case the Government passed the Social Welfare (No. 2) Act of 1989. This re-instated the limitation of the entitlements of married couples and *extended the limitation* to cohabiting couples, making the treatment of married and cohabiting couples formally equal. As well as dealing with the immediate situation of cohabiting couples' claims on the social security system, the Government established a Review Group on the Treatment of Households in the Social Welfare system to examine the wider implications of the Supreme Court decision. In particular, the Review Group was required to focus on the adaptation of social assistance schemes, so that households that might be considered to have similar needs would be treated in an equitable manner. The Group was required to take into account the Irish Constitution's support for married women, the EC Directives on equal treatment, economies of scale in shared household expenditure, and the need to contain Exchequer costs.

The Review Group's report presented four possible scenarios for the future. One was to retain the payment structure in its present form, while the other options were to abolish the limitation, to extend the limitation, or lastly to introduce a household supplement. Given the long-term structural changes required to implement some of these scenarios, the Review Group concluded that only two scenarios could be introduced in the short-term: the *abolition* of the limitation applying to married couples and cohabiting couples, or the *extension* of the limitation to other categories of claimants (Department of Social Welfare, 1991). The structure today is broadly as it was at the time of the Review Group's report.

Ireland's attempt to adapt its social security system according to the EC Directive in sex equality was not conspicuously successful or well thought-out. The result was a 'levelling down' rather than a 'levelling up' of social security standards for some of the most deprived and marginalised families in Irish society. Also, the social security system may be open to *future* Court challenges in that it may still discriminate against married couples compared with other types of households.[9] The legal insecurity of the existing situation means that the full implementation of the EC Directive, let alone the achievement of sex role equality in social security, may still be incomplete.

WOMEN AND POVERTY

Did the developments in social security from the early 1970s onwards have any impact on women's poverty? Was it true, in the first instance, that women had a higher risk of poverty then men? What of the distribution of the family income among men and women in Ireland — is it unequal, and if so, is the inequality so marked as to leave individual women 'poor' even where the total household is above the poverty line? These questions cannot be answered definitively and, in particular, it is by no means straightforward to link the evidence about women's poverty to the performance of the social security system. But enough data is available to place the gender aspects of the social security system in a poverty-related context.

Starting with the broad pattern, Table 6.4 shows that from 1973 to 1987 the risk of poverty among female-headed households declined very markedly and by 1987 the rate was lower than the comparable male rate. This was the period during which substantial improvements were made in the social security arrangements for women — the introduction of new schemes, the removal of the bar on unemployment assistance, and substantial improvements in the real and relative levels of social welfare payments. It was also the period during which the number of financially vulnerable female-headed households — specifically lone mother households — rose. Also, the composition of female headed households shifted towards the more poverty-prone categories of lone mother (unmarried and separated women) and away from widows. That the female rate of poverty declined during this period reflects the very substantial developments in social security that counteracted the wider trends.

Table 6.4: Risk of Poverty (below 50% of average income) by Gender of Head of Household, 1973–1994

Year	Female	Male
1973	29.3	15.7
1980	22.4	15.6
1987	8.9	18.6
1994	24.0	16.8

Source: Callan, Nolan *et al*, (1996), Table, 5.6.

It is also striking from the table that the 1973–1987 trend was reversed in the succeeding seven years. Nolan and Watson's detailed study of women and poverty explains why this happened (Nolan and Watson, 1999). First, and most important, the evolution of social welfare payments from the late 1980s to the mid-1990s was shaped by the report of the Commission on Social Welfare. The Commission had stressed the very low rates of Supplementary Welfare Allowance (SWA) and Unemployment Assistance and the impact of these on the high levels of poverty among the families of the unemployed. Accordingly, the highest rate of increase in benefits went to these families rather than pensioners or lone parents. In relative terms the incomes of lone mothers and older women living on state pensions declined. Second, this policy factor was compounded by some demographic trends — the continued growth in the population of welfare dependent lone mothers, the growth in one-person, older 'female' households and the increased tendency for young adults to depart the family household.

In the period since the mid-1990s the poverty data for 1997 and 1998 shows that the risk (again at the 50% line) rose very sharply for households headed by a person engaged in home duties — these are mostly women: for 1994, 1997 and 1998 respectively their poverty figures were 33.2%, 48.6%, and 58.4% (Layte, Maitre, *et al*, 2001: 24) This suggests a continuation of the trend from 1997 to 1994.[10] The 2001 data shows a slightly higher poverty risk for women, and a noticeably higher risk for women compared to men in the over-65 age group (Whelan, Layte *et al*, 2003).

To set the simple contrast between male and female poverty rates in context it is useful to record some key points from Nolan and Watson's more detailed analysis of poverty rates, which shows the following: (Nolan and Watson, 1999: 17–20)

- First, the *highest* risk of poverty in 1994 was for female, lone parent households (31.7%) and the next highest was female one person households (24.4%): both these figures were very substantial increases on the figures for 1987.
- Second, the *lowest* risk of poverty (10.6%) applied to couples with no children — illustrating the link between the presence of adults and the absence of children with a reduced risk of poverty: the poverty risk for these households remained constant over the period 1987–1994.
- Third, male lone parents had an identical risk of poverty to their female counterparts in 1987, but by 1994 their rate had fallen sharply. Male, one-person households also experience a high rate of poverty — over 20% in both years.

But these risk figures need also to be seen in the light of the *incidence* figures (as defined in chapter three). Close to a half of all poor households (47.6%) are couples with children, reflecting their large share of the population as a whole, and when couples without children are added, the majority of the poor are comprised of couple-households. Female lone parents and female one-person households in that order are the next largest groups within the poor population. The female households have a high *relative incidence* of poverty, however: they comprise a much higher share of the poor than they do of the population in general.

The comparison between men and women is more complicated than the discussion above allows. 'Female-headed' households in the analysis given above are households headed by an adult woman without a spouse, and 'male-headed' households comprise couples with the man defined as 'head'. Therefore, this male/female distinction is also a comparison of households with *different numbers of adults*, and this latter factor is also an important independent influence on poverty. Table 6.5, reproduced from the Nolan and Watson study shows how a range of factors, gender included, affect the risk of poverty for non-couple households (Nolan and Watson, 1999: 46).

Table 6.5 is based on a statistical analysis of the factors that affect the risk of being poor. The table shows the probability of households with specific characteristics being poor and allows detailed comparisons to be made between different households:[11]

- Row A shows that the risk of poverty for a woman aged 25, unemployed, living alone, and from an unskilled working class background is 52%. The corresponding figure for a man with the same characteristics is higher at 64.8%.
- Comparing Row A with Row D, a woman with the same characteristics, but who is older (age 67) and retired, has a 40% risk of poverty.
- Strikingly, if all but one of the characteristics of the woman in row A are held constant, and the poverty rate is instead estimated for an *employed* person, the rate is a mere 4.1%.

Table 6.5: Estimated Poverty Risk for Non-Couple Households with Specified Characteristics

	Characteristics	Risk %
A	Never married woman, age 25, living alone, unemployed, social class 5*	52.4
B	As A, man	64.8
C	As A, widowed	40.2
D	As A, age 67, retired	3.0
E	As A, employed	4.1
F	Female lone parent, age 25, one child, on 'home duties', social class 5*	80.0
G	As F, male	87.0
H	As F, employed	13.4
I	As F, age 40	69.5
J	As F, age 40, widowed	58.2

Source: Nolan and Watson (1999: 46).
* Social class 5 is unskilled manual working class.

- The contrast between row A and rows F and G is also striking. F refers to cases identical to A, except that these women are lone mothers. They have one child and are on 'home duties': here the poverty rate is 80%. In the case of G — male lone parents otherwise identical to case F — the figure is the highest in the selection at 87%.

This analysis clearly shows that gender interacts with other factors in quite complex ways and in ways that suggest that gender is not necessarily the most important variable distinguishing one household from another. On the contrary, employment status is critical, reducing poverty risk to a negligible level, and being older and retired is also associated with a lower level of poverty.

The analysis summarised above is about households rather than individual persons in households or families. It is equally important to see to what extent individual men and women live in poor households (households that are poor taking account of total income in the household and measuring household income on a per capita adjusted basis). Nolan and Watson classify men and women into categories that reflect broad types of family and analyse women's and men's risk of poverty by the type of family and household they live in (Nolan and Watson, 1999: 66). Thus, some men and women are 'unattached': they are unmarried, without children, and not in a couple or marriage situation. These bachelors could be living alone, or with their parents, or one with one parent who might also be a lone parent, or in some other situation. Lone parents might be living alone and be heads of their own household, or be sharing the parental home with one or both parents, or living with others. These patterns will also vary with age.

The figures in Table 6.6 highlight a number of key points:

Table 6.6: Poverty Risk (% Poor) for Male and Female Adults by Living Arrangements and Type of Family, 1994

Males % Poor

Living Arrangements	Unattached, Under 45	Lone Parent	Unattached, 45 or over	Married/ Cohabiting
Head of Household	12.2	11.9	21.1	17.0
With Couple and children	12.2	0.0	6.0	0.0
With Lone Parent	15.7	0.0	0.0	4.6
With other	1.2	0.0	11.5	0.0

Females % Poor

Living Arrangements	Unattached, Under 45	Lone Parent	Unattached, 45 or over	Married/ Cohabiting
Head of Household	9.8	32.7	22.5	17.1
With Couple & children	16.5	10.6	20.4	0.0
With Lone parent	23.5	5.9	15.1	4.0
With Other	3.6	1.7	3.5	0.0

Source: Nolan and Watson, 1999: Table 4.4.

- Individual men and women have a lower poverty risk if they are not heads of households.
- For male and female lone parents in particular there is a markedly lower poverty risk if they are part of a wider household arrangement.
- Younger (<45), unattached women, are an exception to the general pattern — their poverty risk is *lower* where they are heading their own households, bringing the role of employment and economic status into focus.

Table 6.7 shows the poverty risks for young unattached men and women, distinguishing between those in work and those that are not in work. The data confirm that employment status is critical. Poverty rates for young unattached men and women in work are negligible, whether they are heads of their own households or living in wider household units. The differences in poverty rates across different types of household arrangements are also negligible. However, if the men and women not in employment are considered, their living arrangements significantly affect their poverty risk. Being in a wider household substantially reduces the poverty risk for men and women not in work. A woman not in work has a poverty risk of 64% if she heads her own household, and a risk of 27% if she lives with another couple. This differentiation by living arrangements also applies to men.

Table 6.7: Poverty Risk for Young (<45), Unattached Males and Females by Employment Status and Living Arrangements, 1994

Males % Poor

Living Arrangement	Employed	Not Employed
Household head	1.6	43.6
With couple and children	3.7	20.1
With lone parent	6.0	23.8
With other	0.0	3.4

Females % Poor

Living Arrangement	Employed	Not Employed
Head of household	0.0	64.2
With couple and children	3.8	27.0
With lone parent	5.3	33.4
With other	0.0	17.7

Source: Nolan and Watson, 1999: Table 4.5.

What this analysis suggests is that young men and women who are prone to poverty through non-employment are protected from poverty in shared household settings. The dynamic here is unclear. It may be that younger single adults out of work are less likely to leave family homes because of their 'insulation' from poverty there, or that young adults in their own households return to shared households if they become unemployed. The analysis seems to highlight processes that are common to both men and women. It is arguably true that young unemployed men and women that are 'insulated' from poverty in wider households lose some financial autonomy. However, this does not support the general argument that these wider households contain hidden women's poverty. The sharing of households applies to both genders, and the men and women — and the wider households of which they are part — may simply share resources and financial decision-making. To show that this sharing of households results in hidden women's poverty, it would be necessary to show that the women in these settings 'gave up' their incomes to a household head without sharing in the living standard of the whole household. The data summarised above, however, does not reveal anything about the internal allocation and use of households' incomes.

The impact of living arrangements on poverty is directly relevant to one aspect of the social security system — the unit at which the means test is applied. Historically, in the case of social assistance payments, unattached recipients sharing the family home would have been subject to 'benefit and privilege': the 'value' of the shared accommodation was assessed as income and the amount of their payment reduced accordingly. The Commission on Social Welfare argued in principle against this procedure and made recommendations to have its role in the social security system reduced. The rule no longer applies, except in a very limited way to unemployed people living in the parental home. If the role of policy is to structure the social security system to minimise poverty, then the abolition of the 'benefit and privilege' household means test was beneficial. The system now facilitates recipients to reap the economies of sharing a household and to experience a reduced poverty risk, because this sharing does not result in a reduction in their personal social assistance payment.

WOMEN AND INCOME DISTRIBUTION WITHIN THE FAMILY

These final points about women's poverty redirect the focus inside the family. The particular policy concern is that even in families where the total income is adequate those individual women may not have access to the 'family income'. There is not enough research on this topic in Ireland to give a definitive picture or to link the data on intra-family income distribution to policy trends. However, with the limited data available it is possible to throw some light in an Irish context on the concerns articulated in the feminist literature about inequalities and hidden women's poverty within the family. One study has been undertaken in Ireland of the internal management and distribution of households' incomes (Rottman, 1994). This research was informed by the work of Pahl in the UK, whose research identified a number of 'systems' of management of family income (Pahl, 1983). The Irish study examined the financial circumstances of couples and constructed a classification of households' systems of controlling and managing money: (Rottman, 1994: 40):

- About half of the households have a *Whole Wage System*, entailing management of expenditure by one person, unusually the woman.
- A small proportion of the households (about 5%) operate an *Allowance System* in which the main earner, usually the man makes all the routine purchases — this system confers financial control on the main earner.

- Just under 40% use a *Joint Management System* that requires that some regular purchases be made from an allowance or 'kitty', with the remainder made by the main earner.
- One tenth, usually dual-income households, have an *Independent Management System* in which some routine purchases are the responsibility of both partners from their own incomes and others are made form a joint kitty.

According to the study, 'traditional financial management practices' persist, and 'full-fledged wife management is the most common arrangement and expenditure spheres, when divided, tend to be allocated to fit traditional gender roles' (Rottman, 1994; 43). From a social security point of view it is critical to note that families on low incomes tended to have the more traditional forms of financial management. This left the responsibility for managing a low income with the women: the study showed that this has a negative effect on women's psychological health. Joint responsibility and management was associated with higher incomes. Where the woman as well as the man had an income (even in lower income or social welfare households) it conferred greater control on the woman. However, in dual-income families the wives tended to share more of their earnings than the husbands did. The type of financial management system a family operates has implications for the degree of access individual men and women have to 'personal income': men, in general, had greater access to money for personal expenditure. Significantly, the study highlighted the importance of Child Benefit. Among families in receipt of Child Benefit, 58% of the women had no other direct source of income and a further 10% had a small income that was less than Child Benefit.

A central finding in the study was that there was no 'significant reservoir of poverty hidden among the notional affluence of households'. Equally important, however, the study stressed that 'the presence of gender inequalities is not in dispute'. There are clear inequalities in the division of responsibilities between husbands and wives, the power to make major financial decisions and in the differential access to personal and leisure money (Rottman, 1994: 112).

This picture of inequalities between men and women in marriage refers to the early 1990s. However, it receives some support in later studies (Nolan and Cantillon, 1998; Cantillon, 1997). For example, Nolan and Cantillon compared the extent to which husbands and wives were deprived, and specifically measured and compared spouses' degree of deprivation The findings reveal a moderately greater tendency for wives to be deprived in comparison to their husbands, although there were no clear patterns linking this to family income, social class or other significant household characteristics. However, the gap between husbands and wives was less among couples in which the wife had a direct, personal income. This study too confirmed that there is no pattern of individual women in marriages being 'invisibly' poor by virtue of not having access to the family's resources and standard of living.[12] An important qualification to these findings is that they rely on material collected as part of general poverty and income distribution studies. It may very well be that the detection of women's experience of poverty will require the development of more carefully designed indicators.

FUTURE POLICY

Ireland's social security system is now, formally, more gender neutral. But this is not to deny that there are a whole host of gender-specific issues that require debate and policy action. Many of these issues will arise in later chapters. However, there are a number of strategic issues that will continue to generate debate in the future. The first of these is individualisation. A number of reports and studies have touched on this issue in the last decade or so, and it is useful here to briefly re-state the issues (NESC, 1991; Department of Social Welfare, 1991; McCashin, 1999).

Irish social security is still far from conferring individual rights on all women, married and single, and the question remains as to how this can be achieved and to what extent it should be achieved — there is no consensus on this topic. Some of the key points that are made in this debate are as follows:

- Some women still have adult dependant status is the social security system and do not have direct access to an income.
- Women in the labour market can acquire social insurance rights, but it is equally important to confer rights on women who choose to remain in the home, full-time, including women whose spouses are not benefit recipients.
- The tax system is moving in an individualisation direction and will give all taxpayers, including married women, a right to a full standard rate tax band, and the same policy principles should apply to the tax and benefit systems.
- While the current system formally allows married women to have unemployment payments it does this in the context of a complicated definition of dependency.

There is a wide repertoire of reform possibilities here, and whatever policy changes happen are likely to reflect a mix of different principles and priorities. To give a flavour of the possibilities, two reforms, one limited and one comprehensive, can be briefly outlined. One very limited version of reform has been termed *administrative individualisation*. Quite simply this addresses the specific problem of benefit recipients' spouses not having a legal right to the dependant's portion of the payment. In extreme cases in some low-income families this would result in deprivation for spouses and children. Administrative individualisation would ensure that the 'dependant' would automatically receive the dependant's share of the payment, as of right. A variant on this strategy would include an *increase* in the 'adult dependant' rate so that it equalled the personal rate of payment. But this kind of reform deals with only one kind of problem — the lack of an independent income among dependants of benefit recipients.

A different approach would be to introduce a *Home Care Allowance*. In this scenario, the dependant additions would be abolished and the marriage tax credit (and the Home Carer's tax credit) would also be abolished. Instead, all full-time carers in the home, whether men or women, would directly receive a cash allowance. For poorer spouses this would replace adult dependant additions, and for spouses whose partners are in employment the allowance would replace the current tax subsidies to marriage that are paid through the spouse's wage packet. This kind of reform could be comprehensive and applied to all married couples, or narrow, and applied only where there are children in the household. This proposal could also mean that the separate payments to lone parents could be abolished: men and women could simply choose to be full-time carers of children. People could not combine the allowance with receipt of other payments. The scheme would considerably simplify *both* the tax and benefit systems; it would give all home-based carers direct financial recognition, remove the cumbersome adult dependant additions, and enhance gender equity.

The important point here is not the detail, or cost, or feasibility of either of these variants of individualisation, but the fact that individualisation strategies run along a continuum. There are more limited and more radical versions of the illustrations given here. Recently, the Irish social security system has moved some way along the continuum, but the debate about the next step has only begun and it is likely to shape the future evolution of social security.

The second set of issues has been well documented in recent reports for the National Women's Council of Ireland (Murphy, 2003A, Murphy, 2003B). They point out that in spite of the implementation of the EU's Equality Directive there is a range of very specific changes required to adjust the social security system to the reality of women's lives. These changes span a wide area, and in concluding this chapter it is appropriate to note the important recommendations that Murphy proposes for implementation in the next five years. They include abolition of the limitation introduced in the 1990s, payment of full personal rates of non-contributory pensions to spouses, extension of social insurance to relatives assisting in family businesses and farms, and making social insurance credits for persons working in the home retrospective to 1973.

Finally, Murphy also stressed the need for the unemployment payments system and other parts of social security to adapt to the increased presence of women in the workforce. One of the central points here is the importance of part-time work. Many women (and men) with children have a preference for part-time employment. Currently, the unemployment payments structure recognises part-time work in a restrictive fashion. People who are seeing full-time work and can only find part-time work are in principle eligible for an unemployment payment for the days they are unemployed. However, as Murphy points out, the rules do not allow applicants to search for *part-time* work only. Yet for many women, especially those with children and those attempting to re-enter the labour market, part-time work is the preferred and most realistic option. She therefore recommends that unemployment benefit and unemployment assistance be reformed so that availability for part-time work qualifies applicants for a payment.

Notes

1. In addition to these general works there are a number of studies dealing with Ireland: Byrne and Leonard (1997); Daly (1989); Nolan and Watson (1999); Mahon, (1994); O'Connor (1998).
2. The classic work here is Gary Becker's A *Treatise on the Family* (Becker, 1981).
3. Unusually, the government established a special 'follow-up' committee, the Women's Representative Committee to monitor the implementation of the CSW report. The new committee published two reports (Women's Representative Committee, 1976; Women's Representative Committee, 1978) that monitored the implementation of the Commission's recommendations.
4. A fuller account of the material in this section can be found in Cook and McCashin (1997).
5. The full text of the Directive is reproduced in the detailed case study of the Directive published by the Irish Centre for European law (Whyte, 1988: 78–81).
6. The report was NESC Report no. 37 (1978), *Integrated Approaches to Taxes and Transfers*.
7. The Directive allowed a transition period of six years for governments to devise national legislation.
8. For data for the late 1990s and for other family types see Cook and McCashin (1997). In 1997 applying a gradual reduction rather than a cut off changed the definition of dependency.
9. Married and cohabiting couples are subject to the limitation. But, as the Review Group pointed out, couples are now discriminated against relative to *other two person households*, and this too could be legally challenged.
10. Technically the 1997 and 1998 data are not comparable to the 1994 data, as the data for the two later years classifies the households on the basis of the 'reference person' — the respondent in the sample survey who provides the household and personal data on behalf of all the individuals in the household.
11. The technique used in this analysis is logistic regression. It is used to analyse categorical data such as male/female, poor/not poor.
12. The data on which the Rottman, Nolan and Watson, and Cantillon studies were based were collected before the recent very dramatic increase in labour force participation among married women.

7
Lone Parents

INTRODUCTION

This chapter deals with the specific payments for lone parent families. Currently, the most important of these payments is the One Parent Family Payment, a means-tested payment for lone parent families that can be received by lone mothers or lone fathers. As presently arranged, this payment can be combined with other income. The remainder of this introduction deals with problems of definition and the following section gives a brief review of demographic trends. The subsequent section reviews the fundamental policy rationale in this area and this is followed by an account of the early emergence and later development of provisions for lone mothers. The final two sections deal with income poverty among lone mothers and with future policy.

Discussion about this aspect of social security is bedevilled by problems of definition and terminology. In social policy research and public debate the terms 'single parent family', 'one parent family', 'fatherless family' and 'lone parent family' are all used. 'Lone parent family' is the term used here. The adjective 'single' is inappropriate as it invites confusion with 'single' marital status, and the descriptions 'one parent' and 'fatherless' simply ignore the fact that, biologically, children have two parents. 'Lone' is neutral with respect to marital status, it suggests a contrast with the more usual situation of the two-parent family, and it invokes the actual experience of many women in particular — having the sole or prime responsibility for their children in separate households for very extended periods of time, in the absence of a spouse or partner.

The term 'lone parents', taken literally, would describe a significant diversity of households and families. For example, it would encompass an elderly widow living alone with an adult son or daughter; a teenage, unmarried woman (or man) living with and caring for her (his) child; an adult mother or father separated or divorced with custody of the children. In these examples of lone parenthood the sources of the 'lone-ness' are the death of a husband, the absence of a partner and the breakdown of a marriage respectively. Different stages of the life-cycle are also represented here: the widow is in the later stages and does not have young

164

dependent children; the unmarried parent, however, is in the early stage of the family life cycle in terms of her own age and in terms of child dependency. This diversity among 'lone parents' has implications for social security, as lone parents' needs, resources and constraints vary.

An elderly widow may own her own home outright if she is an owner-occupier; she may be entitled to a contributory widow's pension which is at the more adequate end of the range of social security payments and she may also have some savings or an occupational pension related to her late husband's employment. In contrast, a young unmarried mother may not have had an opportunity to acquire independent accommodation, or to accumulate savings, and unless she has access to affordable child care she will be constrained from working full-time and will therefore rely on the social security system as her main source of income. While the father of her child is legally obliged to financially support the child, he has no legal obligation in respect of the mother. Turning to the hypothetical separated parent, s/he is likely to be in the expensive phase of the life cycle, paying for independent housing and supporting school-going children. S/he too faces barriers in attempting to work. The family's income in this situation will depend on whether maintenance is being paid — very little or no maintenance will mean relying on a social security payment.

Given this diversity, it is important to offer a definition of lone parent that can provide a focus for this chapter. O'Higgins' (1987) formulation is adopted here:

> In terms of the primary public policy concerns about lone parent families, a useful definition would require that the parent be non-cohabiting, while the children be below a conventional age of labour market and financial independence (e.g. 16 or 18) with other children included if they are still in full time education, are financially dependent and have their residence in the family home.

This definition clarifies the composition of the category 'lone parents'. Clearly, it excludes older adults with non-dependent adult children, and it excludes those unmarried parents or separated spouses cohabiting with partners. It is important to note that this definition is based on *family units*, i.e. units comprising a parent and one or more dependent children no matter what their *household* circumstances are. Thus, an unmarried woman and her child living with the child's grandparents are defined as a (separate) family unit. It should also be noted that the overwhelming majority of lone parents in Ireland are in fact women and it is acceptable, therefore, in the context of this chapter, to use the terms 'lone parent' and 'lone mother' interchangeably.

The definition of lone parents clearly has implications for their enumeration and for the terms in which lone parenthood is discussed politically. Obviously, the size of the lone parent population will differ according to the definition adopted, and perceptions of the size of the lone parent population are related to policy controversies about the nature, causes and effects of lone parenthood. For example, if too loose a definition is applied it will convey a picture of lone parenthood as comprising a large share of the family population, and tending to support a perception that the scale of lone parenthood has undermined 'the family'. Therefore, definitions and descriptions of lone parents are relevant to wider debates about the family.

LONE PARENTS: DEMOGRAPHIC TRENDS

Before turning to social security policy, the key demographic trends in relation to lone parenthood should be noted. Lone parenthood is not a new phenomenon in Ireland, as Fahey and Russell (2001) have pointed out. The Census of 1926 recorded that 12% of children under 15 years of age had lost one or both parents: as the details below show, this figure is remarkably close to the proportion of children living in lone parent families in the mid-1990s. However, the cause of the loss of one parent in the 1920s was premature death. Over time, as life expectancy rose, this form of lone parenthood diminished and new sources of lone parenthood emerged. Therefore, the first significant demographic change to note is the shift away from widowhood as the route into lone parenthood. In Ireland and internationally non-marital births and marital breakdown have replaced widowhood as the route into lone parenthood.

Non-marital births have risen continuously since the early 1960s in numerical terms and as a proportion of all births. In 1961 non-marital births comprised 1.7 % of all births and by 2002 the figure had reached 31%. It is important to note the conceptual distinction between non-marital *births* and non-marital *lone parenthood*. The figure for non-marital births includes births to non-marital couples — to parents, in other words, that are not 'lone' parents in the terms applied here. Also, many parents will decide to marry or cohabit in the period immediately after a non-marital birth. Furthermore, the route from non-marital birth to lone parenthood historically has been severed by adoption, with very high proportions of non-marital mothers having their babies adopted. In 1971, for example, the ratio of adoptions to non-marital births was 71/100, and as adoptions declined sharply in subsequent decades the ratio fell dramatically, and the link between non-marital births and (non-marital) lone parent families became stronger. Non-marital births and (non-marital) lone parenthood are therefore not coterminous: the non-marital births figure represents the size of the potential inflow to (non-marital) lone parenthood. Teenage births are one important aspect of non-marital births, as these parents are more vulnerable socially. Births to non-marital women under 20 rose rapidly during the 1970s and 1980s, but the increase in the rate of non-marital births stabilised in the early 1990s. In 1981 the rate per 1,000 (unmarried women under 20) was 9.7, it reached 14.5 in 1991 and 17.9 in 2002.

Marital breakdown is the second demographic factor associated with the formation of lone parent families. Ireland experienced a sharp upward trend in marital breakdown (McCashin, 1993; Fahey and Russell, 2001). In 1979 the number of separated persons was 6.1 per 1,000 married persons, by 1997 this figure had reached almost 60 and in 2002 it was 92. As with the non-marital births data, the link between data on the numbers of separated persons and the formation of lone parent families is complex. The figure for the stock of separated persons includes separated people with and without children, and also includes those that are separated/divorced and living in a new relationship. Qualifications aside, the net effect of the three key demographic trends — the fall in widowhood, the rise in non-marital births, and the increase in marital breakdown — has been an increase in the number of lone parent families (as defined above), as Table 7.1 shows.

The number of lone parent families has grown continuously in recent years, both in absolute terms and as a share of all families: the share doubled over the decade 1991–2001 and reached 20% in 2001. These data adopt a restricted concept of child dependency — an age cut-off of 15 for children. If a higher age

Table 7.1: Trends in the Numbers and Incidence of Lone Parent Families (Families with one or more children under 15) 1989–2001

Year	Families (000s)	Lone Parents (000s)	% Change	Lone Parent Families as % of All Families
1989	432.55	39.5	–	9.1
1990	422.10	37.4	–5.3	8.9
1991	423.00	41.4	10.7	9.8
1992	433.40	44.6	7.7	10.3
1993	431.55	46.0	3.1	10.7
1994	447.30	47.2	2.6	10.6
1995	424.10	49.8	5.5	11.7
1996	419.85	52.8	6.0	12.6
1997	424.10	58.1	10.0	13.7
1998	439.70	71.8	23.5	16.3
1999	449.30	78.6	9.5	17.5
2000	448.80	83.2	5.8	18.5
2001	450.20	90.0	8.2	20.0
2002	452.70	97.0	7.8	21.4

Source: Fahey and Russell, (2001) based on Labour Force Survey data and author's calculations based on Quarterly National Household Surveys. Data for 2002 are estimated.

were adopted, it would affect the measure of the size of the lone parent population and its share in the total.[1]

Before turning to the link between lone parenthood and social security some of the key characteristics of the lone parent population should be noted. In relation to their marital status and family circumstances, it is unclear what proportion is separated/divorced, unmarried or widowed: this is because of technical limitations on the Census and Labour Force Survey data. Fahey and Russell's (2001) analysis of the available data suggests that among lone parents with children under 18 about 55% are never married, about 30% are separated or divorced and the balance widowed. Taking the lone parent population as a whole, about 60% of them are economically active, according to the CSO's Quarterly National Household Survey for (December-February) 2001, and labour force participation rates are higher for never married mothers and separated mothers than for married mothers. There is evidence that the socio-economic profile of lone parents is weaker than that of the general population. McCashin's (1997) analysis of Labour Force Survey data for 1995 and Fahey and Russell's (2001) analysis of the corresponding 1997 data both show that the educational and occupational status of lone mothers is lower than that of married mothers, with never-married mothers experiencing the greatest risk of low educational attainment. For example, among women aged 20–24, over 50% of never-married mothers had an educational qualification at Junior Certificate level or lower, whereas the figure for married mothers was 27%: conversely, the rate of third-level attainment was far higher among married than never-married mothers.

Finally, an important demographic aspect of lone parenthood that relates to social security is the *duration* of lone parenthood. It is difficult to offer any definitive data on this topic, but it is important to note that the increasing number of lone parent families in the population recorded above does not reveal anything about the *flows* into and out of lone parenthood. In Table 7.1 above the increase in the number of lone parent families from 2000 to 2001 was about 7,000. This figure is compatible with a range of possible combinations of inflow to, and outflow from lone parenthood. For example, the net change of 7,000 from 2000 to 2001 might result from zero lone parents departing from lone parenthood (through marriage, cohabitation, departure of children, or graduation of children out of dependency) and an inflow of 7,000 lone parents. Alternatively, it could result from an inflow of 10,000 offset by an inflow of 17,000, or any other combination of flows 'in' and 'out' that give rise to a net increase of 7,000. From a policy perspective it would be important to quantify how long different categories of lone parent remain in that status, as this has important implications for the social security system. There is tentative evidence from the Living in Ireland survey that the rate of departure from lone parenthood to marriage/cohabitation is low in Ireland: 91% of the lone parents interviewed in 1994 were still lone parents when re-interviewed after one year (Fahey and Russell, 2001: 37).

It is difficult to offer exact comparisons of the extent of lone parenthood in Ireland and other countries (Bradshaw *et al*, 1996). In terms of the share of lone parent families in the population, Ireland is in the middle range among European countries, with the UK at the top end of the range and the southern Mediterranean countries at the bottom. Most European countries as well as the USA, Canada, Australia and New Zealand have experienced a long-term trend of a growing number of lone parent families.

The number of lone parents in receipt of social security payments has been growing rapidly, reflecting the general trends outlined above.[2] Table 7.2 and Figure 7.1 summarise the trend and show that the number of recipients more than doubled in each of the two decades, and grew over the whole period at an annual average rate of 7.4%. The trend summarised in Table 7.2 reflects underlying social and demographic changes, as well as policy changes that have widened the scope of the recipient population.

Figure 7.1: Lone Parent Social Security recipients (000s), 1981–2002

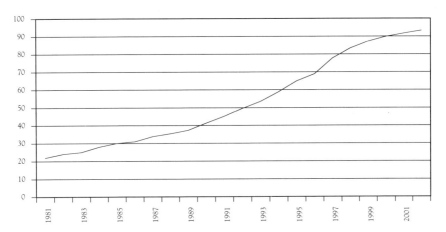

Source: Department of Social and Family Affairs

LONE PARENTS AND SOCIAL SECURITY: POLICY RATIONALE

The rationale for social security benefits relates to the way Beveridge incorporated women in his social security plan, adopted in attenuated form in Ireland. This was outlined in Chapter Six. Marriage was central to the Beveridge system and the construction of lone mothers' social security treatment hinged on the central role he gave to married women's dependence on their husbands (Millar, 1989: 22–32; Brown, 1989: 25–47). In relation to widows first,

Table 7.2: Lone parent Families in Receipt of Social Security in Ireland, 1981–2002

Year	Number (000s)	% Change
1981	21.88	–
1991	45.12	106.2
2001	91.98	103.8
2002	93.26	1.4
Annual Average % change 1981–2002	6.9	–

Source: Statistical Information on Social Welfare Services, Department of Social, Community and Family Affairs, various years.
Notes: The figures for 1981 to 1983 inclusive are estimated. The data incorporate the separate benefits and allowances that refer to specific categories of recipient such as widows, unmarried mothers, and deserted wives.

Beveridge's plan was devised at a time when widows' pensions were already in place and in the Beveridge scheme widows' pensions were incorporated in the new national system of social insurance. The logic here was that in a social insurance system a widow's pension replaced the maintenance from a husband that marriage conferred. In the UK, widows' social insurance pensions had been introduced in 1925 for widows with and without children, and under these arrangements widows were not required to seek employment. Beveridge argued, however, that childless widows should work and support themselves, bluntly asserting that 'There is no reason why a childless widow should get a pension for life: if she is able to work, she should work' (Beveridge, 1942: 64). In the event, Beveridge's argument was not adopted and widows' pensions were included in the general national insurance system.

Turning to separation and marriage breakdown, Beveridge drew an analogy between the risks for married women of separation and of widowhood: both give rise to a loss of maintenance from a spouse. In Beveridge's (1942: 134) terms: 'Divorce, legal separation, desertion and voluntary separation may cause needs similar to those caused by widowhood'. Beveridge reasoned that from a husband's point of view, separation or desertion were not insurable risks (in contrast to unemployment for example), as he could not insure himself against events that occur only through his fault or with his agreement, and if they occur through the 'fault or the consent of the wife' she should not receive an insurance benefit. From the wife's stance, however, loss of 'her maintenance as a housewife without her consent and not through her fault' is a risk and, accordingly, may create an entitlement to social insurance. The net implication of this analysis was a proposal to distinguish between separated women on the basis of whether or not they were at fault, and to treat the 'no fault' cases on the same basis as widows.

This proposal to allow a category of separated women entitlement to an insurance benefit was not implemented. Objections raised to this proposal foreshadowed later debates and complexities, as Brown (1989: 40–43) has shown. How would 'fault' be determined? What if a separation did not result in lost maintenance — a husband at fault might, after all, pay some maintenance, or pay it irregularly? Would this affect the amount of insurance benefit, or entitlement to it? If so, then the 'benefit' would become more like a means-tested allowance. And if a separated woman could become entitled to a benefit without any regard to her spouse's maintenance responsibilities, would this undermine marriage? In the face of these dilemmas separated women were not included in National Insurance, and they were dealt with by National Assistance.

Unmarried women with children received very little attention in the Beveridge Report, and they were left to be dealt with under National Assistance also (Brown, 1989: 43–47). In the Beveridge scheme the unmarried mother in employment would be entitled (as an insurance contributor) to benefit in the event of sickness and unemployment, and could also become entitled to the suite of maternity provisions (Maternity Grant, Maternity Allowance and Attendance Allowance) designed with the married woman in mind. However, there was never any question of providing a national insurance benefit for the unmarried woman with a child not in work because she was caring for her child. The Beveridge system was built on the twin pillars of employment-based contributions and marriage: an unmarried woman out of the labour force and caring for her child was excluded on both these grounds. However, the political debate about these issues had the effect of highlighting the needs of unmarried women with children and creating wider acceptance of their need for national assistance.

The treatment of the various categories of lone parent in the Beveridge report and the subsequent debates about them highlighted the three key issues around which a rationale for social security provision might be constructed. First, should widows be treated differently to other categories of lone parent — by integrating them into the insurance benefits system and consigning other lone parents to means-tested assistance? Second, since other categories of working-age claimant with children (the unemployed, the short-term sick, for example) are required to be available for work should this condition apply also to lone parents? Third, a non-widowed lone mother has a person *outside* the family from whom she might receive financial support — the absent, errant father. But it is not clear to what extent, and how, income from this source should be combined with social security in constructing the incomes of lone mother families.

THE EMERGENCE OF SOCIAL SECURITY FOR LONE PARENTS IN IRELAND

The first official deliberations about lone parent social security provisions after political independence were contained in the *Report of the Commission on the Relief of the Sick and Destitute Poor* (1928). The (O'Connor) Commission was emphatic in its critique of some aspects of the Poor Law and made very clear (although very general) recommendations that encompassed the various categories of lone mother. In relation to widows, the Commission documented the number of widows (and their children) in receipt of Outdoor Relief under the Poor Law and argued for their removal from this 'altogether inadequate' system. It argued firmly in favour of Mothers' Pensions for both widows *and deserted* mothers, referring to the existence of such pensions in some states in the USA: 'We are in favour of a Scheme of Mothers' Pensions payable by the State' (O'Connor, 1928: 57). Mothers Pensions were defined as 'maintenance grants in respect of children under a fixed age to a widowed or deserted mother who has not the means to feed, clothe and house her children adequately'. The Commission envisaged the pension as means-tested and payable until the children reached wage-earning age. Also, the pension would obviate the necessity for and the choice to work outside the home: 'where the children are very young and require constant care and attention the mother is not allowed to work outside her own home'. Pensions were not introduced until 1935 — and then for widows but not deserted wives.

In relation to unmarried mothers, the nineteenth century Poor Law had bequeathed a legacy of institutionalisation of unmarried mothers and their children in workhouses, followed by the boarding out of the children. The 1906 official inquiry on the Poor Law in Ireland pointed to the unsuitability of general Poor Law workhouses and recommended the sub-division of unmarried pregnant women into different types of institutions (Vice Regal Commission, 1906). The sub-division it recommended was moral: on the first 'lapse' women should be sent to special institutions run by religious or philanthropic bodies, and women on their second pregnancy should be contained in one special workhouse in Dublin. In the period between the Poor Law report and the O'Connor Commission the phenomenon of unmarried women with children commanded increasing attention. On the one hand, new 'special institutions' were established by religious orders, becoming known as Mother and Baby homes, and, on the other, the religious and political authorities debated the 'problem' of unmarried motherhood. Sir Joseph Glynn, chairman of the Irish Insurance Commissioners 1911–1933 — later to be a member of the O'Connor committee and later still chairman of a committee dealing with widows' pensions — published a proposal in 1921 setting out a specific model of a 'hostel' type system in which the women would live and work (Glynn, 1921). A clerical contributor to the debate defended the emerging system of intervention by religious organisations that led to the confinement of women in the growing number of special institutions established by religious orders (Sagart, 1922).

The terms of this debate were wholly outside the remit of social security and revolved around the question of *how* to implement a policy of institutionalisation. There was also a strong undercurrent of religious and denominational tension. The 'problem' of unmarried mothers was not only a general moral problem but, for many, a *specific* moral problem of how to restore Catholic unmarried mothers to Catholic virtue: 'This whole subject is of extreme importance, concerning as it does the preservation of a strict standard of moral life in the nation, and the saving from utter ruin of the faith and morality of so many Catholic girls'(Sagart, 1921). Accordingly, for the Catholic authorities, the prime objective was to prevent Catholic girls from being 'rescued' and then proselytised by Protestant charities. This denominational layer to the debate helped to reinforce the separation of unmarried motherhood from wider debates about poverty and the development of social security.

The O'Connor committee's deliberations reflected this moral preference for punitive institutionalisation. Its report devoted a chapter to this topic, starting from its analysis of the large numbers of unmarried mothers (and children) institutionalised in workhouses and county homes (O'Connor, 1928: 68–74). In the late 1920s there were about 1,000 unmarried mothers in institutions, over 700 of these in county homes and former workhouses. The Commission classified unmarried mothers as either 'amenable to reform' or 'less hopeful cases' and proposed that the Boards of Health be allowed discretion in dealing with the first category through the existing Rescue Societies and voluntary organisations. It also recommended that special institutions be established for the second category and for all women that could not be provided for by voluntary organisations. Thereafter, provision reflected this moral framework and during the subsequent three decades unmarried mothers either emigrated or entered an institution, their children being 'boarded out' or adopted. The number of special institutions grew and by the early 1950s there were significantly more women and children in these institutions compared with the County Homes.

Of these three categories of lone mother — widows, deserted wives and unmarried mothers, widows were the first to be assigned a social security payment. The De Valera government established the Committee of Inquiry into Widows' and Orphans' Pensions in 1932 (Glynn, 1933). Sir Joseph Glynn who had served on the Poor Law commission in the 1920s chaired the Commission. It reported in 1933, offering a majority and a minority report. The majority of the commission favoured a contributory social insurance system in principle, but then argued for a non-contributory pension because of the practical limitations of an insurance approach and the low level of coverage that would arise given the limited scope of social insurance. Recognising the potential costs of this approach, it suggested the limitation of pensions to *widowed mothers* in the first instance and the gradual extension of the scheme over time to all widows subject to a means test. The minority report was extremely critical of the majority reasoning, partly on the grounds that a means-tested approach would be a disincentive: 'In a non-contributory scheme not only is thrift not encouraged but it is directly discouraged.' (Glynn, 1933: 43) The minority also questioned the logic of having a separate means-tested payment for poor widows, arguing that such separate provision implied that widows were more deserving than other groups.

In the event, the government introduced *both* an assistance scheme and a contributory widow's pension. The insurance pension applied to those insured under the National Health Insurance code and to permanent employees of central and local government (and some other bodies). However, the means-tested pension was a hybrid of a widow's pension and a widowed *mother's* pension. To be eligible, a widow was required to be at least sixty years of age, or if under that age to have at least one dependent child under fourteen: the age barrier was lowered to fifty-five in 1937 (and lowered again in 1948 and subsequently).

The cumulative effect of these developments was that by the end of the 1940s the only form of lone parenthood commanding a social security response was widowhood. This remained the case after the developments arising from the 1949 White Paper and the 1952 legislation. In striking contrast to the Beveridge report, the White Paper did not even mention deserted/separated wives or unmarried mothers. Nor is there any evidence in the detailed accounts of the 1948–1952 developments that these topics were raised in the drafting of the White Paper or in the debates on the legislation (Cook, 1990; Cousins, 2003; McCullagh, 1998). The White Paper described the provisions for widows as they had evolved from the Glynn committee in the 1930s and proposed the incorporation of the widows' contributory and non-contributory pensions into the proposed national system: the 1952 legislation gave effect to this recommendation. Thus, during the formation of the national social security system, widowhood was incorporated as one the 'risks' to be covered while other lone parents remained invisible.

Unmarried mothers were referred to, however, in a different context at this time. While the institutionalisation of unmarried mothers was well established by the 1950s, the Commission on Emigration alluded to unmarried mothers as a by-product of its concern with emigration, referring to 'the emigration of many unmarried mothers who find it preferable, for one reason or another, to emigrate rather than face all the circumstances of an illegitimate pregnancy and confinement in this country' (Commission on Emigration, 1956: 102). The Commission invited the Department of Health to describe the arrangements for the care of unmarried mothers and published the Department's memorandum as an appendix to its report (Commisssion on Emigration, 1956: 263–265). This short document was a candid statement of official policy and practice and it outlines the administrative framework — the 1939 Public Assistance Act — underpinning the invisibility of unmarried mothers.

This legislation reframed the remaining elements of the nineteenth century Poor Law and integrated it into the local authority-based system of Public Assistance Authorities. Under the legislation the authorities were obliged to provide to persons eligible for public assistance 'such public assistance as shall appear to them to be necessary or proper in each particular case'. The Department of Health pointed out that the services provided included 'accommodation for unmarried mothers and illegitimate children' and the cost of maintenance of illegitimate children in institutions. Also, the memorandum described the *modus operandi* of this system. Local authorities 'endeavour to ensure the most favourable conditions for the moral and social rehabilitation' of the mothers. The mothers are placed in institutions 'under the care of members of religious authorities' from which the children are boarded out at the age of two. This results 'in a stay of two years in an institution for the majority of the mothers'. However, the Department's memo stated that there was 'no general rule to determine the length of stay, which varies with the requirements of individual mothers as assessed by the authorities of the institution in which they are accommodated. There are no legal powers to restrain an unmarried mother from leaving with her child' (Commission on Emigration, 1956: 264).

Neither the Commission proper nor the Department of Health adverted to any possible changes to this system, or to the role that social assistance might play in meeting the welfare needs of unmarried mothers The 1939 Act in principle allowed the authorities to pay direct financial assistance to unmarried mothers, but this practice did not emerge until much later when the need for income maintenance for lone mothers came on to the political agenda.

From the early 1950s until 1970 there were no significant developments — although provision for widows improved continuously, with the age cut-off for childless widows being successively reduced and improvements made in respect of child dependant additions. Then, during the three year period 1970–1973, three specific social security payments were introduced: first, in 1970 a means-tested allowance for *deserted* wives, then, in 1973, a corresponding benefit, Deserted Wife's Benefit, and a third, separate means-tested allowance for unmarried mothers. There has been no detailed research on either the rationale for the design of these new provisions or the political dynamic that led to this flurry of innovation. However, in relation to the design of the provisions a number of points can be made. Deserted wives were treated in an analogous way to widows. For the (means-tested) Deserted Wives Allowance the structure of the means test and the gradation of the allowance in relation to means were the same, and for the Deserted Wife's Benefit the contribution requirements were similar. When first introduced, the Deserted Wife's Allowance was effectively for *deserted mothers* in the case of younger women. Women under 50 were ineligible unless they had at least one dependent child: this age cut-off was reduced to 40 in 1974.

To define desertion three criteria were applied (Commission on Social Welfare, 1986:358–360): First, a woman's husband must have left her and the family home. Second, she must have made 'reasonable efforts' to trace her spouse and to obtain maintenance from him. Third, she must not be in receipt of maintenance from him — in practice, this meant that if she received maintenance greater than the relevant rate of (long-term) unemployment assistance she was considered to be 'maintained'.

To be eligible for a desertion payment a woman had to meet the criteria for at least three months (originally set at six months). All of this was an attempt to put into practise Beveridge's 'no fault' concept. One consequence of this attempt was that Ireland, uniquely, now had a social insurance benefit in relation to one form of marital breakdown.

Implicitly, these new payments assumed that lone mothers were out of the labour market. The means tests gave recipients little scope to undertake paid work in combination with benefit receipt, as the amount of income a recipient could have from earnings without the payment being reduced was miniscule. This combination of provisions put Ireland's developing social security regime for lone parents into an approach clearly recognisable in the international literature (Kammerman and Kahn, 1989; Millar, 1989; Brown, 1989). One group of countries focused on co-ordinated labour market and family policies to achieve greater *gender equity* as an overall policy strategy — Sweden best exemplified this strategy. A second group of countries pursued what Kamerman and Kahn (1989) described as a *universal young child strategy*, the core of which is general (and generous) provision for all families with children (in family allowances, tax allowances, housing benefits and so on). Third, a group of countries followed a policy of *supporting poor lone mothers at home*. Ireland's suite of payments for lone parents was unambiguously in this category. The allowances did not facilitate combining care of children and paid work, and the payment structure was embedded in a wider context of non-participation in paid work among mothers in general, and gender discrimination against women in social security, taxation and employment.

It is difficult to account for the extent and type of policy change that happened, in the absence of historical work in this area. Many of the developments in the wider system of social security in the 1970s formed part of the general programme of social development. In 1969, the *Third Programme for Economic and Social Development*, for instance, explicitly mentioned many of the policy changes that materialised in the following decade, but change in this aspect of social security was not one of them. The Commission on the Status of Women published its report in 1972, and while its analysis and recommendations influenced many aspects of the treatment of women in social security — as Chapter Six showed — there is little convergence between its report and the specific initiatives that were taken affecting lone mothers. For example, the Commission's views about widows' payments and their link to employment echoed Beveridge's: young widowed women should be available for employment and there should be some age or dependency restrictions on payments to widows. This strategy was not adopted. In relation to deserted and separated women, the Deserted Wife's Allowance had already been in place for two years and the Commission (Commission on the Status of Women, 1972: 152) merely noted it as a 'most welcome development', while calling for the initial period of desertion determining eligibility (six months) to be administered on a discretionary basis. The Commission did not recommend — or mention — the type of insurance benefit for deserted wives that was introduced one year later.

One area of policy in which the new provisions coincided to some degree with the Commission's recommendations concerns unmarried mothers. The commission recommended the introduction of an allowance for this category of lone mother. However, it specified that it should be for a period of 'not less than one year after the birth of the child', arguing that the allowance was for the unmarried mother who keeps her child and who needs financial support 'particularly when the child is very young and she cannot resume employment' (Commission on the Status of Women, 1972: 153). This implies that the Commission did not envisage that unmarried mothers should remain out of the labour market on a *permanent* basis. In the event, the allowance was structured so that recipients could receive the payment as long as they had dependent children.

It is more likely that the policy changes were *ad hoc* responses to changing conditions and popular demands, as lone parents became increasingly visible in the 1960s. The popular media had begun to highlight the issue of unmarried mothers at this time and, in particular, the pattern of many women emigrating to the UK and relying on the support of the social services there. Publicity about this reached a highpoint in 1964 with the publication of a widely cited series of articles in the *Irish Times* by a distinguished journalist (Viney, 1964). These articles had an enormous public impact and their influence was reinforced by the changing practices of both the British social services and the Catholic Protection and Rescue Societies. As Viney and others documented, the scale of emigration of young pregnant women was such that in London the authorities constructed a special administrative category, PFI (pregnant from Ireland), in their annual reports on child care (Viney, 1964; Garrett, 2000).

The London Boroughs and the protection and rescue societies significantly increased their emphasis on repatriation at this time. The societies were acutely aware of the fear of long-term institutionalisation that impelled the women to emigrate, and they had also been critical of the practice of long-term incarceration of women in institutions. Their work in the 1960s shows the beginnings of an awareness of the need for some alternative to either emigration or the Mother and Baby Home. Unmarried mothers were therefore becoming visible. Then, abortion became legal in England in 1967. The Catholic Protection and Rescue Societies — as Garrett (2000: 340) has shown — viewed this development with alarm, referring to abortion as a 'temptation of a very serious nature before the distraught unmarried mother'. The availability of abortion created a more urgent context in which the voluntary and statutory services sought to widen the options available to a pregnant unmarried mother — beyond the Mother and Baby Home, emigration or abortion — to include support for the mother to keep her baby and to live independently. This can be gleaned from the content of the first specific policy document on unmarried mothers, *The Unmarried Mother in the Irish Community*, published one year before the introduction of the Unmarried Mother's Allowance (Kilkenny Social Services, 1972).

The 1972 document (a brief document of only sixty five pages) reported the proceedings of a conference about unmarried mothers. This event was held against the background of the Council of Europe's declaration of 1970 on the Social Protection of Unmarried Mothers and was convened by a range of religious, voluntary and professional workers. The Council of Europe (of which Ireland was a member) had spelt out a wide range of policies that member governments should implement, spanning health care, vocational training, access to housing, and so on. The Kilkenny conference reviewed the Irish provisions in the light of the Council of Europe statement and set out a broad agenda of service provision, broadly against a backdrop in which institutionalisation was no longer deemed acceptable. As did the Council of Europe document, the Kilkenny document proposed initiatives across a wide range of services.

This is where the first public, documented references to social security provisions for unmarried mothers can be found. These references were not very specific and alluded to 'economic support during the pregnancy' and to the principle that 'there must be no discrimination in the matter of financial benefits to the unmarried mother'. The only reference to the exact manner in which unmarried mothers might be financially supported is a pointed comment on the unsuitability of social insurance to meet unmarried mothers' needs: 'It is clear that a mother and child must not go unsupported because the appropriate number of stamps on the insurance card have not been accumulated' (Kilkenny Social Services, 1972:47–48). In hindsight, it is interesting that policy developments were fragmented: three separate payments were introduced in a three-year period. The Kilkenny document questioned whether unmarried mothers should be dealt with 'apart from other women with similar problems' and pointed out that 'deserted and unsupported wives, widows, the wives of prisoners are all attempting to bring up children on their own' (Kilkenny Social Services, 1972: 52). However, dealing with all lone mothers as one category for social security purposes was an option that was not seriously considered.

THE DEVELOPMENT OF SOCIAL SECURITY FOR LONE PARENTS

From 1974 to 1989 provisions for lone parents gradually became more integrated, culminating in the introduction of the Lone Parent Allowance. This scheme integrated the separate allowances in respect of unmarried mothers into one payment and gave male lone parents access to a social security payment. (The Deserted Wife's Benefit was retained). These changes were due to a number of factors. In the first instance, the *EC Directive on the Equal Treatment of Men and Women* (see Chapter Six) required that provisions for lone parents allow men and women equal access to a payment. Second, desertion provision proved more problematic in practice than was anticipated. From the introduction of the original payments, 'deserted' women were obliged to wait a period of three months during which they had no support from their spouse before they could become eligible for a payment. This forced women into poverty. Also, the distinction between 'desertion' and 'voluntary separation' proved elusive. For example, it became necessary to invoke the notion of 'constructive desertion' to make a woman leaving a violent spouse eligible for a payment even though her spouse had not 'deserted' her.

Introducing the notion of constructive desertion was an acknowledgement that it was difficult in a social security context to make refined assessments of 'desertion', 'constructive desertion' and 'voluntary separation'. The Commission on Social Welfare's background paper on recipients' experiences of social assistance showed the impact on applicants of the scheme (O'Connor, Hearn and Walsh, 1986: 119–140). Applicants were obliged to discuss very personal matters with administrators who needed to establish the fact of 'desertion'. Decisions were based were based not only on tests of means but also assessments of marital history, and proof that the woman had attempted to obtain maintenance. All of this slowed up the administrative process, leading to high levels of refusal, high levels of appeal against refusals and long delays before successful applicants received the Deserted Wife's Allowance: about 70% of applicants waited four months or longer for a decision (O'Connor, Hearne and Walsh, 1986: 122). The Commission on Social Welfare (1986: 358–361) set out the principles that shaped the Lone Parent Allowance — gender neutrality, and the inclusion of voluntary, 'non-desertion' forms of marital breakdown.

The 1989 reform was accompanied by administrative and legal changes in the way spouse's maintenance obligations were dealt with. From this point onwards, the maintenance obligations on parents in both family law and social security law were broadly convergent and differentiated by marital status. In cases of separation (and later divorce) spouses have maintenance obligations towards each other and to their children, while in cases of non-marital parents the obligation extends only to children. Research by Ward had shown the low level of maintenance awarded to spouses in the courts under the Family Law Maintenance Act of 1976 — many awards were at a level less than state social security payments. In line with the international experience, Ward also showed a very low level of compliance with court orders, and evidence later recorded in the official review of the One Parent Family Payment indicated that maintenance was being paid in respect of 30% and 19% of married and unmarried recipients respectively (Department of Social Community and Family Affairs, 2000: 107–108). Notwithstanding the ineffectiveness of judicial maintenance, women were obliged to make 'reasonable efforts' to obtain maintenance, their entitlement to payments depended on proof of these efforts, and the amount of a payment was conditional on the level of maintenance.

The consolidation of payments begun in 1989 was completed in 1997 with the introduction of the One Parent Family Payment: this integrated the existing schemes and abolished the Deserted Wife's Benefit (for new applicants). At this juncture also the arrangements linking the OPF means-test and maintenance payments were reformed. These arrangements are based on the 'liable relative' principle — that the spouses of lone parent recipients (and the fathers of unmarried recipients' children) of social security payments are liable to contribute to the cost of the social security payment.[3] The legislation was first amended in 1996 so that adequate maintenance was defined as the appropriate level of lone parent payment: in effect, an applicant being adequately maintained would not be eligible for a payment on grounds of means. In cases of separation/divorce this means that a liable relative may be required to contribute up to the full amount of OPF being paid, whereas in non-marital cases only child maintenance arises and there is a specific ceiling on the contribution the parent may be asked to make.

Between 1996 and 2001 important changes were made to the treatment of maintenance and to the means test generally. First, until 1999 the assessment of a liable relative's capacity to pay was done on an administrative basis and in that year this was put on a formal basis. These regulations allow a liable relative an amount in respect of housing costs, additional amounts for personal costs and costs arising from dependent children resident with the liable relative, and mortgage/rent payments to financial institutions in respect of the 'original' family home where it is occupied by a former spouse. Second, the means test for OPFP recipients was also modified. Currently, housing costs up to a maximum of €95 per week are allowed as an offset against any maintenance, and half of the balance of the maintenance above the amount allowed for housing costs is counted as means. This change reflected the recommendation in the review of OFP that recipients should have 'an incentive to pursue maintenance by allowing them to retain at least 50% of any maintenance received' (Department of Social Community and Family Affairs, 2000: 121). In relation to earnings, the first €146.50 per week is not counted as means, and half of the amount between that figure and €293 per week is counted.

Strategically, lone parents' social security provisions rested on traditional assumptions about mothers' non-participation in the labour market. This strategy was fundamentally altered in the 1990s. In policy terms, lone parents henceforth were considered workers as much as mothers, and the design of social security payments (and related provisions) were increasingly geared to facilitating employment. As the details of the current means test suggest, lone parents can now combine a relatively significant element of earnings with receipt of the OPFP payment.

This change in the OPF was embedded in a wider series of changes that cumulatively amounted to a strategy of labour market participation. Notably, the active labour market measures to deal with unemployment that were developed in the 1980s and extended in the 1990s (see Chapter Eight) were widened to include lone parents. Most significantly, the Community Employment scheme was widely taken up by lone parents.[4] In 2000, for example, the weekly number of lone parent recipients on CE was just under 10,000, 27% of all participants, and during that year over 14,000 commenced participation, almost 30% of 'starts' on the scheme. CE facilitated part-time involvement — very often in a recipient's local community, allowing recipients to retain their full OPF while receiving a 'wage', and in some schemes childcare as well as training was provided. CE participants have also been allowed (within limits) to retain secondary benefits such as medical card entitlement and rent supplement.[5]

These developments took place against a background of a growing number of locally based social inclusion programmes focused on lone parents and low income women in general. Community-based, lone parent organisations increased in number during the 1990s, and aside from direct labour market measures a whole host of community development, educational and social inclusion projects emerged, many with state funding. For example, local educational authorities developed programmes for young mothers, the EC's NOW (New Opportunities for Women) programme instigated local training and education initiatives for low income women, the Department of Health established a Teen Parents Support Initiative offering social and family support to teenage mothers, the OPEN (One Parent Exchange Network) organisation emerged as a central body representing the experiences and views of lone parents in national policy forums. There was a wider context again reinforcing the impact of the new OPF and the growing participation of lone parents in local and community projects — the general emphasis from the early 1990s onwards on restructuring the social security and tax systems to improve employment levels.

As Chapter Eight outlines, a central aspect of recent governments' policies has been the focus on 'making work pay', both in the sense of improving the net return to work for those on lower incomes in employment and of increasing the incentive to make the transition into employment for those on social security (Expert Working Group, 1996). A range of *general* changes were made in tax and social security that affected the labour market context of lone parents as well as the wider population: income tax rates were reduced, PRSI contributions were restructured, Family Income Supplement was reformed, Child Dependant Additions to social security payments were reduced in real terms, minimum wage provisions enacted, and a range of transition-to-work measures introduced for social security recipients. In terms of orientation to the labour market, these general measures compounded the effects of the *specific* policies that were directed at lone mothers — such as the revised means test — and offered stronger financial incentives to lone parents to take up and remain in paid work. Employment rates among lone parents did, in fact, increase in the last decade.

LONE MOTHERS AND RELATIVE INCOME POVERTY

The studies of relative income poverty giving data for the late 1980s showed a greater risk of poverty for lone parent families than for households in general. McCashin's data for 1987 showed a higher risk of poverty at the 50% poverty line than for all households — 35% of unmarried lone parents poor in contrast to 13.5% for all households (McCashin, 1993: 50–53). Likewise, the ESRI study for the same year using different data reported a substantially higher risk for lone parent households than for the overall population (Callan, Nolan *et al*, 1989: 97). These studies show too that large two-parent families also have a disproportionate risk of poverty: in fact, depending on the poverty line and the per capita equivalent scale chosen, the rate of two-parent family poverty can be *higher* than that for lone parents. Equally important in these studies is the link between labour market participation and poverty. The pattern of poverty affecting lone parents relative to other family households is reversed once the comparison is confined to those families where the family heads are not in work. Two-parent families in these contexts have a substantially higher risk of poverty, and the larger the number of children the greater the gap in poverty rates. This brings into focus the importance of the relative treatment in social security of lone parent and two-parent families. Specifically, the pattern of social security payments in the late 1980s consigned two-parent families with children to the bottom of the hierarchy of payments (Commission on Social Welfare, 1986).

The review of gender and poverty in Chapter Six showed that the risk of poverty for women and female-headed households fell from 1973 to 1987, in part because of the significant improvements in social security provisions at that time. This trend was reversed in the period from the late 1980s to the mid-1990s, as the risk of poverty for women rose very markedly (Nolan and Watson, 1999). Reflecting this pattern, lone parent poverty also rose. From 1987 to 1994, at the 50% poverty line, the risk for lone parents increased from about 17% to just under 30%, and the *incidence* of lone parent poverty (the share of the poor comprising lone parents) almost doubled. These trends can be attributed to the continued increase in the lone parent population and to changes in its composition. As a sub-group in the population their numbers continued to grow, contributing to their increased poverty incidence, and the profile of the lone parent population continued to shift away from widowhood towards the more financially vulnerable unmarried and separated mothers. However, policy in relation to social security payments also played a critical role in the evolution of poverty rates (Callan, Nolan *et al*, 1996). In response to the report of the Commission on Social Welfare, there was a differentiated approach to increasing benefits and allowances in which the long-term payments on which lone parents rely (Deserted Wife's Benefit, Widows' pensions, Lone Parent allowance) were increased less than the payments prioritised by the Commission. Consequently, lone parents' incomes (overwhelmingly social security payments) declined more significantly relative to the poverty line than the incomes of other groups in the population.

More recent data in relation to lone parents and poverty is summarised in Table 7.3. The first point to note is that the OPF declined significantly relative to the 50% poverty line over the period to 2001: from just under 95% in 1994 it fell to about 70% in 2001. As incomes rose and disposable incomes rose more rapidly again because of falling taxation, the poverty line rose accordingly. Increases in social security payments did not keep pace with disposable income and OPF (Child Benefit included) declined sharply as a proportion of the poverty line. The figures in Table 7.3 suggest that relative income poverty rose from 1994 to 1998. The respective figures are 8.4% and 42.8%. These figures refer to persons in households comprising one adult and one child (where the term 'child' refers to 0–14 year olds), an imperfect reflection of lone parenthood status that may understate the extent of poverty. In recent years certain trends seem to have contributed to a reduction in poverty — the risk fell from 42.8% in 1998 to 37.9% in 2001. First, lone parents, like all other families, benefited from the very substantial rise in Child Benefit — this payment more than doubled in nominal terms over the time period in question. Second, the reformed means test and the freedom of lone parents to retain OPF while receiving a 'wage' under the labour market programmes would have improved the disposable income of many lone parents. Third, lone parents' employment participation increased in a context in which both gross and disposable earnings were increasing significantly.

The data are insufficient to offer a representative picture, but it is reasonable to assume that lone parents reliant wholly on social security experienced an increasing risk of poverty, while some of those in the labour market benefited from the new means-test regime, rising earnings and reduced taxation.[6]

FUTURE POLICY

Chart 7.1 below offers a framework for analysing the key policy issues for the future that have a bearing on the incomes of lone parents and their susceptibility

Table 7.3: Lone Parents and Relative Income Poverty, 1994–2001

Lone Parents and Poverty	1994	1997	1998	2000	2001
Poverty Line: 50% of Average Income €weekly (per capita equivalent)	82.15	104.62	116.20	138.05	156.53
One-Parent Family Payment €weekly (one child; per capita equivalent, Child Benefit included)	77.54	86.13	90.08	96.76	112.28
OPF (per capita equivalent) as % of Poverty Line	94.2	82.3	75.8	70.10	71.7
Poverty Risk: % of Lone Parents below Poverty Line*	8.4	24.0	42.8	39.5	37.9
Poverty Incidence: % of Poor in Lone Parent Households*	6.1	9.5	16.4	12.7	12.0
Lone Parents: Numbers of OPF recipients (000s)	58.8	77.7	83.3	89.9	91.6

Source: Whelan, Layte, Maitre, *et al*, 2003; Department of Social Community and Family Affairs.

Notes: The lone parent poverty risk and poverty incidence figures refer to households identified in the relevant sources as those with '1 adult with children'; per capita scales are 1, 0.66, 0.33; * Poverty estimates based on median income.

Chart 7.1: Lone Parents' Income Sources				
Private		Public Income		
Earnings	Family Maintenance	As Families	As Poor Families	As Lone Parents
Work participation incentives or conditional entitlement?	Role of judicial measures in increasing income	Child benefit — reform of child income support	OPF child dependant additions family income supplement	Cohabitation and the role of individualisation

to poverty. Unlike some other categories of social security recipient, lone parents potentially have income from a number of sources, both public and private, as the chart outlines. Taking private income sources first, earnings (or self-employment income) have become part of the income of some lone parents in recent years, reflecting the policy shift towards employment. In considering the role of employment it is important to note the recent substantial increase in employment participation summarised in Table 7.4. In 2001, the proportion of lone mothers in employment was 55%, having risen from 28% in 1995 — a doubling in the employment rate over the five years. When those unemployed (and seeking work) are added to those in employment, the proportion economically active in 2001 was 60%.

Table 7.4: Employment Participation among Lone Parents 1995 and 2001 (%)

Year	In employment	Unemployed	Not economically active	Total
1995	27.8	6.4	65.8	100
2001	54.5	4.6	40.8	100

Source: Labour Force Survey 1995 and Quarterly National Household Survey, CSO.
Notes: Data refers to lone mothers, excluding those in the later stage of the life cycle whose children are aged 15 or over.

The question for future policy is the role that employment might play in securing incomes for lone parents. Internationally, the trend is towards a greater emphasis on 'activation' in social security generally and this has engendered debates about the labour market role of lone mothers. A recent review of the international experience shows the wide range of policies that might be implemented to increase employment and reduce welfare dependency among lone parents. The United States, for example, implemented policies that combined improved financial incentives with specifically punitive measures that limited entitlements (Waldfagel, Danziger, *et al*, 2001: 37–61). At federal level, the Earned Income Tax Credit introduced in the 1970s to improve the net income of employees with children was very substantially improved in the 1990s, increasing the net return to work: the minimum wage was also improved. The effects of these changes were compounded by the significant shift in welfare policy introduced in the 1996 Personal Responsibility and Work Opportunity Reconciliation Act (PRWORA). This legislation introduced capped block grants for local states to implement time-limited cash assistance for poor families — Temporary Assistance for Families in Need — in place of the long-standing AFDC programme. Under the new system, states were required to apply work requirements and to impose sanctions on welfare recipients in breach of the requirements. They were also mandated to develop childcare programmes for working parents. A time limit of five years was imposed federally for receipt of assistance, but in practice states used the flexibility allowed in the legislation to implement quite varied limits — many states imposed time limits for receipt of welfare that were considerably harsher than the five year limit.

The effects of these changes have been mixed. There has been a large decline in welfare recipiency and increased work participation, and policy has been 'modestly successful in raising incomes for those who work' (Waldogel, Danziger, and Seefeldt, 2001: 59). America's booming labour market was responsible in part for these achievements. However, some lone parents are worse off — in particular those lone parents unable to find or to remain in jobs. Others still have taken up low-paid work and simply 'moved from the ranks of the welfare poor to the working poor', and lone parents remain at a high risk of poverty.

In the Netherlands, too, welfare reform legislation was passed in 1996, and under the legislation all social assistance claimants were given an obligation to seek work. As Dutch commentators on this reform point out, it was 'a major shift in the Dutch motherhood rationale. Instead of perceiving mothers as the main carers of their children, they are now considered as providers' (Knijn and van Wel, 2001: 115). After some controversy about whether the new work requirement should apply to all lone parents the law contained a work requirement where the children were of school-going age (five) or higher. Alongside this legislation a number of other measures were implemented: the proportion of earned income exempt from tax was increased, an earnings disregard for part-time work was introduced and local authorities were given budgets to support child care provisions. Implementation of the new policy was left to the municipalities whose caseworkers administer the work requirements and channel welfare recipients into labour market and employment schemes. Evaluation of these initiatives suggests that there has been little impact on employment rates and some reduction in benefit recipiency — the latter because it has become more difficult to obtain benefit in the first place (Knijn and van Wel, 2001; Millar, 2001). There was considerable reluctance in local municipalities and among lone mothers to actively adopt the work participation strategy, and the local authorities therefore exempted many recipients from work requirements. In the Dutch case, there was a strong adherence to a traditional ideology of motherhood and therefore a lower overall rate of mothers' work participation. This in turn meant that the new policies were being implemented in a historical context that lacked compre-hensive child care and in which many lone mothers had been out of the labour market for long periods.

Variations on these initiatives have been implemented in other countries — Norway, the United Kingdom, Canada and Australia included. These policies include financial incentives to 'make work pay', attempts to support or fund child care provision, and linking of lone mothers to jobs or to labour market schemes, using some combination of compulsion, benefit restriction, and employent support. The exact mix of policies as between incentives on the one hand, and benefit restriction and compulsion on the other, has varied from one country to another. Ireland's shift to a more employment-based policy is therefore broadly convergent with recent international trends.

In considering future policies in Ireland is important to note that employment participation has already reached a high level by historic standards and that lone parents are themselves positively orientated to work and moving off welfare benefits (McCashin, 1996; Russell, Smyth et al, 2002). Studies of lone parents show that they perceive considerable personal benefits from taking up work or training. For many lone parents a move into education, training or employment gives improved personal autonomy and self-confidence, and renewed social contacts and networks, after a period of being out of the labour market, and perhaps enduring difficult personal circumstances. As one lone mother participating in a training course stated (Russell, Smyth et al, 2002: 54):

> I did not get any maintenance and I was my getting social welfare every week. I wasn't very well — I was heartbroken and I'd lost all confidence. Anyway I was [attending a counselling service] and after three or four years I was getting better. I was back in form and I was dying to get out to work. Of course it was because of the money, because I had to pay the mortgage and all that. But it was not just the money either. I wanted to get back with people who could support me and get back my confidence.

This quotation is an apt reflection of the general finding in studies of women and poverty that issues of self-confidence, autonomy, and self-development are as important to their sense of well-being as an improved income. The lived experience expressed here is also supported in the quantitative analysis of women's labour market behaviour. In their study of women returning to the labour market Russell and colleagues show that the likelihood of seeking work or of actually making this transition is positively correlated with receipt of OPF (Russell, Smyth et al, 2002). However, this study — and others in Ireland and internationally — also highlight the constraints on lone parents and the way in which they attempt to realise their desire for independence. There are three issues here. First, independently of financial considerations, lone parents are less likely to re-enter employment when their children are young. Second, whatever an individual woman's preference, her freedom to take-up employment is affected by the availability of affordable childcare. Third, there is considerable variation in the earnings potential of lone parents, reflecting variation in their education. Some lone parents, therefore, may return to low-paid employment and their return to employment may not be a route out of financial poverty.

Extending the logic of recent policy trends in Ireland and internationally would place employment participation right at the core of social security provision for lone parents. This could be done, for example, by making availability for work or training a requirement for some (or all) lone parents. Typically, this could be applied by exempting only those lone parents with children below a certain age from the work obligation, and then dealing on a contingency basis with the income needs of lone parents in the labour market. If a lone parent were unable to find work, or became unemployed, or sick, then h/she would become eligible for a relevant payment such as unemployment benefit. An argument in favour of this strategy is that it would retain lone parents' links with work and give them long-term access to an earned income. Comparisons of the work related social security provisions of different countries point to the lower level poverty among women and children in countries that have historically implemented a work requirement (Millar, 1989; Lewis, 1997).

However, the *context* in which a work requirement is implemented is critical to its impact. Implementing a work requirement in a country — such as Sweden for example — that has comprehensive childcare, labour market and gender equality policies, would be an entirely different matter to implementing it in Ireland. Childcare for working parents in Ireland is by and large in the private market and there is no general subsidy for low-income families. Furthermore, there is a significant problem of low pay among women and among lone parents (Nolan, 1993, Russell, Smyth *et al*, 2002). Enforcing a work requirement on some or all lone parents in Ireland could increase employment levels but would not necessarily address the issue of poverty. In future, therefore, policy in Ireland should continue to build on the lessons of recent experience, which is that a range of measures (such as access to training, means test reform, financial incentives) that tap into women's underlying preference for economic independence will sustain employment levels among lone parents. It is also important to note that employment among lone parents is affected not only by categorical policies directed exclusively at them, but also by wider measures that impinge on low income families and the non-employed. However, it is still the case that lone parents are much less likely (as is also the case with married women with young children) to take up work when their children are young. Their adherence to this preference is one that is very widely supported in Irish debates and sets a natural limit to the extent to which policy should focus on employment participation.

The government's review of the OPF in 2000 essentially supported a strategy of incentives and encouragement rather than compulsion (Department of Social Community and Family Affairs, 2000: 81–85). It recommended a 'proactive approach to employment' and accepted that any form of work test or time limit on benefit receipt 'should not be applied at this time, but that the position should be reviewed when access to child care, training, and education opportunities and progression paths to employment are more supportive, basically when the infrastructure would support such a shift in policy.' Reflecting its aspiration to a pro-active employment policy, the review then recommended a range of administrative and other measures, such as linking recipients to employment facilitators, grant-aiding innovative employment programmes and running information campaigns about employment opportunities.

One specific issue that needs to be addressed is the financial and social vulnerability of young (overwhelmingly unmarried) lone mothers. The research suggests that these women are disproportionately drawn from lower socio-economic groups and their reliance on social security is reinforced by the difficulty of designing labour market and training systems that specifically address their needs (McCashin, 1997).

In relation the role of maintenance payments in securing the incomes of lone parents, current policy is focused on providing incentives to absent parents to pay maintenance. The difficulty in assessing policy here is that there are no representative data on the financial circumstances of lone parent families and the absent parents liable for their support. Existing studies suggest that there may be a high rate of failure to meet maintenance obligations and to adhere to informally agreed and court determined payments (McCashin, 1993; Ward, 1990). The evidence of the official review is that only 2% of unmarried recipients of OPFP are in receipt of maintenance. Of the 29,000 cases of separated liable relatives examined for the review, 23 % could not be traced, and a further 43% were in receipt of a social welfare payment. Only a third were in employment and of these about 14% were deemed 'unable to pay'. The balance of about 8,400 cases comprised of about 7,000 cases under review and over 1,400 where a payment order had been issued under the legislation. The figure for those paying is less than 40% of the number of orders issued (Department of Social Community and Family Affairs, 2000: 112–113).

Could different maintenance arrangements improve the level of maintenance paid and increase the incomes of lone mother families? The details cited above support the conclusion of the review that administration of the liable relatives provisions is lenient: in fact, the review offers an estimate (over €10m) of the annual figure likely to be recouped if existing regulations were more actively enforced. However, it is also clear from the review that there would be significant administrative costs entailed in generating these liable relative contributions. More important, however, is the fundamental objective of any policy change here. Many of the non-contributing liable relatives will have new families, and some will have a low income. If the objective is to reduce poverty and improve the incomes of lone mother families, it is not clear how pursuing liable relatives and redistributing some of their income to their original family can contribute to this objective. It is reasonable to conclude on the basis of existing evidence that policy effort in this area is unlikely to offer substantial scope for underwriting the incomes of lone mother families.[7]

The public sources of income affecting lone parents are child benefit (paid to all families) and the OPF, including its child dependant addition, paid to lower income lone parents, as well as Family Income Supplement for low-income lone parents in employment. There are a number of points to note in relation to future policy. The general structure of child income support (see Chapter Five) has implications for lone-parent as well as two-parent families. The recent restructuring of these supports entailed very substantial increases in Child Benefit, and gave a greater role to Child Benefit and a lesser role to the dependant additions. In turn, this contributed to lowering the ratio of OPF to net earnings during the recent labour market boom when earnings were rising rapidly. If this restructuring continues, with the CDAs held constant in nominal terms, it implies that OPF recipients will need compensating increases in Child Benefit and OPF to ensure that their incomes do not decline. However, it is also clear that the benefits of restructuring of child income support away from the additions in favour of Child Benefit apply with particular force to lone-parent families. Diminishing the role of the CDAs reduces that part of the family's income that is subject to means testing and gives a greater degree of security to the child-related component of a lone-parent's income.

The development of FIS since its introduction in 1984 has also benefited lone-parent, low-paid employees. The payment was extended to part-time employees, the rate of payment was restructured and, more recently, the means-test has been applied on the basis of net income. As Chapter Five pointed out, a wide variety of possible reforms of FIS and of child income support have been advanced and evaluated. Some of these reforms include wholesale simplification, entailing the abolition of FIS and the Child Dependant Additions, and more recent proposals include the introduction of tax credits in place of FIS. These possible reforms are not discussed again here. The point to note here is that any *general* reform in the future in this area will have implications for the income of lone-parent families.

Finally, the role that the cohabitation rule has on lone parents' social security entitlements and its implications for individualisation is relevant. Briefly, it is a condition of OPF that recipients are not cohabiting, and this condition has become increasingly problematic. It is a difficult condition to apply in practice, because social security officials rely on a number of criteria to determine if a couple are living together 'as man and wife', and because the criteria require investigation of inherently private and personal matters[8] (NESF, 2001: 79–96). Furthermore, the operation of the cohabitation rule means that a couple in an ongoing relationship, but not married or living together, where both are social security recipients (for example one on OPF and the other on UA), receive more income in total than if they married or cohabited. This is because the unit of entitlement is based on couples: a couple receives a personal rate and a rate for a qualified adult dependant which is less than two personal rates of payment. (For example, an OPF recipient and a UA recipient would each receive a weekly personal rate of €124.80, totalling almost €250. If they married, or cohabited and declared their cohabiting status, their total rate as a couple would be €207.60, where one would receive the personal rate and the additional rate for a 'dependant'.) This differential may act as a disincentive to marriage and to the natural development of relationships, and may also create an incentive to cohabit without declaration.

More fundamentally, these arrangements are at odds with two other policies. First, the cohabitation rule and the treatment of couples assume, in effect, that an unmarried man living with a woman and her child is supporting her financially. Legally, however, he has no obligation to support an unmarried partner. Second, the tax system treats unmarried couples as separate individuals, and in the case of married couples, official policy is committed to making the income tax system more individualised.

Cohabitation is becoming more widespread and is increasingly a part of the family life cycle, and ideally the tax and social security systems should reflect this reality.[9] However, policy will continue to be affected by the constitutional prerogative for marriage, and this means that any change in the cohabitation rule must be one that does not leave married couples at a financial disadvantage relative to cohabiting couples. In other words, within the existing structure of social security entitlements, the absence of a cohabitation rule would leave married couples at a disadvantage. In future a greater degree of individualisation in social security could get around these constraints. Specifically, if two full personal payments were made to all recipient couples — married and cohabiting — the anomaly to which the cohabitation rule gives rise would be dealt with. Policy-makers are committed to a greater degree of individualisation in the social security system in the immediate future, and if it is implemented in the manner suggested it might create a context in which there would be no rationale for retaining the cohabitation legislation.

Notes

1.   The 0–15 age definition in Table 7.1 is used in the official published data. The present writer used special tabulations of unpublished Labour Force Survey data for 1995 to give an estimate of the lone parent family population based on an age cut-off of 19 for 'children' (McCashin, 1997). The Census data for the 1980s and 1990s are consistent with the LFS and the QNHS data given in Table 7.1, but Census data are not given here as the most recent Census data available are for 1996.

2.   The relationship between data on the lone parent population and lone parent recipients of social security is complicated: the definition adopted for the enumeration of lone parents differs from the legal and administrative criteria for social security eligibility, and the age criteria for child

dependency differ as between the population and social security data. To complicate matters further, the Census, Labour Force Survey, and Quarterly National Household Survey data on the lone parent population may underestimate the population of some categories of lone parent family.

3. According to the Department of Social, Community and Family Affairs (2000: 106), the 1989 provisions were introduced partly because it was suspected that in implementing the relevant family law provisions the Courts were awarding lower maintenance in the light of the potential eligibility of appellants for social security payments.

4. In terms of take-up by lone parents, CE was by far the most significant of the many labour market initiatives. The NESF review of policy on lone parents identifies nine separate initiatives with varying criteria of eligibility (in terms of age, duration of receipt of OPF and so on), and varying rules regarding retention of OFP, treatment of earnings, tax status of income, entitlement to secondary benefits and other issues (NESF, 2001).

5. Details of the CE scheme and how it compares with the other labour market interventions can be seen in NESF (2001).

6. This interpretation is confirmed by the trends in relation to those persons whose economic status is working in the home and who are classified in the poverty data as 'engaged in home duties'. This is an overwhelmingly female category of persons that overlaps with lone parents as a category. At the 50% poverty line the poverty risk for households headed by persons engaged in home duties rose very sharply from 33% in 1994 to 49% in 1997 and 58% in 1998 (Layte, Maitre, Nolan *et al*, 2001:24).

7. The OPF review was careful to note the experience of the UK in which an aggressive policy of pursuit of liable relatives was pursued under the aegis of a separate agency, the Child Support Agency, for a period of time. This proved to be enormously contentious and divisive: the point about the CSA experience is that it was driven by a focus on reducing public expenditure on social security and enhancing personal responsibility rather a focus on poverty reduction (Department of Social Community and Family Affairs, 2000: 118–120).

8. These criteria include co-residence, sharing of household finances, length of co-residence, presence of children.

9. A number of official reports have dealt with aspects of this problem (NESF, 2001; Department of Social Welfare, 1991).

8
Unemployment Benefit and Assistance

INTRODUCTION

This chapter deals with Unemployment Benefit (UB) and Unemployment Assistance (UA). These are the two most important payments for the unemployed. UB is based on social insurance contributions, and UA is for the unemployed that do not have the requisite social insurance contributions, or who have received UB for the maximum amount of time permissible. To qualify for *either* UB or UA applicants must be:

- Unemployed (i.e. at least three days within six days).
- Aged under 66.
- Capable of work.
- Available for full-time work.
- Genuinely seeking work.

The Pay Related Social Insurance (PRSI) requirements for UB are that applicants must have:

- 39 weeks paid PRSI since starting work
- 39 weeks paid or credited PRSI in the relevant tax year (for 2003 applications the relevant tax year is April-December 2001), *or*
- 26 weeks PRSI in the relevant tax year and
- 26 weeks PRSI paid in the tax year previous to the relevant tax year.

UB is payable for a maximum of 15 months and unlike UA it requires that applicants have *lost* employment (a minimum loss of one day's insurable employment including a loss of income). UA is means-tested, although it can be paid indefinitely. Persons aged over 55 who have been receiving either UB or UA for 15 months or more can retire from the workforce and receive the means tested Pre-Retirement Allowance. In the case of both UB and UA an adult dependant addition (ADA) and child dependant additions may be payable. As Chapter Six showed, the definition of dependant is now based on whether or not the recipient's partner has an income. The rules governing this aspect of UB and UA are as follows:

- If the applicant's spouse works and earns less than €89 gross weekly then the full additions are payable for a spouse and children.
- If the spouse's income is between €89 and €197 gross weekly, the full CDA is payable and a reduced ADA based on a sliding scale according to the spouse's income.
- Where the spouse's income exceeds €197 the ADA is no longer payable and only *half* of the CDA is payable.
- Where an applicant's spouse has an income above €76 weekly, half of the spouse's net weekly means are attributed to the applicant and these are offset against the personal rate of payment.

In Ireland, in the last decade, the context in which UB and UA operate changed: in the latter half of the 1990s unemployment fell dramatically and continued to fall until 2001. Reflecting this trend, the number of UB and UA recipients fell by about 150,000 from just under 277,000 in 1992 to about 127,000 in 2002.

The two sections that follow give an overview of the historical development of UB and UA, and the following section looks at the underlying rationale for state provision of unemployment insurance and assistance. The next two sections deal with the particularly controversial issue of the incentive effects of unemployment payments. Then the discussion turns to the link between unemployment payments and broader labour market policies. The final two sections examine poverty trends among the unemployed and briefly note some future policy issues.

THE DEVELOPMENT OF UNEMPLOYMENT BENEFIT

Unemployment insurance in the United Kingdom and Ireland emerged from two general sources. First, in nineteenth-century Europe and the UK the emerging trade union and working class organisations built on the tradition of collective and mutual aid reaching back to the medieval guilds. The first union fund for the unemployed was founded in 1831 by the English foundry men's union and in the following decades union-based schemes proliferated in other European countries. Second, extensive unemployment in Europe and the UK in 1880s led to local government and voluntary responses. In continental Europe this took the form of limited voluntary insurance, in which Switzerland led the way. The city of Berne established such a scheme in 1893 and in Cologne in Germany a scheme was established in 1896. Swiss communes began to subsidise voluntary trade union and friendly society funds. The Belgian city of Ghent in 1901 devised and implemented a system that was to be applied in many parts of mainland Europe for some time — public supplements to unemployed trade union members at the rate of 50% to 75% of benefits paid out of the voluntary fund benefits (Alber, 1981).

Thereafter, there were two broad patterns in the development of countries' systems of unemployment insurance. One group of countries (comprising France, Denmark, Belgium, Finland, Netherlands, Norway, Sweden and Switzerland) initiated voluntary insurance and then later transformed it into national, compulsory unemployment insurance. Norway, for example, established a voluntary system in 1906 and made this compulsory in 1938. The Netherlands did the same in 1916 and 1949 respectively. A second group of countries, (comprising the United Kingdom and Ireland, Italy, Austria and Germany) *started* with compulsory insurance of varying degrees of comprehensiveness. Over the period 1900–1970 all countries, in varying ways and at different times, extended unemployment insurance in the following ways:

- The initially narrow coverage of the schemes was extended so that the schemes became very comprehensive.
- In some countries, benefits in respect of dependants were added to reflect the dependency circumstances of the male employee.
- The duration of benefit receipt was increased.
- Insurance became complemented by means-tested unemployment assistance, either local or national.

Chart 8.1 overleaf, reproduced from Alber's comparative study of unemployment insurance, summarises the key historical data.

As outlined in Chapters One and Two, Ireland's unemployment provisions emerged as a by-product of the evolving British system early in the twentieth century. Lloyd Georges's national insurance legislation arose from the report of the Royal Commission on the Poor Laws and his 1911 legislation was confined to a limited number of trades in which the level of unemployment fluctuated considerably — for example, building and construction, shipbuilding, and saw-milling. In this legislation insurance was compulsory for the designated trades. Employers and employees paid flat-rate contributions into a separate unemploy-ment insurance fund, with the central exchequer contributing one third of the joint employer and employee contribution. Benefits were flat-rate (unrelated to past wages) and limited to one week for every five contributions paid subject to a maximum of fifteen weeks in any one year. Initially, benefit receipt was also conditional on an applicant having been employed for not less than twenty six weeks in the insured trades in the previous five years: this condition was modified in 1914 to the payment of ten contributions. The level of benefit reflected the poverty-relief function ascribed by the Liberal reformers to the emerging national insurance payments; it was set at seven shillings per week (Ir£0.35 in pre-Euro currency) and explicitly designed not to discourage voluntary savings (Farley, 1964; 40–8; Gilbert, 1966).

The scheme was established as a centralised state fund, with the state responsible for its administration and management. Labour exchanges were

Chart 8.1: Chronology of the Development of Unemployment Insurance 1900–1975 in Selected European Countries

Country	Compulsory Insurance	Voluntary Insurance	Dependants Benefits	Extension to Agriculture	Other Core Laws	Added Benefits/ Assistance
Austria	–	1920	1920	1949	–	1926
Belgium	1920	1944	1944	1944	1933/'38/'57/'71	–
Denmark	1907	–	1919	1907	1933/'67	1921
Finland	1917	–	1917	1917	1934/1960	1960
France	1905	1967	1967	–	1934/1960	1960
Germany	–	1927	1927	1927	1956/1969	1918
Ireland		1911	1923	1953	1952/1973	1933
Italy	–	1919	1937	1949	1923/'35/'39/'57	1946
Netherlands	1916	1949	1921	1949	1964	1964
Norway	1906	1938	1938	1949	1959	–
Sweden	1934	–	1934	1934	1941/'44/'53/'74	1916/'73
Switzerland	1924	1976	1924	–	1951	
U.K.	–	1911	1921	1936	1920/'46/'66/'75	1934

Source: Alber   ,   :   :

established to link the payment of benefit to the system for checking claimants' unemployment status. However, the legislation also allowed for trade union offices to act as centres for the registration of claims and the payment of benefits. Officers of the Labour Exchanges decided claims and their decisions could be appealed to a panel of referees comprising workers' and employers' representatives under an independent chairman. (Beyond this panel further appeal could be made to an 'Umpire' — a legal person appointed by the Crown, but independent of the administration of unemployment benefit.) Part of the rationale for the design of the scheme was William Beveridge's attempt to make the large casual, seasonal, and irregular sector of employment in the UK more organised, and to increase the regularity of workers' employment. This led to the inclusion in the scheme of refunds for employers that paid more than a certain number of contributions. Farley (1964: 42) remarks — without citing supporting evidence — that 'it is very doubtful if this provision materially affected the practices of employers regarding the continuity of employment'.

The 1911 provisions in Ireland and the UK were different to the typical European countries' systems in two key respects. First, the benefit system conferred flat-rate benefits at a modest level on employees rather than benefits related to past earnings; the UK and Irish system was explicitly geared to alleviate the poverty associated with unemployment rather than to replace lost earnings. Second, from its inception the UK/Irish system was compulsory and State-led, unlike many of the European countries' systems which remained voluntary for longer and which remained partly in the control of the Trade Unions even after national legislation determined the broad structure of provisions. This difference between the UK and European systems has essentially continued and given rise to the standard classification in the comparative research between 'Beveridgean' (flat-rate) and 'Bismarckian' (earnings-related) social security. Politics was at the heart of this difference. The Liberal reformers had studied the experience of the local and trade union-controlled initiatives in Europe and noted their difficulties (Gilbert, 1966: 231–288). The first local, compulsory provisions (in St. Gallen, Switzerland) had gone bankrupt after two years, for example. More worryingly for the English reformers, the schemes in European countries conferred considerable direct control of unemployment benefit on the highly politicised trade unions.

Strategically, the Liberal reformers wanted a system that would be neither opposed by the unions, nor controlled by them. Also, the scheme could not be deemed to be generous and should offer the potential to manage and organise the labour market to some degree. Beveridge, for example, was strongly committed to the principle of a national network of state-run labour exchanges. The 1911 reform met these criteria, and while the UK/Irish scheme was a centralised state one it allowed direct trade union provision of unemployment benefit. The Act gave a direct financial incentive to trade unions to pay unemployment benefit at a more generous rate than national insurance: unions doing so would be reimbursed three quarters of the amount paid, provided the level of benefit offered was *above* the statutory rate of benefit. This subsidy was paid directly from the Exchequer and not from the unemployment insurance fund, acting as a significant incentive to trade unions to give higher than the standard benefit *and* to support the overall legislation. As Gilbert (1966: 280) observed, 'any trade union opposition to unemployment insurance had been effectively bought off'.

The system of unemployment benefit introduced in 1911 remained largely unchanged until 1920 when the *Unemployment Insurance Act 1920* repealed the 1911 legislation and instituted a much wider scheme. All employees aged 16 and over were included, with certain exceptions (employees in agriculture, domestic service and non-manual employees above a specified income limit). The 1920 Act stipulated that receipt of unemployment benefit required the payment of twelve or more contributions and set out the criteria for payment: application to be made in labour exchanges; applicants must be available for and 'genuinely seeking and unable to obtain employment'; the period of entitlement to benefit must not have expired; attendance at an approved course of training or instruction if required by an Insurance Officer. This legislation excluded workers on strike or those dismissed for misconduct or those who 'voluntarily' quit employment from benefit. In addition, under this legislation employees without any contributions in an insurance year were required to obtain twelve contributions before re-qualifying for benefit, and those without a contribution for five or more years were treated as new contributors on becoming re-employed. No benefit was payable for a period of three 'waiting days' — the first three days of a period of unemployment — although this 'waiting days' provision was not applied if there was gap of less than six weeks between two periods of unemployment. A period of 'continuous unemployment' was defined as two spells of unemployment of not less than two days separated by an interval of not more than two days.

A further modification in 1920 was the discretion given to the state to allow the establishment of 'special schemes' for specific industries. This allowed specific industries to fund and manage separate benefit schemes on the condition that the benefits were no less favourable than the statutory ones. In the event, the freedom to set up separate plans was abolished in 1924, and only one such scheme — for the insurance industry — was established. This continued until the early 1950s when it was subsumed in the national social insurance provisions.

The extended (1920) version of unemployment benefit was far from comprehensive in Ireland, although the effect of the 1920 Act had been to increase the coverage from 2.25 million to 12 million in Great Britain and Ireland as a whole. Notably, the exclusion of agricultural workers had the effect of greatly limiting its applicability to Ireland's workforce. Farley (1964: 45) has estimated that in the mid-twenties about one third of Ireland's employees were covered by the scheme. Against this background, unemployment benefit as legislated for in 1920 had a chequered first decade. In a flurry of legislation in 1920 and 1921, benefit levels were first increased by a third, but then reduced again to the 1920 levels, and the period of waiting days was increased to six. Contributions were increased in the face of escalating expenditure, and additional payments were introduced in respect of the spouses and children of beneficiaries. Cousins' (2003: 35–39) account of unemployment insurance at this time shows how the new Free State government attempted to sustain and adapt unemployment insurance in the face of high unemployment and an absence of alternative policies to either increase employment or offer other forms of income support to the unemployed. It became necessary to increase the duration of unemployment benefit and to extend benefit to demobilised soldiers: consequently, the unemployment fund was subsidised by the exchequer in 1923 and 1924.

Despite pressure to do so, the government refused in 1924 to extend benefit further and after 1924 the numbers in receipt fell sharply. By the late 1920s, the financial situation of the fund had improved to the point where contribution rates could be reduced. However, the salutary state of the unemployment insurance fund did not mirror wider economic realities: registered unemployment rose from 79,000 in 1926 to 145,000 in 1934. The impact of rising unemployment in a context where unemployment insurance was limited was reflected in the increased reliance on the Poor Law (now called Home Assistance). By 1931 the overall rate of Poor Law receipt had risen to 18 per 1,000 of the population from a figure below 14 before World War I. More revealing still was the escalation from approximately 15,000 cases (in 1913) to almost 34,000 cases in 1931 in the actual number of outdoor relief cases (Collins, 1940). Taken together, the financial constraints of unemployment insurance, the practical difficulties of — and political resistance to — large scale public works to provide employment, and the widespread unpopularity of the Poor Law, created the policy momentum that lead to the introduction of unemployment assistance in 1934.

Before turning to UA, the major developments affecting unemployment benefit in the twentieth century should be noted. The post war reforms incorporated in the 1952 Act integrated the separate unemployment fund into the national social security system, extended the period of benefit to six months for those with six months paid contributions, and reduced the waiting day period from six to the original figure of three days. During the 1960s and 70s the duration of unemployment benefit was considerably extended: from six to twelve months in 1967 and to fifteen months in 1976. Also, as Chapter Six records, formal gender discrimination in UB and UA was removed in the 1970s and 1980s.

Viewed comparatively, however, the most significant development in unemployment benefit was the short-lived experiment with Pay-Related Benefit (PRB). In 1974 a second, income replacement element was added to the UB system (likewise to Disability Benefit). PRB, when first introduced, was payable on the following basis. In addition to 'flat rate' benefit, PRB was calculated as a percentage (26%) of 'reckonable weekly earnings', with earnings between a lower tier and an upper ceiling taken into account.[1] This structure moved the UB regime closer to the European model by offering an element of income replacement on top of the basic level of benefit. In 1984, however, policy shifted back towards a flat-rate system and the first of many reductions in PRB were made; for example, the rate of PRB in that year was 25% for the first 141 days and then 20% for the next 234 days. In 1993 prior to its abolition, the rate of PRB was only 12% of (reckonable) earnings.

The abolition of PRB might be ascribed to the influence of the Commission on Social Welfare (1986), which had argued for a Beveridge, flat-rate system of social security. However, the beginnings of the reduction in PRB pre-date the Commission's report and its gradual removal was more likely part of a wide panoply of policies implemented from 1982 onwards, directed at reducing the replacement ratio facing unemployed workers. These policies included incorporation of UB in annual taxable income, introduction of an in-work benefit (Family Income Supplement) for employees with children, and restructuring of child support payments. There was remarkably little debate — still less protest — at the demise of PRB.

THE DEVELOPMENT OF UNEMPLOYMENT ASSISTANCE

Unemployment assistance (UA) introduced in 1933. Prior to the election of the Fianna Fáil government in 1932 on an electoral programme of improved employment and social services the limits of existing systems of income support for the unemployed had become painfully clear. Unemployment benefit had been extended in the 1920s. However, the government was reluctant to simply make access to UB more lenient as a response to the high level of unemployment, although there was no shortage of administrative devices by which this could be achieved. In fact, the focus of policy in the late 1920s was on the solvency of the UB fund. As claimants' benefit entitlements expired, the number of claims in payment fell from 1927 onwards and the financial benefits of this were conferred on the contributors to the UB fund via a reduction in contributions.[2] Alternatives to UB — work schemes for the unemployed and house building programmes — were recommended by a Commission on Unemployment, but because of the costs involved there was official opposition to the idea of work provision on the scale required to have any serious impact on the unemployment problem (Cousins, 2003: 35–52).

This left Home Assistance as the remaining source of support for the unemployed. The Home Assistance authorities attempted to implement a 'work test' as proof of eligibility for outdoor relief, but in reality, as Cook's account shows, the authorities did not have the resources or materials to give the unemployed the opportunity to show their willingness to work and availability for work (Cook, 1990: 66–9). Furthermore, the operation of Home Assistance in the Dublin area aggravated the impact of unemployment. Dublin had been excluded from the provisions of the *Local Government (Temporary Provisions) Act* of 1923 in anticipation of a major reform and the establishment of the Greater Dublin Metropolitan Council. In Dublin, therefore, relief continued to be administered by the unpopular Guardians of the Dublin Poor Law Unions (rather than the local authorities), and when the Dublin Boards of Guardians were permitted to give outdoor relief in 1929 the Guardians imposed both a work test and a two-year residency test. This proved to be highly controversial. Unemployment rose again at the end of the 1920s, giving rise to demonstrations outside the Dail in 1929. The numbers of unemployed caught in the grip of the Poor Law rose sharply in the early nineteen 1930s: the total number of Home Assistance cases nationally increased by 52% from 1931 to 1934.

Against this backdrop, the government provided funding in the 1932 Budget for relief works to be administered by the Department of Industry and Commerce. The unemployed seeking jobs on these relief works were required to register in unemployment exchanges, and this lead to a sharp increase in the live register measure of unemployment. In 1932 Sean Lemass proposed both public works approaches to unemployment and a system of unemployment assistance, entailing a payment to all unemployed persons aged over 18 available for and genuinely seeking work. An Interdepartmental Committee was established to examine the UA proposal and it reported in March 1933. Briefly, the Committee rejected Home Assistance as a suitable means of assisting the unemployed. Home assistance was funded out of local rates and the poorer areas with higher unemployment would be unable to fund HA on the scale required. The Committee also saw Home Assistance as tainted by the Poor Law, deterring many of the unemployed in need from applying. Public works were considered by the Committee, but were deemed to be too costly and ineffective. The Committee contrasted public works with an unemployment assistance scheme: the latter could direct assistance where it was most needed and in budgetary terms would be less costly. In the event, the Committee supported the core of Lemass's original proposal and legislation was enacted in 1934 introducing UA for adults aged between 18 and 70, with separate payment rates for urban and rural areas (Cook, 1990: 71–2; Cousins, 2003: 60–73).

Three critical features of the UA legislation were to be lasting bones of contention. First, the treatment of small farmers. It was not clear how an essentially welfare measure could address the structural basis of small farmers' poverty or how an 'available for work/genuinely seeking work' test could be applied to them. The solution implemented was to allow for Ministerial Employment Period Orders. Under the EPO system small farmers could be excluded from UA in particular areas for particular periods: in practice this was applied in many areas in the summer months until the EPO system was finally abandoned in 1966. Second, the means test provisions assumed that the unemployed should be supported by their families, and this assumption that (typically) single people in the parental home were sharing the family income had the effect of denying many unemployed a payment or giving them only a reduced payment. Over fifty years later the Commission on Social Welfare recommended that the application of this family means test should be greatly limited. Third, the legislation effectively excluded most women. The final version of the legislation excluded married women, and only allowed unmarried women limited entitlement (where they had paid social insurance contributions or had dependent children). This explicit discrimination between men and women began to be removed in the nineteen-seventies.

The broad structure of UA has remained in place since its introduction. The impact of the unemployment crisis in the 1980s led to some further *ad hoc* changes. Notably, the pre-retirement allowance for older workers was introduced, giving the older unemployed less stringent 'available for work' and 'signing on' requirements. Also, the poverty associated with long-term reliance on UA was recognised with the introduction of a separate, higher rate of UA for the long-term unemployed.

POLICY RATIONALE

The financial and social objectives of unemployment payments have always been couched in terms of poverty relief rather than income replacement. This has been reflected in the flat-rate structure of payments, the limited period of entitlement to unemployment benefit (by international standards), and the tiered nature of the social security payments system in which unemployment assistance has been the lowest payment. Ireland shares the universal experience of unemployment insurance being largely a state responsibility. In retirement pensions, provisions for widows, and sickness insurance, for example, there is a thriving *private sector* in many countries. In the case of unemployment provision, therefore, it is useful to re-state the basic analytical rationale for state intervention (see Chapter Ten on pensions).

Is there a private market for unemployment insurance? As the overview of the market failure principles (Chapter Four) suggests, a number of very specific preconditions must hold for markets to supply private insurance (Barr, 1987). In the case of unemployment insurance these are that:

- The probabilities of becoming unemployed are separate for individual workers.
- The probability is less than one.
- The average probability must be known, or at least amenable to calculation.
- There must be no adverse selection.
- There must be no moral hazard.

The first of these conditions raises a wider controversy among different schools of economic thought, but in general it is reasonable to argue this condition is unlikely to hold. The second two conditions are unproblematic, but the last two conditions may not hold. Arguably, a private insurance supplier could avoid adverse selection (contributors with a greater risk of unemployment taking up insurance) by obtaining detailed employment histories from contributors. But the last condition is unlikely to hold: moral hazard does exist to a degree, as individual workers have some control over whether they become unemployed and the duration of their unemployment. This all suggests that all of the pre-conditions for market provision do not hold, giving rise to a case for state provision. But the case outlined here is based on *micro-economic efficiency* principles, not equity or redistribution.

Equity considerations, taken on their own, do not provide a rationale for unemployment insurance. If the objective of policy is to prevent poverty or redistribute income to the poor unemployed, then means tested payments or other transfers out of general taxation are arguably just as effective. However, a system of unemployment insurance may have significant equity side effects. If unemployment insurance is funded out of a progressive structure of social insurance rates, and if unemployment is experienced proportionately more by the poor than the well off, then a powerful form of indirect redistribution is achieved. In practice, the extent to which state unemployment insurance achieves equity depends critically on the detail of the payments system, the financial and family circumstances of the unemployed, and how these relate to the incomes and other circumstances of the community as whole. For example, poverty surveys in Ireland show that the unemployed with dependent children face a very high risk of poverty.

A more general consideration about unemployment insurance is the element of security that UI can confer. In economic terms social insurance generally is an incentive to participate in work. If paid employment brings with it an accumulation of rights, and if workers are protected against the risks of unemployment, this enhances workers' commitment to work and the economy generally. This sense of guarantee is likely to be stronger, the greater the role of UI relative to means-tested UA in the system of unemployment payments. In Ireland's case, the role of UB has been historically more restricted than in European social security systems, due to the late development of the insurance system, the initially restricted scope of social insurance and the limited duration of UB entitlement. Later, in the 1990s, despite the extension of social insurance cover, the continuation of high levels of long-term unemployment (combined with the limited duration of UB) meant that a substantial proportion of the unemployed were reliant on UA rather than UB, and this remains the case today.

Finally, at its introduction, unemployment benefit was viewed (particularly by Beveridge) as having a wider labour market objective. Labour exchanges were not to be simply sites at which payments would be made, but also mechanisms through which labour markets would work more efficiently for the unemployed. Beveridge envisaged that they would have a role in actively helping the unemployed to find work. In both Ireland and the United Kingdom, however, this role has never materialised. Labour exchanges have retained their limited remit as sites where the unemployed register and are paid benefits, but general labour market services such as recruitment, training, manpower planning, and so on, have all remained separate from the administration of UB and UI.

UNEMPLOYMENT PAYMENTS AND WORK INCENTIVES

Market failure analysis gives rise to a rationale for unemployment insurance, and poverty relief objectives support a role for unemployment assistance payments. However, this logic does not *per se* support any *particular* level or structure of unemployment payments. As with other forms of state social insurance, moral hazard can arise: the UB/UA system might affect the probability that an individual is in the category 'unemployed'. Therefore, these payments are structured with a view to ensuring that the system of payments does not weaken the incentive of the unemployed to take paid employment or the incentive of employees to remain in employment or work additional hours.

The terms in which this issue of work incentives are discussed are as follows. Income tax and social security contributions (and other statutory deductions) levied on earnings determine an employee's *net* earnings: when unemployed a worker receives an unemployment payment (and perhaps other statutory income and other welfare supports). If the gap between these two incomes is too small it may affect the incentive to work. In the research literature the relationship between these incomes is the *Replacement Rate*: the ratio of unemployment income to net earnings (RR). If this ratio is too high it can affect work incentives (formally, the labour supply) in a number of ways:

- Those who are unemployed may cease to search for work.
- The unemployed may refuse offers of employment, leading to a higher level and a longer duration of unemployment.
- Workers in employment may work fewer hours, or quit employment.

Each of these effects may result in higher unemployment. In popular discussion — especially at times of high unemployment — illustrations of how very high replacement rates can arise are constructed, and this chain of reasoning is then invoked to establish a link between unemployment payments and the extent of unemployment. Yet this issue remains a contentious one in the research literature and in public and political debate. The controversy is not specifically about the *generosity* (or otherwise) of unemployment payments but concerns the interactions between unemployment payments, earnings, and the general system of taxes and other statutory deductions from pay. Therefore, the policy research and policy debates about unemployment payments overlap with more general concerns about the impact of taxes and all forms of social protection on the labour market generally.

To consider the issue properly it is useful to recall the basic analytical framework in the formal policy literature: this is expressed in terms of an *income effect* and a *substitution effect* (Atkinson, 1993; Stiglitz, 1988). The basic theory suggests that people are more likely to work, or to work longer, the poorer they are; the need of a poor person to work to finance basic consumption is greater than that of a well-off person. Consider the case of a person working only a limited number of hours. If the net return to working extra hours rises because taxes or other deductions fall, or the wage rate per hour increases, this creates a substitution effect. The worker works extra hours and substitutes work for leisure. However, there is also an income effect: the higher return per hour also results in a higher income at the existing number of hours, and this may lead to a reduction in hours worked.

These two effects are theoretical, but their relative sizes, which are central to understanding work behaviour, are an empirical matter. In the real world the effects are complex and vary across individuals and broad categories of workers in the labour market. To extend the discussion, the case of a worker already working a long number of hours can be considered. An increase in the net return per hour here would be likely to create a large income effect — a large increase in income at the same number of hours, and a small substitution effect — a limited tendency to substitute work for leisure. Crudely, for those already working long hours the income effect may outweigh the substitution effect leading them to *reduce* their work hours in response to a rise in the net wage rate. For those working fewer hours the effects will tend to work in the opposite direction.

Turning to unemployment payments, these are a form of unearned income. A change in unearned income induces only an income effect; a rise in these payments will tend to reduce labour supply. In practice, these payments change as other elements in the replacement ratio change (earnings, taxes, and so on). In a case where the replacement rate rises as a result of an increase in unemployment payments and a fall in the net wage per hour (caused, for example, by increased taxes or a fall in the wage rate), the income and substitution effects will tend to work as follows. For those who are unemployed, the rise in unemployment payments confers a straightforward income effect tending to reduce their work incentive. Workers already in employment will suffer a reduced income at their existing number of hours worked and the substitution effect will cause them to reduce work hours in favour of more leisure. However, the sheer need for income for consumption may tend *increase* work hours to achieve an adequate income.

The standard exposition of these principles, it is important to note, emphasises that the analysis of income and substitution effects may suggest results that run against 'common-sense' (Atkinson, 1993). As the logic suggests, it is not obvious that an increase in tax/social security deductions from earnings will reduce work incentives, and to anticipate the findings of the empirical research, the responses of workers vary quite significantly. Women, for example, are more responsive to changes in the tax-benefit system than men.

Before turning to the results of research on this issue, it is important to note some of the limits of the highly formalised framework summarised above. It is based on a rigorous microeconomic logic that abstracts considerably from the real world. Furthermore, the framework makes very simplistic assumptions about the real world of work and the operation of the social security system. Employees do not freely choose their hours of work, nor are workers likely to leave employment to avail of social security payments because the rules of the social security system may not allow this. Not all of the unemployed receive benefits, and those that do may not be in receipt of the maximum payment, and so on. These were the kind of points stressed in one of the widely cited papers that questioned the evidence of incentive effects (Atkinson and Micklewright, 1991).

One of the contentious issues in the discussion of work incentives is the way the replacement rate is defined and measured. Arithmetically, the rate comprises a numerator measuring the unemployment payment and a denominator measuring net earnings. In public commentary, for example, it is often measured simply as the level of UB or UA divided by net average earnings. These kinds of calculations are fraught, however, and a wide variety of approaches can be found in the research. One approach is to attempt some estimate of a *typical* replacement rate. The simplest version of this approach is to take an illustrative case, specify the level of unemployment payment and divide by net earnings. This approach is unrepresentative in principle and all the more so in practice in Ireland, for a number of reasons:

- The ratio will vary according whether other welfare supports are added to UB/UA — for example, the value of housing subsidies that some UA/UB recipients receive, or the implicit income in the value of the means-tested medical card entitlement.

- A critical limitation of the average or typical approach in Ireland is that UB and UA are related to a recipient's family size, as recipients receive additional payments for an adult dependant and a child dependant. Therefore, at any given level of net earnings the ratio will vary by marital status and family size.

- The earnings data in Ireland on which net earnings figures depend may not be wholly representative, as the average earnings data used in these figures refer to industrial earnings (broadly defined) and do not refer to the labour market as a whole.

- A further difficulty with the typical ratio approach is that the unemployed are likely to have had *less than average* earnings and any ratio based on average earnings (however representative the earnings data) may understate the true average ratio.[3]

Notwithstanding these complications, the popular media and some research and official publications use such typical rates. In practice, in many official publications a wide range of rates are given to show the sensitivity of these typical rates to the exact assumptions on which they are based. For example, the Expert Working Group on Integrating Tax and Social Welfare (Expert Working Group, 1996: 162–177) contained a selection of tables in its report comparing net earnings figures, based on average and two thirds of average earnings, with UB and UA for a set of stylised employees (single/married/married with children etc.). These data show, for instance, that the replacement rate, based on average earnings, for a single earner couple with two children receiving UA rose from 49.5% in 1977 to 62.2% in 1994. The respective figures for a single person were 24.1% and 34.5%. Using the data in the report, corresponding rates can be calculated for UB, for lower earnings levels and for different family and dependency circumstances. Giving a wide range of figures in this fashion is a necessary element in such typical rate calculations, but as well as being unrepresentative, it is cumbersome for analysis, as researchers may be attempting to summarise cross-country differences or changes over time.

A second approach is to use *aggregate national accounts data*. Callan and colleagues used this method to analyse trends in the replacement rate in Ireland. (Callan, Nolan and O'Donoghue, 1996). They obtained the earnings data by taking the national accounts figure for total wages and salaries less total income tax and social insurance contributions and dividing this figure by the total number of employees (obtained in Ireland from Census and Labour Force Survey data): this gives a figure for average net earnings. In one data series Callan then divides the maximum rate of UA and UB (weighted by family size and marital status) by the average net earnings figure to yield a ratio called a *Rates-based Replacement Rate*. They also constructed a rate called an *Expenditure-based Replacement Rate*. This is calculated by dividing total expenditure on UA/UB by total recipients, giving an average UA figure, and this is then divided by the net average earnings figure. This exercise shows that the picture of the replacement rate critically depends on the measure chosen: the two rates they calculated differ from each other and they in turn differ from another series based on a variant of the 'typical' approach used by other researchers (Hughes and Walsh, 1983).

Table 8.1 illustrates the differences for one year between various replacement rate measures. As the table shows, the estimates vary widely: even with the comparison confined to unemployment benefit a rate could be cited as high as 61.3% or as low as 29.2%. The source of these sorts of differences is not difficult to identify — the expenditure-based rate, for example, relies on the *actual* amount of benefit paid rather than assuming that all recipients receive the maximum possible benefit. However, the important point to note is that the international research on work incentives is bedevilled by the kind of measurement issues illustrated above with data for Ireland.

Table 8.1: Calculation of the Replacement Rate in 1992 for UB, Various Measures

	Hughes and Walsh	Callan *et al*	Callan *et al*	Working Group
Definition	*Estimated 'typical' rate*, based on maximum UB and net average industrial earnings	*Expenditure-based rate*, using national accounts and total expenditure	*Rates-based replacement rates*, using maximum rates of UB	*Typical rate for illustrative categories*, using maximum rates and net average industrial earnings
Measure	Maximum UB divided by average net (industrial) earnings	Average UB divided by average net earnings (national accounts)	Maximum UB divided by average net earnings (national accounts)	Annualised rate of UB divided by net average industrial earnings
Replacement rate %	46.3	29.2	31.6	**61.3 (married/ spouse and 2 children); 30.3(single person)**

Source: Hughes and Walsh (1983); Callan, Nolan and O'Donoghue (1996); Expert Working Group (1996).

The third broad approach to the RR is the *micro simulation* approach in which large-scale survey data are collected, representative of the income, employment, family and other circumstances of the population. Using these data about people's *actual* circumstances, researchers then construct models of the labour market and of the tax and social security systems (Callan, 1997). RRs can then be calculated in one of two ways — using predicted wages or hypothetical wages for the unemployed. In the former case the wage that would be received by each unemployed person is estimated on the basis of wage equations that predict wage levels using information on individuals' age, education, work experience, gender and so on. Then the person's social welfare income is expressed as a ratio of the wage s/he would receive if in employment (Callan, 1997). These RRs, based on large-scale survey data, are representative. Critically, this approach allows the range of *actual* RRs to be calculated in place of an estimated average for the workforce as a whole. Increasingly, this form of modelling is used in the research on this topic — the results of this kind of research for Ireland will be noted later.

INCENTIVES: THE EVIDENCE

The research on the link between RRs and incentives has given rise to the term *unemployment trap*. This refers to potentially high RRs and to the loss of income (or small increase in income) that might follow from moving from unemployment to employment. A wide variety of research has been undertaken: cross-national studies of countries' unemployment payments, time series analysis within countries or groups of countries, cross-sectional evidence from surveys of poverty and income distribution, experimental evidence from US policy experiments in the 1970s and 1980s, and analysis of the social impact of unemployment. (For reviews of the research see Barr, 1992; Blackwell, 1986; Moffitt, 1992; Atkinson, 1987; Atkinson and Micklewright, 1991; Atkinson and Mogensen, 1993; Pearson and Whitehouse, 1997.) It would be impossible to offer a detailed summary of the international research here, but there are a number of key threads in the research relevant to unemployment payments.

First, the evidence that unemployment payments directly reduce the incentive to work is weak. An improvement in unemployment payments does not seem to lead to voluntary quitting of jobs, although there is clear evidence that increases in unemployment benefit lead to an increase in the *duration* of unemployment. Incentives, where they are affected by UB/UA, seem to be less influenced by the generosity of the payments and more, as Barr has suggested, 'by other aspects of the benefit structure, in particular the maximum duration for which benefit can be received' (Barr, 1992: 767). The association between UB/UA and unemployment duration does not mean that UB is contributing to higher unemployment levels, as workers who take jobs may be simply replacing others who prolong their job search or who are 'voluntarily' unemployed. There is little agreement in the time series research about the effect of UB/UA on the trend over time in unemployment — whether there is one and what its size might be (Blackwell, 1986). One interpretation of the effect of changes in UB/UA is that improvements to the UB/UA regime may create an inflow into the workforce motivated by a desire to qualify for future benefits (an 'eligibility effect'): at a given level of employment the increased labour supply results in higher measured unemployment.

Second, there is general agreement in studies from many countries that there is considerable variation in the effect of unemployment payments (and of taxes and benefits more generally) across different groups in the labour market. Notably, the labour supply responses of women — and more especially married women —

are more sensitive than those of men. A very specific finding is that women married to unemployed men may face strong disincentives in the unemployment payment system. Also, the tax/benefit system has strong effects on the work incentives faced by lone mothers (Walker, 1997).

Third, as the research on this topic has accumulated, the focus of analysis and policy debate has widened beyond unemployment payments *per se* to studies of the links between earnings, taxes and social security, on the one hand, and low levels of employment growth and economic performance generally, on the other. This led to a concern not with the unemployed as such but with those at the lower end of the labour market — in employment and otherwise. The concept of the *poverty trap* captures the focus of this work, it refers to the low rewards that might accrue to employment generally — such as the low return on additional hours work, or the low reward for making the transition into employment. In policy terms this wider analysis is best reflected in the famous OECD *Jobs Study* (OECD, 1995).

This series of reports was completed against a background of slow employment growth in Europe in particular and a concern that the system of social protection was implicated in the high level of long-term unemployment. The OECD offered a wide range of recommendations that are not reported here, but it is clear from its analysis that reform of unemployment and related payments is an element in its prescription for lowering unemployment (OECD, 1995: 48):

> Unemployment insurance and related benefits were originally designed to provide temporary income support to the unemployed during the process of finding a new job. With the growth of long-term and repeat unemployment, these systems have drifted towards quasi-permanent income support in many countries, lowering work incentives. To limit disincentive effects — while facilitating labour market adjustments and providing a necessary minimum level of protection — countries should legislate for only moderate levels of benefit, maintain effective checks on eligibility, and guarantee places on active programmes as a substitute for paying passive income support indefinitely. Possibilities should be explored for making the transition from income support to work more financially attractive, through lowered income tax and social security charges on low earnings and the provision of in-work benefits to low-paid workers, and limiting the extent to which benefit is reduced when beneficiaries take a part-time job.

The general perspective summarised in the above statement influenced governments' social security policies. During the 1990s, Irish policy focused on improving the financial returns to paid work. The instruments used to effect this policy included improved benefits for in-work employees with children, lower taxes and social insurance contributions on the low-paid, the abolition of the remaining element of Pay-Related Benefit, and implementation of a national minimum wage. The cumulative effect of these policies in the context of Ireland's booming economy in which (gross) earnings were rapidly increasing was a significant widening in the gap between unemployment payments and net income from work, and hence a fall in the RR.

Fourth, the research on replacement rates shifted focus and increasingly looked at the wider institutional context in which unemployment payments are embedded. Increasingly, commentators emphasised broader *labour market* policies such as employment services, work search obligations of the unemployed, training and manpower policies and other labour market measures. There is a strong underlying logic to this wider focus (Jackman, Pissarides, and Savouri, 1990). A wide range of factors affect the relationship between the *number of vacancies and the level of unemployment*. For example, two countries with similar vacancy rates might have different levels (or durations) of unemployment and this might be ascribed in part to different RRs, or other differences in the social security treatment of their respective unemployed, or to other features of their labour market arrangements.

The results of this kind of research show that RRs have little effect on the unemployment/vacancy relationship, whereas general labour market policies do. In an analysis of the relative importance of unemployment payments and labour market policies in OECD countries, researchers found little evidence that RRs had an effect, while confirming the findings of much earlier research that the duration of benefit entitlement affects countries' unemployment patterns. Significantly, however, labour market policies and the extent of corporatism are strongly related to countries' experiences in reducing unemployment (Jackman, Pissarides, Savouri, 1990). These researchers suggest that countries with strong labour market policies and strong corporatist commitment to these policies — and corporatist involvement in their design and organisation — are more successful at reducing unemployment. This research, and later comparative research that sets unemployment payments in the context of wider policies and institutions (Layard, Nickell, and Jackman, 1991), highlights the danger of loosely characterising a country's unemployment supports as 'harsh' or 'generous' towards the unemployed. Sweden, for example, has typically had high replacement ratios, but these operate in context of very comprehensive manpower and training policies, a very active enforcement of work search obligations in the social security system and a deep-seated cultural and institutional reinforcement of the work ethic.

WORK INCENTIVES: THE EVIDENCE FOR IRELAND

What is the evidence regarding RRs in Ireland and their impact on work incentives? The historical background is that in the period up to the late 1950s RRs remained low by international standards. From the late 1950s until the mid-1980s they rose continuously, reflecting a growth in unemployment payments relative to earnings and a cumulative increase in taxes and other deductions from gross earnings (NESC, 1975; McCashin and Joyce, 1982; Hughes and Walsh, 1983; Callan, Nolan and O'Donoghue, 1996). This pattern of a long-run increase is consistent across a number of measures of the RR. In the decade from the early 1980s to the early 1990s, RRs remained broadly constant or declined, depending on the measure chosen. Detailed analyses of RRs have been given in recent Irish research (Callan, Nolan and O'Donoghue, 1996: Callan and Nolan, 1997). The central finding in this work is that the earnings the unemployed would receive are, in general, *lower* than average earnings and hence RRs based on average earnings understate actual RRs. Equally important is the finding, summarised in Table 8.2, that in Ireland, in the two years referred to in the table, RRs varied quite widely. Just under 30% of the unemployed have ratios below 50% of net (predicted) wages, a small proportion (under 20% in both years and under 10% in the later year) have RRs in the range above 80%, and the bulk are in the 50–80% range.

Table 8.2 also shows that over the period 1987–1994 there was no dramatic shift in the pattern of RRs, with one notable exception. There was a marked decline in the proportion of the unemployed facing very high RRs: in 1987 one fifth were in the categories above 80% and in 1994 only 7% were in this range. Correspondingly, there was an increase in the numbers in the 60–70% and 70–80% ranges. There are no similar up-to-date data for more recent years but is reasonable to assume that a combination of policy factors and underlying labour market trends will have shifted further shifted RRs in a general downward direction:

• Earnings rose more rapidly than unemployment payments.
• Disposable earnings rose more rapidly still because of reduced taxation and social insurance.
• Earnings at the lower end of lower market became subject to the national minimum wage.
• Child dependant payments for the unemployed did not increase.

A limited picture of these more recent trends is given in Figure 10.1. This updates the official RR estimates in the 1996 report of the Expert Working Group (1996), although these estimates are subject to important limitations as they are (in the terms of Table 8.1 above) unrepresentative, rates-based estimates of recent trends in RRs for recipients of UA. Qualifications aside, the figure reveals a marked downward trend in the RR measured against average earnings.

A number of studies have attempted to quantify the impact of the unemployment support system. Hughes and Walsh (1983) in a detailed study of the duration of unemployment found that unemployment insurance factors were less important than broader macroeconomic factors in explaining the rise in long-term unemployment from 1967–1978. However, they also showed that the extension of unemployment benefit, first from six months to twelve months (in

Table 8.2: Distribution of the Replacement Rate for the Unemployed in Ireland, 1987 and 1994, using Predicted Wages

Replacement Ratio %	1987	1994
0–20	2.7	4.1
20–40	13.6	11.8
40–60	32.1	27.0
60–80	35.5	50.0
80–100	18.4	6.9
100+	1.7	0.1
Total	100	100.0

Source: Based on Callan and Nolan, 1997, Table 6.2.
Notes: The original table in Callan and Nolan showed the RR categories in bands of 10%. These data are based on the assumption that the unemployed who are eligible for FIS would actually claim and receive it in addition to their earnings. See Callan and Nolan, (1997).

Figure 8.1: Replacement Ratio 1981–2001

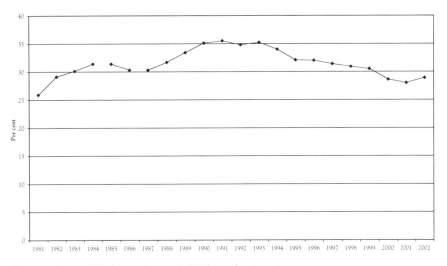

Source: Expert Working Group (1996); author's estimates.

1968), and then to fifteen months in (1976) 'induced longer spells of both UB and total unemployment' (Hughes and Walsh, 1983: 103). Also, the real value of UB and the RR are correlated with the duration of unemployment among men during the first six months of unemployment. In summary, they found that unemployment insurance variables 'exert some significant influence on the duration of unemployment' (Hughes and Walsh, 1983: 106). Later work (Walsh, 1988) also found an association between unemployment compensation and unemployment. In a widely cited paper, Newell and Symons analysed the dramatic rise in unemployment in Ireland from the late 1970s to the mid-1980s and looked at the role of the RR in the context of a full model of the economy. They suggested that unemployment rose because of general demand factors (the UK recession, for example), demography (increased labour supply), and shifts on the supply side of the economy including the supply of labour. One of the latter factors was the rise in the RR over the period 1979–1986 (Newell and Symons, 1990).

Barry and Bradley's analysis, however, emphasised the role of domestic policy (Barry and Bradley, 1991). In particular, rising taxation affected the costs of labour and competitiveness and hence reduced the demand for labour. Later work by Browne and McGettigan was broadly consistent with the Barry/Bradley emphasis on general domestic policies and accorded little significance to the RR in explaining the rise in unemployment from the late 1970s to the early 1990s. However, they did cite the RR in explaining the *persistence* of high unemployment. (Browne and McGettigan, 1993). In a separate study of Ireland and other OECD countries they analysed the link between countries' labour market institutions (broadly defined) and the persistence of unemployment. This study found no correlation between the persistence of unemployment and unemployment payments *per se*. However, in a similar vein to international research, the cross-national variation in unemployment persistence was explained by general institutional factors such as manpower and training policies, the extent of corporatism, the unemployment payment regime, and so on. An International Monetary Fund paper (Santiella, 1994) also suggested that the RR was one factor in underpinning Ireland's prolonged experience of unemployment. In this analysis external factors lay behind the emergence of high unemployment, but high RRs and other aspects of the tax and benefit system contributed to the persistence of unemployment.

The most recent Irish research on this issue is the analysis by Layte and Callan for 1994 and 1997 of the movement out of unemployment of a sample of the unemployed (Layte and Callan, 2001). This representative study carefully incorporated the detailed design of the UB/UA system and used the simulated wages the unemployed would receive as the basis for estimating the RR. Layte and Callan suggest that there *is* an incentive effect but that 'the effects are rather small' (Layte and Callan, 2001: 25). However, this small effect applies to UB only and arises from the duration of UB entitlement: as the cut-off point for UB entitlement approaches, the probability of leaving unemployment increases.

The net implication of all of the above is that unemployment payments had a limited role in Ireland's prolonged experience of high unemployment. This role has been effected partly through the impact of the duration of benefit entitlement on the length of spells of unemployment. An equally important point stressed in the Irish and international research is the role the unemployment payments system and general labour market policies — very broadly defined — had in the persistence of unemployment once it had reached a high level. Interestingly, in Ireland unemployment fell dramatically and was effectively zero by the end of the 1990s. No analysis of this decline in unemployment has attributed it to the *decline* in the RR over this period.

Finally, it is striking the degree to which official policy and policy debate are conducted within the narrow, economic logic of RRs and their potential impact on work incentives. There are two points here. First, quantitative analysis of the link between RRs and incentives does not reveal how the unemployed *perceive and experience* social security and its 'incentives'. Important qualitative research in Northern Ireland by McLaughlin showed that the *source and stability* of income, as well as the *amount* of income, affect the way welfare recipients judge the transition into work. The research also showed that men and women tend to approach these issues differently (McLaughlin, 1991). For example, in many low-income families men judge prospective jobs in terms of earning a *family wage*, a wage sufficient to meet the family's needs without the need for a welfare income. In this social context, then, men will stress their willingness to 'do anything' to get back into paid work, while at the same time categorising some of the jobs available as 'women's work': work that might be suitable, in their minds, as a supplement to a main source of income, but not as a primary income.

McLaughlin's study, and more recent, qualitative research on low income families by Dean and Shah, (2002), shows that families see means-tested in-work benefits, such as Family Income Supplement, as an uncertain source of income. Welfare recipients will fear the loss of these benefits if their earnings increase, and will anticipate changes in the rules and entitlements, seeing them as an insecure source of income. In contrast, an unemployment payment is regular and certain and — however inadequate — it gives recipients a definite framework for financial management. This security is viewed more favourably than the combination of a low-paid job (that might also be insecure) and a means-tested in-work payment. In other words, movement off a welfare income into low-paid employment is seen as a *risk*. McLaughlin's (1991: 496–497) central finding from her study of low-income families is that:

> The families in this study were not simply considering the level of income from work. They were also giving weight to the sources of income and the ways in which relying on different sources could have different consequences. In the case of mean-tested in-work benefits, they could not be sure that they would receive them and how long they would have to wait. The perception of the risks involved in accepting a low-paid job supplemented by and unknown and uncertain quantity of benefits put barriers in the way of adopting the wages-plus-benefits strategy.

Second, unemployment is associated with a wide range of problems for individuals, families and entire communities. Individuals not only experience financial loss, which may pull them below the poverty line, but also loss of social contact, psychological stress, and poorer health (Hakims, 1984; Marsden, 1982; Whelan, Hannan and Creighton, 1991; McLaughlin, Millar, and Cooke, 1989). These very real costs of unemployment have featured much less in the official policy literature. It is striking also that the research on work-related behaviour and incentives is clearly divided into the RR/incentives focus of economists on the one hand, and the social/health/psychological focus of sociologists, on the other, with few studies attempting to integrate 'economic' and 'non-economic' aspects. In Ireland, the Expert Working Group (1996) went to considerable lengths to document RRs and their incentive implications, and built its consideration of incentives exclusively around a review of the *economic* studies of unemployment supports and their incentive effects.

This neglect of the wider impact of unemployment goes beyond the mere division of labour between economics and the other social sciences — it may reflect a more fundamental disagreement about the nature of social behaviour. As Le Grand (1997) in a famous paper suggested, human behaviour can be thought of as the behaviour of a 'knight, knave or pawn'. In this analogy the social behaviour of a knight is benign, unselfish, and socially responsible. If humans behave more like knaves their behaviour, in contrast, is selfish, focused on the short-term, and responsive mostly to personal, short-term financial gain. Therefore, if policy makers and analysts assume that humans behave more like knaves than knights, it is a short step to accepting that the welfare system might lead to a variety of consequences: the unemployed might choose to remain unemployed, or women might choose parenthood outside of marriage, for example. Implicitly, much of the controversy in political debate (between supporters and critics of the welfare system) and in the social sciences (between a narrow financial perspective and a broad social perspective) rests on this fault line that divides intrinsically different understandings of social behaviour.

UNEMPLOYMENT SUPPORTS: FROM INCOME MAINTENANCE TO 'ACTIVATION'

The terms in which income supports for the unemployed are discussed have changed in many countries, reflecting an increased emphasis on potential disincentives and on the costs of income supports generally. Some of the recent developments in income support provisions in Ireland can be seen in the context of this shift to what is variously titled 'welfare-to-work', 'employment-based welfare' or activation. According to a recent study (Anders, Hvinden, and Vik, 1999) the term activation can be defined as:

A broad range of policies and measures targeted at people receiving income support or in danger of becoming permanently excluded from the labour market. Often the aim is to assist the target group to enter or re-enter the labour market through various forms of education, vocational training or re-training, group processes, coaching and practice programmes, and even through the channelling of financial resources. However, the specific objectives of individual measures may vary, as they depend on the starting point of the person concerned. Some have insertion or re-insertion in work as their immediate goal, while others are focused on more limited sub-goals such as developing qualifications, theoretical knowledge, technical skills, self-confidence, or socialising the participant in the routines and expectations of working life.

There are a number of inter-related threads to activation strategies:

- First, active labour market policy (ALMP), identified by a greater overall emphasis on training and substantial state intervention in training, rather than 'passive' policies, as indicated by offering only income support to the unemployed.
- Second, financial incentives, comprising a range of policies affecting pay, taxation, social insurance, and unemployment and other benefits, aimed at reducing replacement ratios and improving the financial returns to work.
- Third, workfare, referring to the use of the benefit system in a coercive fashion, by putting time limits on access to social assistance, for example, making entitlement conditional on participation in menial or very low-paid jobs, or tightening eligibility rules.
- Fourth, social inclusion programmes in local areas and communities, focusing on long-term unemployment and the labour market problems of traditionally non-employed groups such as lone parents, the disabled, and partners of the unemployed.

While individual governments have packaged these elements in varying ways, giving rise to some cross-national variation in activation policies, there is a consistent pattern internationally in the stronger focus on activation, as the following summary of some countries' policy initiatives shows (Sarfatti and Bonoli, 2001).

In the UK, a suite of initiatives called the New Deal has been implemented, giving effect to Prime Minister Blair's principle that 'work is the best form of welfare — the best way of funding people's needs and the best way of giving them a stake in society' (cited in Millar, 2001, 267). The New Deal comprises, first, a range of measures to make it easier for parents to combine work and family life — these include improved maternity provisions, better social protection for part-time workers and a national child care programme — and, second, a programme of area-based initiatives to tackle social exclusion in poor communities. The core of the New Deal, however, is the *compulsory* New Deal for young people unemployed for six months or more. In this scheme benefit receipt is conditional on participation. The scheme incorporates a gateway period of advice and support from a personal adviser in the search for a job. Those who have not found a job by the end of this period are given four options: subsidised employment, full-time education or training, voluntary work or environmental work. If at the end of this period an unemployed person has not found a job, a further process of advice and support follows.

This compulsory programme is embedded in a range of other schemes directed at different target groups A New Deal programme for the Long-Term Unemployed targeted at those aged 25 or over is compulsory for welfare recipients, and there are also New Deal programmes for the Disabled, Lone Parents, and for Partners of Unemployed People. In these latter three cases the programmes of support and advice in job seeking are not compulsory. All of these initiatives have been embedded in a package of financial changes designed to 'make work pay'. Chief among these has been the Children's Tax Credit (replacing the Family Credit, which was in turn a successor to the UK's Family Income supplement). This is paid as a supplement to earnings and provides a guaranteed family income to parents in work: it is paid at a higher level than its predecessor and is paid to the *earner* rather than the carer of children. In addition, in 1997, a national minimum wage was introduced, and there are lower starting rates of income tax and national insurance.

Turning to the Netherlands, a country with a strong commitment to social insurance and an income replacement (rather then poverty relief) approach to social security, a systematic approach to reintegrating welfare recipients into work was introduced in the 1990s (Penning, 2001). The Netherlands does not have a separate unemployment assistance system for those not entitled to benefit: local municipalities provide assistance to the long-term unemployed and others whose income fall below benefit levels. Recent policy changes require each local council to develop a plan each year setting out the detailed arrangements it will make to help people find jobs. Assistance recipients taking a job are given a benefit, which is paid four times annually (€1,818 in 1999) in the period after employment commences. Separate legislation contains measures to help the long-term unemployed into training and work. Job seekers can be posted to private or public organisation and local councils can provide childcare facilities. The legislation empowers local councils to adopt experimental measures by means of exempting individual job seekers from general legislative provisions if this improves the chances of obtaining employment. Unemployment *benefit* recipients now operate under the terms of the 1999 Unemployment Benefits Act. This legislation permits exemptions from the unemployment benefit rules for local initiatives and experimental approaches to job finding. In addition, it allows for retention of benefit where recipients enter self-employment, with 70% of their income deducted from the benefit payment, and payment of a wage supplement for four years where the employment income of a former recipient is less than the benefit payable.

In the Nordic countries, too, the last decade has seen a sharper focus on activation measures, although in the case of Sweden and Denmark this has started from a longer tradition of ALMP. Madsen (2001) uses the term *flexicurity* to describe the combination of labour market flexibility and financial support for the unemployed in Denmark. On the one hand, employees have a lower degree of job security and less protection against dismissal and redundancy, both of which underpin a very high level of labour mobility. On the other hand, unemployment benefit recipients (receipt of benefit in Denmark is linked to Trade Union membership) have historically had very generous replacement ratios (90% in some cases), entitlement to benefit from the first day of unemployment without any 'waiting days', and a four-year period of benefit entitlement. To offset the potential disincentive effect of a high replacement ratio, the requirement to search for work has always been actively enforced, with mandatory full-time activation after 12 months for adults and six months for people under 25.

In 1994 after a period when unemployment rose in Denmark, activation type reforms were introduced. These included a switch to individual action plans for the unemployed, decentralisation of labour market services to regional authorities, and a considerable expansion in the job rotation and leave provisions for employees. Significantly, the general (passive) period of benefit entitlement was reduced in 1996 to two years for adults and six months for young people: for adults this was further reduced to one year in 1999. Currently, therefore, the period of entitlement to passive benefit receipt is now one year, after which activation measures are enforced. Benefit continues for a further three years as long as the recipient is pursuing an individual activation plan. Clasen and colleagues in their overview of Nordic countries' unemployment compensation schemes summarise the Danish approach in the 1990s as a 'more proactive policy involving a firmer link between benefits and employment' (Clasen, Kvist, and Van Oorschot, 2001).

Chart 8.2 summarises the findings of a comparative study of policies in sixteen European countries, Ireland included. The first point to note is that the majority of countries deployed benefit-related measures only. Second, six countries introduced direct activation measures (column 1) and *all* of these combined them with benefit-reduction measures to some extent. Ireland is one such country adopting this 'complementary' strategy (Hvinden, Heikkila and Kankare, 2001: 188). Four of these experienced a rise in labour force participation and a fall in unemployment. Third, Ireland is recorded in the table as implementing only one type of 'reduction' alongside its activation measures, suggesting that its strategy has been less coercive and restrictive than in other countries. The reduction in Ireland's case refers to the abolition of PRB. By contrast, the Netherlands

Chart 8.2: Activation Measures and Labour Market Trends in Selected European Countries in the 1990s

Country	1. Increased activation	2. Benefit reduction	3. Limit benefit duration	4. Tighter eligibility	5. Stricter work availability	6. More means testing	7. Lower unemployment	8. Higher labour force participation
Denmark	X	X	X	X	X		X	
Finland		X		X	X	X		
Norway	X		X	X			X	X
Sweden		+		X	X			
Austria		X		X	X	X		
Belgium		X	X		X			X
France	X	+			X			X
Germany		X	X	X		X		
Luxembourg								X
Netherlands	X	X	X	X	X		X	X
Greece			X			X		
Italy	X				X			
Portugal								
Spain		X		X	X			X
Ireland	X	X					X	X
UK			X	X	X		X	

Source: Hvinden, Heikkila and Kankare (2001).
Notes: See source for definitions. Columns 2–6 refer to benefit policies, and columns 7 and 8 to labour market trends. X denotes a policy of that type, and +indicates that the policy, although introduced, was later rescinded.

implemented policies in all five domains (columns 2–6) of benefit reduction and its active welfare state is now being criticised. One critic suggested that the Dutch 'miracle' of activation might turn into a 'nightmare', and that activation policies have reduced the access of many citizens to social protection as a right, and widened the role of inadequate, means-tested social assistance (Van Oorschot, 2002). Clearly, the specific content of activation policies varies considerably.

Some governments have invoked an activation discourse for what are essentially restrictions on benefits, and others have strategically mixed elements of benefit changes with qualitative improvements in labour market provisions.

The trends depicted above extend beyond Europe. In Australia and New Zealand, too, reductions in social security rights and work-related measures have been introduced and these have impinged in particular on the young unemployed, the long-term unemployed and lone mothers (Sarfati and Bonoli, 2001). Likewise in the United States, the 'welfare reform' provisions of the President Clinton's 1996 legislation made outright reductions in the entitlements of some welfare recipients and implemented a broad strategy of reducing welfare recipient numbers primarily through stricter work requirements.

ACTIVATION POLICY IN IRELAND

In Ireland's case the background to its recent emphasis on activation is its prolonged experience of unemployment (and long-term unemployment in particular) in the 1980s and 1990s. Briefly, up to the mid-1980s ALMP did not feature in Ireland, with training and activation focused either on conventional industrial training and apprenticeship or measures to deal with unemployment as a short-term problem (O'Connell and McGinnity, 1997; Fitzgerald, 1999). The persistence of very high levels of long-term unemployment resulted in the development of a wide range of measures spanning education and general training, skills training, employment subsidies, and direct employment schemes (NESC, 1988; Task Force, 1995; Breen, 1991). From an income maintenance perspective two developments are critical, the first being the Community Employment (CE) scheme, the largest instrument of 'welfare to work' policy.

CE first started in 1984 (as SES, the Social Employment Scheme) at the height of the unemployment crisis and grew to become the largest single program in this area, averaging about 40,000 participants in the 1990s. This is a direct employment measure under which sponsors (these are largely voluntary and community organisations) are given the resources to employ people in half-time jobs. Initially, CE was for the long-term unemployed, but by the late 1990s the largest single category of participant was lone parents (currently, CE is for UB and UA recipients and recipients of the One Parent Family Payment, with a quota of places for the older long-term unemployed). At first, 'pay' for those on CE was half of average earnings (for part-time hours) and this could be supplemented by other part-time work. Later, the 'pay' was modified to parallel the welfare system so that participants receive a personal rate, and also adult and child dependant rates where appropriate. However, lone parents and Disability Benefits recipients on CE retain their benefit *in addition* to their CE income, and Disability Allowance recipients also retain some benefit. Participants also retain secondary benefits such as medical card entitlement.

Labour market analyses of CE point to the poor record of participants in terms of their income levels and employment rates post-CE. The scheme has not been particularly successful in improving skills and helping participants to obtain employment in the open labour market.[4] Aside from the limitations of CE as a labour market measure, its role as an income maintenance measure should be noted. In effect, it creates another social security payment outside of the mainstream payments system, ostensibly on training and activation grounds, but it is not effective in these terms. Moreover, it embodies internal differences among categories of participant that are difficult to rationalise. O'Connell (2000: 70) has pointed out that when all of the labour market schemes are considered the participation rate in these schemes among the unemployed is close to 100%. As participants returning to unemployment after a spell on a scheme are counted as newly unemployed (even if long-term unemployed *before* being on a scheme), the effect of such widespread participation is to give a misleading picture of the mix between short-term and long-term unemployment.

The second critical development is that within social security *per se* a whole range of separate 'welfare to work' schemes has also been developed, summarised in Chart 8.3. This table summarises the key provisions in the social security system to facilitate a transition from welfare dependence to employment (there are other, minor provisions not reported in the table). The net picture conveyed here and confirmed in detailed studies is that these financial — as distinct from training — routes back to employment confer significant net income gains on the participants relative to their original social security payment (Marsden, Murray, and Heaney, 1998). However, an important side effect is the extraordinary complexity of the schemes. This complexity is further compounded if the schemes are considered alongside the long-standing provisions that allow UB and UA recipients to combine welfare receipt with part-time work (these are the rules based on the six-day working week that allow the unemployed to 'sign off' for up to three days to work and to receive benefit for the other days). Also, there are questionable differences in the target groups for the schemes and in their treatment of income and taxation.

The overview of international developments suggested that there are different threads to activation strategies, as follows: general tax and wage policies to improve the financial return to work; active labour market policies in training and skills; social inclusion measures that address local deprivation; and 'workfare' devices that reduce unemployment supports and coerce the unemployed into work. Ireland's strategy has elements of the first three types of policy but not the last. Tax reductions, minimum pay, improved FIS and income maintenance-based work transition measures enhanced the financial return to work; ALMP schemes were implemented by means of CE and a range of other schemes; area based partnerships and a whole host of local social deprivation initiatives pursued a broad social inclusion agenda. However, none of the 'workfare' type policies implemented elsewhere were adopted in Ireland.

Chart 8.3 Summary of Income Maintenance-based Activation Schemes

Scheme	Target Group	Details	Numbers 2001
Back to Work Allowance	Aged 23 and over, unemployed For 15 months and in receipt of UA; also Recipients of other payments (15 months)	Recipients retain percent of benefits on sliding scale for 3 three years — 75%, 50% and 25%; * Recipients retain secondary benefits. BTWA not subject to PRSI or income tax. Employers exempted form PRSI for new jobs; jobs must have a minimum of 20 hours weekly, for 1 year or more, and must not displace existing jobs.	28,483
Back to Work Enterprise Allowance	Recipients of UA/UB, OPFP, Blind Pension Carer's Allowance, Disability Allowance for year or more	Recipients become self-employed in an approved business and receive payment of previous benefit on sliding scale for 4 years (100%, 75%, 50%, 25%), and retain secondary benefits*. Allowance not taxable. Grants available for start-up costs etc. Businesses must be vetted by Area Based Partnerships.	3,708
Back to Education Allowance	Aged 21 or over and in receipt of UA, OPFP, Disability Allowance, Blind pension for 6 months or longer	Recipients enrol in full time day courses with certification in second or third level. For duration of course BTWA paid at same rate as existing benefit. BTWA not means tested, not affected by University maintenance grants; secondary benefits retained*. Annual cost of education lump sum payable.	4,101
Part-time Job Incentive Scheme	Recipients of long-term UA or people on CE	Recipients paid a specific weekly amount (one rate for single, one for married, no additions for children) and allowed take part-time insurable work. Work income is taxable. Duration of PTJI is one year initially.	340

Source: Department of Social, Community and Family Affairs.
Note: The table does not contain all of the details about provisions and eligibility.
*Secondary benefits retained subject to a household income limit.

It is striking, for example, that the general rules governing entitlement to UA and UB have remained largely unchanged in the last decade. Nor has there been a reduction in the duration of UB entitlement or the real value of the payments. The detailed rules determining unemployment status — that a person must be available for work and genuinely seeking work — have also remained intact during this recent period of activation.[5]

UNEMPLOYMENT AND POVERTY

The overview of trends in poverty given in Chapter Three showed that relative income poverty rose during the 1990s. In 1987, 17.5% per cent of all households were below the relative income poverty line of half average income, and in 1994 the figure was 18.6%. During the latter half of the 1990s relative income poverty remained in the region of 20% (Layte, Maitre, Nolan *et al*, 2001; Nolan, Gannon, Layte *et al*, 2002)[6]. Before reviewing poverty trends among the unemployed it is useful to recall the specific changes to unemployment payments that would affect poverty rates:

- From 1987 to 1994 the rate of payment for the long-term unemployed was increased relative to other social welfare payments — this was in response to the Commission on Social Welfare's argument that in *per capita* equivalent terms the unemployed with children were receiving the lowest levels of payment.
- During the 1990s the real value of social welfare payments rose, but at a slower rate than disposable incomes in general, and unemployment payments therefore declined relative to net incomes.
- The last step in the removal of PRB was implemented in 1994.
- The real value of Child Dependant Additions declined, as the discussion of child income support in Chapter Five showed.

Table 8.3 summarises the link between poverty and unemployment payments, giving the figure for the relative income poverty line and the risk of poverty for households headed by an unemployed person. The table also shows the incidence of poverty for the unemployed and the number of UB and UA recipients. As the table shows, the *risk* of poverty rose during this period as the level of unemployment payments declined relative to the poverty benchmark. However, this period was also marked by a steep fall in unemployment, and this resulted in a sharp decline in the *incidence* of unemployment-related poverty. The share of the unemployed among poor households was just over 30% in 1994 and declined continuously to about 10% in 2000.

The risk of poverty for the unemployed increased initially and then stabilised. This begs the question as to why the risk did not continue to rise in view of the declining level of unemployment payments relative to the poverty line. The

Table 8.3: Relative Income Poverty and Unemployment, 1994–2001

Unemployment and Poverty	1994	1997	1998	2000	2001
Poverty Line: 50% of Average Income €weekly (per capita equivalent)	82.15	104.62	116.20	138.05	156.53
Unemployment Benefit — Personal Rate €weekly	77.47	85.73	89.54	98.43	108.59
Unemployment Benefit as % of the Poverty Line	94.3	81.9	77.1	71.3	69.4
Poverty Risk: % of Persons with Unemployed Head of Household in Poor Households (below 50% of median income)	19.1	39.8	41.0	37.3	33.8
Poverty Incidence: % of Poor Households (below 50% of median income) with Unemployed Head of Household	39.5	44.8	31.2	13.9	9.3
Unemployment: Average number of UB and UA recipients, 000s	265.7	23.7	182.1	116.1	126.4

Source: Whelan, Layte, Maitre *et al* (2003); Department of Social and Family Affairs.

booming labour market meant that the number of households or families in which there was no person at work declined significantly. Therefore, in those households in which the head was unemployed, it became more likely over time that in such households other members of the household were at work, reducing the risk of poverty at household level. During 2001 and 2002 unemployment began to rise again, but it is not clear yet what the effect of this will be on the risk and incidence of unemployment-related poverty.

FUTURE POLICY

It is remarkable that the general structure of unemployment provisions has remained largely unchanged since their introduction. Aspects of social security dealt with in other chapters have been the subjects of academic research and policy analysis and, in some cases, intense political debate. But aside from the issue of incentives, the general system of unemployment payments has not featured in policy debates. Against this background, there is no reason to presume that there will be controversial or strategic debate in the near future, but two issues may affect future policy. A combination of labour market trends and policy initiatives have led to a fall in the replacement ratio, to the point where a single person on average earnings faces an RR of about 30%. While unemployment still disproportionately affects those on lower incomes, it may be increasingly the case that unemployment affects higher income earners. If so, then the logic of having *income-related* payments may come into focus again, as some of the unemployed in future may have had substantial earnings, and may therefore have low RRs and face a very large drop in income on becoming unemployed. The point here is that the system of flat-rate benefits may not be appropriate to the kind of economy and labour market Ireland now has. If unemployment payments are low relative to average incomes then a sharp rise in unemployment will bring with it a corresponding increase in relative income poverty (other things being equal).

The history of policy in this area is clear. Income-related benefits were in place for a time, and were then abolished, and there has been no clamour for their re-introduction. However, it possible that the changed circumstances may bring the issue on to the policy agenda again. In a wider context, there has been a sustained debate in Ireland about which social 'model' it should follow — the low-tax, low social spending model of the US, or the high-tax, high spending model more common in Europe. This debate has been largely framed with the health services in mind and is reflected in Wren's (2003) distinguished book on the Irish health service, *Unhealthy State*. Amongst others, Wren has posed the choice (figuratively speaking) between Boston and Berlin. If this debate spills over into social security policy, then Ireland's flat-rate benefit system will be sharply contrasted with the income-related model in many European countries.

The second issue also concerns a change in the labour market — the emergence of part-time employment as an inherent part of the labour market. Historically, the social security system was structured on the basis of full-time employment. For the future, the question is the extent to which the unemployment payment regime has adapted to the reality of widespread part-time work. Murphy's critique from a gender perspective (cited in Chapter Six) suggests that the framework for unemployment payments needs to abandon the *assumption* of full-time work, and actively adapt policy to the reality of part-time employment as a choice for some people. In other words, claimants should be free to claim UB or UA on the basis of being 'available for and genuinely seeking' part-time work. A change such as this is distinctly relevant to women, but it would clearly have general implications. The fact that this policy change is being actively sought on gender grounds, suggests that it is likely to be on the policy agenda in the immediate future.

Notes

1.   In 1974/5 the formula for PRB was as follows. Gross taxable earnings in the previous tax year were divided by 50 to give a figure for reckonable weekly earnings. A figure was taken as the 'floor' and a higher figure as the ceiling, and 26% of the earnings between these figures were calculated as the amount of PRB. PRB was payable as long as UB was in payment ; the total of UB + PRB could not exceed reckonable weekly earnings.

2.   The improved situation of the unemployment fund at this time may also reflect some growth in employment, but the data on employment and unemployment are not adequate to analyse this issue in detail (Cousins, 2003).

3.   O'Mahony (1983) compared typical RRs with those calculated from a random sample of unemployed workers and argued that the actual and typical RRs were highly correlated. Nolan (1987) criticised O'Mahony's methodology and also showed that *changes over time* in a typical RR series correlate quite well with a series based on average benefits paid.

4.   For analyses of CE and other labour market measures see Fitzgerald, (1999), O'Connell (1999), O'Connell and McGinnity (1997). The most wide-ranging evaluation of ALMP in Ireland concludes in relation to CE: 'Thus the the category of active labour market programme which has expanded most rapidly in recent years-direct employment schemes — is the programme type which we have found to be least effective in improving the employment prospects of their participants, and we have shown that the poor performance of such schemes persists even when we take account of the relatively low educational attainment and unfavourable previous labour market experience of participants in direct employment schemes' (O'Connell and McGinnity, 1997: 142).

5.   For a detailed guide to the legal provisions and the statutory regulations see Cousins (1993).

6.   These estimates use the equivalence scale 1.0/0.66/0.33 and are based on average disposable income per capita equivalent, with income (p.c.e.) averaged across households (See Chapter Three).

9
Housing Costs

INTRODUCTION

Governments are involved in housing in a wide variety of ways. These include direct provision of housing, tax incentives and other subsidies to assist people to buy their own homes, means-tested payments for low-income tenants, grants and subsidies to non-profit organisations, and incentives for and grants to landlords. In addition, government affects the quality and quantity of housing through: the planning and land use system; the regulations about minimum requirements in terms of housing density and similar issues; the legislation stipulating tenants' and landlords' rights and responsibilities; and a whole host of other laws and policies.

This chapter addresses the link between *low incomes* and housing costs. The housing needs of those on low incomes are met in a wide variety of ways — the provision of local authority housing, tax allowances and credits, services for the homeless, and so on. Therefore, a discussion of the link between low incomes and housing could open up a discussion of the housing system as a whole and, in particular, of how the system is financed. However, the chapter does not offer an overall review of housing policy but focuses specifically on the way in which the social security and housing systems overlap. Specifically, the chapter deals with the Rent Allowance system that is administered by the local staff of the Regional Health Boards.

Briefly, the Rent Allowance is a discretionary payment administered as part of the Supplementary Welfare Allowances (SWA) legislation. Under the legislation, recipients of benefits and allowances may apply for a Rent Allowance if they are tenants in the private rented sector. Recipients of the allowance receive it in addition to their primary payment. There is a broad national framework that determines whether an allowance is payable and how much is due. Over the last two decades the number of recipients of Rent Allowance has grown significantly.

At the outset it is important to consider why a social security system might provide an allowance earmarked for one category of expenditure. Social security does not have payments earmarked to food, or clothing, or transport. Why is housing the exception? After all, people buy their homes in the same way as they buy other goods and services — in the private market, within the limits of their incomes, on the basis of their needs and tastes. If people are poor and cannot afford to meet these needs, then this is accepted as a general income-distribution problem and social security payments are designed to help meet households' needs, but without any earmarking of social security income to meet *specific* needs.

Housing is different in a number of respects, however. It is a fundamental need and if it is neglected on a large scale it can create significant costs for society as a whole. Furthermore, the pattern of housing costs is exceptional. As the Commission on Social Welfare (1986: 305–306) pointed out, housing costs are often the largest single item of household expenditure, and they can vary significantly from one household to another and within households over time. Housing costs do not adjust, at least in the short-term, to fluctuations in family incomes and changes in family circumstances. For example, a family committed to mortgage repayments whose main earner becomes ill or unemployed is then trapped between fixed housing costs and a greatly reduced income: this trap could also affect tenants in privately rented accommodation.

In a housing system such as Ireland's in which private owner occupation predominates, the cycle of housing costs coincides with the family life cycle and many households experience the burden of child and family dependency and the cost of servicing a mortgage at the same point in the family cycle. Individual households cannot easily or quickly adjust their housing costs. If a family in owner-occupied housing suffers a significant drop in income (as a result of unemployment, for example) it could in theory sell the home. However, this would be costly and time-consuming, and it might be impossible to sell and purchase another home in such a way as to significantly reduce housing costs. In principle, the family could sell and then rent a home, but rents are set by market conditions and for some families rent levels might be higher than mortgage repayments.

Households in private rented accommodation may have greater scope to adjust housing expenditures in response to fluctuating incomes, as the costs of ending one tenancy and embarking on another are small, and it can be done relatively quickly. Some households are in public rented accommodation provided by the local authority and their rents *are* adjusted downwards in the event of a decline in family income. In Ireland, however, local authority tenancies account for less than 10% of the housing stock and therefore only some low-income households have the automatic protection of an income-related rent.

This chapter shows how the means-tested SWA Rent Allowance has become an integral part of the state's response to the housing needs of some low-income persons. The section below gives a brief sketch of the relevant historical and comparative background, and the following two sections document recent background trends and the evolution of the Rent Allowance. The final two sections consider the policy rationale for a rent allowance and the options for future policy.

THE HOUSING SYSTEM

In the international comparative literature, housing systems are characterised as either 'unitary' or 'dualist', and the Irish and UK housing systems are characterised as 'dualist' (Kemeny, 1981; Kemeny, 1995). This characterisation refers to the fault line running through the housing system dividing private ownership from other tenures. Dualist systems are characterised by:

- High levels of owner-occupation.
- Strong social and political preference in favour of ownership and a corresponding devaluation of renting — both public and private.
- Significant social class differences between owners and non-owners and within the owner-occupied sector.
- A limited role for non-profit, social and cooperative housing.

Unitary systems, in contrast, have a more even mix of provision across the different tenures and a less sharp social class divide between tenures, with no social stigma attaching to renting. Critically, unitary systems contain significant non-market elements in the form of large municipal or non-profit/voluntary sectors and a degree of rent control in the private rental market. The standard typologies cite Ireland and the UK as classic examples of dualist systems and Germany and some of the Nordic countries as strongly unitary.

This characterisation of Ireland's housing regime has implications for the link between housing and social security. In a unitary system those on low incomes are likely to be in rental accommodation, in either municipally provided housing or in non-profit or voluntary sector housing. A decline in income or an episode of financial difficulty will be less likely in this context to create problems with the cost of housing. In dualist systems, however, many families on average and below average income are paying for private, owner-occupied accommodation and are vulnerable in the event of unemployment, loss of income, or increases in housing costs due to changes in mortgage interest rates. Likewise in the private rented sector; unregulated market rents would become unaffordable in the event of financial difficulty. The social security system will then have a role in relation to meeting the housing costs of some households.

The development of Ireland's housing over the past four decades has strengthened its dualist character. Table 9.1 below gives the share of the main tenures in the housing system. Owner occupation was the dominant tenure in 1961 and has become the pre-dominant one in the period since then.

At 80%, the share of owner-occupation in Irish housing is very high by international standards. The growth of the economy and the population, commencing in the early 1960s, underpinned the growth in demand for private ownership. However, this growth was also supported by public policy: a wide range of measures encouraged the sector to grow. The taxation of imputed income[1] was abolished in the 1960s, the taxation of residential property[2] likewise in the late 1970s, and mortgage interest relief was permitted in full at taxpayers' marginal rate of income tax (in the 1980s the amount of relief was scaled back and much later was allowed only at the standard rate of tax). Also, capital gains on the sale of principal private residences have been exempt from taxation. Owner-occupation was stimulated further by the introduction (in 1977) of cash grants for first-time buyers of new homes (abolished in 2002), and by the large-scale and continual implementation of generously discounted sales of local authority dwellings to sitting tenants.

In contrast to owner-occupation, the private rented sector was in decline until recently. This long-term trend is common to many countries (Harloe, 1985), but in Ireland is exceptionally marked. The decline from a 17% share in housing in 1961 understates this trend, as the figure in the mid-forties was over 40% (and almost 72% in major cities). The powerful incentives for owner-occupation channelled demand for housing into ownership. This weakened demand for renting was further undermined by the total absence of regulation in the sector until 1992. A small part of the sector was subject to rent control, but this was abolished in the early 1980s when the specific rent control legislation in place was found to be unconstitutional. Rent control exacerbated the long run decline in the sector as it gave landlords no incentive to invest and it targeted the benefits of controlled rents badly (Baker and O'Brien, 1979; McCashin, 2000; O'Brien and Dillon, 1982).

Private rented housing was further emasculated by the growth of large-scale local authority housing provision for low-income families. This happened in spurts: high levels of new stock in the immediate post-war years, a decline in the 1950s, and then significant new provision in the period from the early 1960s to the end of the 1970s. In the late 1980s public provision declined, but resumed again in the early 1990s. Local authority provision displaced private renting as the housing of those on lower incomes. It offered rents related to family income, conferred de facto security of tenure, and gave tenants the right to buy on discounted terms. Furthermore, much of this housing was located in the emerging new sites of industrial employment in towns and cities.

Tax-based incentives to increase the supply of new rented accommodation were introduced in 1981 and these led to a modernisation of the private rented stock at the upper end of the rental market. However, this new apartment sector in renting was not sufficient to offset the long-run decline in the stock; in 1991, the number of private rented units was less than in 1981 when the incentive was introduced (McCashin, 2000). By the early 1990s, notwithstanding the contraction of the sector, demand began to rise, particularly at the lower end of the market. This was

Table 9. 1: Housing in Ireland by Tenure (%)

Tenure	1961	1971	1981	1991	1998
Local Authority Rented	18.4	15.5	12.4	9.7	7.0
Owner Occupied	59.8	70.8	74.4	79.3	80.4
Private Rented	17.2	13.3	10.1	6.3	10.0
Voluntary etc	4.6	2.4	3.0	3.0	3.0
Total	100	100	100	100	100

Source: Census of Population, various. *Quarterly National Household Survey,* 1998.
Note: Some data refer to dwellings, others to households; the shares of the two rented tenures in 1998 are the author's estimates.

due partly to the reduction in local authority provision in the late 1980s and partly to general social trends tending to increase the number of small, separate households. Where, historically, private rented housing was once the tenure of the working classes, over time it became a 'niche' tenure largely for young, small, childless households — a tenure regarded as socially less desirable than ownership, a 'purgatory' to be endured for a time, as the authors of the *After the Celtic Tiger* caustically observed. (Clinch, Convery and Walsh, 2002). However, in the latter half of the 1990s, the private rented stock began to grow again.

Turning to local authority housing, this tenure's share has declined slowly over the period from the early 1960s to the early 1990s. During this period there has been considerable new stock added. Even at its peak, however, newly-built local authority housing has remained a small proportion of total new housing stock: in 1977 it was under one-third of all new housing and it has declined significantly below that level since then. In Ireland, however, local authority rented housing could never have become (as it has in 'unitary' housing regimes) the core of the housing system, even if its share of new housing provision had been much greater. This is because the tenure has acted partly as a gateway to owner-occupation. Most of the houses built by local authorities have been sold to tenants and therefore the stock of rented social housing has not increased in line with the number of units provided, leading to the fall in the share of the tenure in the housing system. This has had the effect of reducing the available stock of local authority rented housing to meet emerging needs, leaving later cohorts of lower-income households less likely to be able to obtain this form of housing and more reliant on private housing. Second, the right-to-buy policy helped to make the tenure attractive relative to private renting (for low-income households). The differential rent scheme in the local authority sector reinforced this effect. Dwellings and flats provided by the local authorities are rented on a 'differential rents' basis, with rents related to income and family size.

Over time, in Ireland and internationally, local authority housing became 'residualised' (Malpass and Murie, 1994; Power, 1987; Power, 1993). This term came to be widely used in the 1980s and 1990s to capture the increasingly negative, residual, role of a substantial part of the sector. Housing in the sector was often provided in the form of large estates, separated from private housing, or in high-rise or multi-storey flats or apartments. The physical environment in these areas, combined with the concentration in them of low-income tenants, meant that these estates and communities eventually became reservoirs of poverty and social problems. As one of the key studies of poverty in Ireland showed, in the mid-1990s the risk of poverty for local authority tenancy households was 49.8% at half the average income poverty line and 74.6% at the 60% (of average income) line (Nolan, Whelan and Williams, 1998: 24). By the early 1990s, local authority rented housing had largely become the preserve of the very poorest households. Much of the housing stock had been sold off into private ownership to the more financially secure tenants, the allocations system channelled the poorest and most socially vulnerable households into this tenure, and the social and environmental quality of the tenure deterred even those in housing need from seeking or accepting housing in the sector (O'Sullivan, 1998).

Voluntary, non-profit housing has played a negligible role in Irish housing. It was only in the late 1980s that official commentaries and policy documents (NESC, 1988) began to recommend an enlarged role for the sector. In contrast to other European countries, the absence of this tenure has meant that low-income households in Ireland did not have the option of non-market housing (other than local authority provision).

The wider housing system has important implications for the analysis of specific instruments of housing policy that affect those on low incomes. Housing subsidies, by-and-large, are regressive, benefiting those on higher incomes most. The bulk of the subsidies go to owner-occupied households, and many independent analyses have stressed that it is difficult to justify the extent of the subsidies on either equity or efficiency grounds. For example, the ESRI argued that the State's direct involvement in the housing sector should be 'confined to social housing' (Fitzgerald, 1999: xiv). In a similar vein, the NESC in its review of housing policy called for 'a more balanced treatment of housing tenures' based on a 'less generous strategy of subsidising owner-occupation' (NESC, 1988: 58–9). The Commission on Taxation described the subsidies to owner-occupation as 'extremely generous' and pointed out that they increased demand above real needs, encouraged over-investment and trading-up in housing, leading to increased house prices (Commission on Taxation, 1982: 138). The difficulties associated with the Rent Allowance and related provisions should be seen against this backdrop — a housing system that is underpinned by a wide range of subsidies that are neither efficient nor equitable.

SOME RECENT TRENDS

Before turning to the rent allowance system it is necessary to briefly note some specific changes in the last decade that have contributed to the growing role of the rent allowance. Chart 9.1 summarises these trends and their impact on housing and on the SWA Rent Allowance. First, from the late 1980s the extent of acute housing need began to grow, because of the growth in the population of especially vulnerable people: former psychiatric in-patients, lone parents, long-term unemployed, and children leaving care, amongst others (O'Sullivan, 1998; Blackwell, 1995). A telling indicator of these trends was the very sharp rise in the official measure of housing need from just over 23,000 in 1993 to 48,000 in 2002: an average annual increase of 8.2%.[3] This led to an escalation in the demand for rented accommodation in the lower end of the market from an increasing number of social welfare dependent households. In turn, this led to a greater role for the rent allowance. The influence of this factor was reinforced by the reduced availability of local authority housing. From the mid-1980s to the mid-1990s the level of new provision was very low — and effectively zero from 1987 to 1990. This channelled demand for housing into the lower end of the private rental market.

In the private, owner-occupied sector, the SWA Rent Allowance began to acquire a role in the mid–1980s because of the unemployment crisis. SWA allowances for assistance with mortgage repayments became a continual part of the income of many families relying on social security benefits. The unemployment crisis helped to institutionalise the allowance as an integral part of the social welfare system. However, when the economic boom arrived in the 1990s it did not diminish the underlying forces giving rise to homelessness and acute housing need. As Chart 9.1 suggests, the economic boom brought new problems. It triggered a marked rise in house prices for owner-occupiers, creating an affordability problem for lower-income households attempting to buy houses. This demand spilled over into the rented sector, generating large increases in rents at all levels in the rental market, creating further pressure on rents, especially for those with low incomes (McCashin, 2000). Bacon's review of the housing market reported annual rates of increase (from 1997 to 1998) in monthly rents between 6.4% and 26.9%, depending on the location and type of accommodation. Rents for older one-bedroom flats increased by 11.8% in that year alone in 'average' locations, for example (Bacon, 1999: 23).

The level of net immigration and changed patterns of migration further fuelled the rise in rents. Ireland's booming labour market in the 1990s attracted a mobile international workforce that saw the rented sector as the immediate source of housing, and at the lower end of the market the growing refugee/asylum-seeking population further fuelled demand. Finally, the rising demand for rented accommodation led to considerable new investment and supply. This resulted in a very significant increase in the number of households in the sector, although it is not clear from the data available what the scale of the increase is or whether the share of the rented sector in the housing system has increased.[4] An important recent development is the stabilisation in rents that began in 2002, arising from the increase in supply. The Price Index for rents decreased by 0.3% from July 2002 to July 2003, in sharp contrast to the rapid increases of recent years. In this context, one recent commentary has suggested that at this point 'the supply of private rented accommodation probably exceeds demand' (O'Sullivan, 2003: 8). There is no evidence, however, that the turnaround in rent levels applies to the lower end of the market to the same extent.

THE EVOLUTION OF THE SWA RENT ALLOWANCE

Under the Home Assistance service that evolved from the Poor Law, local authorities had discretion to offer recipients assistance with rent costs, but the more immediate history of the allowance can be traced to the overall reform of Home Assistance in 1977 and its transformation into Supplementary Welfare Allowances. This legislation set out the right to a legal minimum income, subject to a means test. It also gave the discretion to offer additional regular payments to recipients of SWA and other social welfare payments. The regulations under the Act specified the circumstances under which additional payments could be made; these were rent (defined to include mortgage interest repayments as well as rent), and special heating and dietary needs.[5] Under the core provisions students and persons in employment were excluded from receiving SWA.

The regulations accompanying the legislation set out the terms under which rent supplements would be paid. If a person's post-rent income is less than the appropriate SWA rate minus £6 (€7.20) then a rent supplement can be paid subject to these conditions:

- That the rent is deemed reasonable.
- That the accommodation is suitable.
- That the applicant has a genuine housing need — the latter was not defined in the regulations.

In effect, the scheme requires that an applicant whose sole income comprises the SWA payment meets the first €7.20 rent out of the basic SWA income. In each local area, guideline figures for 'reasonable' rent for households of different sizes are applied annually and the amount of rent supplement is generally determined within that limit. Table 9.2 gives an illustration of how the rent allowance is calculated for two cases — an Unemployment Assistance recipient and a lone parent in receipt of the One Parent Family Payment. In 2002, restrictions were imposed on the Rent Allowance by means of a maximum rent ceiling. Accommodation above this ceiling would not be eligible for the allowance. This may have compelled some recipients to claim the allowance on

Chart 9.1: SWA Rent and Mortgage Allowance; Summary of Key Trends in the 1990s

Trend	Impact on Housing	Effect on Rent/Mortgage Allowance
Rise in Acute Housing Need from late 1980s.	Increased demand at lower end of market.	Rise in claims for rent allowances.
Fall in Local Authority provision from late 1980s.	Demand channelled from local authority to private rented sector.	Increased claims for rent allowances.
High unemployment and long-term unemployment from early 1980s to mid-1990s.	Crisis of affordability for unemployed low-income owner-occupiers.	Rise in demand for SWA allowance for mortgage cost.
Economic boom from mid-1990s onwards.	Rapid rise in house prices — demand spills over into rented sector.	Escalation of rents in private rented sector and increased demand for rent allowance.
Population increase and rise in immigration.	Rise in demand for rented accommodation.	Pressure on rents and on rent allowance expenditure.
Rise in demand for rented housing; increased investment by 'suppliers' from mid 1990s and eventual stabilisation of rent costs.	Growth in absolute numbers of private rented households.	Increase in population of prospective rent allowance recipients.

the basis of a rent that is lower than the rent they are actually paying. These tenants would then have an income lower than the rent-income formula illustrated above.

It was clear to commentators by the late 1980s that broad social and economic changes and other policy developments (noted above) were conferring an expanding role on what was originally intended to be only a supplementary aspect of the SWA scheme. The limited official data suggest that the scheme expanded rapidly. Mills' data records a figure of 8,159 recipients in 1990, and the official figures for 1994 and 2000 respectively are 28,000 and 46,916, an average annual rate of increase of 19% for the whole period (Mills, Smith and Walsh, *et al*, 1991). The trends in expenditure (data available only from 1989), summarised in Figure 9.1, reflect both the increased numbers of recipients and rising rent levels.

Table 9.3 gives fuller details for the period 1994–2002. The year-on-year percentage changes in the scheme's expenditure (in *real* terms) is in the range above 12% from 1994, having declined from the dramatic growth levels of the late 1980s. The growth then slowed considerably in 2000, reflecting a sharp decline in mortgage supplementation. However, in 2001 and 2002 the growth resumed, and in 2002 there was a remarkable rate of increase. Equally important from an income maintenance perspective, however, is that mortgage and rent supplementation has become a core function of SWA, with expenditure on this aspect of SWA accounting for an ever-larger share of the total. In 1989 this share was 15.6% and, as the figures show, the share was 44.6% by 1994 and over 50% in 2002.

SWA was designed as an emergency, stop-gap scheme. However, a high proportion of the supplements become long-term: official data on supplements in payment for six regions of the country in 1999 showed a median duration of eleven months, with 47% in payment for a year or more. These data on duration also suggest that the scheme simultaneously deals with 'two quite contrasting groups of recipients': a large stock of long duration recipients with an increasing age profile, and a large turnover of claimants receiving supplements for short periods (Inter-Departmental Committee, 1999: 7). A related aspect of the scheme is the very specific claimant group it has come to serve. Mills' analysis for 1990, and Guerin's research in three local areas, showed that about 55% of recipients are thirty years of age or under and that the two most common types of claimant are young, unemployed people and lone mothers: these account for about three quarters of the claimant population (Mills, Smith, Walsh, *et al*, 1991; Guerin, 1993; Guerin, 1999). The Inter Departmental Committee noted in 1999 that the composition of the claimant population was changing, with the proportion of the unemployed and young people declining.

Since 1977 there have been two policy developments affecting the context for the rent allowance. In 1982 the legislation underpinning the miniscule rent-controlled segment of the rental market was found to be unconstitutional.[6] This development required a legal response, and the government — instead of introducing a new overall regulatory framework for the rented sector as a whole — responded by introducing a separate, additional social welfare payment for tenants in the newly decontrolled sub-sector. This was on the grounds that these tenants were almost exclusively widows and pensioners reliant on social welfare payments, and that the decontrol entailed very substantial rent increases from very low levels. The new payment was means-tested and linked to a system whereby the landlords and tenants in question agreed the new rent, with a local tribunal system established

Table 9.2: Calculation of the SWA Rent/Mortgage Allowance 2002, € Weekly

Details	Short term UA Recipient	Lone Parent, 1 child
1. Income of Applicant	106.66	127.86
2. Minus SWA Rate	106.66	123.46
3. SWA excess	0.00	4.40
4. Rent Liability	7.20	7.20
5. Rent Contribution (3+4)	7.20	11.60
6. Weekly rent	110.00	200.00
7. Reasonable rent	107.00	238.00
8. Minus Rent Contribution	7.20	11.60
9. = Rent Allowance	98.80	226.40
10. Rent Allowance + Income	205.46	354.26
11. = Total Income	205.46	354.26
12. Total Income minus Rent	95.46	154.26

Source: Department of Social, Community and Family Affairs.
Note: STUA illustration refers to a single person. Rent data are for 2001 in the Eastern Health Board Region.

to deal with disagreements. The introduction of the Social Welfare Allowance for Tenants in Decontrolled Tenancies alongside the SWA Rent Allowance meant that there were now *two* allowances for low-income, private rented tenants, and these in turn co-existed alongside the differential rent system for tenants of local authority accommodation. The 'decontrol' allowance is of very little significance in terms of the housing or social security systems, and is not included in the data on recipients and expenditure or in the policy discussion that follows.

A far more significant development was the 1992 *Housing (Miscellaneous Provisions) Act*. This introduced a modicum of regulation into the private rented sector. The Act gave tenants a legal right to a rent book and a minimum notice to quit. Landlords were obliged under the Act to register their properties with the local authority and the rented properties became subject to minimum standards, with the local authorities having the right to inspect the properties and enforce the standards.[7] In principle, this legislation was important for rent allowance recipients and for policy-makers: it offered a mechanism for them to ensure that the allowance was being paid in return for minimum standards and minimum rights for tenants. However, the 1992 legislation also highlighted a glaring institutional anomaly. Local authorities were responsible for implementing housing services and regulations, while the rent allowance was

Figure 9.1: Real Expenditure (1989 prices) on Rent Allowance

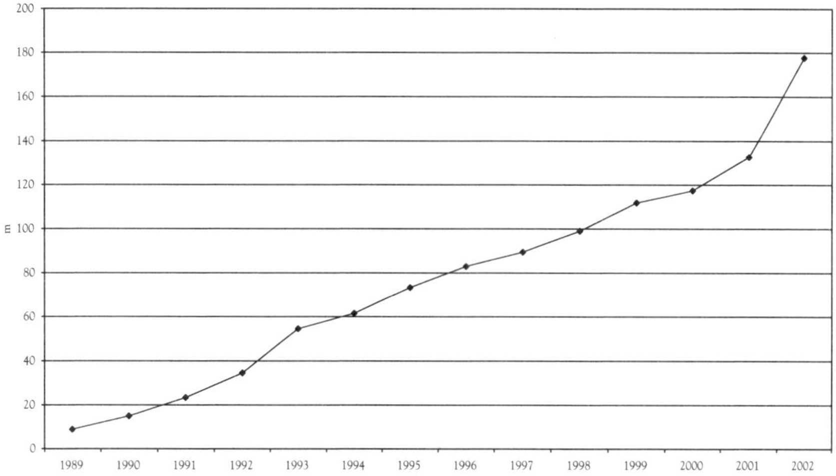

Source: Department of Social and Family Affairs.

Table 9.3: Details of Rent (and Mortgage Allowances) 1994–2002

Year	Total €m (Constant 1994 prices)	% Change	Total as % of all SWA	Rent 000s	Mortgage 000s	All Recipients 000s	% Change
1994	68.6		44.6	28.8	6.8	35.6	
1995	79.7	+16.1	48.1	31.8	7.3	39.1	+9.8
1996	89.0	+11.7	47.4	34.7	7.3	42.0	+7.9
1997	102.6	+15.2	48.6	36.7	7.2	44.0	+4.8
1998	113.4	+10.5	49.4	40.0	6.3	46.3	+5.3
1999	123.3	+8.7	48.7	41.9	5.1	47.0	+1.5
2000	134.5	+9.1	45.9	42.7	4.1	46.9	−0.1
2001	152.2	+13.2	51.1	45.0	4.1	49.1	+4.7
2002	211.8	+39.2	53.6	54.2	4.4	58.6	+8.1

Source: Department of Social and Family Affairs.

being implemented by Regional Health Boards under social welfare legislation on behalf of the DSCFA.

Studies of the allowance revealed a number of problems and anomalies (Fahey and Watson, 1995; McCashin, 2000; Memery and Kerins, 2000; Guerin, 1993; Guerin, 1999):

- The SWA legislation is discretionary. While the Health Boards developed guidelines for the amounts payable, the practice varied from area to area giving rise to differences in treatment for identical cases between one area and another.
- Even after the introduction of the regulations in 1992, it was unclear what the link between the allowance and the regulations was intended to be. Some years after the 1992 Act only a small proportion of the rented stock was registered; furthermore, of the registered stock, only a proportion had been inspected. This suggests that much of the rented accommodation was of a poor standard and possibly in breach of the 1992 legislation. In effect, the escalating rent allowance budget was increasingly subsidising demand in a poor quality, badly regulated segment of the rental market.
- The effect of the allowance became a concern as expenditure and recipient numbers grew. By the late 1990s the allowance was subsidising about 40% of the total rented stock and, by definition, a very much higher per cent of the lower end of the stock. The sheer scale of the support for demand in this part of the market may have exacerbated rising rent levels, with the benefit of the allowance passing on to the landlord in the form of higher rents.
- As its role in the housing system grew, the allowance was not integrated with the wider housing services for those on a low income. For example, the SWA regulations required the applicants to demonstrate their housing need by seeking accommodation from the local authority, but this was not implemented in practice. Also the allowance is not payable to persons in work, whereas low-income tenants in local authority accommodation have their rents subsidised on the basis of income rather than employment status.
- Finally, the allowance had an inherent poverty trap. As persons in employment are deemed ineligible for SWA, a rent allowance recipient taking up a job would lose the allowance and this loss could result in a former recipient having a lower net income after taking up employment. This aspect of the allowance received little attention until the mid-1990s, when government policy focused explicitly on finding ways of facilitating the unemployed to reintegrate into the labour market. In *Budget 2000* a variety of detailed changes were made to deal with this poverty trap: FIS and the Back to Work Allowance were disregarded as income; withdrawal of the supplement would be tapered over four years; additional income paid to those participating in approved training courses would also be disregarded in the means test; and a weekly disregard of income for part-time employees was introduced. These *ad hoc* adjustments, however, made the scheme a good deal more complicated and added a further anomaly by distinguishing between claimants re-entering employment on the basis of *how* they re-entered.

The rent allowance scheme was the subject of three recent official reports. In the first report, *Report of the Review Group on the Role of Supplementary Welfare*

Allowance in Relation to Housing, the emphasis was firmly on the issue of costs —
although some of the issues noted above, such as the poverty trap and the problem
of poor quality accommodation for recipients, were alluded to (Review Group,
1995). For the Review Group the critical problem was the behavioural effect of
the allowance. Noting the high proportion of young people availing of it, the
report suggested, without any supporting evidence, that the scheme had a moral
hazard. The mere availability of the allowance encouraged young people to leave
the parental home and seek independent accommodation. This tendency, it
reasoned, would be reinforced by the 'benefit and privilege' element of the
unemployment assistance means test. This could result in an unemployed person
living in the parental home receiving a reduced unemployment assistance
payment because of the parents' means. The report referred to the 'explosion' in
costs and noted — with remarkable prescience — that expenditure could reach
€127 million by 2000. It identified three significant restrictions on the scheme
that should be considered as ways of reducing expenditure: simply excluding
people under 25 years of age with no dependants; increasing the rent contribution
payable by recipients; and reducing the rent levels deemed reasonable for
determining the amount of the allowance. The report also recognised the
'substantial negative social and financial implications for beneficiaries' of these
measures and refrained from recommending them (Review Group, 1995: 14).

Clearly, the Review Group was alarmed at the way the scheme had expanded
and it gave considerable attention to the social, demographic and economic forces
driving the scheme. It highlighted the fact that the rent and mortgage
supplements had developed into a 'mainstream housing support mechanism
operating outside the framework of housing policy' and argued for 'an integrated
approach to the allocation of housing resources within a single agency' (Review
Group, 1995: 14). In other words, meeting the housing needs of those on low
incomes should be the remit of the *housing* authorities, and not the income
maintenance system. The difficulty with the Review Group's overall approach was
that its emphasis on costs was somewhat misplaced. A significant part of the
growth in rent allowance expenditure was attributable to the rise in housing need
due to the reduction in local authority house-building from the late 1980s to the
early 1990s. The real costs question, therefore, was how much *total* housing
expenditure (SWA rent allowance *plus* subsidies on local authority houses) for
those in housing need had risen, and whether the growth in rent allowance
expenditure was really a substitute for expenditure on direct provision of housing.

The 1999 report of an inter-departmental committee, *Administration of Rent and
Mortgage Interest Assistance,* took up the theme of an 'integrated approach',
reflecting the Department of Social Welfare's view that it should not have a role
in the housing system (Inter-Departmental Committee, 1999). The core
recommendation was that 'rent assistance, where it is appropriate to meet housing
need, should be provided by local authorities as part of, and integrated into,

housing policy'. This Committee (Inter-Departmental Committee, 1999: iii) proposed that:

> Applications for housing or rent assistance should be dealt with in the first instance by local authorities who should provide assistance where appropriate either by way of the provision of social housing accommodation or through rent assistance for appropriate private accommodation.

The model of rent allowance the Committee proposed was one in which the allowance would be subsumed into the local housing services and become one option in the local authorities' repertoire for meeting housing needs. Briefly, the Committee suggested that while local authorities would become the first point of application for housing assistance, those *already in rented accommodation* who become unable to pay the rent would continue to be eligible for rent allowance for a period of one year. At the end the year, the local authority would reconsider the housing assistance required. The existing arrangements would also stay in place for those who apply for housing assistance but wait for a decision — or appeal a refusal of assistance — or for those in immediate danger of becoming homeless. As part of this new regime, the Committee envisaged that local authorities would devise a system of determining housing need based on 'rigorous criteria' and that they would offer rent assistance only where the accommodation conformed to the minimum standards.

It is unlikely, however, that the reform will be implemented because of certain problems with the Committee's analysis. In the first instance, the proposed 'reform' would complicate the system, because it effectively allows for the continuation of two allowances — one for people already in rented housing and another for those who seek housing assistance and are offered an allowance to pay for private rented accommodation. Furthermore, while the Committee's analysis rightly emphasises the central role of local authorities in the housing system, it fails to address the implications of the fact that people seeking housing assistance are also likely to be social welfare recipients. *Prima facie* there is a strong case to be made that the design and administration of an allowance dealing with housing costs should reside in the social security system. The cost of housing for those relying on social welfare has a direct bearing on their risk of poverty and social deprivation, and the structure of any housing-related allowance needs to be devised as much in the context of the tax/benefit system as the housing system.

A Working Group was established in the wake of the Inter-Departmental Committee's Report to develop a framework for implementing its recommendations. This Working Group also completed a report, *Report of the Rental Assistance Planning Group* (DoE, 2002). The Group essentially argued that the rent allowance should not be the main mechanism for meeting housing need, and that long-term housing needs should be dealt with through the provision of housing by the local authorities. In its model of reform, the Group envisaged a 'new supply-based local authority scheme involving the use of Public Private Partnerships' (DoE, 2002: 1). The reform would entail an increase in the supply of rental housing, with the additional supply coming from private landlords or developers who would contract to make the housing available on a long-term basis to the local authority. People with a need for housing could be accommodated in this housing and pay rent on a Differential Rents basis like all other local authority tenants. The strategy envisages a residual role for the rent allowance in meeting short-term housing need.

These reports did not adopt a strategic view of the rent allowance. Rightly, they stressed that the scheme had outgrown its original legislative intent and that it was never envisaged that the DSCFA would take on a significant role in housing. However, this analysis fails to take account of the strategic advantages other governments have identified in rent allowance systems linked to social security (Kemp, 1997: Ditch, Lewis and Wilcox, 2001). These allowances may actually be less costly than direct provision of housing. In fact, the 1995 Review showed that in Ireland the public expenditure costs of the allowance are less for some categories of need (Review Group, 1995: 72): 'rent supplementation is the lower cost option for single people'. The international studies of rent allowances show that governments are moving away from direct provision of housing ('bricks and mortar' subsidies) to subsidies focused on persons and families. This is partly for reasons of cost.

Rent allowances in principle give the recipient some element of choice and allows the authorities to target the allowances by income, family circumstances, and so on. Income-based rather than 'bricks and mortar' subsidies may be more suitable to emerging conditions in Ireland and other countries. Direct provision of housing is difficult and costly to provide on a large-scale without creating ghettos, and it effectively prevents the exercise of choice. Private rental markets are now substantially less regulated than they were 50 years ago and many tenants now require assistance with housing costs. Increasingly, this is seen as an income-distribution problem rather than a housing problem. Finally, giving income-related housing allowances to allow the rental market to work for low-income tenants is likely to suit today's more mobile, flexible labour market and smaller households and families.

RENT ALLOWANCE — POLICY OBJECTIVES

The SWA rent and mortgage supplement has grown in a rapid and unintended fashion. This has impelled policy makers to reconsider the entire rationale for a housing-related allowance as part of the income maintenance system. Currently, policy makers in Ireland are attempting to reduce the role of the SWA Rent Allowance on the grounds that such allowances meet *housing* needs and do not belong in the social security system. It is important therefore to pose the question as to whether there is a rationale for a rent allowance and, if there is, what specific form it should take. To address these basic questions requires a brief review of generally agreed equity and efficiency objectives in housing and social security.

Tenure neutrality is the first such objective[8]. The standard analyses of housing markets stress the importance of neutrality to the efficient functioning of a housing system. If this objective were realistically pursued, policy would ensure that undue subsidisation is not given to one tenure relative to another. In the Irish and British housing systems, which have three main tenures (owner-occupation, local authority housing, and private rented), owner-occupation predominates and policy is not tenure neutral.

Turning to private renting and local authority renting, tenure neutrality would require a broadly equitable approach to the subsidies for these tenures. There are a number of ways in which an equitable system might be approached. Ensuring that the net income after housing costs of comparable tenants in identical accommodation in the two tenures is one possible approach; having a broadly similar framework of housing allowances on the demand side, or construction and other cost subsidies on the supply side is another. Whatever operational definition of neutrality is adopted it is clear that in Ireland (and also in the UK) the private rented sector has not been on a neutral footing with local authority rented accommodation. In Ireland, local authority tenants have had *de facto* security of tenure, in contrast with private rented tenants; likewise, local authority tenants, but not private tenants, have had their rent liability determined within a statutory framework that is related to tenants' ability to pay. The international experience confirms that private renting will be sustained where it is on a relatively equal footing with other tenures (Harloe, 1985). Tenure neutrality, while formally endorsed in some official publications is *not*, in fact, an accepted policy goal in Ireland.

Mobility in the housing system is a second efficiency-related objective. Houses and units of accommodation have a fixed location. Unlike other commodities (clothing, food, personal belongings) a tenant or owner cannot bring housing to another location. It is therefore critically important that the housing market (and tenure-specific markets within housing) is sufficiently flexible to prevent persistent excess demand. Such excess demand can prevent individuals and families adjusting their housing situation to suit their evolving needs and act as a barrier to employees and the unemployed moving geographically within the labour market. A range of policy issues could arise here. For example, low-income persons dependent on local authority housing may be unable to move residence to take up employment in another area if there are strict 'residency' requirements governing eligibility for local authority housing, or people in owner-occupied housing might be slow to change employment if this required a change of residence, because of the transaction and other costs of buying and selling.

A third objective is that the housing system should offer an *efficient quantity and quality* of housing services. Clearly, all of the resources of an economy, or all of an individual's income, cannot be allocated to housing, nor, on the other hand, can there be a zero allocation of resources to housing. Theoretically, the appropriate balance is where the marginal social cost of the resources used for housing equals the value placed on the marginal unit of housing. In practical terms this point may be impossible to identify. It is reasonable to infer, however, that this objective is not being fully attained in Ireland. There is substantial excess *need* for housing as evidenced by the growing waiting lists for local authority housing, and there is a significant problem of *demand*, reflected in the affordability problems in both owner-occupation and private rented. These co-exist with housing consumption in *excess* of needs among many households.[9]

Turning to equity, a variety of objectives can be identified here. First, there is a universally agreed notion *equality of opportunity*. (It is reiterated in the various NAPS documents, for example.) This principle would suggest that generally throughout the population there should be access to the housing system and some degree of choice for the generality of housing consumers. For instance, owner-occupation should not be the exclusive preserve of very wealthy families. Related to this objective is the objective of *minimum standards* in housing. This has a very direct distributional aspect — even those with very low incomes and/or extreme housing needs should be assured a minimum standard of housing (albeit that the definition of this minimum will change over time). It also has a bearing on the efficiency of the housing system: if large segments of the housing system are *not* subject to minimum standards, then this may increase costs on the society and the economy as a whole.

Both these equality objectives impinge on a third set of objectives that deal with *vertical equity*. In other words, the pursuit of housing policy objectives must have regard to the way in which housing is financed and, in particular, to the income-distribution implications of state subsidies and interventions. The exact degree of vertical redistribution to be sought is a matter of judgement, as is the extent to which the pursuit of this objective should be traded off against other objectives. Critically, intervention in housing is related to *poverty* and to the adequacy of social welfare payments. Any view about the adequacy of the payments or the extent of measured financial poverty is based, implicitly or explicitly, on a view about the link between housing costs and social welfare. A payment for one household that is adequate may be inadequate for an identical household with substantially higher housing costs — costs vary greatly and in the short-term households cannot change them. Put another way, the pattern and extent of measured poverty might be substantially altered if poverty were defined in terms of *disposable income net of housing costs*.

Is it necessary to intervene in the housing market to meet equity and efficiency objectives? To consider the rationale for, and the nature of, policy interventions in rented housing the distinction between three broad categories of intervention should be noted: regulation of the *physical quality* of the stock, interventions to affect *demand*, and interventions to sustain and increase *supply*. The first two of these are directly relevant in this context.

The question of regulation of the quality of housing is uncontroversial. There are no advocates of market approaches that stretch their advocacy of market provision to the point of rejecting regulation for basic physical standards. The underlying logic derives from both equity and efficiency principles. Equity is an important consideration here, as many housing consumers will have low income, some will have poor education, and so on. Such housing consumers are unlikely to have the capacity to enforce publicly agreed standards in relation to the physical and structural quality of landlords' accommodation. There is, in other words, an imbalance of power in the marketplace rather than a perfectly competitive market of equal buyers and sellers. This logic does not, of course, clarify what the appropriate *specific* standards should be in any given context.

The efficiency issues are more general. To leave the market fully unregulated assumes that the appropriate conditions for perfectly competitive markets apply. One key condition is *perfect information*. Individuals renting housing can not be assumed to know the structural quality of the dwelling, the quality of the plumbing, electrical work and fittings, and so on. Nor is it a reasonable assumption that individuals will even know the prevailing official standards. Dwellings and housing units are heterogeneous, non-standard commodities, infrequently bought or rented, and consumers therefore have little opportunity to learn about housing standards in the marketplace. Renting a home, put simply, is not the same as renting a car or a television.

A more important consideration is information about *prices*. In a competitive market for many goods (food, clothes, and so on) a consumer will have information about the costs of one choice relative to another. However, renting a home and consuming 'housing services' takes place over a period of time. In a totally unregulated market the supplier (landlord) might alter the price (rent) at a date after the initial transaction. If this happens, the tenant and landlord may agree on an adjusted price. But, whether this is the case or not, the fact that tenants would not know the rent over the likely period of future consumption is a departure from the preconditions for market provisions and, on efficiency grounds, is a justification for intervention. (A more common example of this type of reasoning in policy analysis is the private pensions market. Purchasers of pensions cannot be expected to have information about current and future inflation rates, interest rates and other financial and economic variables that affect the quality of the pension they might buy. This is seen as justification for regulation of the private pensions industry.)

Market failure is the final efficiency issue. The central concept here is *merit goods*. These are goods in respect of which the state supersedes the normal presumption of consumer choice and sovereignty (basic education is compulsory for example, no matter what the wishes of the parents or children). Analytically, this arises because the welfare of the well off that pay taxes is affected more by the consumption of the 'poor' than by the income of the poor (formally, if there are consumption externalities). In other words, the affluent are more willing to redistribute consumption *directly* in the form of housing or education, than *indirectly* by means of income distribution. Housing and education, and some other services, are viewed as 'good' consumption by taxpayers. In these circumstances, a strong justification arises for some mechanism to ensure a minimum level of consumption. This could take the form of direct state provision of goods, or imposing minimum standards for market-provided goods, or 'earmarking' redistributed income to specific merit goods (a grant for third-level education is one example of the latter, a housing benefit or allowance is another).

It is clear that there are *a priori reasons* for accepting a departure from simple, unregulated market provision in the housing system as a whole and in the private rented market. The first general — and uncontroversial — conclusion is that regulation and inspection of minimum standards is necessary in all areas of the housing system.

Turning to *demand*, the two principal means by which Government might attempt to directly affect demand are rent regulation or subsidies to tenants in respect of their rent (variously called Rent Allowances, Housing Allowances, or Housing Benefit). These forms of intervention have been particularly contentious and they are discussed separately in the next two sections.

RENT CONTROL

Rent regulation has historically been the most common intervention on the demand side of the market. In the circumstances of today's housing market in Ireland it might be suggested that rent control is justified on the basis of the widely agreed objectives of housing policy. It could be argued that to pursue equity objectives the price of rented housing should be controlled, that tenants may not even have enough market information to act as sovereign consumers, that especially vulnerable groups can be discriminated against in the market, and that 'uncontrolled' market rents will act as inflationary pressures in the economy. However, the historical experience in many countries, Ireland included, seems clear. Governments have increasingly deregulated rents on the grounds that comprehensive regulation has not historically achieved either equity or efficiency objectives. On the contrary, rent regulation in the form of rent control has been associated with the decline of private renting and with poor quality rented housing for low-income tenants.

It is useful to examine how the relevant analytical principles have been applied to private rented housing (Albon and Stafford, 1988; Albon and Stafford, 1987).

The usual exposition of the basic principles takes the form of conventional supply/demand curves: these show that rent control leads to a reduction over time in the *quantity* of rented housing supplied and in the *quality* of housing supplied, without a reduction in excess demand. This clearly violates the basic objective of adequacy in relation to the quantity and quality of the housing stock. The logic of the analysis also suggests that, if there is rent control, landlords have to use *non-price* mechanisms to choose between prospective tenants. This in turn is more likely to generate discrimination on ethnic or other non-price criteria. Rent control, furthermore, does not distinguish between tenants on the basis of either landlords' or tenants' *incomes* and is therefore ineffective in advancing equity objectives. In a dynamic analysis (and in historical experience) comprehensive rent control, once established, leads to demands for the exclusion of *new* dwellings or tenancies from regulation. A clear horizontal inequity is then built into the structure of the rented housing market: tenants with identical incomes and in identical relevant circumstances can face very different housing costs. In addition, the differentiation between 'new' and 'old' tenancies creates a tendency to immobility among those in the rent-controlled stock: this can be both a *housing immobility* and wider *geographical or labour market immobility*.

Rent control gives landlords an incentive to evict, as they are restricted in the rents they may charge. Historically, this has lead governments to introduce *tighter* security of tenure provisions, thus widening the gap between tenants in regulated and unregulated tenancies. In these circumstances, a black market emerges in the access to regulated tenancies — a phenomenon known as 'key money' (as in Sweden, for example). This entails prospective tenants paying substantial lump sums informally to landlords and sitting tenants, where the sitting tenant wants to move and the prospective tenant wants to rent the rent-controlled accommodation. The sitting tenant then uses the lump sum to engage in a similar transaction for new accommodation. Experience in Sweden and elsewhere suggests that tenants with higher incomes may be best placed to operate in this market context. Furthermore, if strict rent regulation is combined with security of tenure, landlords can then only respond by minimising their costs in the areas of maintenance and refurbishment. Over the long run this leads to a cumulative deterioration in the *quality* of the stock — a very inefficient outcome.

Some commentators combine this type of reasoning with the historical observation that the private rented sector has been in decline in countries with extensive regulation. They then advance trenchant conclusions about regulation being the 'cause' of the decline. Albon and Stafford (1988: 20), for instance, summarise their work as follows:

> In conclusion, the effects of rent control are many: reductions in the quantity
> and quality of the rental stock; the stimulus to various 'sharp', illegal and

unpleasant practices; and the serious effects on the mobility of people. . . . If rent control is removed, the quantity of housing demanded may well be reduced, but the overall consumption of housing in the short run, since the supply is relatively inelastic, would not be affected. . . . In addition, rent control diminishes the incentive to 'ration' accommodation, because it encourages the continued occupation of large houses by small families, who would, in a free market, either sub-let or move to smaller dwellings. Moreover, a rent that denies a return competitive with alternative investments is clearly not going to encourage either new construction for rental or new lettings from the existing stock.

Basic market logic and international experience seem to argue against rent regulation, but a number of additional points are relevant here. Harloe's (1985) detailed comparative study points out that while there is an association between regulation and decline across various countries, it is by no means as direct as might be expected. Some countries had active private rented tenures long *after* regulation was in place; in other countries the decline in the sector commenced *before* regulation was introduced. Other accounts (Doling, 1997: Donnison, 1982) argue that while the persistence of rigorous regulation contributed to an acceleration of decline, other structural factors (notably, the increasingly favoured treatment of owner occupation) were also important. In their review of the British experience Coopers and Lybrand (1989, para. 4.5) concluded that:

> There is neither conclusive evidence nor general support for the proposition that the Rent Acts have been the major *cause* of the decline of private renting, although there is considerable evidence that they have played a significant *role*. (Emphasis in original.)

It is also important to note that one of the assumptions in the standard economic model of the impact of rent control is that the landlord is a profit maximiser. Recent empirical studies of landlords (Kemp, 1998; Crook *et al*, 1992) show that this may not be the case. In the UK, Canada, and Ireland for example, landlords are generally small-scale landlords with only one or two properties. Their knowledge of market conditions and regulations is incomplete, and their behaviour is not wholly consistent with a profit maximising approach.[10] This suggests that landlords' behaviour may be affected by a wide variety of considerations — such as freedom to remove difficult tenants, problems in securing rent arrears, the benefits of having their property tenanted by 'good' tenants who will care for the property, keeping the property within the family, and other considerations.

A further point is that the conventional analysis of rent costs does not distinguish, as Barr (1987) points out, between a *dwelling* and a *home*. A landlord rents accommodation to a tenant and then the tenant turns the accommodation into a home by investing human capital and adding value. For example, by developing friendships, enrolling children in local schools, discovering the most convenient route to travel to work, locating near extended family and so on. These aspects of the 'value' of the tenancy are not transferable to other, similar accommodation at a similar price located elsewhere. In this logic, the landlord is conferred a form of monopoly power when the rent is being renegotiated. The tenant's 'investment' has created part of the value of the tenancy for the tenant. If the landlord were a profit maximiser, then the tenant's investment could be built into the landlord's demand for a higher rent than comparable dwellings of identical physical quality would obtain. For the sitting tenant the accommodation has become a *home* and for the (profit maximising) landlord it is a *dwelling*. This analysis does not suggest that rents should be controlled, but that *changes in the rent of sitting tenants* could justifiably be linked to an appropriate benchmark.

The discussion of rent controls drawn on above does not take account of the variety of rent control regimes or of the wider regulatory context for rented housing. Increasingly, research on the impact of rent controls takes account of the specific forms of rent control, incorporates other features of the regulatory regime, and adopts a dynamic perspective that analyses the response of landlords to rent regulation. Recent research along these lines distinguished *twelve* variants of rent regulation and offered conclusions on the likely effect of each variant on the quantity and quality of private rented housing (Kutty, 1996). For example, rent control may be permanent or temporary; control can take the form of set annual increases in nominal terms or as maximum percentage increases, or many other forms; control may or may not be combined with minimum standards; minimum standards may or may not be accompanied by grants or other incentives for maintenance and refurbishment. The conclusion of one recent analysis is that it is critical to study rent control in the context of all of its provisions and of the housing market environment. Specifically, Kutty (1996: 86) concludes that the:

> negative impact of rent control on maintenance can be mitigated by policies that revise the rent ceiling upwards and policies that link rent increases to increases in the value of housing services (such as a policy of increasing rents by the market value of housing services that have been added through maintenance). Also, policies that enforce high quality standards and at the same time make compliance with the standards not unprofitable (through a maintenance subsidy, as practised in the Netherlands and Belgium) can lead to improvements in housing quality under rent control. These results suggest that countries that practice rent control can protect the quality of rental housing by including in the rent regulation a built-in response to changes in quality, a return on investment in housing maintenance and rehabilitation, and quality code enforcement.

The conclusion in relation to rent regulation is that it can be used as a mechanism to subsidise demand. It is important to stress that the historic form of rent control, with rents levels set for all tenants for long periods would *not* be appropriate. However, a form of rent regulation that allows the market to determine the rent that landlords and tenants agree on at the beginning of a tenancy, and that regulates the terms on which rents are *increased*, would be equitable and efficient. Internationally, the trend for the last four or more decades has been to abandon the old-fashioned form of rent control that was repudiated in Ireland. Countries (Germany, notably) that retain good quality, private rented sectors use some form of indexation for rents, and within the indexation formula allow rents to be related to changes in the quantity and quality of housing services obtained by the tenant.

RENT ALLOWANCES

Rent regulation, however, is only one form of subsidy to demand in the private rented market. An increasingly common form is a housing allowance: an addition to the income of tenants linked, typically, to their rent and income, and family or dependency circumstances. There are principled arguments in favour of this approach. Rent allowances are better than general rent regulation on equity grounds. The amount of subsidy can be tailored quite specifically to the incomes of tenants and to other relevant circumstances. They are also more efficient than rent control or direct provision of housing: they do not interfere directly with the market but allow the market to function, giving tenants some degree of choice, and supplementing the *incomes* of tenants. In addition, the *cost* of supplementing tenants' incomes may be a good deal less than the cost of providing housing in specific circumstances — as the Review Group's report showed for single people in Ireland.

The housing allowance approach is becoming more popular internationally. Policy makers have been driven not only by the logic of this approach, but also by the political drift to targeting in social policy generally and by the decline in the last two decades in support for non-market and collective provision of services generally (Ditch, Lewis and Wilcox, 2001). Housing allowances also have one practical advantage — they allow policy makers the option of grafting a housing allowance on to the main system of social security, and this is quite important where a large proportion of the prospective recipients are likely also to be recipients of social security.

In practical terms, however, a number of policy elements must be in place if the theoretical advantages of a rent allowance are to be realised:

- Rent regulation and rent allowances need to be considered and implemented jointly. If tenants are subsidised for their rent costs, some framework of regulation for standards and for rent indexation is also necessary, otherwise the allowance will simply end up subsidising poor quality accommodation for which high, and unregulated rents are charged.

- The adoption of a housing allowance should not be driven solely by a focus on cost reduction. Market-determined rents are likely to be high relative to the income of social security recipients or people on lower incomes, and an inadequate allowance will simply redirect housing need back into publicly provided housing. The adoption of a housing allowance should therefore be a *strategic choice in social security and housing policy* rather than an *ad hoc* response to changes in the housing system.

- The exact structure of rent regulation and rent allowance needs to be designed with the supply side of the rental housing market in mind. If the *supply* of rented housing is inelastic — not responsive to changes in price — then the effect of a housing allowance may be to simply increase demand; as a result, rents may rise and the benefit of the subsidy conferred, in part, on the landlord. In the Irish private rented sector this point may be especially important as the stock of rented dwellings was relatively stable (and may have declined) while the number of recipients of SWA rent allowances grew in the period from the late 1980s onwards. The observed rise in rents at the lower end of the rental market during this period may have been due to some extent to the subsidisation of demand.[11]

FUTURE POLICY

Finally, what direction should Ireland's rent allowance take in the future? One approach is that being proposed by the Inter-Departmental Committee and the Working Group. This effectively involves an abandonment of the rent allowance as an income maintenance responsibility and its absorption into the local authorities' housing services. On balance this seems misguided. The principle that *all* housing services — including financial assistance with rent and mortgage costs — should be part of one seamless housing service seems sensible, but the administrative simplification this might bring seems to be far outweighed by general policy considerations. The rent and mortgage allowance offers an element of choice to tenants, and it is a cheaper way of meeting housing need than the alternative of direct provision for some tenants. Since many of those currently or prospectively requiring assistance with housing costs are in the social security system, including a rent-allowance-type payment in the main social security system seems practical and efficient.

The argument in support of the retention and development of an allowance carries even greater force in the light of the broader institutional changes taking place in the private rented sector. As pointed out earlier, the 1992 Act introduced some regulation into the sector regarding minimum rights for tenants, minimum standards of housing, landlords' obligations to register properties, and so on. The long-term direction of policy now is to follow the recommendations of the recent Commission on the Private Rented Residential Sector: implementation of these will strengthen regulation, improve supply and develop the sector generally (Commission on the Private Rented Residential Sector, 2000). In particular, the Commission's recommendations will allow for a degree of rent regulation, and will improve security of tenure, and establish an institutional framework (a Private Residential Tenancies Board) for the management and development of the sector. *The Private Residential Tenancies Bill 2003* incorporates the Commission's recommendations, and if the Bill becomes law it will considerably alter the context in which the private rented market operates.

In this new context, some form of rent allowance makes considerable sense. Where the sector is now managed and regulated — as it increasingly will be — it minimises the potential problems and enhances the benefits of direct financial assistance to tenants. This assistance will be given in a context where minimum standards are in place, where supply is also being improved, and where landlord-tenant relations are properly governed. In brief, the future setting for a rent allowance will be qualitatively more suitable than that in which the SWA rent and mortgage allowance emerged.

If the strategy of retaining an allowance is accepted, further consideration is required of the *specific form* an allowance should take. One option here is to simply *retain* the SWA Allowance in its current form as a supplementary payment largely for recipients of social welfare payments. In this scenario, the one reform that should be considered is the discretionary nature of the scheme. As the legislation is discretionary, some variation may arise in the determination of entitlement to the allowance and the amount of the allowance — notwithstanding the guidelines at local health board level about reasonable rents and supplements payable.

A second variant is to expand the SWA allowance into a *housing benefit* as recommended by the Commission on Social Welfare (Commission on Social Welfare, 1986: 305–19). The Commission approached the issue from a social security perspective and argued that a separate, explicit payment in relation to housing costs is an integral part of a social security system that attempts to offer a minimally adequate income. Even where the main social security payments are adequate the wide variation in housing costs will mean that some households will have very inadequate incomes after housing costs have been paid. The Commission proposed (Commission on Social Welfare, 1986: 31) that a:

> nationally uniform housing benefit should be established. This scheme should be based on an explicit judgement as to an adequate income after housing costs have been met. The scheme should be locally administered but should not be discretionary — the entitlement and the amount of the payment should be statutorily defined. The scheme would apply in the private rental and owner-occupied sectors in respect of mortgage and rent costs and would comprehend

employees as well as social welfare payments, subject to income and rent criteria.

The Commission also envisaged that in the long-term the housing benefit would be coordinated with the local authority differential rent system, so that there would be equal net housing subsidies for families of identical circumstances across the private and local authority sectors.[12] A more immediate and important implication of the Commission's proposal is that it would not confine the benefit to social welfare recipients but extend it to all employment statuses on a means-tested basis. This approach has much merit in the light of the glaring poverty trap in the current system: full-time employees are not entitled to SWA, although this problem has been ameliorated recently by extending the allowance to part-time employees and allowing some people returning to work to retain the allowance on a transitional basis. The Commission's approach has the potential to be more efficient (by removing a disincentive to take up employment) and more horizontally equitable (by treating all tenants on the basis of income rather than employment status).

This option, while abolishing one poverty trap, could create another: it would add a further means-tested payment to the nexus of taxes and benefits affecting those on low incomes. Currently, those on modest incomes are affected by taxes and social insurance contributions that affect their disposable incomes and by means tests for Family Income Supplement (if they have children), for differential rent (if they are local authority tenants), and for medical card eligibility (if their income is in the range of Category 1 eligibility for Health Services). Clearly, the exact way in which an employee might be affected would depend on the details of the means test, but the potential would be there for large numbers of employees to become subject to a very high marginal tax/benefit withdrawal rate. The Commission's option could be designed to avoid this problem. However, introducing a further means-tested payment could complicate the task of coordinating the tax and benefit system and might give rise to disincentives.

Finally, any consideration of the future of housing or rent allowances should consider the evolving tax treatment of mortgage interest relief and rent. In relation to interest relief, this now takes the form of a tax credit, with the relief being claimed at the standard rate of tax for all taxpayers. The tax allowance for private rented tenants was originally introduced only for tenants aged over 55 but is now available for all tenants, again at the standard rate of tax.

The Rent Allowance and the tax-based allowances for rent and mortgage interest could be restructured into a *housing tax credit*, encompassing both the rented and owner-occupied sectors. In this model, the tax credit could be adjusted annually and differentiated by family size or a range of other housing-related variables. From a broad policy perspective it would also introduce some degree of tenure neutrality for owning and renting.

A reform of this type is not currently on the policy agenda. Policy proposals that entail any limitation on the preferred treatment of owner-occupation have historically received little support. However, the rent tax allowance has now acquired a role alongside the SWA scheme and the supports for owner-occupation. Simultaneously, the tax system is incrementally moving towards a greater reliance on tax credits. This new context puts a housing tax credit scheme within easier reach as a policy reform. One complication of this model is that a housing tax credit scheme would not be suitable for those dependant on social welfare (Disability Allowance or long-term Unemployment Assistance recipients, for example). Some form of less comprehensive rent allowance might still be required.

Notes

1. Imputed income is the money the 'occupier' pays to the 'owner', analogous to the rent a tenant pays to a landlord. Where the owner and occupier are the same person and money is not actually paid, this notional transfer is, in effect, a form of income and in some countries this income is taxed.
2. This taxation was commonly referred to as 'rates'. A new tax, Residential Property Tax, was introduced in the early 1980s, abandoned again and reintroduced temporarily in the 1990s, but this tax applied to only a very small proportion of the housing stock and yielded insignificant revenue.
3. These are the figures reported in the Department of the Environment's bulletins of Housing Statistics; the DoE is legally obliged to undertake an assessment of homelessness every three years and these figure record the results of the assessments.
4. McCashin (2000) notes that the Labour Force Survey and the Census data for 1997 and 1991 respectively suggest a 61.5% increase in the number of private rented households during this period, and cautions against the use of this figure for technical reasons.
5. The legislation is S.11 of the 1977 *Supplementary Welfare Allowances Act*. The SWA legislation was later subsumed into the *Social Welfare Consolidation Act* of 1993. The 1977 Act also gave discretion to pay 'one-off' lump sums for emergency needs.
6. For an account of the rent controlled sector of the private rental market in Ireland see Threshold's report *Private Rented: The Forgotten Sector* (O'Brien and Dillon, 1982).
7. A description and critique of this legislation can be found in Ryall (1997), Ryall (1998) and Ryall (1999).
8. Formally, tenure neutrality exists when competitive markets leave individuals indifferent between buying and renting accommodation, with no artificial distortion through subsidies. An approximate example of is the case of television rental and purchase (Barr, 1987: 365).

9.   It is useful to distinguish between *need* and *demand*. Need refers to the amount of housing required to accommodate a population of a given size, age and so on, at an agreed minimum standard, without taking into account the individual households' income or ability to pay for housing. Demand, however, refers to the amount of housing households can afford.

10.   The research to date does not offer any clear account as to why this might be the case. Kemp (1998), however, suggests that it may be related to the advanced age of the typical landlord, to the fact that landlords do not use equity or debt to finance their ownership of properties, or that they view the properties as extensions of their own or their families' property. Work by Memery and Kerrins (2000) on landlords in Ireland suggests that a range of factors affect landlords' decisions and behaviour.

11.   In relation to the *supply* of private rented accommodation, a similar theoretical issue arises about the effect of supply side subsidies such as general subsidies for existing tenancies. Whether they increase supply critically depends on the elasticity of demand.

12.   The Commission also listed a range of specific questions that would need to be dealt with in devising a national housing benefit system, such as the desirability of a limit on the duration of the payment, the need for a limit to the amount payable, and other issues (Commission on Social Welfare, 1986: 319).

10
Old Age Pensions

INTRODUCTION

This chapter deals with the main social security provisions for old age. These are the Retirement Pension, the Old Age Contributory Pension (OACP), and the Old Age Non-Contributory Pension (OANCP). The first two of these are based on social insurance and the latter is a means-tested, social assistance payment. Both the Contributory and the Non-Contributory Pensions are payable at age 66, whereas the eligible age for the Retirement Pension is 65.

There are two central aspects of old age pension provision that distinguish it from other areas of social security. The first of these is the role of private provision. State-provided pensions exist alongside a structure of *private* provision, and much of the policy controversy is about the relative importance of state vis-à-vis private provisions and the ways in which they overlap. Second, in pensions policy there is a wide acceptance of an *income replacement* goal for policy. The National Pensions Board (NPB) pointed out (1998: 84) that while poverty is one of the key issues in pensions policy, it is also important to ensure that older people have an income that reflects their acquired living standard so that they do not 'suffer a sharp drop in their living standards' on retirement.

The next two sections below give a brief description of social security pensions and a sketch of other important pension provisions. The subsequent section gives an overview of the development of social security pensions, and then the discussion turns to a particular controversy in pensions policy: the debate about whether pensions should be pre-funded or paid for out of current revenue. Then the focus turns to future policy, paying particular attention to the recent report of the National Pensions Board (NPB), *Securing Retirement Income* (NPB, 1998). This document has set the framework for the future evolution of pensions policy in Ireland.

Discussion about pensions policy is often couched in terms of 'pillars' or 'tiers'. These terms refer to the implicit hierarchy in the pensions system. The first pillar refers to the basic state provisions under social insurance and social assistance, and the second to occupational pensions from employers. The third pillar refers to private income from investments and interest. Increasingly, the term 'fourth pillar' is also coming into use. In some countries governments are responding to the ageing of populations by exhorting or requiring older people to continue to work beyond pensionable age, and hence earnings is a potential fourth pillar of income provision.

THE CURRENT PENSION SYSTEM: SOCIAL INSURANCE AND ASSISTANCE

Chart 10.1 summarises the features of the first pillar and Table 10.1 gives the aggregate figures for recipients and expenditure in 2002.

Table 10.1: Social Insurance and Assistance Pensions in 2002

Pension	Recipients (000s)	Expenditure (€m)	Expenditure (%)
Contributory	105.3	868.7	39.3
Retirement	83.1	803.4	36.3
Non contributory	87.8	537.3	24.3
Total	276.2	2,209.4	100.

Source: Statistical Information on Social Welfare Services, 2002.
Note: These data do not include the Pre-Retirement Allowance for the long-term unemployed aged 55 or over (see Chapter Eight).

Total expenditure in 2002 was over €2.2 billion (2.1% of GNP), in respect of approximately 276,000 pension recipients. Social insurance pensions now considerably outstrip the non-contributory pension in terms of recipient numbers and expenditure. As the chart suggests, the contribution requirements are complex: they are structured around rules about when pensioners commenced contributions, their average yearly contributions, and the age at which they commenced employment.

There are two important points not specifically noted in the chart. First, since 1994 time spent working in the home (with dependent children under 6 or dependent relatives) has been disregarded for purposes of calculating yearly average contributions. This has limited, although not eliminated, the loss of a social insurance record for the time spent in the home. Second, there are also complex arrangements for credited (as distinct from paid) contributions: the most important of these are the credits acquired at times of unemployment and sickness. Credited contributions can help to sustain an insurance record in the absence of an income from which to pay PRSI.

The non-contributory pension is also payable at age 66, subject to a means test. An important feature of the means assessment is the treatment of savings and property. The family home in which a pensioner resides does *not* count as means, although any property yielding an income is assessed. To assess the value of savings the first €12,500 (approximately) is disregarded in the case of a single person (double for a married couple), and for savings above that figure a weekly income is imputed and assessed as means. For example, with savings of €25,000 a single pensioner has the first €12,500 disregarded, and for every €1,270 above that threshold (to €25,400) means of €1.27 per week are imputed. At higher levels of saving a higher weekly rate of means is imputed. The pension payable is reduced according to means and the levels of pension payable are in bands. Pensioners can have a substantial level of savings while still retaining entitlement to a pension.

THE CURRENT PENSION SYSTEM — OCCUPATIONAL PENSIONS

Social security pensions exist alongside a system of occupational pensions and personal pensions. The NPB (1993: 5) defines occupational pensions as an 'arrangement organised by an employer to provide pensions and/or other benefits to one or more employees on retirement or to surviving dependants on death'. Personal pensions refer to arrangements made by individual self-employed people, or employees who are not members of occupational schemes. Occupational pensions are far more common. There are two types of occupational pensions — Defined Benefit and Defined Contribution pensions:[1]

- *Defined Benefit* pensions are particularly common in the public service. Under this arrangement an employee's pension is defined in some way in relation to his/her salary or pay: the pension could be half of final (pensionable) salary, for example.
- *Defined Contribution* schemes offer pensions that are wholly related to the benefits purchased by the employee through contributions, and the amount of the pension will depend on value of the pension fund (or the value of the annuity that might be purchased from the proceeds of a policy).

In Ireland at present, according to the official survey of pensions coverage among adults aged 20 to 69, 43.3% of employees have an occupational pension, 5.4 % have a personal pension and a further 3.5% have both a personal pension and an occupational pension (CSO, 2002). This gives a total coverage among employees of 52.2%. Among the self-employed, the total coverage is 44% (by definition, all personal pensions).

Membership of occupational pension schemes varies considerably. It is higher among men than women, higher for public than for private sector employees, and higher also for full-time than for part-time workers. The details of pension coverage will be discussed again below. As regards the type of scheme employees

Chart 10.1 : Summary of Social Security Pensions Provisions

Pension (€ per week, single person, under 80)	Age	Retirement Condition?	Insurance Contributions Required	Means Test	Other Rules
Contributory (€157.30)	66	No	Commenced paying contributions before age 56; at least 156 full-rate contributions paid, or, if the yearly average is between 10 and 19, at least 260 contributions paid; a yearly average of at least 48 full-rate contributions paid and/or credited from 1979 to end of the tax year before age 66 or a yearly average of at least 10 full-rate contributions paid and/or credited from 1979 to the end of the tax year before age 66.	N/a	A yearly average of 10 full-rate contributions is required for a minimum pension, and an average of 48 for the maximum.
Retirement (€157.30)	65	Yes	Commenced paying PRSI before age 55; at least 156 full-rate contributions paid; a yearly average of at least 48 full-rate contributions paid and/or credited since 1979 to end of the tax year before age 65 or a yearly average of at least 24 full-rate contributions paid and/or credited from 1953, or the time employment commenced, to the	N/a	A yearly average of 24 full-rate contributions required for a minimum pension and an average of 48 for the maximum.

					end of the tax year before age 65; if retirement commences between 2002 and 2012 a minimum of 260 full-rate contributions is required.	Specific provisions for sale of home and purchase of other home; also special rules for sale of home and entry to nursing home.
Non-contributory (€144.00)	66	No	N/a			Means include: cash income, earnings, value of savings and investments above €12,500, value of property (own home excepted); amount of pension is related to assessed means.

Notes: The retirement condition for the retirement pension allows pensioners, both employees and self-employed, to work on a very limited part-time basis: the retirement condition for the retirement pension ceases at age 66. There are special rules allowing a half social insurance pension for those with pre-1953 contributions, and further rules allowing pro-rata pension for those with higher incomes who were not contributing before 1974 (when the income limit was abolished).

belong to, the ESRI pensions survey shows that among employees that are scheme members a very large majority (85%) are in defined benefit schemes and the remainder in defined contribution schemes (Hughes and Whelan, 1996). However, the proportion of public sector employees in defined benefit arrangements is significantly higher than for private sector employees.

From a policy standpoint, there are three important points to note about the link between social security pensions and occupational pensions:

- First, at the level of households and individual pensioners, pension income at any given time may come from a mix of sources, and the mix may change over time. Therefore, any trends or patterns that might be observed in relation to pensioners' incomes reflects the operation of the *pensions system as a whole* and not just social security pensions.

- Second, many occupational pension schemes in both public and private sector schemes are *integrated* with the social security pensions system. Briefly, the amount of the occupational pension paid on retirement takes account of the value of the state pension. Changes in the design and level of the state pensions have implications for the occupational pension entitlements of employees and also pensioners in receipt of occupational pensions.

- Third, the costs of the social security and occupational pensions need to be viewed as a totality. Occupational pensions are supported by *tax reliefs*. The employer and employee contributions to (occupational) pension funds are tax deductible, investment income from pension funds is tax exempt, pension 'lump sums' are tax exempt, but pension income in the hands of the recipient is taxable. The net effect of this tax treatment is to generate considerable tax expenditures. These indirect expenditures have grown significantly in recent years, and the policy choices in relation to improving pensions need to reflect the indirect costs of the tax reliefs and the direct cost of the social security pensions.

How important are the different sources of income to the pensioner population? The key trends up to the mid-nineties revealed in the ESRI survey were:

- A long-term growth in the number in receipt of social security pensions.
- A growth from a very low base in the number of occupational pensions.
- A decline in the importance of farming, self-employment and earnings.
- An increase in the number receiving an income from interest and dividends, although it comprises a low share, on average, of the income of older households.

The most recent data on income sources in older persons' households are summarised in Table 10.2. These are representative figures taken from the Household Budget Surveys and they show that state social welfare payments are

Table 10.2: Income from pensions as a percentage of total income for households headed by older people

Sources of pension income	1987	1994/95	1999/2000
All state social welfare sources, age 65–74	43.0	37.0	47.9
All state social welfare sources, age 75+	44.0	40.9	48.3
Occupational pensions, age 65–74	15.7	20.8	23.5
Occupational pensions, age 75+	16.3	26.8	20.6

Source: Connell and Stewart, 2004, based on Household Budget Surveys.

the most significant element in older persons' incomes. The role of occupational pension income increased from 1987 to the end of the 1990s, but most of this growth took place from 1987 to 1994–5. One interesting detail is the *decline* in the share of occupational pensions in households' incomes in the older (age 75+) category, from 26.8% to 20.6%. This may indicate the absence of indexation in some occupational pensions and a decline in the share of these pensions in the overall incomes of the elderly.

THE DEVELOPMENT OF SOCIAL SECURITY PENSIONS

The evolution of pensions up to the present day can be divided into three broad phases, as follows: first, the period from 1908 until the early 1960s, at which point the contributory pension was introduced; second, from the early 1960s until the early 1980s, during which time both of the social security pensions expanded, and policy debate focused on the possibility of a state income-related pension; third, the period since then, in which the current strategy has evolved of attempting to develop occupational pensions and private pensions rather than a second-tier state pension.

The first period commenced with the introduction of the Old Age Pension in 1908 in Ireland and Great Britain. In its first two decades the pension had a colourful history by the standards of social security development in Ireland. In the context of the Irish economy of the time the pension was generous in two respects. First, the pension levels were set with the earnings and living standards of the British working class in mind. When transplanted into the Irish context, the pensions were high relative to the earnings of Irish workers and to the lower costs of living in Ireland (Ó Gráda, 2002; Guinnane, 1993). Second, at a macro-level, the share of the older population in Ireland was higher than in the UK and the combination of pension levels and the large population of recipients meant that the pension represented a substantial fiscal transfer from Britain to Ireland, as Guinnane (1993: 272) pointed out: 'The Irish being older and poorer than the English, Ireland had far more pensioners per capita.'

The registration of births had not been introduced until 1864 and it was therefore very difficult to enforce the main stipulation about the pension: applicants had to have reached 70 years. The historical evidence suggests that there was, indeed, intentional misreporting of age (Ó Gráda, 2002: Guinnane, 1993). Also, it was difficult to implement a test of means in a predominantly agricultural, self-employed economy, and as a result a large majority of the pensioners received the maximum payment. In 1909, in the face of the cost of providing pensions the government undertook a more searching assessment of pension claims. This resulted in the withdrawal of 38,945 pensions in Ireland.

The popularity of the new pension was in marked contrast to the official concern about costs and age-misreporting. Not only was the pension generous, but it also offered older persons an alternative to the Poor Law workhouse, and the extent of both indoor and outdoor relief declined among the old after the pension was introduced. For the Poor Law guardians too, the pension led to savings as a result of the decline in Poor Law relief among the elderly. Although the means test for the pension took into account the value of the 'benefit and privilege', a pensioner received from living with his/her family, the pension was still a boon for the families of the elderly. It was a direct financial boost to the family's budget to have an older person in receipt of a pension, and the pension also removed the pressure on families to admit older persons to the workhouse (Ó Gráda, 2002).

Some modifications were made to the pension prior to political independence. The residency requirement of 20 years was relaxed and the exclusion of former poor relief recipients was abolished. More significantly, the Blind Persons Act of 1920 extended the pension to blind persons aged 50 and over, and the rate of pension was doubled. However, the new Free State Government inherited the original structure of the pension. At the time of its introduction, nationalist politicians had been very aware of the costs of the pension. This awareness, combined with a continuing unease about age-misreporting, may have contributed to the government's willingness to use the pension as a source of economies in the 1924 budget. This budget imposed significant reductions in the pension: the maximum rate was reduced by 10% and the means test was tightened. As a result, the total number of pensions fell from 122,845 in 1924 to 115,817 in 1925. More dramatic still was the fall in the number of maximum pensions in payment: from just over 112,000 to under 30,000 (Ó Gráda, 2002). Critics of this retrenchment contrasted it with the reductions in tax rates on higher incomes and in death duties on larger estates.

The reduction in the pension was restored in 1928, but pensions were now highly politicised and became 'something of a defining issue between Fianna Fáil and Cumann na nGaedheal' (Ó Gráda, 2002: 155). In fact, the government was defeated in the Dail in 1929 on a pensions issue. The opposition proposed the removal of the clause in the 1908 Act that required the means of pensioners' families to be taken into account. The opposition did not press its victory and allowed the proposed legislation to lapse. However, the pension featured as an election issue in 1932 (and again in 1933) and early in the life of the Fianna Fáil government important changes were made to the old age pension:

- The 'benefit and privilege' clause taking account of the means of resident family members was abolished.
- The bar on elected representatives making representations about pension applications was removed.
- The Poor Relief disqualification was finally abolished.
- The age of qualification for blind persons was reduced from 50 to 30.

Fianna Fáil governments administered pensions legislation more leniently. Successful appeals by applicants on grounds of age increased significantly after 1932. Also, the Department of Local Government encouraged appeals in cases where applicants had been denied a pension on the grounds that they had deliberately disposed of assets in order to acquire a pension. This leniency was rationalised in terms of the need to allow older farmers to transfer the family farm to younger family members: however, the formal 1908 legislation disallowing pensions on the transfer of assets remained in place.

In the 1930s and 1940s the pension became less politically contentious. Proof of age was no longer problematic from the mid-1930s, removing one of the bones of contention and one source of appeals. The legislative changes and the more lenient administration together defused the politics of pensions. Pensions were integrated with the newly introduced provision for widows in the late 1930s, so that a widow in receipt of a contributory pension at age 70 would become entitled, irrespective of means, to a maximum old age pension. The final significant act in the early development of the pensions was the legislation of 1951 allowing farmers (with farms below a certain valuation) to assign the farm to children without affecting the right to a pension. This change and other changes to the means test for blind persons' pensions were brought in by William Norton as part of his attempt to secure political support for the wider social security plan outlined in the 1949 White Paper (see Chapter Two). In the event, although the White Paper had proposed comprehensive social insurance pensions, these were not part of the 1952 Act.

The second phase in the development of pensions began with the 1960 Social Welfare Act. This act legislated for the OACP, which was introduced in 1961 by a Fianna Fáil government. The government was criticised by William Norton, leader of the Labour Party in 1961, largely on the same grounds as in 1952. The 1952 legislation, Norton pointed out, contained no provisions for pensions, and the 1960 Act contained only limited provisions (Cook, 1990: 112). Coverage of the OACP was confined to persons insured under the social security legislation, thereby excluding the self-employed, public servants and people above the income limit for social insurance contributions. From the early 1960s until the early 1980s, pensions developed within the framework of the OACP and the OANCP. In the

1970s, the pace of change quickened, reflecting in part the emphasis on social security issues of the 1973–7 Labour-Fine Gael coalition government. A Retirement Pension (RP) was introduced in 1970, and then in rapid succession during the years of Coalition government the age of eligibility was reduced from 70 to 66 for the OACP and the OANCP, and 65 for the RP. The long-term potential pool of social insurance pensioners also expanded with the abolition of the income ceiling for contributors to social insurance.

In the mid-1970s, the policy debate changed. The question at that point was how far the development of social security pensions should proceed, given that the direction of change was towards comprehensive social insurance provision. The first official contribution in this new phase of policy development was the Green Paper *A National Income Related Pension Scheme* (Department of Social Welfare, 1976). This came in the wake of significant real improvements in the value of the OACP and OANCP and a reduction in the age of eligibility for these pensions, and the momentum towards extension and development of the state pensions was strong at that time.

The Green Paper identified the following as the shortcomings of the system at the time; inadequate coverage of occupational pensions among both employees and the self-employed; exclusion of the self-employed from social insurance; lack of protection of pension rights for members of occupational schemes; the absence of an income-replacement element; and uncertain and mixed arrangements about indexation of pensions. The Green Paper started not only from a pragmatic recognition of the deficiencies of the current arrangements, but also with a firm statement of the importance of income replacement as a central feature of any future pensions system (Department of Social Welfare, 1976: 62):

> Fundamentally what is needed is the basing of the pensions to be provided in a national system on the concept that pension is in replacement of lost income or earnings and should, therefore, be related to the level of such income or earnings. Flat-rate pensions cannot achieve this as, while they may replace a very high level of the earnings for the lower-paid workers, their replacement value declines as the earnings level rises. In these circumstances, the flat-rate pensions must be regarded as inadequate unless they are wedded to a supplementary pension that is earnings-related in one way or another.

Having offered this argument in favour of an income-related pension, the Green Paper proceeded to offer models of how such a system might apply in the Irish context of the time. Briefly, it set out three model illustrations of an income-related pension system, as follows:

Model A. This would entail a single-tier system, providing purely earnings-related pensions, not differentiated between single persons and those with spouses and dependants. The pension would subsume existing occupational pensions and the social insurance pension, and would move in line with average earnings.

Model B. This would be a two-tier system in which the first tier would be based on the existing social insurance pension and the second tier would comprise an earnings-related, supplementary pension. In the first tier, the payment would be structured according to marital and dependency status, and in the second, the supplementary pension would apply to those above an earnings limit, and (as in the case of PRB) the supplementary pensions would be related to a lower earnings 'floor' and an upper earnings 'ceiling'. In one version of this model, employers and employees would have the right to 'contract out' of the second-tier provided they had supplementary pension arrangements of a specified standard.

Model C. Essentially this would be a variant of Model B. Here there would be a basic social insurance pension (differentiated by marital status) and a supplementary pension. However, in this model, the second tier pensions would only encompass employees with earnings up to a level around average earnings, leaving the higher-income employees to be catered for in occupational pension schemes.

The Green Paper then gave illustrations of pension levels under these models and forecasts of their budgetary costs and contribution requirements. It also offered a review of the arguments about how pensions should be funded, whether on a pay-as-you-go (PAYG) or funded basis (with contribution income being set aside into a fund from which future pension liabilities will be met). The Green Paper was ambivalent. It fully acknowledged the deficiencies of the contemporary system and firmly argued a role for an income-replacement dimension to pensions. This, combined with the detail it offered of possible new designs and their cost and contribution requirements, implied that at the time the government might be strongly disposed towards an income-related pension. However, it also pointed out that the analysis of costs and models in no way implied a decision to proceed with income-related pensions. It outlined what it saw as the potentially negative consequences of higher (pension) contribution rates on employers and employees, and argued that an expanded pension system based on PAYG principles could displace national savings and investment.

There was considerable public and political interest in the policy issues raised in the Green Paper. A White Paper was drafted but never published, and by the early 1980s the likelihood of income-related pensions had receded from public and political view. In fact, policy developed in an entirely different direction. After the Green Paper was published, the existing social security pensions were further improved (further lowering of the pension age and increases in the real value of the payments) and a further Green Paper *Social Insurance for the Self-Employed* was published (Department of Social Welfare, 1978). In the early 1980s the economy entered a period of rising unemployment and escalating levels of national debt. There was a change of government in 1977 and further elections in 1981, and again in January 1982 and November 1982. A Labour-Fine Gael coalition government took office in 1982 and the Labour party was again assigned responsibility for social security. However, a new twist was put on pensions policy in the early 1980s when the lack of regulation in occupational pensions led to some widely publicised crises of standards, funding and accountability. Taken together, these new circumstances led to a decisive shift in policy.

In 1985, the then Minister for Social Welfare publicly outlined the likely development of pensions in the future, suggesting that the priority issues were: the social insurance coverage of the self-employed; the need for regulation of occupational pensions; and the necessity to sustain the value of the existing state pensions. In relation to income-related pensions, the Minister stated that (Minister for Social Welfare, 1985: 16):

> The main emphasis in the State scheme will have to remain on aiming to ensure that flat-rate pensions achieve a reasonable relationship with earnings. That is not to say that the issue of pay-related pensions can or will be ignored. But the options there have to be considered in terms of what the economy can afford at a time when the overriding priority is unemployment.

The Minister then announced (in the same speech) the establishment of a National Pensions Board and outlined the proposed Board's terms of references. Quite independently of the emergence of the NPB, the Commission on Social Welfare offered an overview of pensions and of social insurance more generally. The Commission broadly concurred with the Green Paper's analysis of the deficiencies of the pensions system and welcomed the establishment of the NPB. It suggested that an earnings-related pension was not a priority and that the main objective of policy 'should be to use limited resources to improve the income position of all categories of social welfare recipients' (Commission on Social Welfare, 1986: 328).

The establishment of the NPB in 1986 ushered in the third and most recent phase in the evolution of pensions. Policy moved quickly from the mid-1980s onwards, with the NPB producing a succession of reports that fed directly into policy (NPB, 1987; NPB, 1988; NPB 1989; NPB, 1993). In 1989 the self-employed were included in the social insurance system: this development followed the recommendations of both the NPB's (1988) report on the subject and the Commission on Social Welfare's report.

In 1990 the Pensions Act was passed, and became law in 1991. The legislation followed closely the NPB's reports on the regulation of occupational pensions and the implementation of the EU's Equal Treatment Directive as it pertained to occupational pensions. Briefly, the Pensions Act put the NPB on a statutory footing as the overarching regulatory and advisory body, and constructed a new legislative framework for occupational pensions, setting out detailed legislation about:

- Funding standards, including actuarial practices and financial monitoring.
- The role and responsibilities of Pension Trustees.
- The rights of pension fund members to information, and the disclosure requirements of pension fund trustees.
- Preservation, revaluation and transfer of pension contributions and benefits on changing jobs.
- Legal obligations on trustees to members on the winding-up of a pension scheme.
- Equal treatment between men and women in relation to contributions, eligibility for scheme membership, benefits and retirement ages.

The extension of social insurance to the self-employed was one element in the emerging pension regime, and the new regulatory regime for occupational pensions was another. These elements, however, were only part of the wider pensions system for which the NPB was given policy responsibility. In 1993, the NPB (1993) issued its final report, *Developing the National Pension System*, giving detailed recommendations about all aspects of the pensions system, but more importantly offering a view about the long-standing question of income-related pensions. The majority of the NPB did *not* agree that there should be a state income related pension and the Board recommended that 'the coverage of occupational schemes and personal pension arrangements should continue to be encouraged, in particular the existing tax treatment should be encouraged' (NPB, 1993: 202). Also, the NPB repudiated the idea of *compulsory* second-tier pensions, whether in a state scheme or compulsory occupational and private pensions. However, there were familiar lines of disagreement. The Trade Unions expressed a preference for state income-related pensions funded by additional percentage PRSI deductions, while business and employer interests expressed opposition to compulsory income-related pensions 'under any circumstances' (NPB: 203).

The NPB's final report sparked further policy debate, the first round in which was the official publication, *National Pensions Policy Initiative: Consultation Document* (Department of Social Welfare, 1997). In this document the government and the NPB jointly attempted to engender debate on the overall structure of pensions provision in Ireland, and raised again, very explicitly, the fundamental questions that had driven policy debate since the 1970s Green Paper. It invited readers and participants to consider questions such as the role of the state in pensions provision, the desirability of an income-related pension, the possibility of compulsory occupational coverage, and so on. The consultation document set out broad policy options, reviewed some relevant international experience, and listed relevant policy criteria, just as the 1976 Green Paper did. However, while the discussion in the consultation document was studiously neutral, the stances already expressed by the various interests in the NPB's 1993 report were firmly re-stated: the trade unions advocated a role for a state income-related pension, and the business and employer organisations expressed opposition to any obligatory second-tier pension.

From the point of view of the future development of policy, the key point in the consultation document was the NPB's separate statement of its preferred policy. This statement reiterated in full the view the NPB had outlined in its 1993 report (Department of Social Welfare, 1997: 59):

> The Board concluded that, having regard to existing levels of coverage, international experience and the number of small employers in Ireland, it is highly unlikely that comprehensive pension cover, which would maintain established standards of living, can be achieved under the present national pension system (compulsory social insurance for flat-rate pensions and voluntary occupational or personal pension arrangements providing supplementary pension cover).

The Board also had serious reservations as to whether a second tier income-related pension scheme under social insurance would be sustainable in the longer term, in the light of the demographic projections and the projected level of contributions required to finance first tier social insurance pensions.

Accordingly, the Board recommended that occupational and personal pension cover arrangements should continue to be encouraged. It also recommended that the Pensions Board should monitor, and report on, the coverage and scope of pension provision at regular intervals.

In short, the Board adhered to the view that voluntary and private provision (underpinned by regulation and tax relief), rather than state provision, should be the source of any future second tier pension arrangements. One year later in *Securing Retirement Income* (NPB, 1998), the NPB set out in greater detail the logic of this strategy and outlined a full range of proposals for future pension provision. These proposals were adopted by government and their broad thrust was implemented on a phased basis from 1999 to 2002. The *Securing Retirement Income* proposals are dealt with fully later.

EQUITY AND EFFICIENCY

One of the differences between pensions and other areas of social security is that pensions are provided both by the market and the state. As the discussion above showed, it is the boundary between public and private provision and their relative roles and treatment that are at the core of policy choice and debate. It is necessary, therefore, to review the equity and efficiency principles outlined in Chapter Four as they apply to pensions.[2]

Taking *efficiency* first, the essential question is whether the basic principles point to market or state provision. The standard assumptions (Barr, 2003) that are required for market provision of pensions are: perfect competition, absence of market failures and perfect information. Broadly, the first two assumptions hold. If there are no barriers to market entry, there will be multiple competing providers. There are no serious market failures with pension products: pensions do not have the technical characteristics of public goods nor do they impose externalities (costs or benefits on people other than pension purchasers). In the area of perfect information, however, the standard assumption does not hold. One obvious point here is the sheer complexity of pensions. While commercial advertising of pensions often uses the term 'product' to refer to a pension, pensions are legally and financially complicated, and lower-income consumers will be disproportionately disadvantaged by confusion or lack of information. Furthermore, there is likely to be an imbalance of information between the supplier of pension 'products' and the average consumer. This information problem is not a justification for state provision. However, it does offer strong grounds for state regulation of pension products and how they are marketed and sold.

The problem of inflation introduces a more serious departure from the perfect information condition. A supplier of a private insurance product must be able to estimate the average probability of the insured event happening (for instance a fire or a car accident) in order to determine a premium (the price of insurance). With pensions the key event is the likelihood of inflation: purchasers are attempting to ensure a certain *real* standard of consumption during retirement. Pension providers cannot estimate the probability distribution of different levels of price change, and therefore inflation is effectively an uninsurable risk.

A further complication is that for the perfect information assumption to hold the probabilities of the insured event for one consumer must be *independent* of the probability for any other. This does not hold in the case of inflation (or unemployment, to take another example). If prices rise for one person, they rise for them all. Private insurance can deal with individual events but not with general social events. As private pension provision is unable to offer indexation against inflation, there is a role for the state on efficiency grounds of guaranteeing an indexation element in private pensions. The standard theoretical treatment of this question concludes: 'Thus there is an efficiency argument, at a minimum, for state intervention to assist private schemes with the costs of unanticipated inflation once pensions are in payment. The state is able to offer such a guarantee because it can use current tax revenues on a pay-as-you-go basis.' (Barr, 2003: 211–2)

The underlying efficiency logic therefore supports a theoretical case for state intervention. But is there an argument for *social insurance*? First, social insurance is usually compulsory (for the generality of the population for a wide range of risks). This means that there is no problem of adverse selection with the 'bad risks' opting out: the premiums can then be determined on a pooled basis. There are also significant practical arguments for state or quasi-public organisation of insurance: lower administrative costs and administrative simplicity.

Turning to *equity* issues, poverty amelioration is one of the relevant objectives. If retired persons were left to obtain pensions exclusively in the private market lower-income persons might have no pensions or only very inadequate ones. This would give a case for some form of state provision, either directly as a state pension, as a supplement to a private pension, or as a tax support for private provision. Historically, the evidence shows that the introduction of state pensions was associated with a decline in poverty among the elderly. This basic equity reason, combined with the efficiency limitations of private pensions, give a rationale that both justifies and explains the existence of state social insurance and assistance pensions.

However, if this reasoning is accepted another fundamental issue arises. *How* should pensions be provided? The essential task of a pension is to redistribute living standards over the life cycle. Clearly, it is not possible to achieve this directly by storing up goods and services for future use (housing is an exception to this), and future consumption must be shared somehow. Should today's pensioners' incomes be provided out of current income on a pay-as-you-go (PAYG) basis, or should it be on a funded basis, out of savings made in the past? PAYG schemes such as the non-contributory old age pension or the pensions paid by the state to retired employees do not pay pensions out of an accumulated fund: the state taxes the current generation of workers and uses part of the proceeds to pay pensions to the retired. One point of confusion here is that many countries, Ireland included, have social insurance pensions. Entitlement to these is based on contribution rules, and the employers and employees pay specific contributions into a separate fund. However, the term 'social insurance' may convey an impression that such schemes are funded in the sense described above. These are PAYG pensions. Contributions are really earmarked taxes rather than insurance premiums, and the current income in the fund pays for the *present* generation of pensioners.

One point to note about the equity aspect of social insurance pensions is that social insurance *may* be redistributive. It could be directly redistributive if, for example, the structure of contributions is related in a progressive way to workers' incomes. In practice, however, the detailed distributive effects of social insurance are complex and not readily transparent. A wide range of variables have distributive effects: credited contributions, differential life expectancy, and a host of detailed rules about contributions and their link to entitlements.

In a funded scheme, an individual pays contributions into a pension fund (often matched by an employer's contribution) managed by a commercial company or by a non-profit body such as an occupational pension. On retirement, the contributions (along with interest and capital gains) amount to a capital sum. This is usually converted into an annuity, i.e. an annual payment for life.[3] As the earlier descriptions pointed out, funded schemes can be either defined benefit or defined contribution in nature. Defined benefit pensions are usually organised at company or sector level: here the pensioner is given an annuity on retirement related to the employee's pre-retirement wage and length of service. In effect, the pension is indexed to wages up until the point of retirement. The employee's contribution is usually a percentage of pay. In these circumstances the employer bears the risk that the rate of return on pension fund assets is not sufficient to permit indexation of the pension to wages after the employee retires, and the employer's contribution may need to be adjusted.

With defined contributions the employee's pension (the annuity purchased with the accumulated capital) depends wholly on the value of the accumulated fund. Here the employee bears any risk associated with fluctuating rates of return on pension funds during his working life. The employee also bears the risk of any inflation over and above the inflation rate built into the pension contribution.

There has been a continuing controversy about which of the two approaches to financing pensions, PAYG or funding, is the most desirable. This is, in part, a theoretical question. However, the question has assumed considerable policy significance internationally in the light of the growth in the elderly population and the need to pay for the rising cost of pensions. Funding future pension liabilities, it is being increasingly argued, provides a mechanism to pay for the growing number of pensioners. The view is widely expressed that funding is intrinsically more prudent, simply 'saving for old age'. This is true for individuals, but not for *society as a whole*. From a social and economic standpoint, today's workforce produces the consumption of today's pensioners, and the function of pensions is to divide output between workers and pensioners

The formal theoretical treatment of this subject shows that, in a fundamental economic sense, there is no difference between funding and PAYG. It can be shown that under certain simplifying assumptions PAYG and funded arrangements lead to identical results (Barr, 1993; Barr, 1997).[4] Clearly, pensioners can only consume what the workforce produce and do not consume themselves, and pensioners rely on the succeeding generation of workers to produce the goods they consume. However, this theoretical reasoning adopts quite specific assumptions:

- The number of workers remains unchanged.
- Output per worker is constant over time.
- Output per worker is not affected by the choice of pension system, funded or PAYG.

What if the first assumption fails and the number of workers (and output) declines? Under a PAYG system, taxes or social insurance contributions simply redistribute total output between workers and pensioners. With funding, pensioners will have accumulated savings, but (other things being equal) these savings together with workers' consumption will exceed the level of output. Pensioners will have accumulated money, but where the total of this money and workers consumption exceed the level of output then prices will rise, reducing the *real* value of pensioners' savings.

However, this analysis does not apply if the second assumption does not hold. Output per worker may *rise* over time. If output per worker rises sufficiently then the smaller workforce can produce the same total output as before. Historically, of course, productivity per worker rose over a long period of time, and, in policy terms, in many countries with ageing populations the real issue is the balance between a declining workforce and trends in output per worker.

The third assumption is the most controversial. Output per worker may *depend on the type of pension system*. Specifically, it has been argued that PAYG pensions result in lower rates of national saving and hence lower national investment and output than funded pensions. This argument can be traced to a famous paper (Feldstein, 1994) that showed that the US (PAYG) social security system was implicated in the US's depressed rate of national and personal savings. Before noting the evidence about this contention it is useful to summarise the chain of reasoning involved, and to consider each link in the chain separately. Chart 10.2 outlines the argument.

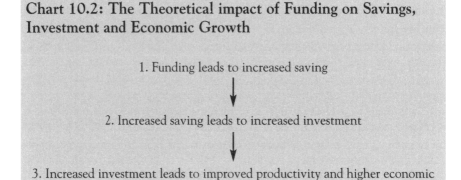

Chart 10.2: The Theoretical impact of Funding on Savings, Investment and Economic Growth

1. Funding leads to increased saving

2. Increased saving leads to increased investment

3. Increased investment leads to improved productivity and higher economic growth.

- The first assertion is that *funded pensions generate higher savings than PAYG*. This point certainly holds for any cohort of pensioners during the build-up phase, but when the cohort retires it begins to 'dissave'. In other words, in steady state, the savings of workers are offset by the 'dissavings' of pensioners. There is also a more general point about motives for savings. If a worker's pension contribution is switched from PAYG to a funded pension, then savings increase if the worker's voluntary savings are unchanged. However, if the worker offsets the switch to funding with a reduction in voluntary saving of the same amount then savings remain the same.

- The second link in the argument is that funding leads to *higher investment*. This is not necessarily the case. Pension savings might be used to buy non-productive assets.
- Third, it is argued that funded pensions lead to *higher productivity and output* than PAYG. Here, too, the argument may not be valid. Pension fund managers in either funded state or private schemes will not necessarily make more efficient investment choices.

Theoretically then, the view that funding is superior to PAYG is arguable. The issue of funding versus PAYG has moved from the realm of theory to policy because of the growing share of the elderly in the population of many developed economies and the consequent concern over the sustainability of pensions. It has also become a politically contentious issue because of the influence the pro-funding arguments have had in the last two decades on pensions policy. In its influential report *Averting the Old Age Crisis*, (1994) the World Bank adopted a broadly pro-funding stance, influencing the recent pensions policies of many governments. The World Bank's report and the policy developments it has shaped have been sharply criticised by a wide range of pensions commentators in many countries, partly because the World Bank recommends funding as a general strategy across a wide range of countries, developed and undeveloped, and partly because funding does not address poverty and inequality among the elderly (Blackburn, 2002; Minns, 2001; Davies, Land, *et al*, 2003; Hughes, 1996).

Unfortunately, empirical research has not resolved the theoretical debate or the political controversy. Since Feldstein first published his influential paper a considerable amount of research has been undertaken, but the results of the research are inconclusive. Reviews of the international research by the International Monetary Fund (1995) and the World Bank (1994), as well as academic researchers (Atkinson, 1987; Barr, 1992; Barr, 1993; Cartwright, 1984; Hughes, 1996; Munnell, 1986B) all acknowledge that the empirical evidence is mixed. The safest policy conclusion to draw is that countries with an ageing population should not rely wholly on funding as a method of securing adequate incomes for the aged.

The funding versus PAYG controversy has become particularly acute in the last decade because many developed countries began to experience rising pension costs in the context of an ageing population. But if funding rather than PAYG is not a solution, what policy options are available? In theory, a government could respond to a declining working-age population by reducing the demand for goods and services among workers (by increasing taxes or social insurance contributions) or among pensioners (by allowing their income to decline relative to average incomes). Alternatively, policy could focus on increasing output by increasing the number of workers or the output per worker, or both. Among the relevant policy instruments are the following: improving the productivity of the workforce through education and training; increasing the size of the labour force through later retirement or higher immigration; and improving the quality and quantity of capital. The point about funding as a solution to a growing elderly population is that it might address only the last element on this agenda — and even then it would do so indirectly.

Taking equity and efficiency considerations together, if efficiency principles do not point unambiguously to a preferred form of pension provision, and if the empirical research on the impact of funding versus PAYG is unclear and contentious, then there is strong justification for weighting equity very highly in policy deliberations about pensions systems. The important point is that the evidence about how to achieve equity (in the form of poverty reduction and high levels of income replacement) is *not* ambiguous: comprehensive social insurance combined with second-tier pensions (state or private) is more effective than systems built around residual state schemes supplemented by private provision (Davies, Land, *et al*, 2003; Falkingham and Rake, 2003: ILO, 2000).

CURRENT TRENDS AND POLICIES

This section deals with recent trends in Ireland and internationally, and then outlines the specific strategy adopted in Ireland in the wake of the National Pensions Policy Initiative (NPPI).

First, Table 10.3 shows that the share of older people in the population fell from 1991 to 2001. However, the ratio of social security pensioners to the elderly population has risen in the last decade. This is the net outcome of a decline in the numbers of OANCP recipients and a significant rise in the population of OACP and RP pensioners due to the maturing and expansion of the social insurance system. The ratio of pensions expenditure to GNP fell significantly over the decade, because of the exceptional growth of incomes and the decline in the level of the state pensions relative to earnings. This last point is illustrated in the final row of the table: the ratio of the contributory pension to net earnings was about 40% in the early 1990s and 36% in 2002.

Second, pensioner poverty has been growing. Table 10.4, based on the Living in Ireland surveys, shows the proportions of older households below the 50% and 60% relative income poverty lines.[5] At the lower of these two poverty lines the poverty rate rose almost five-fold, and at the higher rate it rose more than seven-fold from 5.9% to 44.1% over the 1994–2001 period. The very high rate at the higher poverty line is indicative of a general problem of low income in older households: more detailed data on income by the age of household head shows a very sharp decline in income at age 65 and a further decline at age 75 (Connell and Stewart, 2004).[6]

Table 10.3: Trends in Pensions 1991–2001

Pensions	1991c.	2001c.
Population 65+ as % of Total Population	11.4	11.2
No. of Pensioners (000s)	241.0	264.3
Pensioners as % of Population 65+	59.8	61.7
OACP as % of Net Earnings	40.3	36.4
Pensions Expenditure as % of GNP	8.2	2.1

Source: Department of Social, Community and Family Affairs, Central Statistics Office.
Note: The data in the last two rows refer to 1992 and 2002.

Table 10.4: Percent of Persons 65+ Below the (Relative Income) Poverty Line 1994–2001

Poverty Line	1994	1997	1998	2000	2001
60% of Median Income	5.9	24.2	32.9	38.4	44.1
50% of Median Income	2.8	2.6	5.7	12.0	18.2

Source: Whelan, Layte, Maitre *et al*, 2003.

Third, Ireland's demographic situation is relatively benign by comparative standards. In 2001, the share of persons aged 65 and over in the total population was 11.2% and the ratio of the working-age population to the older population (the 'support ratio') was 5.27:1. According to the projections in the most recent actuarial review of the social insurance fund, the latter ratio will rise in the short-term and then decline. The decline is projected to be gradual from 2006 to 2011 and steep thereafter (DSFA, 2002). Figure 10.1 summarises the central projection. The reduction in the working-age population relative to the older population will be accompanied by a fall in the child-dependent ratio. When the two dependent categories are combined the 'total support ratio' is projected to increase until 2011 and then to fall very gradually.[7] To put Ireland in context, the share of the elderly in the population of many developed economies is already in the range above 20%, and Ireland will not reach that point until the second decade of this century.

The actuarial review also quantified in considerable detail the financial implications of the demographic projections. Currently, the funding model for social insurance is PAYG. In the future under PAYG arrangements, if pensions are indexed to prices, the review suggests that pensions expenditure as a share of GNP will remain almost unchanged, rising from approximately 1.5% of GNP in

Figure 10.1: Ratio of Working Population to Dependent Population

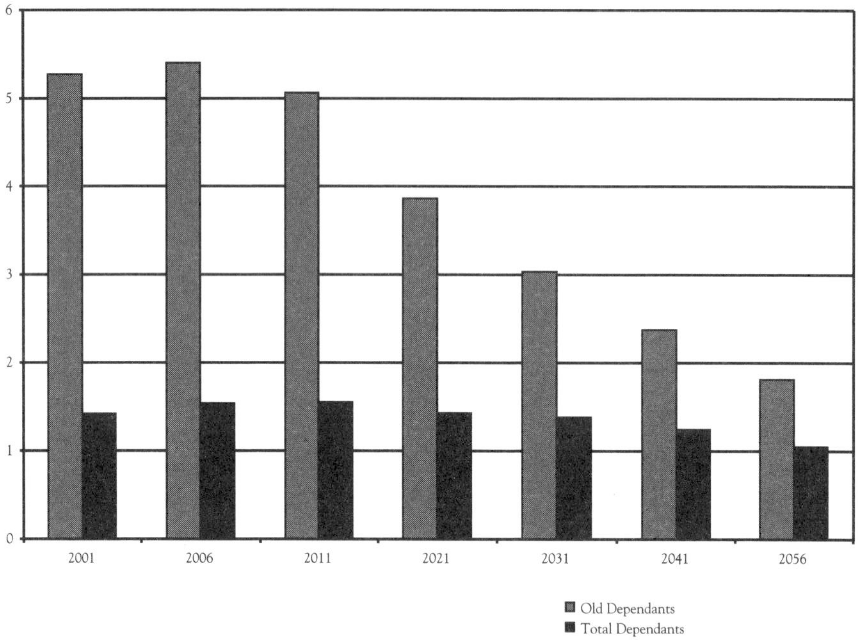

Source: Department of Social and Family Affairs.

2001 to just over 2.1 % in 2056. Price indexation, however, would imply (given the assumptions adopted about the future evolution of prices and incomes) that pensions would decline relative to incomes. This could lead to a rise in relative income poverty. However, if indexation to earnings rather than prices is adopted expenditure will grow over the same period to 6.5% of GNP. These alternative scenarios have implications for the contribution rates for social insurance. Under price indexation these can be maintained and even lowered, whereas earnings indexation (without an Exchequer subvention to the social insurance fund) would necessitate continual increases in the contribution rates, beginning in the next decade.

On the international front, pensions policy in the last decade has been overshadowed by the ageing of the population in many developed economies: in some European countries in particular the economic challenge of ageing has been compounded by persistently low levels of economic growth. The authoritative review of international pensions policy conducted by the International Labour Organisation (ILO) summarises the types of policy change that have been implemented in response to the growing size of the elderly population (ILO, 2000: 576–97):

- There is a discernible trend towards a *reduction in social security pension benefits*. These reductions are usually indirect, and phased, and would include changes to the details of pension indexation formula (United Kingdom), adjustments to the earnings base governing the initial pension benefit (Australia), and greater targeting, through tax claw-backs and means tests, of universal pensions (Finland; Sweden).
- Many countries are *increasing their social security contribution rates*. This is being done in some cases through outright increases in the core contribution rates (France, Canada) and widening the income base on which contributions are levied (Japan; Norway).
- Governments are implementing measures that result, directly or indirectly, in an *increase in the age at which pensions are paid*. The US, for example, effectively reduced pension benefits by phasing in an increase of two years (from 65 to 67) in the normal pensionable age (starting for workers aged 62 in 2002). The traditionally lower pension age for women is also being phased out: Portugal, Greece and the UK are all implementing equal pension ages, by raising the age for women. Also, in the 1990s, the historic trend towards lower pension ages and earlier retirement came to an end. Instead governments are offering (actuarially) reduced pensions at early retirement and increased pensions for deferred retirement.
- Nearly one third of the OECD countries reviewed in the ILO's study adopted *privatisation measures*, broadly defined. In some cases this has entailed permission to contract out of state second-tier pensions (the UK), and in others (The Netherlands; Switzerland) mandatory participation by employers and employees in industry-wide pensions schemes. Australia introduced a privatised retirement income scheme based on mandatory contributions by employers, employees and the state to private defined contribution funds. In time this will partly replace the means-tested social security pension.
- There is a shift *towards defined contribution* arrangements in the occupational pensions sector and *notional* defined contributions in some countries' social security pensions. In the latter case (Sweden and Italy are examples) pension benefits were historically based on a proportion of earnings, but these have been changed so that contributions are notionally paid into an individual's account; the account is revalued annually using an index such as GDP growth. Individuals' pension benefits are determined by the fund and a conversion factor that varies according to the age at retirement. The conversion factor is the key variable in the system — in the Italian case this may be modified every ten years in the light of economic and demographic circumstances.

Against this international background, the NPB (1998) produced its *Securing Retirement Income* document as the framework for the future evolution of Ireland's pension system. In all, the document contains forty-seven recommendations, some of these are strategic and others entail quite specific proposals about state, occupational or private pensions. These are the key elements in the pensions strategy:

- An improvement in — although not an extension of — the state pension.
- Retention of the tax treatment of occupational pensions.
- Development of a larger private pension sector.
- Some element of funding for social security pensions.

In terms of the historic debate about whether the state should provide a second tier pension, the strategy firmly repudiated this option and also rejected the option of mandatory occupational pensions in the private sector. To deal with the problem of low coverage of personal and occupational pensions, the NPB advocated the introduction of Personal Retirement Savings Accounts (PRSAs). These are private, individual retirement accounts into which employees make (tax deductible) contributions that are 'portable' from employment to employment. What are the implications of the pensions regime advanced by the NPB (and now broadly accepted as the agreed framework for pension provision in the future)?

THE NATIONAL PENSIONS BOARD STRATEGY

Taking the recommendations about the state pension system, the central one is that policy should aspire to a *minimum social security pension of 34% of average industrial earnings*. Specifically, the proposal entails the phased achievement of this target over a five to ten year period. The proposal did not specify how the state pension should be indexed once the target had been reached. However, the NPB's analysis recognises that price indexation over the long run would not be sufficient to avoid pensioner poverty and that it would be desirable to increase pensions in line with the growth in earnings. This framework for the level and indexation of pensions led the NPB to conclude that an explicit *funding* mechanism would be necessary to pay for future pensions.

This element of the NPB's strategy is important, as it offers a benchmark for the adequacy of pensions and, if implemented in full, it would imply a significant increase in the incomes of those relying wholly or largely on the state's pensions. Against the recent background of pensions and (benefits generally) falling behind earnings, it would be a more equitable policy.

In the case of the *occupational pensions*, the most important proposal concerned their treatment under the tax system: there should be no alteration in the tax regime. Employer and employee contributions are tax deductible, investment income from pension fund and capital gains are exempt from tax, one and a half years remuneration as a lump sum on retirement is tax free, but pension income received by pensioners is assessable for income tax.) The NPB (1998: 17) described the current tax regime as 'long established' and argued that any change to taxation in this area would introduce uncertainty and 'act as a major deterrent to private pension provision'. Viewed against its own policy criteria this proposal can be questioned.

The overall strategy of the NPB is to expand occupational and personal pension membership: in fact, the NPB aspires to an ultimate coverage rate of 70% of the workforce (aged 30 and over) having some form of second tier pension. It did not recommend *mandatory* occupational coverage for the private sector and it is therefore relying on the tax incentives to expand occupational coverage. However, it is not clear that the tax incentives have been effective, as the pension coverage rates have persistently remained in the region of 50%. If *mandatory* occupational pensions were being recommended as a device to increase coverage in some or all of private sector, then the tax revenue foregone via the tax incentives would be linked with some increase in coverage.

The tax treatment proposals need to be viewed also in the light of *cost* and *equity* considerations. In 1999–2000 the revenue foregone from the tax incentives was €1,274 million. To put this figure in context, the respective figure for social security pensions was €1,449 million. Over the last decade, as Figure 10.2 shows, the tax expenditure cost as a percentage of direct pension costs has been rising continuously, and is now in excess of 80%. Remarkably, *Securing Retirement Income* contains no projections of the future costs of the tax incentives, while offering detailed projections of the direct expenditure costs of social security pensions in

Figure 10.2: Tax Expenditure on Occupational Pensions as % of Direct Expenditure on State Pensions, 1990–1999

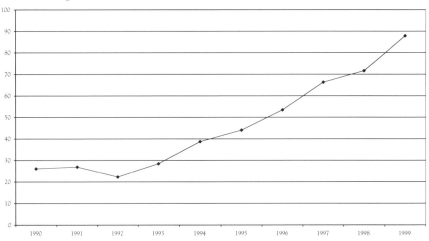

Source: Revenue Commissioners.

the future. This is all the more remarkable given that the NPB's proposed new PRSA pension is also tax deductible.

As regards equity considerations, coverage is skewed towards the higher income groups. Figure 10.3, reproduced from Hughes's (2001) research on occupational pensions, shows that at the lowest-income levels, membership of pensions schemes is extremely low (less than 1%), and therefore the benefit of the tax incentives to low income employees is negligible. Conversely with higher-income employees: there is over 90% coverage among the highest tenth of wage-earners. This imparts a very regressive profile to the distribution of the financial benefits of the tax incentives, and the fact that tax deductibility applies at marginal rates of tax — conferring larger tax savings on higher income taxpayers — exacerbates the inequitable distribution of the tax expenditures. Hughes (2001: 49) summarised his estimates of the income distribution effects of tax expenditures as follows, 'the top 20% of employee taxpayers receive more than 60% of the tax expenditure while the bottom 20% receive less than 0.5% of it'.

The NPB (1998: 123) explicitly rejected the option of an earnings 'cap' on tax deductibility of employer and employee contributions, whereby contributions in excess of the 'cap' would not attract tax relief. This would ameliorate both the cost and the inequity of the tax regime for occupational pensions. The NPB accepted that the idea of a cap would need to be reviewed, and the representatives of the Ministers of Finance and of Social and Family Affairs, seemed to indicate unease at the inequity of the tax regime by suggesting that the introduction of a cap 'should be examined in detail' (NPB, 1998: 123).

Figure 10.3: Percentage of Employees with Pension Entitlements by Income Decile

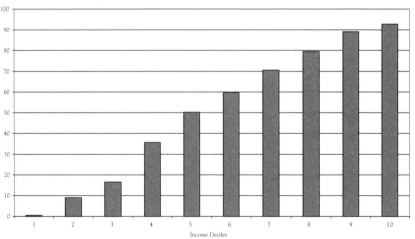

Income Deciles

Source: Hughes (2001).

The third thread in the NPB strategy is the new system of *PRSAs*. These are defined contribution retirement accounts provided by financial institutions. Under the relevant legislation, *Pensions (Amendment) Act 2002*, employers not offering occupational pensions (or excluding certain employees from an occupational pension) are legally obliged to facilitate access to these accounts for individual employees. This legal obligation came into effect in September 2003. The critical aspects of PRSAs are as follows:[8]

- They are not confined to standard employees and may be taken up by the self–employed, carers, casual and part-time employees, and so on.
- PRSA holders may move between employers and remain as contributors to the same fund or transfer the funds to an occupational scheme, and under certain conditions an occupational scheme member may transfer pension benefits to a PRSA.
- The contributions made are tax deductible, the proportion of income that can be contributed is tiered according to the age of the contributor and there is freedom for contributors to cease, defer and change their contributions.
- Employers may, but are *not* obliged to contribute to an employee's PRSA.
- Employers must facilitate employees' contributions through payroll deductions and must also make reasonable arrangements to allow employees access to advisors and financial advice during working hours — however, a PRSA contract is between an individual and the financial institution providing the PRSA.
- PRSAs are regulated in a variety of important respects — all PRSA products and their providers must be approved by the NPB: there are detailed regulations about charges, minimum contributions, investment procedures, contributors' rights in relation to disclosure, and transfer of funds, and contributors have access to a Pensions Ombudsman. (The 2002 legislation established a Pensions Ombudsman.)
- The value of the fund is wholly dependent on its investment performance and there are no guarantees offered to contributors. On retirement, contributors may take 25% of the fund as a tax-free lump sum and use the balance to buy an annuity (or leave the funds in the PRSA to withdraw later, or transfer the balance to an Approved Retirement Fund).

Clearly, PRSAs may offer some scope to improve pensions coverage as they offer flexible, portable, easy-access pensions. Also, their introduction has been accompanied by a substantial publicity programme raising awareness about pensions generally, and about the details of PRSAs and the strong regulatory framework in which they will operate. But will PRSAs lead to an increase in pensions coverage? One critical factor here will be the cost; if the minimum contributions are high relative to the disposable income of potential subscribers, then presumably cost will be a deterrent. An important additional consideration in the Irish context, for many individuals, is that paying off mortgage debt and becoming a homeowner is the most important saving commitment. Until home ownership is achieved (or largely achieved) other forms of long-term saving may not be an option. The fact that employers are not obliged to contribute will not help to increase the take-up.

The more fundamental consideration, however, is that pensions products — even well-designed, accessible and widely publicised ones — seem complex, even obscure, to many people, and in particular to those on low incomes. This fact, combined with the defined contribution nature of the PRSAs and the absence of a pension guarantee, may result in a low take-up. Finally in relation to PRSAs, the public may simply not accept the underlying principle of *personal* rather than collective responsibility for second-tier pensions. It may be the case that, given the choice, those currently without pensions would opt for a second-tier state pension or mandatory occupational provision rather than individual retirement accounts.

The fourth element in the NPB strategy concerns *funding*. Briefly, the NPB (1998: 110) recommended the establishment of an 'explicit mechanism to fund, at least partially, the prospective substantial growth that is projected to occur in social welfare and old age pensions, if they grow in line with earnings'. In 2000 the Government established the National Pension Reserve Fund under the management of the National Treasury Management Agency (NTMA) to fund future social security and state occupational pensions. The legislation obliges the state to set aside into a fund 1% of GNP annually, giving the NTMA the legal and managerial autonomy to invest in funds that will accumulate into a long-term reserve to meet future pension liabilities. Under current legislation, the government may not draw on the funds until 2025. This arrangement is a recognition that pre-funding may offer a contribution to the cost of future pensions, but it does not reflect a commitment to a purely funded approach to overall pensions provision.

The funding issues that have engendered public and academic debate concern the financial and organisational aspects of the NTMA: whether the '1% rule' is appropriate from a macro-economic perspective, and whether the specific organisational structure of the NTMA guarantees its independence (Lane, 2001). One specific social policy issue is that the legislation leaves open the possibility of separating the fund into two funds: one dealing with the state occupational pensions and the other with social security pensions. If the funds were split in this way it is unclear what implications this would have for the current social insurance fund.

FUTURE POLICY

For the present, the broad structure of the pensions system has been consolidated. However, future events may open up some fundamental questions again. For example, if the partial funding system under the NTMA does not offer the requisite long-term real returns the funding issue might be re-opened. In the immediate future, it remains to be seen what progress will be made in the expansion of pensions coverage. It is important to note that there are alternatives if the NPB's strategy does not succeed. As one of the foremost analysts of Irish pensions policy has argued, there is an alternative to the strategy of partial privatisation and funding (Hughes, 1996: 59):

> In the absence of persuasive evidence that increased reliance on funding would increase national savings rates we should not count on the supposed benefits of privatising pensions to provide a solution to the problems posed by an ageing population. We should be wary of proposals for radical reform of pension systems which have no role for social insurance. If occupational pension coverage is to be extended, either on a voluntary or mandatory basis, the full costs to the Exchequer of maintaining the favourable tax treatment of occupational pensions should be made explicit. The problems posed by an ageing population can be dealt with effectively and equitably by spreading the burden of pensions among different social groups through a mixture of fiscal and employment policies.

This trenchant critique of trends in pensions policy raises some questions of a more political nature. Given its circumstances, with a low share of the elderly in the population and a broadly benign economic scenario, why did Ireland draw so heavily on the funding and private provision aspects of recent international experience? Has recent Irish pensions policy been overly influenced by the perspectives of global financial institutions which have such a large stake in pensions systems worldwide? The answer to this question must await future research on the history of pensions policy in Ireland.

Notes

1. There are also mixed or hybrid schemes, although these are rare.
2. This section relies heavily on Barr, (1993; 2003).
3. An annuity is an income stream for life in which the present value of the income stream is equal to the capital sum for an individual with the average life expectancy.
4. Barr (2003) contains detailed arithmetic examples of funded and PAYG systems.
5. The disposable income figures on which the poverty estimates are based do not include the cash value of non-cash benefits.
6. If households are divided into seven categories by age the lowest incomes (1999–2000) are in the age groups 65–74 and 75+; the average income (per

capita equivalent) for all households was €238 per week and the respective figures for the two older age groups were €191 and €172. These figures are lower than the corresponding figure (€239) for the age category 15–24 (Connell and Stewart, 2004).

7.   These figures summarise the central projection. The Actuarial Review also reports variations on the assumptions underpinning the central projection. It is important to note that a number of population projections have been undertaken in recent years, including the NPB's (1993; 1998) projections in relevant publications and the earlier actuarial review published in 1997. The detailed figures in these various projection exercises differ for technical and methodological reasons, but the projected pattern in relation to the age structure of the population is broadly consistent across the various studies, i.e. a declining share of the elderly in the total population in the immediate years ahead followed by a gradual and continuous rise.

8.   A complete guide to PRSAs, *Personal Retirement Savings Accounts*, is available on the National Pensions Board's website, www.pensionsboard.ie.

11
Sickness and Disability

INTRODUCTION

This chapter reviews the social security arrangements relating to loss of income and lack of income arising from illness and disability. These are quite complex, comprising a range of different benefits focused on different needs. The next section describes the social security provisions in this area, and the sections following give a brief historical account of the development of policy in this area, and a review of the policy rationale. The final section discusses future policy.

CURRENT PROVISIONS

Chart 11.1 summarises current provisions. The first point to clarify is the use of the term *Disability Benefit* (DB) in the first row. 'Disability' is somewhat of a misnomer here. DB is in fact the payment to people in employment absent from work through illness, it is *not* directed at people with underlying, long-term disabilities (of course, a disabled person in mainstream insurable employment could receive DB if absent from work through illness in the normal way). As the Chart shows, DB is based on social insurance contributions and is payable as a flat-rate benefit at the same level as UB. *Invalidity Pension* (IP) is the long-term counterpart of DB. It is payable to persons formerly in receipt of DB who are *permanently* incapable of work; the payment is at a higher level than DB and it attracts the additional benefits-in-kind that attach to the various old age pensions.

The *Occupational Injuries* (OIB) scheme is a self-contained suite of payments for persons injured or ill as a result of their employment-related activity. Like IP and DB it is based on social insurance contributions. A defining feature of OIB is the range of ancillary benefits it encompasses. Most important of all, a Disablement Pension is payable in addition to benefit, if an employee suffers a loss of faculty. The pension is awarded on a sliding scale related to the degree of disablement. Where the percent degree of disablement is below twenty a lump sum is payable: if it is above this threshold, a pension is payable.[1] However, the amount of the pension is not affected by any benefit the recipient has or any earnings received

Chart 11.1 Summary of Provisions for Sickness and Disability

Scheme	Category of Recipient	Eligibility	Other Details	Weekly Personal Rate € (and other benefits)
Disability Benefit	Employees aged under 66 absent from work	Based on social insurance; core rules are 39 weeks PRSI since work commenced and 39 weeks in relevant tax year; medical certificate required	DB included in taxable income: duration of entitlement related to PRSI record; recipient *may* be allowed to have limited employment; recipients allowed access to various back-to-work schemes after 3 years	€124.80; adult and child dependant additions where applicable: *half* of DB personal rate may be paid with another benefit/allowance
Invalidity Pension	Employees permanently incapable of work, or over 60 and seriously ill, or unable to work for past 12 months and likely to be so next 12 months	Based on social insurance; core rules are a total of 260 weeks paid PRSI and 48 weeks paid or credited in relevant tax year	IP included in taxable income; no limit on duration of payment if illness continues; medical condition may be reviewed; recipients may be allowed limited work or training; recipients may access some of the back-to-work schemes.	€130.30 (under age 65), higher rates for older recipients; adult and child dependant additions payable where applicable: also Living Alone Allowance and Fuel allowance may be payable

Occupational Injuries Benefit	Employees ill or injured at work	Employees in insurable jobs (separate treatment for civil servants); illness must last a minimum of 4 days (Sundays excluded); medical certificate required.	OIB included in taxable income; Payable for 26 weeks; after 26 weeks recipients may apply for DB; recipients may take paid employment for rehabilitative purposes (max. of 20 hours) or approved training if unable to pursue usual occupation	€124.80; adult and child dependant additions, where applicable; half of OIB personal rate may be payable with other benefits; Disablement Benefit also payable for loss of physical or mental faculty; if DB is *not payable and Disablement Benefit is awarded,* Unemployability Supplement is payable; Constant Attendance Allowance for Disablement Pension recipients needing care
Disability Allowance	Adults with disease, or physical or mental disability, or illness lasting one year or more	Based on means and medical certificate; means test exempts some income from training, and some income from spouse; payment continues unless disability ceases	DA recipients may access back-to-work schemes	€124.80; adult and child dependant additions where applicable; if married couple are both disabled two payments made; recipients may receive Living

Blind Pension	Persons aged 18 and over, blind or with low vision	Based on similar means test to DA, and medical certificate	May access back-to-work schemes; separate Mobility Allowance and Blind Welfare Allowance for some disabled (from Health services); Blind Person's Tax Allowance	€124.80; adult and child dependant additions if applicable; same extra benefits as DA; BP recipients may qualify for other benefits if under 66	Alone and Fuel Allowances and other allowances (electricity, phone rental etc.)

Source: Department of Social and Family Affairs.

on returning to work. Also, the OIB scheme allows for the payment of a Constant Care Attendance Allowance in the case of a seriously disabled person requiring continuing care at home for their personal needs.

The fourth row refers to the *Disability Allowance* (DA), formerly known as the Disabled Person's Maintenance Allowance. DA is a payment for people permanently 'disabled' and unable to work, and is based on a medical assessment and a means test. DA would also be a 'fall back' allowance for employees whose social insurance records would not allow entitlement to DB. The *Blind Pension* is the only benefit directed at a particular category of disability. The means test and benefit level are broadly the same as for DA.

Clearly, there are a range of objectives implicit in this mix of benefits and allowances:

- Alleviating poverty among workers absent from work sick (DB).
- Providing long-term sickness pensions to workers who become chronically sick and unable to return to work (IP).
- Providing income and other services to workers injured at work and requiring employers to contribute to these employment-generated costs (OI).
- Compensating workers injured or disabled at work (Disablement Pension).
- Supporting seriously incapacitated workers with the costs of personal care services (Constant Care Allowance).

Table 11.1 records the aggregate data on these provisions. In 2002 there were 185,000 direct recipients of these payments, and expenditure totalled €1.28 billion. To put these figures in context, there are 2.64 million people in Ireland aged between 15 and 64: of these, 271,000 have a disability/longstanding health problem, a 'disability rate' of 10.2 %.[2] How comprehensive is the social security system in giving income support to those who are ill or disabled? The number of long-term social security payments (for the same age group) in respect of a longstanding illness or disability is 126,073, a coverage rate of 46.5% of the population. If this calculation were based only on the disabled classified as 'unemployed' and 'not economically active', the coverage figure would be 77.7%.

These figures show the *size* of the population of the long-term benefit recipients (DB excluded) and the self-reported 'disabled' population. However, they should not be taken as an index of 'how good' the benefit system is. In the first place, the benefit recipient numbers and the population numbers are based on different definitions; the benefits data record the numbers in receipt of a benefit, having been medically assessed, while the population figures are based on self-reported disability. The survey data give a point-in-time (cross-section) estimate, but disability is a dynamic process and people's health and disability status changes. A cross-section survey cannot quantify the flows (in and out) of the status 'disabled'. A more important issue is that the benefits system deals with the *financial losses and costs* of sickness and disability. Assessing how well the

Table 11.1: Sickness and Disability in 2002: Recipients and Expenditure

Scheme	Recipients 000s	Expenditure €m	Expenditure %
Disability Benefit	54.6	385.4	29.9
Invalidity Pension	52.1	403.6	31.3
Occupational Injuries Benefit	13.1	77.0	6.0
Disability Allowance	62.8	407.6	31.6
Blind Pension	2.1	14.2	1.1
Total	184.7	1,287.8	100

Source: Statistical Information on Social Welfare Services.

social security system fulfils this role would require more than a simple comparison of these aggregate figures.

Before proceeding to review the development of benefits, the definition of disability must be considered. The critical point is the distinction between the *medical and social* concepts of disability (Oliver, 1990). In the former case disability refers to a physical condition (for example, loss of a leg) and the impact this has on physical functioning (reduced mobility), and consequently on a person's capacity to work and to participate in society generally. The social model, however, stresses the general social response to medical conditions and their physical consequences. For example, loss of a limb and impaired mobility need not reduce social participation if there is accessible, affordable transport. Modern disability rights activists articulate this emphasis on the social context. They stress the role of the wider social framework in preventing (merely) physical conditions and impairments from becoming 'disabilities' in terms of exclusion from education and work, and consequently lack of income.

This is relevant to social security. Benefit access is medically determined and the role of the benefits is to respond to the financial consequences of sickness or disability. One important issue therefore is the extent to which the benefit system deals with the costs of illness and disability. A key consideration here is the loss of earnings. The current system partly replaces lost income, and how well it does this is essentially a question of how adequate benefits are in relation to average incomes: this issue is relevant of course to all categories of benefit recipient. But there are specific extra costs that may arise in the case of disability: heating, dietary, mobility and other costs (Glendinning and Baldwin, 1988). These costs are by no means easy to quantify, but the sophistication with which the social security system deals with these costs is one of the factors that may prevent those with medical conditions and physical impairments from becoming disabled in the wider social sense. Ensuring that these costs are dealt with allows those with 'disabilities' to start on an equal footing with the population at large.

One wider implication here is that the social security system is only one policy instrument — and not necessarily the most important one. Transport policy, education, rehabilitation, training, and so on, are all clearly relevant. Social security, however, is related to these wider policy areas in one specific sense. It must be structured so that the benefit system reinforces the impact of whatever positive policies there are in relation to training and rehabilitation, and other policies. At a minimum, the system should not compound recipients' difficulties in accessing training and employment (by making means tests very restrictive or making benefit receipt conditional on not being active, for example).

HISTORICAL DEVELOPMENT

DB emerged from the earliest social insurance initiatives introduced at the beginning of the twentieth century. Initially, the benefit was administered through the mechanism of approved societies overseen by the Irish Insurance Commissioners. By the early 1930s there were sixty-five approved societies, varying greatly in size and financial status. In 1933 the National Health Insurance Act amalgamated the societies into the National Health Insurance Society (NHIS). This society became responsible for the administration of sickness benefit (as it was then called) and was managed by a committee representing the government (specifically, the Minister for Local Government and Public Health), employers and trade unions. In 1950 this regime ended with the transfer of the NHIS's functions to the Department of Social Welfare, leading to the incorporation of sickness benefit into the emerging national system of social insurance.

From 1952 onwards the scheme was part of the wider system of social insurance and was affected by general developments in the social security system as a whole. The level of benefit and the structure of benefit evolved in parallel with that of UB. In 1974 the introduction of PRB incorporated DB as well as UB; likewise, in the 1980s when short-term benefits became included in taxable income this too included disability benefit. During the 1950s and 1960s the rate of claims and the duration of claims were broadly static, but they rose significantly during the 1970s and gave rise to concerns that the level of DB and PRB combined was inducing a greater incidence of absence from work and higher levels of DB expenditure (Hughes, 1982). The most significant development after the 1952 Act was the introduction of the Invalidity Pension in 1970. This offered a long-term pension, based on social insurance contributions, to people with a long-term incapacity.

The Occupational Injuries scheme has a somewhat different history. It originated in the Workmen's Compensation system first introduced in the last decade of the nineteenth century (Farley, 1964: 8–15). Under the 1897 *Workmen's Compensation Act* employers became liable to pay compensation at fixed rates (related to earnings, and subject to a maximum) to workers injured in the course of their work: employers were also obliged to pay a lump sum in the event of a worker's death. At first, this legislation applied to only a limited number of hazardous employments, but over the course of the subsequent half-century the legislation was extended to agricultural workers, and non-manual workers. In 1906 an important change was made extending the liability of employers to cases of death and incapacity arising from specified industrial diseases. This legislation also introduced the legal power to amend and add to the schedule of specified industrial diseases.

The workmen's compensation arrangements relied in part on employers taking out insurance against their liabilities, but where this did not happen workers had to rely on the courts to obtain compensation. This in turn required proof of negligence on the employer's part. The legislation allowed a role for the courts where agreement between employer and employee, or arbitration, failed to resolve compensation claims. Also, the Circuit Court had a role in reviewing the amount of an ongoing weekly payment, in deciding whether employers could redeem their liabilities by paying a lump sum, and in other ways.

Workmen's Compensation came to an end in 1965. The Labour Party, as a member of the 1954–1957 Inter-Party government, had persuaded its partners in government to establish the Commission on Workmen's Compensation. The commission reported in 1962, but its report was not unanimous. A majority recommended retention of the existing scheme, proposing some reforms, such as compulsory insurance for employers, improved compensation for widows, and allowances for the cost of care. The minority report proposed a social insurance scheme, invoking the logic of the Beveridge report in its argument — the need for adequate benefits, comprehensive cover, and a unified, national system of administration. In its report the minority pointedly referred to the role of the private insurance companies, noting that very little of the premiums paid by insured employers actually passed on to injured workers as compensation, and observing that it 'was a profitable branch of their business and that its loss would be a serious blow' (Commission on Workmen's Compensation, 1962: 199). In contrast, the majority stated that it was 'strongly influenced by the arguments in favour of the status quo and the undesirability of interfering with the established private enterprise system unless substantial advantages could thereby be achieved' (Commission on Workmen's Compensation, 1962: 190). The minority Fianna Fáil government repudiated the majority view and legislated for the introduction of OIB as part of the overall social insurance system.

Disability Allowance was originally part of the health care system, under the title Disabled Person's Maintenance Allowance. In 1996 this payment was integrated into the income maintenance system and its title changed to Disability Allowance. Simultaneously, the means test was reformed and the scope of the allowance widened.

The Blind Pension (BP) was introduced in 1920 as an adjunct to the Old Age Pension. Blind people aged over fifty were awarded a pension on the same basis (and subject to the same means test) as persons aged seventy or over were awarded an old age pension. Over time the age threshold was reduced to eighteen. The BP is now analogous to the DA (in terms of the payment rates and means test), which is available to the majority of those with long-term disabilities.

Finally, recent trends in recipient numbers are summarised in Figure 11.1. The figures refer to the *stock* of recipients at a point during the year rather than the flow of cases in and out of the benefit system. There are two notable trends. First, there is a continuous growth in the Invalidity Pension numbers. These recipients are largely in the older age categories, with over 77% aged over fifty. Second, the Disability Allowance scheme is growing at an exceptional rate in recent years. In 1996 there were just over 37,000 recipients, and by 2002 the number had reached 62,783, an annual average rate of increase of 8.8%. In the case of Blind Pension beneficiaries (not shown in the figure) the number is marginally above 2000 and has been declining very slowly but continuously in the last decade.

Figure 11.1: Recipients of Main Sickness/Disability Payments, 1992–2002 (000s)

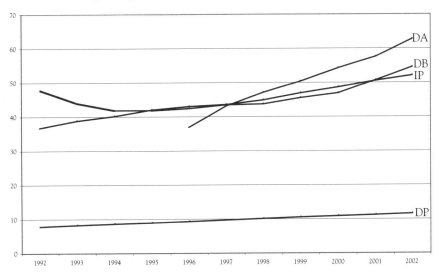

Source: Department of Social and Family Affairs.

POLICY RATIONALE

Is there a clear rationale for the state disability (DB) and invalidity payments (IP) to deal with short-term and long-term illness respectively? Could insurance against loss of income from sickness absence be provided in the private market, given that conditions have changed since the introduction of national insurance almost one hundred years ago? The same underlying principles apply here as in the case of unemployment benefit, although the conclusion is less clear-cut. For the private market to provide sickness insurance efficiently a number of pre-conditions must hold (Barr, 1997):

- First, individuals' probabilities of sickness-related absence from work should be unrelated. This would hold in the case of sickness absence insurance, but not in the case of unemployment in which entire occupations and sectors can be affected simultaneously.
- Second, the probability of work absence for any given time period should be less than one. This pre-condition would also hold as a generalisation.
- Third, there should be no problems of adverse selection or moral hazard. Insurance companies can deal with adverse selection (disproportionate self selection into insurance by those most likely to claim) and moral hazard (deliberate unjustified claims) through inspection and screening procedures.

This suggests that *theoretically* there is a clear case for market rather than state provision. There are wider considerations, however. There is, as Chapter Eight pointed out, a definitive case for state organisation of unemployment insurance. Therefore, there are powerful practical advantages for employers, workers and the state in organising a state system that covers both sickness absence and unemployment. Furthermore, the historical experience prior to national insurance in Ireland and the UK was that non-state provision was at best incomplete and inadequate. This raises equity issues also. If market provision is incomplete (because of its cost, for example) it is likely to be lower income workers (those more prone to illness) that will be left without sickness absence insurance.

One important point here is that *employer provided* sick pay has grown since the establishment of DB as part of the social security system. However, the limited evidence available (Hughes, 1988) suggests that sick pay cover is low outside of the state sector, and is very much lower in small, private sector companies. These considerations acquired a very immediate relevance in Ireland in the late 1980s. In 1987 the government announced its intention to reform DB by making employers responsible for paying absent employees for the first 13 weeks of sickness absence. Undoubtedly, the proposed reform was influenced by the introduction of Statutory Sick Pay in the UK in 1983: this had shifted the responsibility for sick pay to employers for the first eight weeks of sickness. There were also significant policy concerns in Ireland about the growth in expenditure on DB and about the 'moral hazard' of DB payments acting as an incentive to employees to be absent from work.

The proposed reform did not proceed. However, Hughes's (1988) contribution to the short-lived debate on the state's role in relation to sickness payments highlights some fundamental issues in relation to DB:

- First, the impact of such a change critically depends on *how* the restructuring would take place. If the state were to simply refund individual employers for their payment of sick pay for an initial period it would not necessarily reduce sickness absence or public expenditure on DB; neither employer nor employee would have an incentive to economise on sick pay.
- Second, the debate about the proposal highlighted the low coverage of occupational sick pay outside certain segments of the workforce, and employers without such arrangements might have been ill equipped to implement a scheme of short-term sickness benefit in place of DB. This consideration might still apply.
- Third, the concerns being expressed about abuse of DB (the moral hazard) not being controlled proved unfounded: the statistical evidence about the impact of the state's medical inspection system showed that it is an effective method of detecting questionable claims.
- Fourth, the argument that the replacement ratio for DB was too high, giving an incentive to claim, did not seem to be supported by the evidence. Since then the replacement ratio has fallen in tandem with the ratio for unemployment payments.

None of this is to suggest that the role of the state in providing income for short-term and long-term sickness absence from work should never change. But it is clear that the conditions that would be required for employers or private insurers to successfully assume the state's current responsibilities may not currently hold. If poverty is brought into consideration this raises even further questions. The original objective in introducing benefit for sickness absence was to prevent financial destitution among sick workers. Any proposed alteration in the structure of disability and invalidity provisions would have to consider this central question.

Turning to Occupational Injuries, a somewhat different set of issues arises. Historically, this scheme emerged because of the costs and ineffectiveness of the Workmen's Compensation system. There has been no critique of the fundamental logic of the OIB scheme. As the Commission on this subject acknowledged, there is considerable scope to debate the theoretical advantages of a state social insurance model. Whatever the merits of these arguments, there are considerable practical and institutional advantages to integrating occupational illness and injury provisions into the overall state scheme.

The OIB regime, however, co-exists alongside other contributory benefits and means tested allowances for disability. In effect, the social insurance basis of OIB confers a distinctly superior suite of provisions for the occupationally ill and disabled as opposed to other forms of disability. Barnes and Baldwin's (1999: 172) critique of the UK system may be relevant to Ireland's arrangements: they point to 'too much emphasis on the origins of disability rather than its effects'. This question of the separate treatment of the occupationally injured has a gender dimension. Historically, the lower rate of work participation among women meant that disabled women in the home (including those 'occupationally injured' while engaged in 'housework' or caring) would receive only a means tested payment for DA, and this would be based in part on a spouse's means, where this applied. The formal gender inequalities in social insurance have of course been largely dealt with, and over time women in the work force will begin to acquire rights to OIB including the long term Disablement Pension. This all reveals the anomalies that arise from the mix of policy objectives underpinning the various schemes.

In the case of the Blind Pension and the Disability Allowance, the former pre-dates the DA and its precursor the Disabled Person's Maintenance Allowance. At this point, it is difficult to construct a rationale for separate payments, and arguably the BP could be integrated into the more general payment for the disabled. In principle, the DA meets the needs of those with long-term disabilities, but its structure ignores the central question of the *costs* of disability. Social security for the disabled should ideally address two related problems. First, if a long-term disabled person is not economically active then the DA can meet the need for income maintenance. Second, the disabled have additional needs and costs. Special provision is required to bridge the gap between what it takes for a disabled recipient to achieve a given standard of living as opposed to a non-disabled person with the same income. In other words, the disabled and non-disabled should, figuratively, have a level playing pitch. The disabled person at *any level of income* should have a non means-tested payment that recognises the additional costs arising from disability. The DA does not achieve this. The payment is at the same level as UB and DB rather than the old age or other pension, and there is no specific payment dealing with disability related costs.

There is little disagreement in the policy literature on the general principle of costs (Barnes and Baldwin, 1999; Glendinning and Baldwin, 1988). Nor is there disagreement about the sources of these costs: lower earnings (even for those economically active); the costs of special services; and, extra living costs (such as clothing, heating, and transport). However, it is by no means clear how these costs should be measured, and, having been measured, how they should be reflected in a payment to meet these costs. On the question of measurement, a number of approaches are possible: direct questioning of disabled people to ascertain how much extra they spend; completion of detailed expenditure diaries by disabled and non-disabled, and; measurement of the standard of living of the disabled as indicated by ownership of consumer durables, ability to save and participation in social activities (Reith, 1994).

In Ireland, there has been no research on the costs of disability. The Commission on the Status of People with Disabilities (1996) supported the principle of recognising the costs of disability, but disappointingly, gave no evidence on this topic. Tubridy's sociological study of the disabled in Ireland

(Tubridy, 1996) did not analyse the income, costs or expenditures of the respondents. If policy makers wished to incorporate the costs of disability in a reformed structure, how would this be done? A reform should attempt to achieve a number of goals (Reith, 1994):

- Equity between disabled and non-disabled people.
- Equity among the disabled regardless of the source or type of disability.
- Equity between disabilities based on the severity and financial *effects* of the disability.

This could be achieved in the Irish case by retaining the DA in its present form and then implementing a Disablement Supplement for all the disabled, untaxed and without a means test. A supplement of this nature should be based on an assessment of an individual's capacity to engage in normal daily activities and the degree of difficulty entailed in doing so. This would then allow the supplement to be tiered according to the severity of disability. In principle, this approach could also offer a mechanism for the disabled to meet the costs of care services.

FUTURE POLICY

In considering future policy a useful starting point is the poverty data summarised in Table 11.2. These figures highlight the far higher risk of relative income poverty among the disabled: the figure of 48.3% is the highest of all the labour force status categories. Furthermore, this figure represents a very dramatic increase on the figures in earlier years.

Clearly, the high rate of poverty mirrors the general trend of benefit levels declining over time relative to disposable incomes. It also raises the issue, mentioned earlier, about the structural position of the DA payment in the benefit system overall. Many DA recipients receive it as a long-term source of income, like Invalidity and Old Age Pension recipients, and there may be a case for bringing DA into the category 'long term' and increasing the benefit level accordingly. This might help to bring the poverty rate among the disabled closer to the rate experienced by the retired.

However, the high poverty rate cannot be viewed in isolation from the low rates of employment participation. Figure 11.2, based on the CSO survey of disability, highlights the gap in employment levels between the disabled and non-disabled. An analysis of employment policy and disability would go beyond the remit of this chapter, but a number of points are directly relevant. Historically, the segregation of the disabled within the education system effectively led to their exclusion from the labour market. This is now beginning to change and the increased access of the disabled to mainstream education may lead to a long-term upward shift in their employment rates. Also, the wider social and cultural impact of the disability rights movement with its emphasis on the empowerment of the

Table 11.2. Percentage of Persons Below Poverty Line (50% of Median Income) by Labour Force Status of Head of Household, 2001

Labour Force Status	% Poor
Employee	2.9
Self employed	10.6
Farmer	12.0
Unemployed	33.8
Retired	15.3
Home Duties	31.2
Ill/Disabled	59.0
All	12.9

Source: Whelan, Layte, Maitre *et al* (2003).

Figure 11.2: Percentage Employment Rates for Disabled and Non-Disabled, by Age, 2002

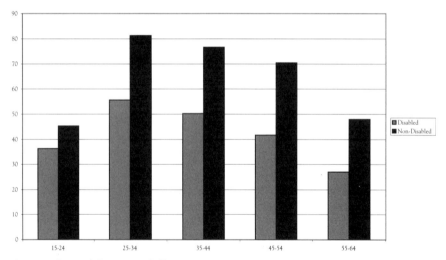

Source: Central Statistics Office.

disabled and their inclusion, as equals, in social and economic life may alter the attitudes of employers, and the disabled themselves, towards employment.

Against this wider background, the specific instruments of policy to increase employment may be less important. The first of these is the 3% quota on civil and public service jobs, originally adopted as a voluntary quota in 1977. The second policy is the provision of employment in sheltered workshops — just under 8,000 people in 215 workshops, and the third is the administrative arrangement by government departments to facilitate approved, rehabilitative work by benefit recipients. In addition, the recipients of the various allowances have been free to participate in the general activation, welfare-to-work initiatives. The *Employment Equality Act 1998* added a fifth policy instrument. This legislation requires employers to make adjustments to the workplace so that disabled employees can work and compete on an equal footing with other employees (Conroy, 2003). Aside from any questions about the scale or effectiveness of these measures, there may be a fundamental tension between policies that view the disabled as mainstream employees, and those that require them to identify themselves as 'disabled'.

The argument in favour of a Disablement Supplement to meet the costs of disability has implications for employment. A non-means tested supplement would not create poverty traps or disincentives, and would be consistent with a stronger employment focus in future policy. It is possible that in the immediate future there will be a policy initiative about the costs of disability. A working group was established in 2000 to consider the issue and has not yet reported. The Group's deliberations take place against a background of limited research and disagreement in principle between the Commission on Social Welfare (1986) and the Commission on the Status of People with Disabilities (1996): the former did not accept the notion of a supplement, while the latter supported it in principle.

Finally, the self-employed are still excluded from the various insurance-based payments. As they are now social insurance contributors, a logical development in the future that would improve the sickness and disability payments system would be to extend Invalidity Pension entitlement to them.

Notes

1. The maximum rate of Disablement Pension is €155.90 weekly in respect of 90% disablement or greater. The pension is on a sliding scale, with 20% disablement resulting in a weekly pension of €31.20. Where the degree of disablement is below 20% a lump sum is payable (maximum of €10, 910). An example of 100% disablement would be the loss of both hands; the loss of two fingers of one hand would be a 20% disablement.

2. The estimates given here are based on the results of a special disability module in a Quarterly National Household Survey in 2002. The figures refer to the number of respondents in the survey reporting a longstanding health or disability problem.

Part Three

12
The Future: A New System?

INTRODUCTION

In part two the focus in each chapter was on one aspect of the social security system. This concluding chapter looks at the social security system as a whole. Over the last quarter of a century a number of analyses of social security in Ireland and across the world have considered alternative systems and offered differing conclusions. In Ireland in the last decade the Conference of Religious of Ireland (CORI) has campaigned for the abolition of the current system and its replacement by a fundamentally different system called Basic Income (BI). CORI's campaign has engendered some debate and evaluation of BI and more recently it led the government to establish an official working group on the topic. This group produced a series of working papers, and the government published a Green Paper on BI in 2002, *A Basic Income*. The Green Paper and its associated documents, and the general arguments about reform, are the subject of this final chapter.

Firstly, the chapter outlines in general terms, without detailed description or evaluation, the alternative type of social security system on which BI is based. Then the discussion summarises the strategic and theoretical logic that has been invoked in support of fundamental reform and briefly notes the link between this logic and actual policy developments. The focus then turns to the detail of the Green Paper and the evidence it offers about the possible costs, benefits and effects of BI. The final section considers the potential of the current system to adapt to future challenges and reviews the specific issues that will pre-occupy policy makers in the near future.

INTEGRATED APPROACHES TO SOCIAL SECURITY

Systems of social security fall into one of two broad categories — categorical or universal. The first of these entails payments based around qualifying conditions of some sort (for example contribution requirements for social insurance benefits or means tests for social assistance allowances). Universal schemes, in contrast, provide one system applicable to all — with the possible exclusion of a very small number of exceptional cases. Negative Income Tax (NIT) and Basic Income schemes are the two purest forms of such universal strategies. The concept of NIT originated in the US in the 1960s, advocated most cogently by the conservative economist Milton Friedman in *Capitalism and Freedom* (published in 1962) and again in *Free to Choose* (Friedman, 1979: 149–159). A programme of detailed research and policy experimentation grew up around the NIT concept in the United States and Canada (Munnell, 1986A).

Abstracting from the detail of Ireland's current system of taxes and benefits, the rationale for NIT as a replacement for more conventional systems is as follows. Persons liable for income tax are entitled to tax credits or allowances, but low-income earners who are not liable for income tax obtain no benefit from these. In fact, if the tax system is structured around allowances in a system with varying marginal rates, then higher income tax payers (with higher marginal tax rates) benefit more in cash terms that than those on lower incomes with lower tax rates (or a zero tax rate).[1] NIT counteracts this problem by reversing the taxation mechanism and paying supplements (negative taxes) to those taxpayers whose income is so low that it is *less* than the total of their tax allowances or credits.[2] In this way the income tax system is divided into two parts: those with incomes above the total of the allowances or credits would pay tax and those below would be paid a supplement — a 'negative tax'. By definition, there is a break-even point at which no tax is payable and no negative tax received. The theoretical attractions of NIT are that:

- It considerably simplifies tax and benefit systems by effectively integrating income maintenance functions into the tax system.
- It can remove poverty traps, thereby improving work incentives, by abolishing means tests and having one positive/negative tax rate.
- It can address poverty by establishing a guaranteed minimum income and by using the tax system to supplement the incomes of the working poor.

NIT proposals vary in their details but there are three defining features of NIT:

- A tax rate or benefit reduction rate on earned income.
- A minimum income for all families or individuals with no other income.
- A break-even point at which no net tax is paid or negative income tax (supplements) received.

These features of NIT are interrelated, so that any one of the three variables is jointly determined by the other two, and this interrelationship is central to the policy trade-offs in designing such schemes. Figure 12(a) illustrates the operation of NIT. In the figure, the diagonal dotted line represents a neutral case in which there is no tax or benefit and net income is the same as pre-tax income. The break-even point is where this line intersects the net income line Y_1. A person with a pre-tax income Y would also have a net income Y in the absence of a benefit. With NIT the negative tax fills the gap between Y and a minimum, Y_1.

Figure 12.1 NIT schemes

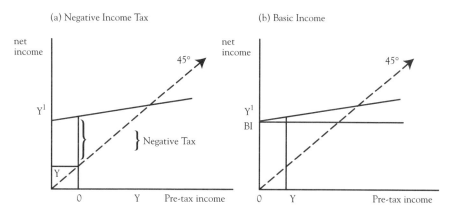

(a) Negative Income Tax

(b) Basic Income

This would apply with all cases of Y up to the breakeven point. At higher levels of Y pre-tax income would be past the breakeven point, and with 'positive' tax paid the net income line would be below the neutral line.

The second form of universal integrated approach is variously titled Basic Income (BI), Social Dividend, and Citizen's Income. As Figure 12(b) suggests, this strategy is analytically similar to NIT, and is comprised of the same three elements. It entails a minimum income guarantee in the form of a payment to *all* citizens and a proportionate tax levied on all income other than the universal BI. As the horizontal line in Figure 12(b) shows, the BI is paid to all persons, no matter what there pre-tax income level is. If pre-tax income is 0, then the BI brings the person up to the BI level. Above the break-even point, the tax paid is greater than the BI and below it the BI is less than the tax paid. If pre-tax income is Y, then the combination of the Basic Income and the earned income after tax gives a net income of Y_1.

The analytical logic underpinning BI and NIT is similar and in the illustration the outcome in terms of net income is identical. NIT and BI also have broadly similar policy implications: both systems entail the abolition of pre-existing social insurance and assistance payments. However, there is an important practical difference between these two variants of integration. Strictly speaking, the BI version is an income *guarantee*, as it is paid directly and unconditionally to everybody, at all levels of pre-tax income. The minimum guarantee under NIT, however, is a net outcome *after* the interactions of earnings and (positive or negative) taxes.[3]

INTEGRATED APPROACHES: FROM MODELS TO POLICY

Neither of these schemes has been implemented in the pure form outlined above. However, the general approach has influenced the analysis of social security in many countries, and a wide variety of reforms has been proposed — and some limited reforms implemented — that reflect this approach of attempting some integration of tax and social security. In the US and Canada, the NIT approach gained considerable academic currency and detailed evaluations and programs of research on NIT were undertaken. Policy experiments were undertaken in which NIT was introduced for experimental groups in the population and the results monitored. Much of the research arising from these experiments focused on the incentive effects of replacing traditional welfare provision for the poor. This research generated considerable — and inconclusive — academic controversy about the impact of NIT on the incomes and employment participation of the poor (Munnell, 1986).

In the UK in the mid-1960s the first specific policy proposal invoking the NIT concept was advanced (Lees, 1967). This proposal was directed at families with children. In the context of a system paying Family Allowances in cash and also offering Child Tax Allowances, the proposal entailed integrating support for families into a negative tax of 50%. A family whose income fell below their total tax allowances would receive a supplement of 50% of the difference between their income and the allowances. This idea would have improved the net incomes of some poorer families, at little budgetary cost, but with uncertain administrative and incentive implications (Atkinson, 1969). In 1970 the Conservative Party election manifesto referred to NIT and in 1972 the Conservative government published a Green Paper, *Proposals for A Tax Credit Scheme*. The Green Paper offered a comprehensive approach to integrating the tax and social security systems. It proposed a series of tax credits (fixed amounts to be deducted from tax liabilities), to replace personal tax allowances, Family Allowances and means-tested Family Income Supplement for low-paid employees. All income (credits excluded) would be taxed at 30% and credits would be added to income: at low levels of income the credits could exceed gross tax liability and the net effect would be a negative tax on those with the lowest incomes.

This Green Paper generated wide debate, political as well as academic (Atkinson, 1973; Judge, 1980; Sandford, 1980). While the tax credit proposals were not implemented, the Green Paper and its aftermath had two effects. First, evaluations of the proposals clarified the basic difficulty with NIT-type proposals. It is difficult to replace all of the social security system and the tax system, and to do so while simultaneously improving the incomes of the poor and sustaining work incentives, without incurring significant costs (Atkinson, 1973; Sandford, 1980; Collard, 1980). Second, the debate crystallised the reform advocates in the UK into two broad camps. One group of reformers focused on ways to implement integrationist proposals, The other group argued for a retention of a Beveridge-style system, but with more adequate benefits, improved Family Allowances, and a reduced role for tax allowances: this reform strategy became known as the 'Back-to-Beveridge' strategy. Third, while both sets of proposals had some concerns in common — reducing reliance on means-tests and dealing with the inequalities of tax allowances — the differences between the reform strategies rested in part on very different policy emphases and different social and political perspectives. Broadly, integrationists tended to emphasise incentives while proponents of reform within the social insurance system were more focused on poverty and benefit levels, than on the structure of the system.

During the 1980s, the UK debate tended to mirror these two broad camps and further, more elaborate, programs of overall reform were advanced. One, for example, offered a critique of the social insurance system and advanced a detailed program of policy change that would lead to a full-blown BI (Parker, 1989). Another study, equally critical of social insurance, set out a detailed scheme that would replace much of the conventional benefit system with a targeted system of credits administered through the tax system (Dilnot, Kay and Morris, 1984). The debate in the UK continued into the 1990s with the Borrie Commission's report and the debate it occasioned (Borrie, 1994). Borrie embraced a new approach to social insurance (a 'participation income') rather than an NIT or BI strategy. In practice, in the UK both the pace and the content of policy change in social security has been at a considerable remove from the aspiration to sweeping reform and theoretically pure proposals.

Some of the insights of integrated approaches have influenced governments' policies in a variety of ways, however. Increasingly, policies have recognised the inequity of tax allowances (for the elderly, for children, and so on) that co-exist with cash benefits, and the policy trend has been to subsume the allowances into cash payments or transform the allowances into credits. Likewise, policy makers increasingly evaluate social security contributions and income taxation *jointly*. While these have been kept as separate taxes in most countries, governments now attempt to coordinate income tax and social security so that their combined effects contribute to employment, distributional and other policy goals. Also, NIT and BI critiques have highlighted means tests and their potentially negative impact. This has led governments to find alternatives to means-tests for those in work with low incomes, and to reform the sometimes complex systems of means-tests for social security that can overlap with means-tests for health, housing and other social services.

Turning to Ireland, international debates and analyses have been reflected in official policy documents, academic research and policy advocacy. In each of the last four decades integration of the tax and social welfare systems has been the subject of policy review — although never of widespread public or political controversy. The NESC published its report *Integrated Approaches to Taxes and Transfers* in 1978 (NESC, 1978). This study first identified a series of policy problems arising from the lack of integration of social security and tax systems, as follows: the gradual convergence of benefit levels and tax-free allowances giving rise to incentives problems; the proliferation of tax-free allowances valued at taxpayers' marginal rates conferring substantial, indirect benefits on higher-income taxpayers; the imposition of social security contributions on employees and employers and levying this 'tax' on a different and narrower tax base than income taxes; the narrowing over time of the differential between assistance allowances and insurance benefits, eroding the link between insurance contributions and benefits. Then the study illustrated three options for policy change that would, in varying degrees, integrate the social security and income tax systems. One of the options outlined was a BI-type scheme, and the other options were versions of a tax credit scheme, but there were elements common to all three schemes:

- A replacement of tax allowances by tax credits.
- A broadening of the 'tax' base on which social security contributions are levied so that income tax and social security contributions are levied on the same base.
- An extension of the income tax base through a reduction or abolition of tax allowances and tax deductions (for items such as mortgage interest payments, private health insurance and so on).

In the event the government rejected the option of attempting reforms along these lines.[4]

Later, in the 1980s, two government commissions, The Commission on Taxation and the Commission on Social Welfare, considered the need for full integration of tax and social security. The First Report of the Commission on Taxation acknowledged the theoretical attractions of NIT and BI schemes but concluded that 'any attempt to solve the problem of poverty with a single comprehensive system of income maintenance which is integrated with the income tax system would be very costly' (Commission on Taxation, 1982: 322). Accordingly, the Commission argued for the continued separation of the taxation and social security systems and proposed a reform of the tax system that included some elements of integration: the abolition of tax allowances for special categories such as the elderly and children; the introduction of personal credits rather than allowances; the removal of tax deductions for expenditures such as health insurance; the imposition of a single (low) rate of income taxation on all income, and; the conversion of the social insurance contribution to a social security tax on all income. In this model of reform, poverty would remain the remit of the social security benefit system, and the inequities and incentive problems of the tax system were to be dealt with by abolishing tax allowances and applying a single (low) rate of tax.

The Commission on Social Welfare was equally emphatic in its rejection of full integration, citing some of the reasoning given by the Commission on Taxation, while offering a particular emphasis of its own (Commission on Social Welfare, 1986: 172–185). In its pre-occupation with poverty, the Commission saw increases in benefits and allowances as central to any reforms, and the scale of the required increases meant that it would be very costly to incorporate the benefit levels into a universal scheme. The Commission argued that a social insurance, contingency-based scheme is not only less costly than a universal one (for any given level of benefit), but also that it is a 'more effective means of directing social security payments to persons in need of an income without actually undertaking means tests' (Commission on Social Welfare, 1986: 181). Furthermore, in the Commission's view, simple, mechanical systems such as BI or NIT would be too inflexible. On the benefits side, BI could not reflect diversity in needs, and in taxation NIT would be too rigid a system of income support for many on low incomes, as their circumstances and needs fluctuate in a way that an NIT regime could not reflect. In short, the Commission embraced a Beveridgean strategy, arguing for an extended social insurance system, more adequate benefits, and improved child income support.

In the 1990s, notwithstanding governments' rejection of sweeping integrationist reform, the analysis and debate continued, due in large measure to the advocacy work of the Conference of the Religious of Ireland. In a series of publications CORI argued a principled case for a pure BI system for Ireland and set out details of the proposed benefit levels, tax rates, and costings (Healy and Reynolds, 1994: Healy and Reynolds, 1995; Clark and Healy, 1997). Also in the 1990s, researchers offered detailed critiques of the cost and distributional implications of reform proposals drawing on representative models of the population and the tax and benefit system (Callan, 1991; Callan, O'Donoghue and O'Neill, 1994).

A further official examination of social security and tax systems was completed in 1996 by an Expert Working Group (Expert Working Group, 1996). The Working Group's terms of reference were explicitly directed at the 'interaction of the tax and social welfare systems' and with the reforms necessary 'to achieve greater coordination/integration of the two systems' (Expert Working Group, 1996: 2). In response to the earlier reports on taxation and social welfare, policy in these areas had developed in an uncoordinated fashion, the Group argued, and the broad thrust of its report was to identify problems arising from the lack of coordination and to suggest reforms. In line with the Commission on Taxation's analysis, tax policy had been informed in part by reductions in the scope of tax deductions and reduced rates of taxation: this pattern tended to favour higher, rather than lower income tax payers. However, in the area of social security, the Commission on Social Welfare's report informed the extent and pattern of increased benefits.

The Expert Group showed that the combination of increased social welfare payments and the lack of indexation of tax allowances in the period from the late 1980s to the mid-1990s had led to a narrowing of the gap between net income from work and unemployment payments, leading to high replacement ratios and potential incentive problems. Also, the system of child income supports for welfare recipients exacerbated this problem. Some of the uncoordinated changes in tax and social security in the decade to 1996 designed to improve policy had, in the Group's analysis, worsened the problems arising from the lack of integration. For example, the introduction of FIS in 1984, and its gradual extension over time, had created a poverty trap for some low-paid workers with families because of the way the FIS means test interacted with tax and social insurance contributions and with other means tests.

The Expert Group's report studied replacement ratios in detail and identified reforms that would lower these ratios, ameliorate poverty traps for low-paid employees, and underpin return-to-work. A radical shift to a fully integrated system would not achieve these objectives, the Group argued, and like the commissions before it, the Group opted for reform within the broad framework of separate tax and social security systems. Some of the key reforms it proposed were: the coordination of budgetary policy so that the gap between net take home pay and unemployment payments would not rise; reform of child income support to make it more neutral as between work and unemployment; and the gradual integration of the additional employment and health levies into the tax system proper.

Since 1996 the broad thrust of policy has reflected this report's emphasis on incentives: tax rates have been lowered and the tax allowance system has been partially converted to a tax credit system; child income support is more neutral; changes in means tests have been modified and specific welfare-to-work schemes introduced. However, the possibility of sweeping reform of the system as a whole has continued to shape analysis of social security. The nationally negotiated *Partnership 2000* document contained a commitment to establish a Working Group on Basic Income. The report of this group was completed in 2000 and arising from this work a Green Paper and a series of associated Working papers were published; a further policy pamphlet advocating a BI scheme for Ireland was also published (Government of Ireland, 2002; Clark, 2002). The details of these studies are reviewed later. However, before turning to these proposals it is important to place BI and NIT ideas in a wider context. While there are no indication that governments adopt radical, clean-sweep reforms, the theoretical designs of integrated systems stubbornly continue to influence policy analysis. The next section discusses *why* this approach continues to have influence.

RATIONALE FOR ALTERNATIVE APPROACHES

For many advocates of BI or NIT, the strategic policy issue is the inherent unsuitability of social insurance for today's conditions. Recalling that the Irish social security system derived from Beveridge, a useful way of presenting the rationale for a new social security system is to outline Hermione Parker's celebrated case for an abandonment of social insurance in the UK and its replacement with BI (Parker, 1989).

Parker points out that the Beveridgean system was predicated on a particular conception of social security. In the Beveridge model, social security is concerned with securing an income interrupted or forgone through retirement, sickness, unemployment or widowhood. Primarily, this means security of income up to a *minimum*, and the provision of a minimum in such a way as to ensure that the 'interruption' of earnings ends as quickly as possible. Beveridge applied this definition of social security and adopted three assumptions about the broader framework of social provision in post war UK: the existence of universal child income payments; public provision of comprehensive health care; and the maintenance of full employment. Then Beveridge also embraced what Parker has described as five 'implicit assumptions' about social security strategy (Parker, 22–30):

- Poverty is primarily due to interruption of earnings, and as long as earnings are supplemented by child allowances for workers with families then social security benefits can be confined to those who are not working.
- Society consists of 'normal' family units such as married couples in stable relationships, widows and (heterosexual) single persons living alone or with their parents.
- Married women are financially dependent on their husbands.
- Government can — and ought — to maintain full employment: a system of unemployment benefit can only operate practically if unemployment is short-term and at a low level.
- Full employment means regular, full-time work for men in the prime age groups, with few job changes and minimal need for re-training.

The increasing irrelevance of these assumptions is central to the advocacy of a different system. In the British case, the argument for change was strengthened by the failure to *implement* Beveridge's plan properly. Although child allowances were introduced, they were not age-related as Beveridge had recommended, and were less than the recommended payment. To compensate for these inadequacies, child dependant allowances for the poorest of families — welfare recipients — were introduced. In turn, this created the mixed system of child income support that gave higher child support to those on unemployment benefit and created poverty and unemployment traps for those with children. Also, the level of insurance benefits that underpinned the post-war UK system was below subsistence level. Furthermore, the unemployment benefits system envisaged by Beveridge did not materialise. Beveridge did not intend a specific time limitation on entitlement to benefit, but stressed that the indefinite duration of entitlement that he recommended should be linked to a requirement to take re-training in the context of state-provided training.

In the verdict of Parker and other commentators (Atkinson, 1969; Judge, 1980; Field, Meacher and Pond, 1977) the poor implementation of Beveridge, combined with the growing irrelevance of his assumptions, created serious systemic problems. Among insurance recipients reliance on means-tested social assistance grew because of the inadequacy of the benefits; the inadequate child allowances led to family poverty among low-paid employees; the mixed system of child income support created unemployment and poverty traps; the emergence of new circumstances and needs not recognised in the core assumptions (lone-parenthood, long-term unemployment, new work patterns of work such as part-time jobs) lead to an unanticipated dependence on means-tested allowances. For advocates of radical reform these problems with social security engendered a qualitative social change — the emergence of an 'underclass' (Parker's terminology) relying in whole or in part on means-tested payments and semi-permanently excluded from employment and mainstream social life (Parker, 1989: 38–60).

Debate about tax-benefit integration is also embedded in a wider argument about the nature of citizenship in contemporary societies in two ways. First, it has been argued that many mature developed economies are in transition from being industrialised, full-employment economies to a new status as service-based, flexible economies. (Standing, 1984: Offe, 1984). According to this reasoning, many European economies in particular are chronically prone to lower levels of economic growth and higher unemployment. This is due to a number of factors such as the loss of competitiveness to emerging economies in other regions of the world, and the demographic burden of pensions and health care provisions for the elderly. A central impact of these changes has been the emergence again of long-term, mass unemployment and the growth of entire sub-sets of the population that are habitually on the fringes of the labour market. This is not a transient phenomenon. The basic economic paradigm has changed and the core of the 'old' economy — secure public or quasi-public employment and stable life-long employment in private sector manufacturing — is shrinking. In its place a flexible labour market is emerging. This is characterised by greater employment insecurity, a significant role for part-time and atypical employment, a higher risk of low paid work and greater wage inequality, and the presence in the labour market of women (and men) attempting to balance employment and family responsibilities.

The implication of this scenario is that welfare states can no longer use employment-based social insurance as the guarantor of income security. As Standing has suggested, to allow the 'new' labour market to operate efficiently 'social policy should *decouple income security from the labour market*' by providing to each person 'a guaranteed basic income, essentially an individual share of national income, a 'social dividend' as a right of citizenship' (Standing, 1994: 57–58, her italics). Proponents of this viewpoint then cite a litany of benefits that would flow from this new form of income security. A guaranteed basic income would:

- Facilitate and encourage labour flexibility.
- Encourage self-employment.
- Remove the stigma of unemployment and abolish the paradox of benefits for the unemployed only if they remain unemployed.
- Avoid the rigid institution of retirement and inflexible notions of retirement age.
- Eliminate the need for state intrusion into citizen's lives by abolishing the need to monitor sickness, unemployment and availability for work, cohabitation, etc.
- Equalise the economic status of men and women, and of individuals of different marital statuses and sexual orientation, by conferring income security as a right on all citizens.
- Reduce administrative costs substantially through the simplification of the social security system.
- Avoid the stigma of benefit receipt and the problem of low take-up of benefits by removing means tests.

The second aspect of the citizenship debate concerns the universal and unconditional nature of the income guarantee in BI proposals. This requires some justification and a number of advocates BI, notably Van Parijs, have developed highly formalised ethical and philosophical arguments (Van Parijs, 1992; Van Parijs, 1995; Jordan, 1994; Offe, 1994). Van Parijs' reasoning is similar to the modern theories of social justice elaborated by liberal-egalitarian thinkers such as John Rawls (Van Parijs, 1992). Van Parijs also sets out a full micro-economic exposition of the theoretical link between the level of basic income, taxation and national income.[5] Summarising his logic, a free and just society has a well-enforced structure of rights and each person has the greatest possible opportunity to do whatever s/he might want to do (Van Parijs, 1995: 25). This latter condition — 'maximin opportunity' in Van Parijs's terminology — distinguishes real freedom from merely formal freedom. According to Van Parijs (1992: 229):

> Although it does make sense to formulate justice in terms of a maximin criterion, what it is to be 'maximinned' cannot be income alone. It must, rather, be something like the real freedom (as opposed to the sheer right) to do whatever one might like to do with one's life, including consume, get a job, and perform enjoyable activities.

This approach contrasts with the more conventional analysis of the link between work, poverty and social security. Conventionally viewed, if those out of work are poor, then benefits should be increased to alleviate poverty. However, the lowest net wages could then exceed benefit levels. In this analysis, there is an inherent conflict between employment objectives and poverty objectives. But this ignores 'the right not to work, or the right not to do work one does not like doing' (Van Parijs, 1992: 228). Fairness is not simply about increasing the income of the poor; the degree of fairness cannot be simply read off from the distribution of income. An increase in the incomes of the poor that is obtained by pressurising into work those who place a higher value on leisure or free time would not increase fairness. It could be an unfair discrimination against those with a lesser taste for income and consumption.

Therefore, income and consumption, access to work, and freedom, must all be considered when discussing justice. Basic Income speaks to all three, according to Van Parijs. BI underpins basic consumption, but as it is paid irrespective of income from other sources, it also can act, in effect, as an employment subsidy for the recipient. It would enable those who attach importance to paid work or self-employment *per se* to accept work at a lower wage than they would accept in the absence of a basic income. Also, a basic income would give each individual the option *not* to work — not to accept any job for which they have been deemed to be suitable — as it is paid unconditionally.

However, while Van Parijs attempts a rigorous analytical justification for BI the philosophical and political basis of BI is somewhat eclectic. As Van Parijs acknowledges, there are in fact 'competing justifications' for a basic income (Van Parijs, 1992: 3–43). A range of philosophical stances — Marxist, Libertarian, Post-Materialist, and Communitarian — can be invoked. Libertarians, for example, emphasising individual freedom and the coercive power of the state, may see BI as a substantial reduction in state intervention in people's lives. Post-materialists can present it as being 'non-productivist', designed to improve sustainability by reducing the emphasis on work participation and economic growth (Offe, 1994). Communitarians will highlight the divisions between the socially excluded, dependent for long periods of time on 'conditional' welfare built around means tests and categories of need, and those in the mainstream with secure incomes and access to social insurance rights. BI offers a way of integrating the socially excluded by providing unconditional welfare to all (Jordan, 1986; Jordan, 1994).

BASIC INCOME IN IRELAND

But are these various levels of argument — policy, strategic and philosophical — relevant to the reform of social security in Ireland? Clearly, the policy critique of social insurance offered by Parker and critics of social insurance has a distinct resonance in the Irish context: the assumptions she identifies and the problems occasioned by persisting with these assumptions have been outlined in earlier chapters. However, it is valid to question the extent to which Parker's type of critique necessarily justifies abandonment of social insurance and its replacement with BI. Some of the problems inherent in the Irish (and UK) social insurance system have been addressed — at least in part–within the framework of the current system. The social insurance system has redressed the gender imbalance to some degree, although the system is still not fully based on individual rights, and care work is still imperfectly recognised. Likewise, the child income support system has been reformed, and the social insurance contribution system is now more coherently related to income taxation.

For Parker and other advocates of BI, a decisive indicator of the failure of insurance and assistance systems is the growth of means testing and the problems this brings: low take-up, poverty traps, and — in the British case at least — a large segment of the population dependent on means-tested payments and outside of the insurance based system of rights for long periods of time. This central point does *not* apply with equal force to Ireland. In the wake of the limited social insurance legislation enacted in 1952, the Irish system was largely a means-tested one. However, the social insurance system grew rapidly in later decades and the proportion of recipients and expenditure as between insurance and means-tested payments has been shifting historically towards insurance. In 2001, the share of insurance recipients across all schemes was 56% and in the core areas of provisions for widows, pensioners, the sick and the unemployed, the balance has become less means-tested and more insurance-based than in the past.

The adaptation of Ireland's social insurance regime to cope with its deficiencies has made the Irish system very complex, however. There are now eight categorical schemes in social insurance and seven separate means-tested allowances, including the 'last resort' SWA scheme. The unit of entitlement is a hybrid of individuals and families and the governing contribution rules are highly complex. The annual reports of the Office of the Ombudsman record the large volume of social security cases referred to it, and the reported cases show the administrative and legal complexity of the present structure. In brief, the policy critique offered by Parker and others does highlight some of the problems of the social security system in Ireland. However, the critique does not amount to a definitive case for BI, in part because the failure or success of social security is a matter of degree, and in part because it has proven possible to address the critique within the framework of the social insurance and assistance model.

What of the strategic analysis of the changing nature of the economy? The context outlined by Standing, Offe, Parker and others is one that clearly resonates in the old 'Bismarckian', early-industrialising welfare states. The Irish campaigners for BI have embraced this vision. For example, in their call for a BI as part of a 'new paradigm' CORI states (Healy and Reynolds, 1994: 29):

For decades socio-economic policy has been built on a simple framework or paradigm. This paradigm envisages a world in which full-time jobs are available for everyone seeking them, in which these jobs provide adequate income for people holding them and their 'dependants' and in which good social insurance is available for people who are sick, unemployed or retired. In this way every person is meant to have meaningful work, adequate income and to participate in national development. This paradigm is seen more and more as a spectacular failure.

For these advocates of BI, the paradigm failure is world-wide and driven partly by the projected growth in the world's population: 'Simply to keep the numbers unemployed in the world at their present level would obviously demand levels of job creation which are clearly unsustainable' (Healy and Reynolds, 1994: 30). A related publication refers again to the conventional paradigm and points to its failure: 'Much effort and financial resources have been expended in pursuit of this goal but analyses of the results produce the clear conclusion that this paradigm has been spectacularly unsuccessful in achieving its goals. Unemployment is higher than at any time in the history of the state' (Healy and Reynolds, 1995: 44). It is understandable that this analysis was offered in the mid-1990s when unemployment in Ireland was high (12.1% in 1995) and had been at a very high level for a decade or more. Within five years unemployment had fallen to a very low level (3.7% in 2001) and the employment growth was not confined to 'atypical', low-paid, service-type employment. In fact, the employment growth has been characterised as 'occupational upgrading', with employment increasing substantially in middle and higher grade occupations (O'Connell, 2000). Unemployment rose again to just under 5% in 2003, but this does not portend an inescapable return in the short or medium term to the double-digit rates of unemployment and high levels of long-term unemployment of the 1980s and 90s.[6]

None of this is to suggest a triumphal account of the Celtic Tiger economy or to adopt a casual stance about likely levels of unemployment in the future. The analytical point is that CORI transplants into the Irish context a perspective articulated by a number of commentators (Jordan, 1994; Standing, 1994; Van Parijs, 1994) about the economic and employment problems of some European countries. This perspective essentially focuses on the demise of large-scale, manufacturing employment and the apparently intractable problem of high unemployment in these countries. This analysis is hardly applicable to Ireland. On the contrary, comparative studies of the Irish economy highlight that it is not the same *type* of economy as the large, early industrialising economies. In O'Riain's terms it is a 'flexible developmental state', a state that has strategically integrated Ireland into the global economy and successfully pursued employment creating policies across a wide range of areas — taxation, industrial policy, labour market policy, education, and so on (O'Riain and O'Connell, 2000; O'Riain, 2000). From a social security standpoint, the critical question is whether the case for BI in Ireland rests wholly or substantially on the view of Ireland's economic and employment prospects held out by Healy and Reynolds. To the extent that it does, this case is distinctly weakened.

As regards the wider ethical and philosophical questions about BI, the central issue is the justification for unconditional welfare. BI proponents recognise the importance of paid employment, of course. Van Parijs suggests that a job is in fact the most important asset in today's world — an asset that is likely to be extremely unequally distributed. He then argues, in effect, for a tax on all earnings, self-employment, and profits, at a rate that maximises the tax yield, with the revenues supporting an unconditional basic income. This model accepts the right to a job but gives effect to this right by taxing job 'rents' and redistributing them as an unconditional basic income.[7] This case can be challenged along the lines advanced by Ian Gough (Gough, 2000). As Gough points out, contributing to socially productive activity in its widest sense is a defining feature of human nature and of individuals' membership of society. He argues that 'the principle that all able bodied persons should be enabled to contribute, and then should actually contribute, to the common wealth is a powerful component of intuitions about justice' (Gough, 200: 212). For Gough and critics of BI, reciprocity is the relevant principle. Work and leisure are not simply morally equivalent, and able-bodied people should have both the right and the duty to participate in productive activities.

BI breaches the principle of reciprocity because, as Gough explains, it would be paid to everybody (Gough, 2000: 215). There is a further point about the right to work. Some people — through sheer misfortune — may not be able to enforce that right, but a basic income does not specifically compensate for this, as it is paid to the voluntarily as well as the involuntarily unemployed. BI is therefore non-reciprocal and indiscriminate. According to this reasoning, the appropriate policy is to give all citizens a real right to work and to tie benefits to participation — but not necessarily to participation in conventional paid employment. This perspective on work and participation suggests a further point. BI does not acknowledge that the *source* of income may be an important factor in people's welfare. Income associated with productive activity and participation — as distinct from unconditional income — may contribute more to individual and collective welfare. Arguably, work and participation can reinforce self-respect and personal identity, enhance personal development, create opportunities for social contact and relationships, and sustain and develop skills.

One final, general point about Van Parijs' argument is its emphasis on *income* as the main instrument of individual and social welfare. His analysis relies heavily on the importance of consumer rationality and freedom of choice and hence he visualises a limited role for collective provision of public and social services. He explicitly allows for some obvious instances of market failure (public provision of police, basic education etc.). However, the degree of rationality he imputes to individual behaviour does not logically allow him to accept direct state provision of goods and services. He does not extend this argument to its logical conclusion or consider in detail the implications of this approach for non-cash welfare such as health, education and housing.

In its advocacy of BI in Ireland, CORI draws heavily on the philosophical work of Van Parijs and derives from this philosophical base the following set of policy principles (Healy and Reynolds, 1995: 30–34):

- Nature and its resources are available *for the benefit of all.*
- All citizens have a right to an *adequate income.*
- The adequate income should be a guarantee for *all citizens.*
- The adequate income should be *penalty-free* — without stigma, or coercion or control.
- The adequate income system should contribute to *horizontal and vertical equity* and its cost should be shared equitably.
- The system should be *efficient* in the broadest sense by having a positive impact, relative to the status quo, on the welfare of society and on the situation of the worst-off in society.
- The adequate income guarantee should be *simple* to understand and administer;
- The adequate income guarantee should *promote autonomy and reduce dependency.*

According to CORI, the existing social insurance and social assistance regime does not reflect these principles and should be replaced by a BI scheme. The key elements in the CORI plan reflect the theoretical design of integrated approaches outlined earlier, and the details of its 1995 proposals are as follows:

- Replacement of all current benefits and allowances by a *basic income for all citizens* — without reference to means, personal circumstances, marital status, employment status or any other qualifying criteria.
- Establishment of a set of *basic income payments tiered according to age*, with adults' payments in ascending order by age category (20–64, 65–79, 80+) and the two older age groups receiving the current age-differentiated Contributory Old Age pension.
- Payment of a separate *basic income in respect of children* (0–20), incorporating the child dependant allowances and child benefit into an enhanced child benefit.
- Introduction of a *Social Solidarity Fund* (in place of the existing Supplementary Welfare Allowances) to offer 'top-up' payments to those relying wholly on the basic income.
- Reduction of employers' Pay-Related Social Insurance contributions by a quarter and conversion of employers' PRSI into a *Social Responsibility Tax* payable at one rate on all wage income.
- *Abolition of all personal allowances and discretionary allowances* (for mortgage interest, private health insurance, and so on) in the income tax code. ,
- *Abolition of other earmarked taxes* on personal income.

- *Removal of income tax exemption* limits.
- Imposition of a *single rate of tax of 50% on all income* without exemptions deductions, or allowances.

CORI then offers contrasts between the net incomes of particular types of households and families under the existing and proposed systems and illustrates the kinds of gains and losses that would arise from the reform. Clearly, the very lowest income groups under the existing system — people relying on the lowest social welfare payment in the existing system — would tend to gain, as would low-income couples with children because of the payment to each individual and the improved income for children. Likewise, some higher income taxpayers would lose because of the uniformly high rate of tax and the abolition of tax allowances and reliefs of all kinds. However, the pattern of gains and losses would be very mixed.

Before proceeding to look at the Green Paper and the most recent analysis of the costs and effects of BI, some general points about the CORI arguments should be noted. The principles CORI sets out are difficult to reject at a very general level at least, and some of the individual elements in its reform package can be justified for quite specific policy reasons. For example, the current tax system is made less efficient and less equitable because of the proliferation of allowances and reliefs; the level of some benefits is low and a reduction in relative income poverty requires improvements in some payment levels. However, it is not clear that the broad strategy CORI advocates follows from the principles it sets out, and some of the details of its proposed system are at odds with the general objectives CORI purports to support. In relation to the principles, the difficulty with the campaigning literature is that it nowhere offers an evaluation of the range of possible systems against the principles. BI is simply taken to reflect the principles, and no mention is made of any other possible strategy. It would be possible to argue, for example, that a generous means-tested system ('capped universalism' is the term used to describe this strategy, which is historically associated with Australia) would equally advance the principles CORI sets out.

More generally, the argument does not consider the relative importance of the various principles and the potential trade-offs between them. For example, a BI system is undoubtedly simple because it gives every citizen the same payment: but it might be easier to achieve the *adequate income* guarantee by giving a higher payment to those without an income or with a low income. Simplicity is achieved by forgoing higher improvements on payments targeted at the poor. Likewise, vertical equity might be better advanced through a conventional benefits system (built around means-tests or insurable contingencies) combined with a tax system with a progressive structure of tax rates.

In applying its general policy principles, CORI criticises the existing system in very general terms, but the criticisms lack supporting evidence about the actual operation of the existing system. For example, it argues that currently many people are 'forced to do nothing as a condition of receiving their social welfare entitlements' and that this contributes to 'the creation of a dependency culture' (Healy and Reynolds, 1994: 44). The current system, because of its complexity, also leads to 'confusion, delays and unintended victimisation' (Healy and Reynolds, 1994: 44). The argument about dependency and recipients being 'forced to do nothing' is not based on an adequate description of the system; the structure of the system is far more balanced and allows a wide range of recipients (the unemployed, lone parents, pensioners, for example) to combine employment and welfare receipt. In so far as the point about doing 'nothing' and 'dependency' relates to the unemployed and the incentive to work, the general terms of CORI's critique are at odds with the very complex evidence about work incentives in Ireland and internationally.

CORI's references to 'dependency culture' are again offered in very general terms, but they imply a cultural view of poverty in which the welfare system creates a separate culture of passivity and lack of motivation among the poor. The notion of a culture of poverty has been intensely controversial in social research and policy debate, but CORI's general endorsement is not based on any systematic consideration of the evidence. In particular, there is no empirical support for the argument that the Irish social welfare system has the social consequences that CORI imputes to it. It is also not clear what CORI's policy logic is here: if the current system creates a dependency culture, would a BI at a higher level than current social welfare payments strengthen or weaken this culture? Similarly, the general assertions about 'confusion' and 'victimisation' are not supported by empirical evidence. In fact, there is remarkably little systematic evidence available in Ireland about the detailed operation of the social welfare system or of recipients' experiences.

The BI proposals emphasise the need for *adequate* incomes, but do not consider how adequacy relates to systematic variations in people's *needs*. Housing costs are a case in point: some people have zero costs and for other people their mortgage or rent payment is their largest single expenditure. Many countries have found it necessary to devise some specific way to incorporate housing costs into their social security regimes. BI does not allow for this complexity. Similarly with illness and disability: the current system in Ireland, for example, pays an Invalidity Pension to qualified insured persons with long-term illnesses that preclude them from work. This pension is at a higher level than many other payments, reflecting — albeit imperfectly — the different needs of the long-term ill in relation to diet, heat and transport, for example. BI trades off these complexities in favour of simplicity.

In relation to the critical issue of adequacy, CORI does not offer an *independent* calculation of an adequate income, but adopts an existing social security payment (the old age pension) as the core of its BI framework. This means that the BI system confers the same level of income on the largest group of social security recipients (pensioners), although the CORI proposal allows for supplementary payments through its proposed Social Solidarity Fund. Presumably, one of the issues here is cost. Giving an adequate payment to the entire adult population requires a tax rate of 50%. However, an independent analysis of what constitutes an *adequate* income might suggest a payment *higher* than CORI's proposed payment, and this in turn would imply a higher tax rate. This highlights the dilemmas in the design of BI schemes: if the basic payment is to ensure adequacy for all, it pushes up the cost and the required tax rate; if the payment is scaled back, then it compromises on the critical objective of providing adequate payments to prevent poverty.

Curiously, one critical aspect of social security policy that CORI does not mention in its campaign is the implication it would have for gender equality. The proposal envisages a far-reaching change, as BI would be paid independently of marital and personal circumstances to all men and women. In the Irish context this would resolve the historic problem of the family and dependency-based nature of the system and the lack of personal rights for women that this has entailed. Ireland has redressed some of this historic inequity, but the system is still dogged by complexity and controversy about the relative treatment of men and women, and of married and cohabiting persons.

There is broad agreement in the various assessments of BI that it requires higher tax rates than the current system. The CORI proposals in the mid-1990s suggested that a tax rate of 50% would underpin the costs of their proposed scheme. A number of detailed papers offered estimates of the costs and taxation implications of BI (Callan, O'Donoghue and O'Neill, 1994; Honohan, 1987; Clark and Healy, 1997; O'Toole, 1995; Ward, 1994). The evaluation of Basic Income by researchers at the Economic and Social Research Institute, for example, showed that for the tax/benefit year 1993/4, a BI set at the level of the lowest social welfare payment would require a tax rate of about 68% (Callan, O'Donoghue and O'Neill, 1994). However, before turning to the detail of the most recent assessment of BI in the 2002 Green Paper, a number of points should be noted about the related issues of costs, tax rates and benefit levels.

First, there are methodological differences in the way proposals are costed.[8] Second, the detailed design of BI affects its cost.[9] Third, there are a wide range of BI strategies. The simple, universal scheme discussed above is only one variant. It is important to note that in Ireland analyses have been undertaken of significant variations on the simple BI strategy. For example, in their analysis for 1993/4, Callan and his colleagues, illustrate the effect of giving couples a lower level of BI than two single persons (while still conferring each person with a personal right to half of the couple's total basic income). This reduces the cost so that the required tax rate becomes 63% rather than 68%. An even more significant variation is Partial Basic Income (PBI). This entails paying a very much lower payment to all citizens, while retaining the existing structure of social security payments. PBI has been assessed in Ireland by Callan (Callan *et al*, 1994), and in her study of the UK Parker (1989) set out detailed proposals for a partial scheme as an intermediate step towards a full BI.

THE GREEN PAPER

CORI continued its campaign for BI during the 1990s. In 2000 the government responded to this and agreed, as part of the national partnership agreement *Partnership 2000 for Inclusion, Employment and Competitiveness*, that a full evaluation of the costs and implications of BI be undertaken. In undertaking this evaluation, teams of researchers produced a series of Working Papers and the government published a Green Paper (Government of Ireland, 2002). The Working Paper and the Green Paper do not discuss the theoretical and philosophical issues, but focus specifically on the costs, the tax rate required to fund a BI, the impact on poverty, and the labour market and economic implications. This section gives an overview of the material.

The basic income working group set out to produce definitive calculations that would command agreement among both BI campaigners and independent analysts, and the working papers start with a set of common assumptions about population size and distribution, the evolution of earnings, price inflation and so on. One working paper by an advocate of BI (Clark, 1999) then gives costs and tax rates (for 2001) and a second, by researchers at the ESRI, then adopts the same assumptions and produces estimates. Both estimates are based on the age-tiered payment system summarised earlier and both adopt identical assumptions about payment levels: for example, the weekly BI payments in 2001 would be €128.65, €95, and €121.92 for persons aged respectively 80+, 21–64, and 65–79, with substantially lower payments for children and younger adults. Table 12.1 summarises the key points in the two exercises. The ESRI's analysis suggests that a BI requires a tax rate of about 51%, while the estimate by Clark points to a tax rate of 47.2%.

The sources of the differences in the estimates are identifiable from Table 12.1. Clark makes upward *ad hoc* adjustments to an original estimate of the tax base. There are also differences in the figure for the savings that arise from the abolition of some existing schemes (third-level grants, community employment schemes etc) and a difference in the amount of tax revenue set aside for general exchequer purposes. Clark also makes an additional calculation. Noting the size of the current budget surplus, he estimates the required tax rate on the basis of abolishing the surplus (€2.71bn approximately) and allowing the contribution to the general exchequer to be funded from this source. This reduces the contribution from income tax to the general exchequer from €4.97 billion to €2.27 billion. In turn, this significantly reduces the net cost and the estimated tax rate then becomes 40.2%. However, this arithmetical adjustment is a fundamental alteration to the

Table 12.1: Comparison of ESRI and CORI/ Clark Estimates of BI Costs and Tax Rates for 2001 (€m)

Basic Income Details	ESRI	CORI/Clark
1. Cost of BI payments	15,201	15,246
2. Exchequer Contribution	6,205	4,975
3. Savings	–456	–723
4. Administration and Social Solidarity Fund	–	598
5. Total Expenditure (1+2+3+4)	20,945	20,096
6. Social Responsibility Tax	1,956	1,956
7. Revenue from Flat-rate Tax (5–6)	18,994	18,140
8. Income Tax Base	36,839	38,384
9. Tax Rate %(7/8)	51.6	47.3

Source: Based on Callan, Nolan, Walsh *et al* (2000) and Clark (1999).
Note: The original figures were expressed in Irish punts.

fiscal framework in which the BI is being assessed: in effect, comparing a BI scheme funded partly by the elimination of the budget surplus with the existing tax-benefit system would not be comparing like with like. The appropriate comparison between the estimates, therefore, is between the 52% and 47% tax rates.

The proposed scheme would have effects on the distribution of income and on poverty rates and both sets of analysts offer their respective estimates in some detail. For Clark, the key finding here is that the average income of all households would rise because of the combination of BI and underlying increases in income (Clark, 1999: 19). Comparing *average* household income in each decile in 2001 under the existing and BI regimes he shows that the average high-income household would lose and the average low-income household would gain. Correspondingly, the average income of the lowest income households would rise relative to the poverty line, so that even in the lowest tenth of the income distribution average income would be greater than the poverty line.

The ESRI researchers' results offer quite a different emphasis. They compare the BI scenario with a benchmark scenario, based on the evolution of recent tax and social welfare policy.[10] On *average* the incomes of the lowest sixth deciles would be higher, and that of the top four lower, under BI. However, there are some households that lose and some that gain *within* each income category. Briefly, of the estimated 1,990.6 million tax/benefit units, over 1 million are estimated to lose, about 740,000 to gain, and the balance experience no change. Average losses and gains are lower and higher respectively in the lowest income ranges. Single employees tend to lose, as do dual earner couples without children. Most lone parents lose, and so too do a large majority of dual earner couples without children. The source of these losses resides in the proposed BI structure. Young single employees would be subject to tax at 50% and (if under 21) would be receiving a lower payment than 'adults', and losing the various tax allowances. Young unemployed people receiving the lower proposed payment fare less well than under the current UA/UB system. Lone parents currently receive a payment at the higher end of the benefit hierarchy and also higher Child Dependant Additions: if they are employed they receive a married tax credit. BI would result in a relatively lower benefit payment and taxation of all lone parents' employment income at 50%. Some single retired people would also lose. The BI system would abolish the current Living Alone Allowance and the aged-related tax allowance. As the additional income that pensioners might have (investment income, occupational pensions) would be taxed at 50%, they could pay more tax under the BI than the current system.

These points all highlight the difficulty of replacing the entire tax-benefit system with one simple system without creating complex patterns of gains and losses. It is possible of course — as both Clark and the ESRI analysts point out — to make compensating changes in the BI scheme to redress the losses. The ESRI analysts set out a detailed 'compensation plan' to modify the impact of the losses and they show that, while remaining within the broad parameters of the BI, it is possible to reduce the overall number of losers and increase the number of winners.[11] However, large numbers stand to lose even under the 'BI plus compensation' regime, and the single most important source of the persistent losses is the system of lower payments to younger adults.

The ESRI researchers also offered detailed estimates of the poverty impact of BI. Table 12.2 summarises some key data from this analysis.

BI would significantly reduce income poverty relative to the benchmark especially at the 40% and 50% lines. At the 50% line the proportion poor would fall from about 20% to 15%. Its impact is much more muted at the higher line, with less than a one-percentage point reduction in the poverty rate. When the BI is modified to include compensation for the 'losers', the poverty reduction impact is more significant. The researchers' detailed calculations showed that at the 40% line a very significant factor in the reduction is due to the effect BI would have on raising the income up to BI level of those who would currently receive only a Qualified Adult additional payment. At the higher lines, however, the significant effect arises from the receipt of BI by adults who would not be in receipt of a payment under the current system. These may be employees in low paid jobs, or the spouses of low-paid workers.

An equally important impact relates to the alternative poverty measures in the final two rows of the table: these measure the *depth* of poverty. The poverty gap measure is an index of how far the poor are below the (50%) poverty line on average: the weighted measure takes account of the distribution of the poor below the (50%) line, giving greater weight to the those further below the line. Both of these measures would fall very substantially under a BI system. Finally, the analysis

Table 12.2: Estimates of Poverty Impact of BI in 2001

Poverty Measure	Benchmark	BI	BI + Compensation
% Below 40% Poverty Line	10.6	6.6	4.8
% Below 50% Poverty Line	19.8	15.5	13.0
%Below 60% Poverty Line	30.3	25.2	24.4
Poverty Gap (50% line)	0.041	0.028	0.023
Weighted Poverty Gap (50% line)	0.012	0.007	0.005

Source: Callan, Nolan, Walsh *et al* (2000: 41–46).
Note: The poverty data refer to the proportion of individuals experiencing relative income poverty.

also shows the expected gender impact (Callan, Nolan, Walsh, *et al*: 37). A substantial proportion of individual women (48%) gain from BI — a direct reflection of the fact that under the current system many women do not receive an income. However, some of this impact is *between spouses or partners*: a frequent scenario might be that an employed married man would lose personal and marriage tax credits and pay a higher tax rate on all his income, while a non-earning wife would receive the full BI.

What of the incentive effects of BI? Clark offers no definitive answer. He accepts that BI would be 'expected to have an impact on the supply and demand side of the labour market' (Clark, 1999: 38). He suggests that for the low-paid BI would reduce the disincentives to take up work and to work longer hours, and for the higher-paid there might be disincentives because of the higher tax rate. In addition, he notes that a BI could affect the way wage rates are determined and thus indirectly affect employment, and he points to the possibility that it could also affect participation in education, mobility between jobs, and migration. The reports for the Working Group also contain papers that examine the international labour market literature and its implications for BI in Ireland (Callan, Boyle, McCarthy *et al*, 2000).

The Working Group's review of the extensive research in the US and Canada on NIT and BI schemes advises caution about drawing inferences for Ireland in relation to work incentives: this is for technical reasons and also because of the vast differences in context. The review suggests two conclusions. First, the experimental research on NIT and BI, combined with later studies, seems to suggest that BI does indeed have a negative effect on labour supply, but this is small. Second, a consistent finding is that the employment decisions of women — and in particular married women — are much more responsive to financial incentives than that of men.

In considering the likely effect of BI in Ireland, the working papers consider the main routes through which employment incentives might be affected. One route is through the impact on incentives to work among the unemployed because of the higher replacement ratio (net income from welfare/net income from work). Here the working papers offer valuable detail. Among the unemployed, BI would eliminate the possibility of net wages exceeding the BI: in other words, the new system would not generate replacement ratios in excess of 100%. This change would affect very small numbers. The bigger change would be the shift in the overall distribution of ratios. There would be a fall in the number of unemployed facing low ratios (30% or less) and a rise in the proportions with moderate or high ratios: the proportion with a ratio in excess of 70% would fall from 19% to 16%.

An important point to note is the quite different impact of BI on those working in the home. Their ratios tend to rise. Under BI, the proportion of this category facing ratios in excess of 70% rises markedly from just over a third to nearly a half (Callan, Boyle and McCarthy et al, 2000: 26) The significance of the (predominantly female) working-in-the-home group is that their employment decisions are especially responsive to financial incentives, and BI would therefore seem likely to reduce their labour supply. This would tend to compromise the potential of BI to achieve greater gender equality. Individual rights to a personal income for all men and women would be a core element of BI, but the much larger number of women in the home facing greater financial disincentives might reduce the scope for some women to achieve economic independence through paid employment.

The other route through which BI could influence work incentives concerns those in employment. Here, the broad pattern is an upward shift in replacement ratios. There would be fewer facing low ratios and a substantial rise in the number of moderate ratios (30%–70%). However, the proportion experiencing ratios in excess of 70% would rise by four percentage points to 19%, although no employees would have ratios in excess of 100%. The replacement ratio, comparing welfare income with net employment income, is one aspect of work incentives for employees. An equally important one is the marginal tax-benefit withdrawal rate (MTBWR). This measures the relationship between a change in gross income and a change in net income after taking account changes in income tax, PRSI, and means-tested benefits (an MTBWR of 50% means that a €100 increase in gross pay leads to increased taxes/loss of benefits of €50). Under the conventional system a majority of individuals (57%) at work have marginal tax rates of 30% or less, taking into account PRSI and means-tested benefits. By definition, BI would result in a twenty percentage points increase in the marginal tax rate of these employees, as all income other than the BI would be taxed at 50%.

The working papers also point to other mechanisms through which BI could affect the labour market and the economy. Migration could rise if the BI were higher than the benefits available in other economies; the higher overall tax rate might have a negative effect on economic growth, while greater labour market flexibility and a less unequal distribution of income could enhance growth; if participation in paid employment fell, it could facilitate a growth in the social economy with greater participation in voluntary work and socially useful (currently unpaid) activities. It is less clear what the magnitudes of these possible effects are. It seems reasonable to infer — given the likely impact on employees' marginal tax rates and replacement ratios and on many women's replacement ratios — that BI would reduce employment participation, as one of the working papers concludes: 'we conclude that a fall in labour supply is more likely than an increase' (Callan, Boyle, McCarthy *et al*: 2000: 71).

The general implication of the working papers is that, at best, the employment and economic impact of BI would be uncertain and, at worst, would reduce employment participation and, through this mechanism and others, would reduce the future growth of the economy. If it were confidently established that employment participation would fall, is this a definitive argument for abandoning BI? For advocates of BI, the key points presumably are that it would lead to some reduction in poverty, and that the fall in employment and its consequential effect on economic growth are inherent and *desirable* parts of the scheme. As the discussion above suggested, a central part of the case advanced by proponents of BI is the case for freedom: freedom to choose non-employment in the context of an adequate income guarantee. For those concerned primarily with conventional economic and social goals such as full employment and economic growth, the probable fall in employment participation and the uncertainty of other impacts would outweigh any distributional and other advantages of BI. A basic difficulty in evaluating BI is that it would be a fundamental, qualitative change in the social and economic framework rather than an incremental change in the tax-benefit system. Therefore, any general predictions about its effects should be interpreted with caution.

The Green Paper is studiously neutral for the most part. It gives the background to the debate and a summary of the findings of the various working papers. In the conclusion, in what comes closest to a statement of the government's view about BI, the Green Paper reiterates the relevant points in the *Agreed Programme* of the present government. It stresses the government's commitment to the poverty reduction targets of the revised anti-poverty strategy and points to the government's priority in taxation — to ensure that all those on the minimum wage 'are removed from the tax net and 80% of all taxpayers pay tax only at the standard rate (currently 20%)' (Government of Ireland, 2002: 47). This clear statement of priorities is clearly at odds with the adoption of a BI strategy. However, the Green paper also welcomes debate on tax and welfare policy and, curiously, calls for debate on policies that might increase the likelihood of achieving the benefits of BI while seeking to 'minimise those effects that might be regarded as less desirable'.

FUTURE DEVELOPMENTS

Before discussing the specific issues that will shape policy in the immediate future two final points about the BI debate should be noted. First, there is little evidence that the case for BI has support in government, the political parties, or in civil society generally. Second, it is striking that in the flurry of research and evaluation of BI there has been little recognition of the enduring logic in support of conventional systems of social security, and very little attempt to systematically evaluate the arguments in favour of the current social insurance system. As the relevant chapters in part two suggest, there may be good reasons for having the current system. The failure of private markets in pensions, unemployment payments, and sickness insurance gives rise to a *prima facie* case for social insurance; the nature of housing costs requires a specific social security response; the divergence between the private and social costs of children and the needs associated with the family life-cycle give strong justification for a system of family support payments. These are examples of the arguments in support of the current social security system.

Policy logic and political realities suggest that in the immediate future, the government will not be attempting to introduce a new tax-benefit system, and that future policy developments and debates are likely to take place within the framework of the evolving social insurance and assistance regime.[12] These concluding paragraphs outline what the key policy debates might be in the near future.

Indexation has been a recurring aspect of policy since the Commission on Social Welfare's report. The Commission did not agree on whether or how there should be a formal system of indexation. It set out a framework that informed policy to some degree: its original financial targets for payment levels (updated for inflation) were incorporated in the various national partnership agreements from 1987 to the present day. Relative income poverty grew, however, because of the unforeseen growth in incomes and the reductions in taxes that together led to an unanticipated increase in average disposable incomes during the 1990s. In the period since the Commission's report the economy has moved to a different level of development. The lesson of the past decade has been that it is just as necessary in periods of prosperity, as in periods of economic difficulty to have a policy mechanism for monitoring and adjusting payment levels. At this point the question is: how should payment levels relate to evolving living standards?

The opening contribution to the future debate on this question was offered in the recent report on indexation (Government of Ireland, 2001). The contributors to this report did not agree on the issue. One point of view noted in the report is that there should not be a formal mechanism of indexing payments and a second, opposing point of view was that, as a matter of right, all benefits and allowances should be indexed to earnings: proponents of this view offered specific targets in relation to the level of benefits. A majority of the contributors to the indexation report agreed that in the short-term it was reasonable to adopt a target of 27% of Gross Average Industrial Earnings for the lowest benefit, with this target to be achieved by 2007. The impact of this report lies in the fact that it arrived at a specific, medium-term target and that it was derived in the context of government/union/employer discussions. In the future, the outcome of the indexation report may act as a catalyst for policy debate and initiative in relation to benefit levels in the same way as the Commission on Social Welfare's targets for payment levels shaped policy in the past.

A second set of issues concerns *child income support*. Recent policy here has been to enhance the role of Child Benefit and reduce the role of Child Dependant Additions. The question for the future is to what extent this restructuring can and should continue. The answer to this may depend to some extent on the future level of unemployment. If it rises significantly and the number of families with children receiving benefits rises accordingly, it will make the abandonment of CDAs and the transition to a unified system of child income support more difficult. The policy logic of moving to a unified system is as relevant now as it was when policy reforms in this area were first mooted. If this part of the social security system is reformed, it will simplify the system and it may reduce child poverty and remove poverty traps for the unemployed with children.

Child income support is also related to the wider debate on tax-benefit integration. The instrument for supporting low-paid employees with children is FIS. The problems with it are well documented and, as Chapter Five suggested, one solution would be to move to a child tax credit system for employees. If this tax credit were made refundable, it would be progressive in its overall impact because it would disproportionately affect lower income families. The positive outcomes in terms of child poverty in the UK associated with the switch to tax credits is likely to reinforce policy-makers in Ireland in their initial moves towards tax credits — the government has already established a Steering Committee on Refundable Credits. If this form of child income support for employees is introduced and the unification of Child Benefit and Child Dependant Additions materialises, then the system of child income support will be transformed. This change would also have an interesting institutional implication. The Revenue Commissioners would administer refundable tax credits and, insofar as the credits are about poverty and distributional issues, their introduction would have the effect of making poverty policy more central to the design and implementation of tax policy.

A further contentious issue that will command attention is *individualisation*. The tax system has been individualised to some degree, but the implications of applying the individualisation principle to the benefits system are only beginning to be considered. Individualisation could take a number of forms, as Chapter Six suggested: from a 'weak' version, administrative individualisation, to a 'strong' version, full individual payments to all qualified adult partners and means tests that rely on personal rather than marital incomes. At the time of writing the government is committed to individualisation in the weak sense, but once this is in place the momentum towards a stronger version may build up and the controversies aired in the 1991 Review Group and elsewhere may be revisited.

Individualisation is essentially a gender issue. The other gender-related question concerns women's access, as individuals, to old age and widows' *social insurance pensions*. This question may become more salient as the impact of the recent rise in women's employment participation makes itself felt. In principle, this will lead over the longer run to some women acquiring 'male' social insurance contribution profiles. However, as Chapter Six noted, the way in which women's work in the home is being recognised for social insurance purposes is still somewhat limited. Women that returned to work in mid-life might find in the coming decade that the contribution rules for pensions may still preclude them from insurance pensions in their own right. Administratively, a problem like this would be easy to solve: contribution rules can be changed and particular categories of women can be 'blanketed in' for pensions. However, as the population-profile ages and the gap in life expectancies (between men and women) leads to more and more older women relying on social security in their old age, the costs of these *ad hoc* solutions will rise. But the strategic question for public policy here is that the state is committed to a system of social insurance — at least in the implicit sense that it has not actively sought to develop alternatives. There is likely to be continuing interest in pushing out the margins of social insurance so that it is as widely encompassing as possible.

Finally, social security *pensions* will become increasingly important in the coming decade, as Ireland's elderly population gradually begins to grow. For now, the state's policy is to have, firstly, some element of pre-funding for pensions and, secondly, to extend private pension provision through occupational pensions and personal retirement savings accounts. It is possible that the reliance on occupational and personal pensions will be misplaced — more specifically that low-income workers may still lack occupational or personal pension membership. If this turns out to be the case, then the debate about pensions may be opened again. Whether a renewed debate about pensions would raise again the option of a second-tier state pension is another matter. History suggests that Ireland's adherence to a limited, Beveridge-style system is very strong and that public interest is not easily mobilised around strategic issues in social security.

Notes

1.   To illustrate, a tax allowance of €1,000 would be worth €500 (1,000 × 50%) to a taxpayer paying a marginal rate of tax of 50%, while it is worth zero to a taxpayer whose income is below the tax exemption limit and whose marginal rate of tax is therefore 0%.

2. The argument here ignores the fact that there may also be an income exemption limit below which all income is excluded from taxation.

3. Technically, the BI scheme is an *ex-ante* minimum income while the NIT type scheme is an *ex-post* minimum.

4. The official government statement referring to the NESC study acknowledged that it presented 'an interesting case for the integration of the present income tax and social welfare code'. In a reference to the BI type scheme illustrated in the study — a scheme that would have entailed additional costs — the government pointed out that acceptance of the proposals would depend on 'the extent to which the community would be willing to bear both the substantial additional taxation and the redistribution of the tax burden which a significant step towards an integrated system would entail' (Department of Economic Planning and Development, 1978).

5. Briefly, there is a point between 0% and 100% at which the tax rate to fund BI can be set which maximises the BI payable and beyond which point per capita GNP may fall. Likewise, there is an ethical position that maximises the amount of basic income relative to GNP per capita. This 'Rawlsian' ethical position can be contrasted with a pure egalitarian position that would actually equalise basic income and GNP per capita, or a pure libertarian one in which the basic income is set at zero and BI expenditure as a share of national income is zero.

6. The most recent medium-term review of the Irish economy offers a benchmark forecast of economic growth, employment and unemployment levels. This review suggests that GNP growth could be 3.1% in 2004 and in the range of 5% to 6% through to 2010, and that unemployment will fall again back to its 2002 level of 4.2% (Fitzgerald, Cullen, Duffy *et al*, 2003).

7. The argument by Van Parijs (1995) in *Real Freedom for All?* is more complex. It models jobs as scarce assets that generate what are technically termed 'economic rents'. Jobs should therefore be auctioned to the highest bidder and the rents then taxed to fund the basic income.

8. The analyses of BI by the researchers at the Economic and Social Research Institute rely on a quantitative model of the tax-benefit system based on large-scale social survey data about individuals and families. Other analysts use aggregate administrative and official data. In his examination of the costs of BI, O'Toole (1995) points out a difficulty with the latter methodology: there is a significant divergence between the estimates of the total income available for taxation (the 'tax base') as between the Revenue Commissioners' administrative data and the Central Statistics Office's figures on national income.

9. For example, in one analysis CORI points out that its scheme would logically make a number of existing expenditure programmes unnecessary. The system of higher education grants, and some income supports to farmers

are cases in point. If these programmes were abolished in the context of the introduction of a BI this would result in 'savings' that affect the affordability of the reform.

10. This benchmark is derived from a very detailed specification about how the tax and social welfare system would evolve without BI. Briefly, the benchmark entails no benefit increase above inflation with the exception of old age pensions and meeting the Partnership 2000 commitments in respect of the target rate for the lowest payments. On the tax side, the benchmark is labelled a 'mixed tax cuts' strategy reflecting a continuation of adjustments to allowances and bands of the previous years. The benchmark specifies the amount of resources that would be allocated to tax adjustments and social welfare increases.

11. The details are that the overall number of losers would fall from over 1 million tax/benefit units to 875,000 and the number of winners would rise from 737,000 to 916,000. This is achieved by: giving higher BI payments in respect of third and subsequent children; replacing the living alone allowance with a weekly €12.7 allowance for those living alone with only the BI payment and those in need of care who are in a household with no income source other than BI; giving a payment of €63.5 weekly for those doing 'socially useful' work, and granting a tax allowance in respect of the income from occupational pensions.

12. The history of the political and official responses to BI points consistently to an unwillingness on the part of governments and political parties to embrace a strategy of this nature. The 1994 CORI pamphlet, for example, contains the views of the political parties (Healy and Reynolds, 1994). One of the parties, the Green Party, agreed that BI was a good idea in principle and that it should act as benchmark for future policy.

Some Useful Websites

www.welfare.ie This is the Department of Social and Family Affairs' site. It gives an excellent guide to the Irish system of cash benefits, and contains a page with the most recent Budget information. The annual statistical report is also available there in PDF format.

www.combatpoverty.ie The Combat Poverty Agency has a statutory remit to advise the Irish government on poverty policy. Its site is useful as a source of comment and it also offers very good links to sources of official and other publications about poverty and social policy.

www.cso.ie The Irish government's statistical office (CSO) has a wide range of statutory duties in relation to the compilation and publication of official statistics. The CSO's site contains general data on incomes, prices, employment, and so on. It also publishes the results of special surveys conducted as part of the routine Quarterly National Household Survey and many of these are directly relevant to social security. The site currently contains survey results on pensions, disability, and child care amongst other topics.

www.pensionsboard.ie The National Pensions Board is responsible for pensions policy and for the regulation of occupational and private pensions. Its annual reports are on the site. The site also has very comprehensive information about pensioners' rights and the operation of pension schemes.

www.ilo.org This is the site of the International Labour Organisation based in Geneva. It gives detailed information on the various international agreements and conventions about labour standards and social security provision. The site is very useful as a source of comparative information and as a guide to the ILO's publications.

www.issa.int/engl.homef.htm The International Social Security Association's site has a database on social security in different countries and this offers links to many sites concerned with specific aspects of policy such as pensions.

www.ssa./gov/statistics The US government's Social Security Administration compiles a very detailed document *Social Security Programs Throughout the World*. This document can be accessed here and is a very useful tool for international comparisons.

www.citizensincome.org This site is of particular interest to those wishing to conduct research on Basic Income.

www.dwp.gov.uk This is the site for the main UK government department responsible for social security, the Department of Work and Pensions.

(There is a four page list of relevant UK and international website addresses in the Appendix to Millar, J. (2003) ed. *Understanding Social Security*. Bristol: The Policy Press.)

Bibliography

Abel-Smith, B. (1982), 'Sex Equality in Social Security' in Lewis, J. (ed.), *Women and Social Policy*. London: Croom Helm.

Alber, J (1981), 'Government Responses to the Challenge of Unemployment: The Development of Unemployment Insurance in Western Europe' in Flora, P. and A. Heidenheimer, (eds.), *The Development of Welfare States in Europe and America*. New Brunswick: Transaction Inc.

Albon, R. and D. Stafford (1987) *Rent Control*. London: Croom Helm.

Albon, R. and D. Stafford (1988) 'Rent Control: Its Costly Repercussions'. *Social Policy and Administration*, Vol. 22, No. 1, pp. 10–21.

Allen, K. (2000), *The Celtic Tiger: The Myth of Social Partnership in Ireland*. Manchester: Manchester University Press.

Anders, J., B. Hvinden, and K. Vik (1999), 'Activation Policies in the Nordic Countries' in Kautto, M., M. Heikkila, B. Hvinden, S. Marklund, and N. Ploug, (eds.), *Nordic Social Policy: Changing Welfare States*. London: Routledge.

Atkinson, A.B. (1969), *Poverty in Britain and the Reform of Social Security*. Cambridge: Cambridge University Press.

Atkinson, A.B. (1973), *The Tax Credit Scheme and Redistribution of Income*. London: Institute for Fiscal Studies.

Atkinson, A.B. (1987), 'Social Insurance and Income Maintenance' in Auerbach, A. and M. Feldstein (eds.), *Handbook of Public Economics* Vol. 11. Amsterdam: North-Holland.

Atkinson, A.B. (1993), 'Work Incentives' in Atkinson, A.B. and G.V. Mogensen, *Welfare and Work Incentives*. Oxford: Clarendon Press.

Atkinson, A.B. and J. Micklewright (1991), 'Unemployment Compensation and Labour Market Transitions: A Critical Review'. *Journal of Economic Literature*, Vol. 29, No. 2, pp. 1679–1727.

Bacon, P. and Associates (1999), An Economic Assessment of Recent House Price Developments. Report submitted to the Minister for Housing and Urban Renewal. Dublin.

Baker, T.J. and T.M. O'Brien (1979), *The Irish Housing System: A Critical Overview*. Dublin: Economic and Social Research Institute.

Baker, J. (1986), 'Comparing National Priorities: Family and Population Policy in Britain and France'. *Journal of Social Policy*, Vol. 15, No. 4, pp. 421–442.

Baldwin, P. (1990), *The Politics of Social Solidarity*. Cambridge: Cambridge University Press.

Barnes, H. and S. Baldwin (1999), 'Social Security, Poverty and Disability' in Ditch, J. (ed.), *Introduction to Social Security*. London: Routledge.

Barr, N. (1987), *The Economics of the Welfare State*. London: Weidenfeld and Nicholson.

Barr, N., (1992), 'Economic Theory and the Welfare State: A Survey and Interpretation'. *Journal of Economic Literature*, Vol. 30, pp. 741–803.

Barr, N. (1993), 'Retirement Pensions' in Barr, N. and D. Whynes (eds.), *Current Issues in the Economics of Welfare*. London: Weidenfeld and Nicholson.

Barr, N. (1997), *The Economics of the Welfare State*. (Third edition.) Oxford: Oxford University Press.

Barr, N, and D. Whynes (1993), *Current Issues in the Economics of Welfare*. London: Macmillan.

Barrett, A., J. Fitzgerald and B. Nolan (2000), 'Earnings Inequality, Returns to Education and Low Pay' in Nolan, B., P.J. O'Connell, and C.T. Whelan, *Bust to Boom. The Irish Experience of Growth and Inequality*. Dublin: Institute of Public Administration.

Barret, A., C.T. Whelan, and J.J. Sexton (2001), *'Employability' and its Relevance for the Management of the Live Register*. Dublin: Economic and Social Research Institute, Policy Research Series, Paper No. 40.

Barrington, R. (1997), *Health, Medicine and Politics in Ireland 1900–1970*. Dublin: Institute of Public Administration.

Barry, F. and J. Bradley (1991), 'On the Causes of Irish Unemployment'. *Economic and Social Review* Vol. 22, No. 4, pp. 253–286.

Beveridge, W. (1909), *Unemployment: A Problem of Industry*. London.

Beveridge, W. (1942), *Social Insurance and Allied Services*. London: HMSO. Cmd.6404.

Bew, P. and H. Patterson (1982), *Sean Lemass and the Making of Modern Ireland*. Dublin: Gill & Macmillan.

Blackburn, R. (2002), *Banking on Death or Investing in Life. The History and Future of Pensions*. London: Verso.

Blackwell, J. (1986), *Unemployment Compensation and Work Incentives*. Commission On Social Welfare, Background Paper No. 2. Dublin: Commission on Social Welfare.

Blackwell, J. (1988), 'Family Income Support: Policy Options' in Healy, S. and B. Reynolds (eds.) *Poverty and Family Income Policy*. Dublin: Conference of Major Religious Superiors.

Blackwell, J. (1994), 'Changing Work Patterns and their Implications for Social Security' in Baldwin, S. and J. Falkingham (eds.), *Social Security and Social Change. New Challenges to the Beveridge Model*. Hemel Hempstead: Harvester Wheatsheaf.

Blackwell, J. (1995), 'Is There a Need for Change in Housing Policy' in Convery, F. J. and A. McCashin (eds.), *Reason and Reform. Studies in Social Policy*. Dublin: Institute of Public Administration. pp. 243–261.

Booth, C. (1889–1903), *The Life and Labour of the People of London* (17 volumes). London: Macmillan.

Borrie, Sir Gordon (1994), *Social Justice. Strategies for National Renewal: The Report of the Commission on Social Justice*. London: Vintage.

Bradshaw, J. (1986), 'A Useful Policy Analysis'. *Administration* Vol. 34, No. 4 (Annals).

Bradshaw, J., J. Ditch, H. Holmes, P. Whiteford (1993), *Support for Children: A Comparison of the Arrangements in Fifteen Countries*. London: HMSO.

Bradshaw, J. and D. Piachaud (1980), *Child Support in the European Community*. London: Bedford Square Press.

Bradshaw, J, S. Kennedy, M. Kilkey, S. Hutton, A. Corden, T. Eardley, H. Holmes, and J. Neale (1996), *Policy and the Employment of Lone Parents in 20 Countries. The EU Report*. York: Social Policy Research Unit, University of York (European Observatory of National Family Policies).

Brannen, J. and G. Wilson. (eds.) (1987), *Give and Take in Families. Studies in Resource Distribution*. London: Allen and Unwin.

Brannen. J. and P. Moss. (1991), *Managing Mothers*. London. Allen and Unwin.

Breen, R. (1991), *Education, Employment and Training in the Youth Labour Market*. Dublin: Economic and Social Research Institute.

Briggs, A. (1961), *Social Thought and Social Action: A Study of the Work of Seebohm Rowntree 1871–1954*. London: Longmans.

Brittain, J.A. (1972), *The Payroll Tax for Social Security*. Washington: The Brookings Institute.

Brown, J.C. (1989), *In Search of a Policy. The Rationale for Social Security Provision for One Parent Families*. London: National Council for One parent Families.

Brown, J.C. (1990), *Victims or Villains? Social Security Benefits in Unemployment*. York: Joseph Rowntree Memorial Trust.

Browne, F. and D. McGettigan (1993), *Another Look at the Causes of Irish Unemployment*. Central Bank of Ireland. Technical Paper.

Burchardt, T. (2000),'The Dynamics of Being Disabled'. *Journal of Social Policy*, Vol. 29, No. 4, pp. 537–552.

Burchardt, T. (2003), 'Disability, Capability and Social Exclusion' in Millar, J. (ed.), *Understanding Social Security Issues for Policy and Practice*. Bristol: Policy Press.

Burke, H. (1987), *The People and the Poor Law in Nineteenth Century Ireland*. Dublin: Women's Education Bureau [Arlen House].

Callan, T., B. Nolan, and B.J. Whelan, D.F. Hannan with S. Creighton (1989), *Poverty, Income and Welfare in Ireland*. Dublin: Economic and Social Research Institute, General Research Series, Paper No. 146.

Callan, T. (1991), *Income Tax and Welfare Reforms. Microsimulation Modelling and Analysis*. Dublin: Economic and Social Research Institute.

Callan, T. (ed.) (1997), *Income Support and Work Incentives; Ireland and the UK*. Dublin: Economic and Social Research Institute, Policy Research Series No. 30.

Callan, T. (1997), 'SWITCH: the ESRI TAX-Benefit Model' in Callan, T. (ed.), *Income Support and Work Incentives: Ireland and the UK*. Dublin: ESRI. Policy Research Series. No. 30.

Callan, T., G. Boyle, T. McCarthy, B. Nolan, J. Walsh, J. Nestor, D. van de Gaer (2000), *Dynamic Effects of a Basic Income: Phase 2 of a Study for the Working Group on Basic Income. Final Report*. Dublin: Department of An Taoiseach.

Callan, T., M. Keeney, B. Nolan, and J. Walsh (2001), *Reforming Tax and Welfare*. Dublin: Economic and Social Research Institute, Policy Research Series, No. 42.

Callan, T., M. Keeny, J. Walsh (1993), 'The Distributive Impact of Budgetary Policy' in Callan, T., D. Madden, and D. McCoy (eds.), *Budget Perspectives 2003*. Dublin: Economic and Social Research Institute and Foundation for Fiscal Studies.

Callan, T. and B. Nolan (1994). 'The Meaning and Measurement of Poverty' in Nolan, B. and T. Callan, (eds.), *Poverty and Policy in Ireland*. Dublin: Gill & Macmillan.

Callan, T. and B. Nolan (1997), '.Microsimulation Analyses of Replacement Rates in Ireland' in Callan, T. (ed.), *Income Support and Work Incentives in Ireland*. Dublin: ESRI: Policy Research Series, No. 30.

Callan, T., B. Nolan, and C. O'Donoghue (1996), 'What has Happened to Replacement Rates?' *Economic and Social Review*, Vol. 27, No. 5, pp. 439–457.

Callan, T., B. Nolan, J. Walsh, G. Boyle, T. Mc Carthy, R. Nestor, D. van de Gaer (2000), *Dynamic Effects of a Basic Income: Phase 2 of a Study for the Working Group on Basic Income*. Dublin: Department of the Taoiseach (Working Paper).

Callan, T., B. Nolan and C.T. Whelan (1996), A *Review of the Commission on Social Welfare's Minimum Adequate Income*. Dublin: Economic and Social Research Institute, Policy Research Series, Paper No. 29.

Callan, T., B. Nolan, B.J. Whelan, C.T. Whelan, J. Williams (1996), *Poverty in the 1990s*. Dublin: Oak Tree Press.

Callan, T., B. Nolan, J. Walsh and R. Nestor (1999), 'Income Tax and Social Welfare Policies' in Kearney, C. (ed.), *Budget Perspectives*. Dublin: Economic and Social Research Institute and Foundation for Fiscal Studies.

Callan, T., C. O'Donoghue, and C. O'Neill (1994), *Analysis of Basic Income Schemes for Ireland*. Dublin: Economic and Social Research Institute, Policy Research Series, Paper, No. 21.

Callan, T., C. O'Neill, and C. O'Donoghue (1995), *Supplementing Family Income*. Dublin: Economic and Social Research Institute. Policy Research Series.

Cantillon, S. (1997), 'Women and Poverty: Differences in Living Standards within Households' in Byrne, A, and M. Leonard (eds.), *Women and Irish Society. A Sociological Reader*. Belfast: Beyond the Pale Publications.

Cantillon, S. and B. Nolan (1998), 'Are Married Women More Deprived than their Husbands?'. *Journal of Social Policy*, Vol. 27, No. 2, pp. 151–171.

Cartwright, W.S. (1984), 'Saving, Social Security and Private Pensions'. *International Social Security Review*, Vol. 37, pp. 123–138.

Castles, F.G. (1998), *Comparative Public Policy*. Cheltenham: Edward Elgar 1998.

Castles, F.G. and R. McKinlay (1979), 'Does Politics Matter: An Analysis of the Public Welfare Commitment in Advanced Welfare States'. *European Journal of Political Research*, Vol. 7, pp. 169–186.

Child Benefit Review Committee (1995), *Report to the Minister for Social Welfare*. Dublin: Department of Social Welfare.

Clark, C. (1999), 'Report for the Working Group on Basic Income'. Dublin: Department of the Taoiseach (Working Paper).

Clark, C. (2002), *The Basic Income Guarantee*. Dublin: The Liffey Press.

Clark, C. and S. Healy (1997), *Pathways to a Basic Income*. Dublin: Conference of Religious of Ireland.

Clasen, J. (1999), 'Beyond Social Security: The Economic Value of Giving Money to Unemployed People'. *European Journal of Social Security*, Vol. 1, No. 2, pp. 151–180.

Clasen, J., J. Kvist and W. Van Borscht (2001), 'On Condition of Work: Increasing Work Requirements in Unemployment Compensation Schemes' in Kato, M., J. Fritzell, B. Hinder, J. Kvist, and H. Uusitalo (eds.), *Nordic Welfare States in the European Context*. London: Routledge.

Clinch, P., F.J. Convery, and B.M. Walsh (2002), *After the Celtic Tiger*. Dublin: O'Brien Press.

Collard, D. (1980), 'Social Dividend and Negative Income Tax' in Sandford, C., C. Pond and R. Walker (eds.), *Taxation and Social Policy*. London: Heinemann.

Collins, J. (1940), 'Public Assistance in Irish Social Services: A Symposium'. *Journal of the Statistical and Social Inquiry Society of Ireland*, pp. 107–143.

Commission on Emigration and Other Population Problems 1948–1954 (1956), *Report*. Dublin: Stationery Office.

Commission on the Private Rented Residential Sector (2000), *Report*. Dublin: Stationery Office.

Commission on Social Welfare (1986), *Report*. Dublin: Stationery Office.

Commission on the Status of People with Disabilities (1996), *Report: A Strategy for Equality*. Dublin: Stationery Office.

Commission on the Status of Women (1972), *Report to the Minister for Finance*. Dublin: Stationery Office.

Commission on Taxation (1982), *First Report: Direct Taxation*. Dublin: Stationery Office.

Commission on Vocational Organisation (1943), *Report*. Dublin: Stationery Office.

Commission on Workmen's Compensation (1962), *Report*. Dublin: Stationery Office.

Commission on the Family (1998), *Report*. Dublin: Stationery Office.

Connell, P. and Stewart. J. (2004), 'Incomes of Retired Persons in Ireland: Some Evidence from Household Budget Surveys' in Stewart, J. and G. Hughes, *Reforming Pensions in Europe*. London: Edward Elgar.

Conniffe, D. and G. Keogh (1988), *Equivalence Scales and Costs of Children*. Dublin: Economic and Social Research Institute.

Conroy, P. (1994), 'Income Maintenance and Social Protection'. *Paper to Combat Poverty Agency and National Rehabilitation Board Conference on Disability, Exclusion and Poverty*. Dublin.

Conroy, P. (1997), 'Lone Mothers: the Case of Ireland' in Lewis, J. (ed.), *Lone Mothers in European Welfare Regimes. Shifting Policy Logics*. London: Jessica Kingsley.

Conroy. P. (2003), 'Employment' in Quin, S. and B. Redmond (eds.), *Disability and Social Policy*. Dublin: University College Dublin Press.

Cook, G. (1986), 'Britain's Legacy to the Irish Social Security System' in Drudy, P.J. (ed.), *Irish Studies 5: Ireland and Britain since 1922*. Cambridge: Cambridge University Press.

Cook, G. (1990), *The Development of Social Security in Ireland (Before and After Independence)*. London: University of London, Dissertation.

Cook, G. and A. McCashin(1997), 'Male Breadwinner; a Case Study of Gender and Social Security' in Byrne, A. and M. Leonard (eds.), *Women and Irish Society: A Sociological Reader*. Belfast: Beyond the Pale Publications.

Cook, J. (1986), 'Pragmatic Consensus rather than Radical Critique'. *Administration*, Vol. 34, No. 4 (Annals).

Coopers and Lybrand Associates Ltd. (1989), *Ways of Reviving the Private Rented Sector*. London: Housing Research Foundation.

Cousins, M. and G. Whyte (1993), *A Guide to Unemployment Payments and Employment Schemes*. Dublin: Free Legal Advice Centres.

Cousins, M. (1995), *The Irish Social Welfare System. Law and Social Policy*. Dublin: The Round Hall Press.

Cousins, M. (1999), 'The Introduction of Children's Allowances in Ireland 1939–1944'. *Irish Economic and Social History*, Vol. 26, pp. 35–53.

Cousins, M. (2003), *The Birth of Social Welfare in Ireland, 1922–1952*. Dublin: Four Courts Press.

Crook, A.D.H. (1992), 'Private Rented Housing and the Impact of Deregulation' in Birchall, J. (ed.), *Housing Policy in the 1990s*. London: Routledge and Kegan Paul.

CSO (2002), *Quarterly National Household Survey: Pensions*. Dublin: Central Statistics Office.

Daly, M. (1989), *Women and Poverty*. Dublin: Attic Press.

Daly, M. (1995), 'The Operations of Famine Relief, 1845–1847' in Poirteir, C. (ed.), *The Great Irish Famine*. Cork: Mercier Press.

Daly, M. (ed.) (2001), *Care Work. The Quest for Security*. Geneva: International Labour Office.

Davies, B., H. Land, T. Lynes, K. Macintyre, and P. Townsend, *Better Pensions: The State's Responsibility*. London: Catalyst.

Davies, H. and H. Joshi (1994), 'Sex, Sharing and the Distribution of Income'. *Journal of Social Policy*, Vol. 23, No. 3, pp. 301–340.

Dean, H. and A. Shah (2002), 'Insecure Families and Low-Paying Labour Markets'. *Journal of Social Policy*, Vol. 31, No. 1, pp. 61–80.

Department of the Environment (2002), *Report of the Rental Assistance Planning Group*. Dublin: Department of the Environment, unpublished.

Department of Social Welfare (1949), *Social Security*. Dublin: Stationery Office.

Department of Social Welfare (1976), *A National Income-Related Pension Scheme: A Discussion Paper*. Dublin: Stationery Office.

Department of Social Welfare (1978), *Social Insurance for the Self-Employed: A Discussion Paper*. Dublin: Stationery Office.

Department of Social Welfare (1991), *Report of the Review Group on the Treatment of Households in the Social Welfare Code*. Dublin: Stationery Office.

Department of Social Welfare (1997), *National Pensions Policy Initiative: Consultation Document*. Dublin: Department of Social Welfare.

Department of Social, Community and Family Affairs (2000), *Review of the One Parent Family Payment*. Programme Evaluation Report No. 7. Dublin: Stationery Office.

Department of Social, Community and Family Affairs (2002), *Actuarial Review of the Financial Condition of the Social Insurance Fund as at December 2000*. Dublin: Stationery Office.

Dilnot, A., J. Kay and C.N. Morris (1984), *The Reform of Social Security*. Oxford: Oxford University Press.

Ditch, J. (1986), 'A View from the North'. *Administration* Vol. 34, No. 4 (Annals).

Ditch, J. (ed.) (1999), *Introduction to Social Security: Policies Benefits and Poverty*. London: Routledge.

Ditch, J., A. Lewis and S. Wilcox (2001), *Social Housing, Tenure and Housing Allowance: An International Review*. London: HMSO, Department of Work and Pensions.

Dixon, J. (1999), *Social Security in Global Perspective*. Westport, Connecticut: Praeger.

Dixon, J. (2000), 'A Global Ranking of Social Security Systems'. *International Social Security Review*, Vol. 53, No. 1.

Doling, J. (1997), *Comparative Housing Policy: Government and Housing in Advanced Industrialised Countries*. New York. St. Martin's Press.

Donnison, D., (1982), *Housing Policy*. London: Penguin.

Dowling, B. (1986), 'Paper to Symposium on the Report of the Commission on Social Welfare'. *Journal of the Statistical and Social Inquiry Society of Ireland*, Vol. 25, Part 4, pp. 1–20.

Drew, E., R. Emerek, and E. Mahon (eds.) (1998), *Women, Work and the Family in Europe*. London: Routledge and Kegan Paul.

Dropping, J., B. Hvinden, and K. Vik, (1999), 'Activation Policies in the Nordic Countries' in Kautto, M., M. Heikkila, B. Hvinden, S. Marklund, N. Ploug (eds.), *Nordic Social Policy: Changing Welfare States*. London, Routledge and Kegan Paul.

Esping-Andersen, G. (1985), *Politics Against Markets*. Princeton: Princeton University Press.

European Commission (1995), *Social Protection in Europe*. Brussels: European Communities.

European Commission (2001A) *Social Protection in the Member States of the Community [MISSOC]*: Brussels: Commission of the European Communities.

European Commission (2001B), *EU Employment and Social Policy, 1999–2001: Jobs, Cohesion and Productivity*. Luxembourg: Office for Official Publications of the European Communities.

Eurostat (1999), *First Results from the European Community Household Panel Survey*. Luxembourg: Office for Official Publications of the European Communities.

Evason, E. and L. Spence, 'Women and Pensions: Time for a Rethink'. *Social Policy and Administration*, Vol. 37, No. 3, pp. 253–270.

Expert Working Group on the Integration of the Tax and Social Welfare Systems (1996), *Report*. Dublin: Stationery Office.

Fahey, T. (1998A), 'Child Care Policy Options' in Callan, T., D. Duffy, T. Fahey, B. Nolan, J. Walsh, S. Scott, B. Feeney, P. O'Connell (eds.), *Budget Perspectives*. Dublin: Economic and Social Research Institute.

Fahey, T. (1998B), *The Agrarian Dimension in the History of the Irish Welfare State*. Dublin: Economic and Social Research Institute, Seminar Paper.

Fahey, T. and J. Fitzgerald (1997), *Welfare Implications of Demographic Change*. Dublin: Oak Tree Press.

Fahey, T. and H. Russell (2001), *Family Formation in Ireland: Trends, Data Needs and Implications*. Dublin: Economic Social and Research Institute, Policy Research Series.

Fahey. T. and D. Watson (1995), *An Analysis of Social Housing Need*. Dublin: Economic and Social Research Institute.

Falkingham, J. and K. Rake (2003), 'Pensions Choices for the 21st Century: Meeting the Challenges of an Ageing Society' in *Social Policy Review 15. UK and International Perspectives*. Bristol: The Policy Press.

Farley, D. (1964), *Social Insurance and Social Assistance in Ireland*. Dublin: Institute of Public Administration.

Feldstein. M. (1974), 'Social Security, Induced Retirement and Aggregate Capital Accumulation'. *Journal of Political Economy*, Vol. 82, pp. 905–926.

Field. F., M. Meacher and C. Pond (1977), *To Him Who Hath: A Study of Poverty and Taxation*. London: Penguin Books.

Finch, J. and D. Groves (1983), *Labour and Love: Women, Work and Caring*. London: Routledge and Kegan Paul.

Fitzgerald, E. (1999) 'Unemployment' in Quin, S., P. Kennedy, A. O'Donnell, and G. Kiely (eds.), *Contemporary Irish Social Policy*. Dublin: University College Dublin Press.

Fitzgerald, E., G. Kiely, C. Carney, and P. Quinn (1994), *The Cost of a Child*. Dublin: Combat Poverty Agency.

Fitzgerald, J., I. Kearney, E. Morgenroth and D. Smith, (1999), *National Investment Priorities for the Period 2000–2006*. Dublin: Economic and Social Research Institute. Policy Research Series No. 33.

Fitzgerald, J. and Fahey, T. (1997), *Welfare Implications of Demographic Trends*. Dublin: Oak Tree Press.

Flora, P. (ed.) (1986), *Growth to Limits: The Western European Welfare States Since World War 2*. Berlin and New York: Walter de Gruyter.

Flora, P., and A. Heidenheimer (eds.) (1981), *The Development of Welfare States in Europe and America*. London: Transaction Publishers.

Fukayama, F. (1999), *The Great Disruption*. London: Profile Books.

Fraser, D. (1973), *The Evolution of the British Welfare State: A History of Social Policy Since the Industrial Revolution*. London: Macmillan.

Friedman, M. (1962), *Capitalism and Freedom*. Chicago: University of Chicago Press.

Friedman, M. (1980), *Free to Choose*. London: Pelican Books.

Garrett, P. (2000), 'The Abnormal Flight: The Migration and Repatriation of Irish Unmarried Mothers'. *Social History*, Vol. 25, No. 3, October, pp. 330–343.

George, V. and P. Wilding (1976), *Ideology and Social Welfare*. London: Routledge.

Giddens, A. (1998), *The Third Way*. Cambridge: Polity Press.

Gilbert, B. (1966), *The Evolution of National Insurance in Great Britain*. London: Michael Joseph.

Ginsburg, N. (1979), *Class, Capital and Social Policy*. London and Basingstoke: Macmillan.

Glendinning, C. and S. Baldwin (1988), 'The Costs of Disability' in Walker, R. and G. Parker, *Money Matters: Income, Wealth and Welfare*. London: Sage.

Glenndinning, C. and J. Millar (eds.) (1992), *Women and Poverty in Britain: The 1990s*. Hemel Hempstead: Harvester Wheatsheaf.

Glynn, Sir Joesph (1921), 'The Unmarried Mother'. *Irish Ecclesiastical Record*, Vol. 18, Fifth Series, pp. 461–467.

Glynn, Sir Joseph (1933), *Committee of Inquiry into Widows' and Orphans' Pensions*. Dublin: Stationery Office.

Gough, I. (1979), *The Political Economy Economy of the Welfare State*. London: Macmillan.

Gough, I. (2000), *Global Capital, Human Needs and Social Policies*. Basingstoke: Palgrave.

Government of Ireland (1969), *Third Programme for Economic and Social Development 1969–1972*. Dublin: Stationery Office.

Government of Ireland (1985), *Building on Reality*. Dublin: Stationery Office.

Government of Ireland (1987), *Programme for National Recovery*. Dublin: Stationery Office.

Government of Ireland (1991), *Programme for Economic and Social Progress*. Dublin: Stationery Office.

Government of Ireland (1997), *Sharing in Progress: National Anti-Poverty Strategy*. Dublin: Stationery Office.

Government of Ireland (2000), *Partnership 2000 for Employment, Inclusion and Competitiveness*. Dublin: Stationery Office.

Government of Ireland (2001), *Final report of the Social Welfare Benchmarking and Indexation Group*. Dublin: Department of the Taoiseach.

Government of Ireland (2002), *Basic Income: A Green Paper*. Dublin: Stationery Office.

Gray, P. (1995), 'Ideology and the Famine' in Poirteir, C. (ed.), *The Great Irish Famine*. Cork: Mercier Press.

Guerin, D. (1993), *Claiming Rent Supplement: Theory and Practice in Cork City*. Dublin: Threshold.

Guerin, D. (1999), *Housing Income Support in the Private Rented Sector: A Survey of Recipients of SWA Rent Supplement*. Dublin: Combat Poverty Agency.

Guinnane, T.W. (1993), 'The Poor Law and Pensions in Ireland'. *Journal of Interdisciplinary History*, Vol. 24, No. 2, pp. 271–291.

Hakim, C. (1984), 'The Social Consequences of High Unemployment'. *Journal of Social Policy* Vol. 11, No. 4, pp. 433–467.

Harloe, M. (1985), *Private Rented Housing in the United States and Europe*. Croom Helm: Beckingham.

Harris, J. (1977), *William Beveridge: A Biography*. Oxford: Clarendon Press.

Healy, S. and B. Reynolds (1994), *Towards an Adequate Income Guarantee*. Dublin: Conference of Religious of Ireland.

Healy, S. and B. Reynolds (1995), *An Adequate Income Guarantee for All*. Dublin: Conference of Religious of Ireland.

Heclo, H. (1974), *Modern Social Politics in Britain and Sweden*. New Haven: Yale University Press.

Honahan. P. (1986), 'Comments to Symposium on the Report of the Commission on Social Welfare'. *Journal of the Statistical and Social Inquiry Society of Ireland*, Vol. 25, Part 4, pp. 1–20.

Honohan, P. (1987), 'A Radical Reform of Social Welfare and Income Tax Evaluated'. *Administration*, Vol. 35, No. 1 pp. 69–82.

Hughes, G. (1982), *Social Insurance and Absence from Work in Ireland*. Dublin: Economic and Social Research Institute.

Hughes, G. (1985), *Payroll Tax Incidence, the Direct Tax Burden and the Rate of Return on State Pension Contributions in Ireland*. Dublin: Economic and Social Research Institute, General Research Series, Paper No. 120.

Hughes, G. (1988), *Disability Benefit Reform*. Dublin: Economic and Social Research Institute, Policy Research Series, Paper No. 8.

Hughes, G. (1996), *Pension Financing, The Substitution Effect, and National Savings*. Conference Paper to European Network for Research on Supplementary Pensions. Munster: ENRSP.

Hughes, G. (2001), 'The Cost and Distribution of Tax Expenditure on Occupational Pensions in Ireland' in Feldstein, M. (ed.), *Thirty-First Geary Lecture*. Dublin: Economic and Social Research Institute.

Hughes, G. and B. Whelan (1996), *Occupational and Personal Pension Coverage 1995: A Report Prepared for the Department of Social Welfare*. Dublin: Economic and Social Research Institute.

Hughes, J.G. and B.M. Walsh (1983), 'Unemployment Duration, Aggregate Demand and Unemployment Insurance: A Study of Irish Live Register Survival Probabilities 1967–1978'. *Economic and Social Review*, Vol. 14, No. 2, pp. 93–118.

Hvinden, B., M. Heikkila and I. Kankare (2001), 'Activation, Social Protection and Employment' in Kautto, M., J. Fritzell, B. Hvinden, J. Kvist and H. Uusitalo (eds.), *Nordic Welfare States in the European Context*. London: Routledge.

ILO (2000), *Social Security Pensions: Development and Reform*. Geneva: International Labour Office.

Inter-Departmental Committee on Family Allowances (1942), *Report*. Dublin: Department of the Taoiseach.

Inter-Departmental Committee (1999), *Administration of Rent and Mortgage Interest Assistance*. Dublin: Stationery Office.

International Monetary Fund (1995), *World Economic Outlook*. Washington D.C.: International Monetary Fund.

Jackman, R., C. Pissarides and S. Savouri (1990), 'Labour Market Policies and Unemployment in the OECD'. *Economic Policy*, October.

Jenkins, S.P. (1991), 'Poverty Measurement and the Within-Household Distribution: Agenda for Action'. *Journal of Social Policy*, Vol. 20, No. 4, pp. 457–483.

Jordan, B. (1986), 'The Reform of Social Security'. *Administration*, Vol. 34. No. 4, pp. 207–220.

Jordan, B. (1994), 'Efficiency, Justice and the Obligations of Citizenship' in Ferris, J. and R. Page (eds.), *Social Policy in Transition*. Aldershot: Avebury.

Judge, K. (1980), 'Beveridge: Past, Present and Future' in Sandford, C., C. Pond and R. Walker, *Taxation and Social Policy*. London: Heinemann.

Kaim-Caudle, P.R. (1973), *Comparative Social Policy and Social Security: A Ten Country Study*. London: Martin Robertson.

Kamerman. S. and A. Kahn (1989), *Single Parent, Female-Headed Families in Western Europe: Social Change and Response*. Geneva: International Social Security Association.

Kemeny, J. (1981), *Sweden Rental Housing Subsidies: Policies and Problems*. Birmingham: Centre for Urban and Regional Studies, University of Birmingham.

Kemeny, J. (1995), *From Public Housing to the Social Market: Rental Policy Strategies in Comparative Perspective*. London: Routledge.

Kemp, P., (1998), 'Private Renting in England'. *Netherlands Journal of Housing and the Built Environment*, Vol. 13, 3.

Kennedy, F. (1989), *Family, Economy and Government in Ireland*. Dublin: Economic and Social Research Institute.

Kennedy, K., T. Giblin, and D. McHugh (1988), *The Economic Development of Ireland*. London: Routledge.

Kilkenny Social Services (1972), *The Unmarried Mother in the Irish Community: A Report on the National Conference on Community Services for the Unmarried Parent*. Kilkenny: Kilkenny Social Services.

Kinealy, C. (1995), 'The Role of the Poor Law During the Famine' in Poirteir, C. (ed.) *The Great Irish Famine*. Cork: Mercier Press.

Kirby, P. (2002), *The Celtic Tiger in Distress: Growth With Inequality in Ireland*. Basingstoke: Palgrave.

Knijn, T. and F. van Wel (2001), 'Does it Work? Employment Policies for Lone Parents in the Netherlands' in Millar, J. and K. Rowlingson, *Lone Parents: Employment and Social Policy*. Bristol: Policy Press.

Kutty, N., (1996), 'The Impact of Rent Control on Housing Maintenance: A Dynamic Analysis'. *Studies*, Vol. 11, No. 1.

Land, H. (1975), 'The Introduction of Family Allowances: An Act of Historic Justice' in Hall, P., H. Land, R. Parker and A. Webb (1975), *Change, Choice and Conflict in Social Policy*. London: Heinemann.

Land, H. (1994), 'The Demise of the Male Breadwinner: In Practice but Not in Theory' in Baldwin, S. and J. Falkingham (eds.), *Social Security and Social Change: New Challenges to the Beveridge Model*. Hemel Hempstead: Harvester Wheatsheaf.

Lane, P. (2001), 'The National Pensions Reserve Fund: Pitfalls and Opportunities' in Feldstein, M. (ed.), *Thirty-First Geary Lecture*. Dublin: Economic and Social Research Institute.

Layard, R., S. Nickell and R. Jackman (1991), *Unemployment: Macroeconomic Performance and the Labour Market*. Oxford: Oxford University Press.

Layte, R. and T. Callan (2001), 'Unemployment, Welfare Benefits and the Financial Incentive to Work'. *Economic and Social Review*, Vol. 32, No. 2.

Layte, R. B. Maitre, B. Nolan, D. Watson, C.T. Whelan, J. Williams and B. Casey (2002), *Monitoring Poverty Trends and Exploring Poverty Dynamics in Ireland*. Dublin: Economic and Social Research Institute, Policy Research Series, Paper No. 41.

Lee, J. (1989), *Ireland 1912–1985: Politics and Society*. Cambridge: Cambridge University Press.

Lees, D.S. (1967), 'Poor Families and Fiscal Reform'. *Lloyds Bank Review*, October, pp. 1–16.

Le Grand, J. (1997), 'Knights, Knaves or Pawns? Human Behaviour and Social Policy'. *Journal of Social Policy*, Vol. 26, No. 2, pp. 149–170.

Le Grand, J. and Robinson, R. (1984), *The Economics of Social Problems*. Second edition. London: Macmillan.

Lewis, J (1992), 'Gender and the Development of Welfare Regimes'. *Journal of European Social Policy*, Vol. 2, No. 3, pp. 159–173.

Lewis, J. (1993), 'Introduction: Women, Work, Family, and Social Policies in Europe' in Lewis, J. (ed.), *Women and Social Policies in Europe*. London: Edward Elgar.

Lewis, J. (ed.) (1997), *Lone Mothers in European Welfare Regimes: Shifting Policy Logics*. London: Jessica Kingsley.

Lewis, J. (2001A), 'Legitimising Care Work and the Issue of Gender Equality' in Daly, M. (ed.), *Care Work: The Quest for Security*. Geneva: International Labour Office.

Lewis, J. (2001B), 'Orientations to Work and the Issue of Care' in Millar, J. and K. Rowlingson, *Lone Parents, Employment and Social Policy*. Bristol: Policy Press.

Lister, R. (1975), *Social Security: The Case for Reform*. London: Child Poverty Action Group.

Mahon, E. (1994), 'Ireland; A Private Patriarchy'. *Environment and Planning*, Vol. 26, pp. 1277–1296.

Madsen, P. (2001), 'The Danish Model of Flexicurity: A Paradise with Some Snakes' in Sarfati, H. and G. Bonoli (eds.), *Labour Market and Social Protection Reforms in International Perspective*. Aldershot: Ashgate.

Malpass, P. and Murie, A. (1994), *Housing Policy and Practice* (Fourth edition.) London: Macmillan.

Marsden, D. (1973), *Mothers Alone: Poverty and the Fatherless Family*. London: Penguin.

Marsden, D. (1982), *Workless: An Exploration of the Social Contract Between Society and the Worker*. London: Croom Helm.

Marsden, H., C. Murray, and C. Heaney (1998), *Welfare to Work: The Financial Benefits of Taking up Employment*. Dublin: Irish National Organisation of the Unemployed.

Marshall, T. H. (1975) *Social Policy*. Fourth Revised edition. London: Hutchinson.

McCashin, A. (1982), 'Social Policy 1957–1982' in Litton, F. (ed.), *Unequal Achievement: The Irish Experience 1957–1982*. Dublin: Institute of Public Administration.

McCashin, A. (1988), 'Family Income Support in Ireland: Trends and Issues' in Healy, S. and B. Reynolds (eds.) *Poverty and Family Income Policy*. Dublin: Conference of Major Religious Superiors.

McCashin, A. (1992), 'The Politics of Social Security in the Republic of Ireland: A Case Study of the Report of the Commission on Social Welfare'. Paper to Conference on the State of the Irish Political System. University College Cork (unpublished).

McCashin, A. (1993), *Lone Parents in the Republic of Ireland: Enumeration, Description and Implications for Social Security*. Dublin: Economic and Social Research Institute.

McCashin, A. (1996), *Lone Mothers in Ireland: A Local Study*. Dublin: Oak Tree Press.

McCashin, A. (1997), *Employment Aspects of Young Lone Motherhood*. Dublin: TREOIR and National Youth Federation.

McCashin, A. (1999), 'The Tax/Welfare Treatment of Households' in *Report of the Working Group Examining the Treatment of Married, Cohabiting and One-Parent Households under the Tax and Social Welfare Codes*. Dublin: Stationery Office.

McCashin, A. (2000), *The Private Rented Sector in the 21st Century: Policy Choices*. Dublin: Threshold and St. Pancras Housing Association.

McCashin, A. and H. Donoghue (1979), 'A Discussion Document on the Evaluation of the 1975 Supplementary Welfare Allowances Act'. Dublin: National Committee on Pilot Schemes to Combat Poverty (unpublished).

McCashin, A. and L. Joyce (eds.) (1982), *Poverty and Social Policy in Ireland*. Dublin: Institute of Public Administration.

McCullagh, D. (1998), *A Makeshift Majority: The First Inter-party Government*. Dublin: Institute of Public Administration.

Mishra, R. (1998), *Globalisation and the Welfare State*. Cheltenham: Edward Elgar.

McKay, S. and K. Rowlingson (1999), *Social Security in Britain*. London: Macmillan.

McKee, E. (1989), 'Church-State Relations and the Development of Irish Health Policy: the Mother and Child Scheme'. *Irish Historical Studies* Vol. 25, No. 98, pp. 159–194.

McLaughlin, E, J. Millar, and K. Cooke (1989), *Work and Welfare Benefits*. Aldershot: Avebury.

McLaughlin, E. (1991), 'Work and Welfare Benefits: Social Security, Employment and Unemployment in the 1990s'. *Journal of Social Policy*, Vol. 20, No. 4, pp. 485–508.

McLaughlin, E. (1999), 'Social Security and Poverty: Women's Business' in Ditch, J. (ed.), *Introduction to Social Security: Policies, Benefits and Poverty*. London: Routledge and Kegan Paul.

McLaughlin, E. (2001), 'Ireland: From Catholic Corporatism to Social Partnership' in Cochrane, A., Clarke, J. and S. Gewitz (eds.), *Comparing Welfare States*. London: Sage.

McManus. A. (2003), 'Social Security and Disability' in Quin, S. and B. Redmond (eds.), *Disability and Social Policy in Ireland*. Dublin: University College Press.

Memery, C. and L. Kerrins (2000), *Gatekeeping Housing Supports: Discretion in the Operation of Rent and Mortgage Interest Supplement*. Threshold: Dublin (unpublished).

Millar, J. (1989), *Poverty and the Lone Parent Family: the Challenge to Social Policy*. Aldershot: Avebury.

Millar, J. (2001), 'Adjusting Welfare Policies to Stimulate Job Entry: the Example of the United Kingdom' in Sarfati, H. and G. Bonoli (eds.), *Labour Market and Social Protection Reforms in International Perspective: Parallel or Converging Tracks?* Aldershot: Ashgate.

Millar, J. and K. Rowlingson (2001), (eds.), *Lone Parents, Employment and Social Policy: Cross-national Comparisons*. Bristol: Policy Press.

Mills, F. (1999), 'Income Maintenance' in Quin, S., P. Kennedy, A. O'Donnell, and G. Kiely, *Contemporary Irish Social Policy*. Dublin: University College Dublin Press.

Mills, F., E. Smyth and J. Walsh with H. Tovey (1991), *A Review of Supplementary Welfare Allowance*. Dublin: Combat Poverty Agency.

Minister for Social Welfare (1985), *Address by the Minister for Social Welfare at First Annual Conference of the Retirement Planning Council of Ireland*. Dublin: Department of Social Welfare.

Minns, R. (2001), *The Cold War in Welfare: Stock Markets Versus Pensions*. London: Verso.

Moffitt, R. (1992), 'Incentive Effects of the US Welfare State: A Review'. *Journal of Economic Literature*, Vol. 30, pp. 1–61.

Munnell, A.H. (ed.) (1986A), *Lessons from the Income Maintenance Experiments: Proceedings of a Conference Held in September 1986*. Washington: Federal Reserve Bank and The Brookings Institution.

Munnell, A. H. (ed.) (1986B), 'The Impact of Public and Private Pension Schemes on Saving and Capital Formation'. *International Social Security Review*, Vol. 39, No. 3, pp. 244–257.

Murphy, M. (2003A), *Valuing Care Work*. Dublin: National Women's Council of Ireland.

Murphy, M. (2003B), *A Woman's Model for Social Welfare Reform*. Dublin: National Women's Council of Ireland.

National Pensions Board (1987), *First Report*. Dublin: Government Publications.

National Pensions Board (1988), *Report on the Extension of Social Insurance to the Self-Employed*. Dublin: Government Publications.

National Pensions Board (1993), *Developing the National Pension System*. Dublin: Government Publications.

National Pensions Board (1998), *Securing Retirement Income*. Dublin: National Pensions Board.

NESC (1975), *Income Distribution: A Pilot Study*. Report No. 11. Dublin: Stationery Office.

NESC (1977), *Towards a Social Report*. Report No. 25. Dublin: Stationery Office.

NESC (1978), *Integrated Approaches to Taxes and Transfers*. Report No. 37. Dublin: Stationery Office.

NESC (1980), *Alternative Strategies of Family Income Support*. Report No. 47. Dublin: Stationery Office.

NESC (1988), *The Nature and Functioning of Labour Markets. A Survey of International and Irish Literature and a Statement of Research Priorities for Ireland*. Dublin: Stationery Office.

NESC (1989), *A Review of Housing Policy*. Dublin: Stationery Office.

NESC (1991), *Women's Participation in the Irish Labour Market*. Dublin: Stationery Office.

NESC (2003), *An Investment in Quality: Services, Inclusion and Enterprise*. Dublin: Stationery Office.

NESF (2001), *Lone Parents*. Forum Report No. 20. Dublin: Stationery Office.

Newell, A. and J. Symons (1990), 'The Causes of Ireland's Unemployment'. *Economic and Social Review*, Vol. 21, No. 4, pp. 409–429.

Nicholls, G. (1898), *A History of the Poor Law*, Vol. 2 (New Edition) London: P.S. King.

Nolan, B. (1987), 'More on Actual Versus Hypothetical Replacement Ratios in Ireland'. *Economic and Social Review*, Vol. 18, No. 3, pp. 159–172.

Nolan, B. (1993), *Low Pay in Ireland*. Dublin: Economic and Social Research Institute. General Research Series.

Nolan, B. (1995), *Ireland and the Minimum Income Guarantee*. Dublin: Combat Poverty Agency.

Nolan, B. (1999), 'Income Inequality in Ireland' in McCashin, A. and E. O'Sullivan (eds.), *Irish Social Policy Review 1999*. Dublin: Institute of Public Administration.

Nolan, B. (2000A), *Child Poverty in Ireland*. Dublin: Oak Tree Press.

Nolan, B. (2000B), *Income Distribution in Ireland*. Dublin: Oak Tree Press

Nolan, B. and B. Farrell (1990), *Child Poverty In Ireland*. Dublin: Combat Poverty Agency.

Nolan, B., B. Gannon, R. Layte, D. Watson, C.T. Whelan, J. Williams (2002), *Monitoring Poverty Trends in Ireland. Results from the 2000 Living in Ireland Survey*. Dublin: Economic and Social Research Institute, Policy Research Series, Paper No. 45.

Nolan, B., P.J. O'Connell and C.T. Whelan (eds.) (2000), *Bust to Boom*. Dublin: Institute of Public Administration.

Nolan, B. and H. Russell (2001), *Non-Cash Benefits and Poverty in Ireland*. Dublin: Economic and Social Research Institute, Policy Research Series, Paper No. 39.

Nolan, B. and D. Watson, (1999), *Women and Poverty in Ireland*. Dublin: Oak Tree Press.

Nolan, B., Whelan, C.T. and J. Williams (1998), *Where are Poor Households? The Spatial Distribution of Poverty and Deprivation in Ireland*. Dublin: Oak Tree Press.

Nozick, R. (1974), *Anarchy, State and Utopia*. Oxford: Basil Blackwell.

O'Brien, L. and Dillon, B. (1982), *Private Rented: The Forgotten Sector of Irish Housing*. Dublin: Threshold.

O'Connell, P.J. (1996), *The Effect of Active Labour Market Programmes in Ireland*. Dublin: Economic and Social Research Institute, Working Paper No. 72.

O'Connell, P.J. (1999), *Are They Working? Market Orientation and the Effectiveness of Active Labour Market Programmes in Ireland*. Dublin: Economic and Social Research Institute, Working Paper No. 105.

O'Connell, P.J. (2000), 'The Dynamics of the Irish Labour Market in Comparative Perspective' in Nolan, B., P.J. O'Connell and C. T. Whelan (eds.) *Bust to Boom? The Irish Experience of Growth with Inequality*. Dublin: Institute of Public Administration.

O'Connell, P. J. and F. McGinnity, *Working Schemes? Active Labour Market Policy in Ireland*. Aldershot: Ashgate.

O'Connor, C. (1928), *Report of the Commission on the Relief of the Sick and Destitute Poor*. Dublin: Stationery Office.

O'Connor, J., R. Hearne and K. Walsh (1986), *Social Assistance: Experiences and Perceptions of First-time Applicants*. Dublin: Commission on Social Welfare, Background Paper, No. 3 (unpublished).

O'Connor, J. (1995), *The Workhouses of Ireland: The Fate of Ireland's Poor*. Dublin: Anvil Books.

O'Connor, P. (1998), *Emerging Voices: Women in Contemporary Irish Society*. Dublin: Institute of Public Administration.

O'Cinneide, S. (1999), 'The 1949 White Paper and the Foundations of Social Welfare' in Lavan, A. (ed.), *50 Years of Social Welfare History*. Dublin: Department of Social, Community and Family Affairs.

OECD (1992), *Private Pensions and Public Policy*. Paris: OECD, Social Policy Studies, No. 9.

OECD (1995), *The OECD Jobs Study. Facts, Analysis, Strategies*. Paris: OECD.

Offe, C. (1994), 'A Non-productivist Design for Social Policies' in Ferris, J. and Page, R. (eds.), *Social Policy in Transition*. Aldershot: Avebury.

Ó Gráda, C. (2002), *'The Greatest Blessing of All': The Old Age Pension in Ireland*. The Past and Present Society, Oxford.

O'Higgins, M. (1987), 'Lone Parent Families: Numbers and Characteristics' in *OECD Conference on Lone Parents, The Economic Challenge of Changing Family Structures, Conference Paper No. 3*. Paris: OECD (unpublished).

O'Hearn, D. (1998), *Inside the Celtic Tiger*. London: Pluto Press.

Okun, A. (1978), *Equality and Efficiency: The Big Trade Off*. Washington: Brookings Institute.

Oliver. M. (1990), *The Politics of Disablement*. London: Macmillan.

O'Mahony, D. (1983), 'A Study of Replacement Ratios Among a Sample of Irish Workers'. *Economic and Social Review*, Vol. 14, No. 2, pp. 77–91.

O'Riain, S. (2000), 'The Flexible Developmental State, Globalization, Information Technology and the 'Celtic Tiger''. *Politics and Society*, Vol. 28, No. 3, pp. 3–37.

O'Riain, S. and P. J. O'Connell, 'The Role of the State in Growth and Welfare' in Nolan, B., P.J. O'Connell and C.T. Whelan (eds.), *Bust to Boom: The Irish Experience of Growth with Inequality*. Dublin: Institute of Public Administration.

O'Sullivan, E. (1998), 'The Other Housing Crisis' in *The Fiscal Treatment of Housing: Proceedings of the Thirteenth Annual Conference of the Foundation for Fiscal Studies*. Dublin: Foundation for Fiscal Studies.

O'Toole, F. (1995), ' The Costings of a Basic Income Scheme' in Healy, S. and B. Reynolds (eds.), *Towards an Adequate Income Guarantee*. Dublin: Conference of Religious of Ireland.

Pahl, J. (1983), 'The Allocation of Money and the Structuring of Inequality within Marriage'. *Sociological Review*, Vol. 31, No. 2, pp. 235–262.

Parker, H. (1989), *Instead of the Dole*. London: Routledge and Kegan Paul.

Pascall, G. (1986), *Social Policy: A Feminist Analysis*. London: Tavistock.

Pedersen, S. (1993), *Family, Dependence and the Origins of the Welfare State: Britain and France, 1914–1945*. Cambridge: Cambridge University Press.

Pennings, F. (2001), 'A Critical View of Incentives to Help Benefit Recipients into Work in the Netherlands' in Sarfati, H. and G. Bonoli (eds.), *Labour Market and Social Protection Reforms in International Perspective: Parallel or Converging Tracks?* Aldershot: Ashgate.

Pearson, M. and E. Whitehouse (1997), 'Making Work Pay: The OECD Study of Taxes, Benefits, Employment and Unemployment' in Callan, T., (ed.), *Income Support and Work Incentives: Ireland and the UK*. Dublin: Economic and Social Research Institute, Policy Research Series, No. 30.

Piachaud. D. (1979), *The Cost of A Child*. London: Child Poverty Action Groups.

Pierson, P. (1994), *Dismantling the Welfare State*. Cambridge: Cambridge University Press.

Powell, F.W. (1992), *The Politics of Irish Social Policy 1600–1900*. Lewiston, New York: The Edwin Mellen Press.

Power, A. (1987), *Property before People*. London: Allen and Unwin.

Power, A. (1993), *Hovels to High Rise. Slum Housing in Europe Since 1850*. London: Routledge.

Quadagno, J. (1984), 'Welfare Capitalism and the Social Security Act of 1935'. *American Sociological Review*, Vol. 49, No. 4, pp. 632–647.

Rathbone. E. (1940), *Family Allowances*. London: Allen and Unwin.

Reith, L. (1994), 'Exploring the Links between Poverty and Disability: the Extra Costs of Disability.' *Paper to Combat Poverty Agency and National Rehabilitation Board Conference on Disability, Exclusion and Poverty*. Dublin: Combat Poverty Agency.

Review Group on the Role of Supplementary Welfare Allowance in Relation to Housing (1995), *Report to the Minister for Social Welfare*. Dublin: Stationery Office.

Riordan, S. (2000), "A Political Blackthorn': Sean MacEntee, the Dignan Plan and the Principle of Ministerial Responsibility'. *Irish Economic and Social History*, Vol. 27, pp. 44–62.

Rimlinger, G. (1971), *Welfare Policy and Industrialisation in Europe, Russia and America*. London: John Wiley.

Rottman, D. (1994), *Income Distribution within Irish Households: Allocating Resources within Irish Families*. Dublin: Combat Poverty Agency.

Rowntree, S. (1901), *Poverty. A Study of Town Life*. London: Macmillan [Centennial 2001 edition].

Ruggie, M. (1984), *The State and Working Women*. Princeton: Princeton University Press.

Russell, H., E. Smyth, P.J. O'Connell and M. Lyons (2002), *'Getting Out of the House'*: Women Returning to Employment, Education and Training. Dublin: The Liffey Press.

Ryall, A. (1997), 'Recent Developments in Residential Tenancy Law (Part 1)'. *Conveyancing and Property Law Journal*, Vol. 2, No. 4.

Ryall, A. (1998), 'Recent Developments in Residential Tenancy Law (Part 2)'. *Conveyancing and Property Law Journal*, Vol. 3, No. 1.

Ryall, A. (1999), 'Residential Tenancies: Enforcement and Control'. *Conveyancing and Property Law Journal*, Vol. 4, No. 2.

'Sagart', (1922), 'How to Deal with the Unmarried Mother'. *Irish Ecclesiastical Record*, Vol. 20, pp. 145–153.

Sandford, C. (1980), 'The Tax Credit Scheme' in Sandford, C., C. Pond and R. Walker. *Taxation and Social Policy*. London: Heinemann.

Sainsbury, D. (ed.) (1994), *Gendering Welfare States*. London: Sage.

Sainsbury, R. (1999), 'The Aims of Social Security' in Ditch, J. (ed.), *Introduction to Social Security*. London: Routledge.

Santiella, J. A. (1994), *Unemployment in Ireland: A Survey of Features and Causes*. Washington: International Monetary Fund.

Sarfati, H. and G. Bonoli (eds.) (2001), *Labour Market and Social Protection Reforms in International Perspective*. Aldershot: Ashgate.

Second Commission on the Status of Women (1993), *Report*. Dublin: Stationery Office.

Schmid, G. and B. Reisser (1996), 'Unemployment Compensation and Labour Market Transitions' in Schmidt, G., J. O'Reilly and K. Schomann (eds.), *International Handbook of Labour Market Policy and Evaluation*. Cheltenham: Edward Elgar.

Skocpol. T. (1995), *Social Policy in the United States: Future Possibilities in Historical Perspective*. Princeton: Princeton University Press.

Skocpol, T. and E. Amenta (1985), 'Did Capitalists Shape Social Security?'. *American Sociological Review*, Vol. 50, No. 4, pp. 572–575.

Standing, G. (1994), 'The Need for a New Social Consensus' in Ferris, J. and R. Page (eds.), *Social Policy in Transition*. Aldershot: Avebury.

Stiglitz, J. (1988), *Economics of the Public Sector*. New York: W.W. Norton.

Task Force on Long Term Unemployment (1995), *Report*. Dublin: Stationery Office.

Thurow, L. (1971), 'The Income Distribution as a Pure Public Good'. *Quarterly Journal of Economics*, May, pp. 327–336.

Titmuss, R. (1956), 'The Social Division of Welfare' in *Essays on the Welfare State*. London: George Allen and Unwin.

Townsend, P. (1979), *Poverty in the United Kingdom*. London: Pelican.

Tubridy, J. (1996), *Pegged Down*. Dublin: Institute of Public Administration.

Van Oorschot, W. (2002), 'Miracle or Nightmare? A Critical review of Dutch Activation Policies and their Outcomes'. *Journal of Social Policy*, Vol. 31, No. 3, pp. 2002.

Van Kersbergen, K. (1995), *Social Capitalism: A Study of Christian Democracy and the Welfare State*. London: Routledge and Kegan Paul.

Van Parijs, P. (1992), *Arguing for a Basic Income*. London: Verso.

Van Parijs, P. (1995), *Real freedom for All: What, if Anything, Can Justify Capitalism?* Oxford: Clarendon Press.

Vice Regal Commission (1906), *Poor Law Reform in Ireland*.

Veit-Wilson, J. (1998), *Setting Adequacy Standards: How Governments Define Minimum Incomes*. Bristol: Policy Press.

Viney, M. (1964), *No Birthright: A Study of the Irish Unmarried Mother and her Child. The Irish Times Articles*. Dublin: Irish Times.

Vogler, C. and J. Pahl (1994), 'Money, Power and Inequality Within Marriage'. *Sociological Review*, Vol. 42, No. 2, pp. 262–288.

Vroman, W. (2001), *Unemployment Insurance and Assistance: A Comparison*. Washington: The Urban Institute.

Waldfagel, J., S. Danziger, K. Dandier, and K. Seeded (2001), 'Welfare Reform and Lone Mothers' Employment in the US' in Millar, J. and Rowlingson, K., *Lone Parents, Employment and Social Policy*. Bristol: Bristol Press.

Walker, I. (1997), 'Work Incentives, Taxes and Transfer Programmes' in Callan, T. (ed.) *Income Support and Work Incentives: Ireland and the UK*. Dublin: Economic and Social Research Institute.

Walsh, B.M. (1974), 'Income Maintenance Payments in Ireland, 1953–1971: Cyclical Variations and Long-Term Growth'. *Economic and Social Review*, Vol. 5, No. 2, pp. 213–225.

Walsh, B.M. (1988), 'Why is Unemployment so High in Ireland Today?' in *Perspectives on Economic Policy*. Dublin: Centre for Economic Policy Research, University College Dublin.

Ward, S. (1994), 'A Basic Income System for Ireland' in Healy, S. and B. Reynolds (eds.), *Towards an Adequate Income for All*. Dublin: Conference of Religious of Ireland.

Ward, P. (1990), *The Financial Consequences of Marital Breakdown*. Dublin: Combat Poverty Agency.

Whelan, C.T., D. Hannan and S. Creighton (1991), *Unemployment, Poverty and Psychological Distress*. Dublin: Economic and Social Research Institute.

Whelan, C.T., R. Layte, B. Maitre, B. Nolan, D. Watson, and J. Williams (2003), *Monitoring Poverty Trends: Results from the 2001 Living in Ireland Survey*. Dublin: Economic and Social Research Institute.

Whyte, G. (ed.), (1988). *Sex Equality, Community Rights and Welfare Law: The Impact of the Third Equality Directive*. Dublin: Irish Centre for European Law, Trinity College.

Whyte, J. (1972), *Church and State in Modern Ireland 1923–1970*. Dublin: Gill & Macmillan.

Wilensky, H. (1975), *The Welfare State and Equality*. Berkeley, California: University of California Press.

Women's Representative Committee (1976), *Progress Report on the Implementation of the Recommendations in the Report of the Commission on the Status of Women*. Dublin: Stationery Office.

Women's Representative Committee (1976), *Second Progress Report on the Implementation of the Recommendations in the Report of the Committee on the Status of Women*. Dublin: Stationery Office.

World Bank (1994), *Averting the Old Age Crisis: Policies to Protect the Old and Promote Growth*. Oxford: Oxford University Press.

Wren, M. (2003), *Unhealthy State*. Dublin; New Island.

Wynn, M. (1970), *Family Policy*. London: Pelican Books.

Yeates, N. (1997), 'Gender and the Development of the Irish Social Welfare System' in Byrne, A. and M. Leonard (eds.) *Women and Irish Society: A Sociological Reader*. Belfast: Beyond the Pale Publications.

Yeates, N. (2001), *Globalisation and Social Policy*. London: Sage.

Index